No truck with the Chilean junta!

Trade Union Internationalism, Australia and Britain, 1973-1980

No truck with the Chilean junta!

Trade Union Internationalism, Australia and Britain, 1973-1980

Ann Jones

PRESS

Published by ANU Press
The Australian National University
Canberra ACT 0200, Australia
Email: anupress@anu.edu.au
This title is also available online at http://press.anu.edu.au

National Library of Australia Cataloguing-in-Publication entry

Author:	Jones, Ann, author.
Title:	No truck with the Chilean junta! : trade union internationalism, Australia and Britain, 1973-1980 / Ann Jones.
ISBN:	9781925021530 (paperback) 9781925021547 (ebook)
Subjects:	International labor activities--History Labor movement--History. Labor unions--Australia. Labor unions--Great Britain. Labor unions--Chile--Political activity.
Dewey Number	322.2

All rights reserved. No part of this publication may be reproduced, stored in a retrieval system or transmitted in any form or by any means, electronic, mechanical, photocopying or otherwise, without the prior permission of the publisher.

Cover design by Nic Welbourn and layout by ANU Press

Cover image © Steve Bell 1987 - All Rights Reserved. http://www.belltoons.co.uk/reuse.

This edition © 2014 ANU Press

Contents

Acknowledgments vii
List of abbreviations ix
Introduction 1

Britain

1. The 'principal priority' of the campaign: The trade union movement 25
2. A 'roll call' of the labour movement: Harnessing labour participation 63
3. 'Unique solidarity'? The mineworkers' delegation, 1977 89
4. Pinochet's jets and Rolls Royce East Kilbride 117

Australia

5. Opening doors for Chile: Strategic individuals and networks . 155
6. 'Chile is not alone': Actions for resource-sensible organisations 181
7. 'Twelve Days in Chile', 1974 201
8. 'Not one pound of wheat will go': Words and actions 223
Conclusion 255
Appendix 265
Bibliography 269
Index 299

Acknowledgments

This book would not have been possible without the generous thoughts and memories of the oral history participants. Those who gave liberally of their time are acknowledged in the footnotes as contributors to this history.

I would especially like to thank Mavis Robertson and Mike Gatehouse, whose generosity, kindness and consideration surpassed my expectations.

I acknowledge the goodwill of the Rolls Royce East Kilbride Shop Stewards (2007), Mick Wilkinson, Colin Creighton, Barry Carr, Gustavo Martin Montenegro and Mike Gonzalez, who gave me access to their records.

The professionals of the archives deserve a special mention for their attentiveness and endurance. I would specifically like to thank Darren Treadwell at the People's History Museum (Manchester), Carole McCallum at the Glasgow Caledonian University Archive, Penny Pemberton at the Noel Butlin Archives Centre (Canberra) and John Callow at the Marx Memorial Library (London). I also thank those archives and others acknowledged within which have granted permission to re-print images of the time.

I am indebted to Professor Paul Pickering, whose patience was exemplary throughout the process. The publication of this work would not have been possible without the contribution of The Australian National University's Publication Subsidy Committee.

The work towards this book has been the product of the curiosity, respect, social conscience and work ethic instilled in me by Helene and Garry Powell, and it is to them that I dedicate these words.

List of abbreviations

ABB	Australian Barley Board
ABCF	Association for British–Chilean Friendship
ABS	Australian Bureau of Statistics
ACCC	Australian Competition and Consumer Commission
ACTT	Association of Cinematograph, Television and Allied Technicians (UK)
ACTU	Australian Council of Trade Unions
AEU	Amalgamated Engineers Union (later AUEW) (UK)
AFL	American Federation of Labor
AFULE	Australian Federated Union of Locomotive Enginemen
AI	Amnesty International
AICD	Association for International Cooperation and Disarmament (Aust.)
ALP	Australian Labor Party
AMIEU	Australasian Meat Industry Employees Union
AMWSU	Amalgamated Metal Workers' and Shipwrights Union (Aust.)
AMWU	Amalgamated Metal Workers' Union (Aust.)
APEX	Association of Professional, Executive, Clerical and Computer Staff (UK)
ARU	Australian Railways Union
ASIO	Australian Security Intelligence Organisation
ASIS	Australian Secret Intelligence Service
ASLEF	Associated Society of Locomotive Engineers and Firemen (UK)
ASTMS	Association of Scientific, Technical and Managerial Staffs (UK)
ATTI	Association of Teachers in Technical Institutes (UK)
AUEW	Amalgamated Union of Engineering Workers (UK)
AUEW TASS	Amalgamated Union of Engineering Workers Technical, Administrative and Supervisory Section (UK)
AWB	Australian Wheat Board
BLF	Builders Labourers' Federation (Aust.)
BLP	British Labour Party
BWIU	Building Workers' Industrial Union (Aust.)

CAC	Chile Action Committee (Sydney, Aust.)
CCCD	Canberra Committee for Chilean Democracy (Aust.)
CCHR	Chile Committee for Human Rights (UK)
CEPCH	Confederación de Empleados Particulares de Chile (Chilean Employees' Confederation)
CIA	Central Intelligence Agency (US)
CICD	Campaign for International Cooperation and Disarmament (Aust.)
CIO	Congress of Industrial Organizations
CITU	Catholic International of Trade Unions
CPA	Communist Party of Australia
CPGB	Communist Party of Great Britain
CPSA	Civil and Public Services Association (UK)
CSC	Chile Solidarity Campaign (UK)
CSCC	Chile Solidarity Campaign Commission (UK)
CSC EC	Chile Solidarity Campaign Executive Committee (UK)
CSCP	Committee for Solidarity with the Chilean People (Aust.)
CUT	Central Unica de Trabajadores (Trade unions congress of pre-coup Chile)
DINA	National Intelligence Directorate (Chile)
EETPU	Electrical, Electronic, Telecommunications and Plumbing Union (UK)
ETUC	European Trade Union Council
FCC	Free Chile Committee (Aust.)
FCO	Foreign and Commonwealth Office (UK)
FDU	Firemen and Deckhands Union (Aust.)
FEDFA	Federated Engine Drivers and Firemen's Association of Australia
FIEMC	Federation of Building Workers
FINM	Federación Industrial Nacional Minera (Chilean Mineworkers' Federation)
FTAT	Furniture, Timber and Allied Trades (UK)
GCDC	Glasgow Chile Defence Committee
GDR	German Democratic Republic (East Germany)
GMWU	General and Municipal Workers Union (UK)
ICFTU	International Confederation of Free Trade Unions

ILO	International Labour Organisation
IMF	International Metalworkers Federation
IMG	International Marxist Group (UK)
IS	International Socialists (UK)
ISTC	Iron and Steel Trades Confederation (UK)
ITF	International Transport Workers' Federation
ITT	International Telephone and Telegraph Company
JWG	Joint Working Group (UK)
LCPC	London Co-op Political Committee
LCS	London Co-operative Society
LCS-PC	London Co-operative Society Political Committee
LHASC	Labour History Archive and Study Centre (Manchester)
LPYS	Labour Party Young Socialists (UK)
MAPU	Movimiento de Acción Popular Unitario (Popular Unitary Action Movement) (Chile)
MIF	International Federation of Miners
MIR	Movimiento de Izquierda Revolucionaria (Movement of the Revolutionary Left) (Chile)
MWU	Miscellaneous Workers' Union (Aust.)
NAFTA	North American Free Trade Agreement
NALGO	National Association of Local Government Officers (UK)
NATFHE	National Association of Teachers in Further and Higher Education (UK)
NATSOPA	National Society of Operative Printers and Assistants (UK)
NCB	National Coal Board (UK)
NGA	National Graphical Association (UK)
NOLS	National Organisation of Labour Students (UK)
NSWBLF	New South Wales Builders' Labourers Federation
NUDBTW	National Union of Dyers, Bleachers and Textile Workers (UK)
NUGSAT	National Union of Gold, Silver and Allied Trades (UK)
NUJ	National Union of Journalists (UK and Ireland)
NUM	National Union of Mineworkers (UK)
NUPE	National Union of Public Employees (UK)
NUR	National Union of Railwaymen (UK)

NUS	National Union of Seamen (UK)
NUSMW	National Union of Sheet Metal Workers (UK)
NUTGW	National Union of Tailors and Garment Workers (UK)
PGEUA	Plumbers and Gasfitters Employees Union of Australia
PLP	Parliamentary Labour Party (UK)
POEU	Post Office Engineers Union (UK)
PSNC	Pacific Steam Navigation Company (UK)
RREK	Rolls Royce East Kilbride
RREKSS	Rolls Royce East Kilbride Shop Stewards
RREKWC	Rolls Royce East Kilbride Works Committee
RRSSEK	Rolls Royce Shop Stewards East Kilbride
SLADE	Society of Lithographic Artists, Designers, Engravers and Process Workers (UK)
SOGAT	Society of Graphical and Allied Trades (UK)
SPA	Socialist Party of Australia
STUC	Scottish Trades Union Congress
SUA	Seamen's Union of Australia
SWL	Socialist Workers' League (Aust.)
SWP	Socialist Workers' Party (UK)
SZOT	Hungarian Solidarity Campaign
TGWU	Transport and General Workers' Union (UK)
TGWU GEC	TGWU General Executive Council
TUC	Trades Union Congress (UK)
TWU	Transport Workers' Union (Aust.)
UCATT	Union of Construction, Allied Trades and Technicians (UK)
UDM	Union of Democratic Mineworkers (UK)
ULS	University of London Students
UNESCO	United Nations Educational, Scientific and Cultural Organisation
UNHRC	United Nations Human Rights Council
UP	Unidad Popular (Popular Unity Government)
USDAW	Union of Shop, Distributive and Allied Workers (UK)
WCL	World Confederation of Labour
WFTU	World Federation of Trade Unions

WUS	World University Service (UK)
WWFA	Waterside Workers' Federation of Australia
YCL	Youth Communist League (UK)

Introduction[1]

Figure 1 Chile Solidarity Campaign sticker.

Source: *No Truck with the Chilean Junta*, Chile Solidarity Campaign [hereinafter CSC], Box 1—Collecting tins, postcards, stickers, leaflets, People's History Museum, Manchester. The slogan 'No Truck' was used in other contexts with other graphics. See, for example: *Stop Chilean Copper Entering Britain*, CSC CSC/16/1, Labour History Archive and Study Centre [hereinafter LHASC], Manchester.

As a lorry driver in Northampton pulls himself up into the seat of his cab on a brisk morning before sunrise, he might not seem like an international political actor. But he is. As he reverses and glances through the back window of his truck, he looks past stickers. One of them reads: 'NO TRUCK WITH CHILE!!'

It's a seemingly inconsequential sticker, but it articulates something very grand in concept: that workers on one side of the world could alleviate the suffering of workers living under a dictatorship on the other.

On 11 September 1973, an alliance of the Chilean Navy, Air Force, Army and police seized power after attacking the Presidential Palace in the capital, Santiago. Their supporters legitimised the coup as being a people's rebellion against an oppressive government.[2] In reality, they had ousted a democratically elected coalition of socialists, communists, other left radicals and some centre-aligned groups. Together, the coalition was called Unidad Popular (UP, or Popular Unity).[3] Salvador Allende was the leader of the UP and a member of the Socialist Party of Chile; he was a Marxist who promoted socialist reforms. Trade unions had formed a strong support base for Allende's government, and were integrated

---

1 Please note: dates of archival titles are entered as written on the original source to aid identification of the document. Thus dates as a part of archival identification do not necessarily follow the academic guidelines of [day] [month] [year]. The [year] has been deleted in the citation if it is implicit within the title of the document. The titles of items in the archives had been italicised in order to aid comprehension.
2 Brian Loveman, *Chile: The Legacy of Hispanic Capitalism* (New York: Oxford University Press, 2001), 105.
3 Samuel Chavkin, *Storm Over Chile: The Junta Under Siege* (Westport, Conn.: Lawrence Hill & Company, 1985), 45.

firmly into sections of the administration.⁴ Popular Unity's program of reforms was referred to as *'la vía chilena al socialismo'* (the Chilean road to socialism), a unique path towards socialism particular to the Chilean situation. This peaceful and parliamentary way was part of a wave of alternative ideas that had begun a surge of popularity throughout the world, and the eyes of the global political left had turned to the slender Latin American country and its experiment.

After coming to power, Allende implemented a platform of reforms including the nationalisation of large industries. Consequently, there was an increase in hostility towards his government from several sources: the political right wing in Chile, multinational companies with interests in Chile, landowners and even the Roman Catholic Church. Meanwhile, those more radical than Allende criticised him for idealising institutions (such as the armed forces) as 'classless' and 'professional'.⁵ Allende believed that both his government and those institutions would respect the democratic process that had brought him to power. It was a fatal mistake.

The election of Allende in 1970 had been a 'political and psychological blow' to the United States of America.⁶ Henry Kissinger, Assistant to the American President for National Security Affairs, famously said, 'I don't see why we need to stand by and watch a country go communist due to the irresponsibility of its own people'.⁷ American manipulation in Chile followed years of involvement in the Vietnam War, which was also opposed by progressives, and to them Chile became another example of the evils of imperialist intervention. The actions of imperialist forces contributed to Chile's instability and were embodied (for the international political left) by multinational companies such as International Telephone and Telegraph.

The United States invested US$8 million opposing the election of Allende, and President Richard Nixon made it clear that there was more money available to the opponents of the Allende Government.⁸ Opposition parties were funded and

---

4 Ronaldo Munck, *The New International Labour Studies: An Introduction* (London: Zed Books, 1988), 172.
5 The political ultra-left viewed the military as a bourgeois institution and potentially harmful to the success of the revolution. Salvador Allende, 'The Role of the Armed Forces', in *Salvador Allende Reader: Chile's Voice of Democracy*, ed. James Cockcroft (Melbourne: Ocean Press, 2000), 86–8.
6 Paul E. Sigmund, *The United States and Democracy in Chile* (Baltimore: The Johns Hopkins University Press, 1993), 217.
7 Ibid., 103. The United States justified its interference in Chile because of the possible snowball effect that would spread socialism throughout the Western Hemisphere. The unstable economic and political nature of Chile's neighbouring countries gave credence to the snowball theory, and President Nixon and his security advisor, Henry Kissinger, resolved to get rid of 'that son-of-a-bitch Allende'. Paul Jensen, *The Garotte: The United States and Chile, 1970–1973* (Aarhus: Aarhus University Press, 1988), 18–19; Nixon, as quoted in Sigmund, *The United States and Democracy in Chile*, 55.
8 Simon Collier and William F. Sater, *A History of Chile: 1808–1994* (Cambridge: Cambridge University Press, 1996), 355; see also p. 115.

the media was manipulated.⁹ Of course, Chileans did have their own agency, and the crisis leading up to the coup was stimulated by a strike that congested the country. The Central Intelligence Agency (CIA) supported a truck drivers' stoppage in October 1972 and again in July–August 1973, shutting down this essential transport system.¹⁰ Sympathetic shopkeepers, whole sectors of commerce, doctors, engineers, bankers, gas employees and lawyers later joined the drivers on strike, thereby worsening the crisis that was enveloping Chile. The impact of the boycotts on the Government was compounded by the congressional rebellion of the extreme left and right wings of the UP administration. The relationship of the Christian Democratic Party and the rest of the UP started to disintegrate under the pressure.

The time was ripe for a coup.¹¹

On the day of the military uprising, the president and a handful of supporters fortified themselves in the palace. Allende broadcast a final speech to the citizens of Chile before the radio station was bombed.¹² He said: 'Long live Chile! Long live the people! Long live the workers! These are my last words.'¹³ Soon after, it was announced that the president had died during a full-scale military assault that all but flattened the Presidential Palace.

As the events recorded in this book were unfolding through the 1970s, the repression in Chile persisted. Decree 228 was put in place after the first wave of arrests, stating that the country was in a state of siege. Disappearances of citizens, summary trials and executions started and did not stop. In December 1973 Decree Law 198, which limited trade union function, was established. Within a year of the coup, the National Intelligence Directorate (DINA) was set up and the state apparatus for political oppression became permanent. During the dictatorship in Chile, 100 000 people were detained in prison and 3000 people were 'disappeared'.¹⁴

---

9   See: Sigmund, *The United States and Democracy in Chile*, 51–2, 64, 71; Chavkin, *Storm Over Chile*, 45; Loveman, *Chile*, 248; Jensen, *The Garotte*, 21, 217.
10 Sigmund, *The United States and Democracy in Chile*, 69–70.
11 The United States had cut off formal support to all sectors of Chile except for the armed forces during Allende's term. Military officers were trained at the School of the Americas where the syllabus included 'counterinsurgency' techniques and pro-United States rhetoric. A military coup was seen as the first chance of mobilising the full military detachment of Chile in 100 years. Loveman, *Chile*, 259; Sigmund, *The United States and Democracy in Chile*, 66; Chavkin, *Storm Over Chile*, 70–1; Mark Ensalaco, *Chile Under Pinochet: Recovering the Truth* (Philadelphia: University of Pennsylvania Press, 2000), 27.
12 Patrick Adams, 'Deadly Politics: Salvaging Memories in Santiago', *Duke Magazine* (September–October 2005).
13 James D. Cockcroft, ed., *Salvador Allende Reader: Chile's Voice of Democracy* (Melbourne: Ocean Press, 2000), 241.
14 *Report of the Chilean National Commission on Truth and Reconciliation*, Vol. I/II (Notre Dame, Ind.: University of Notre Dame Press, 1993), 1122. Many people estimate this number to be much higher, for example: Chavkin, *Storm Over Chile*, 42.

The intensity of images of these events initiated a wave of Latin American solidarity throughout the world, though radical engagement with Latin America was by no means new. Bands of men had left Britain in the 1800s to fight in Simón Bolívar's war, and in the nineteenth century groups of Welsh settlers moved to Argentina, where they hoped to maintain their culture away from English influence.[15] From Australia, William Lane led a socialist utopian group to settle in Paraguay, and Western engineers and other workers travelled to the southern cone of Latin America to seek their fortune in the railway and mining industries.[16] These activities, plus their portrayal in popular fiction and media, contributed to the consistent idealisation of Latin America in the Anglophone world. Latin America was imagined as a continent full of commercial and sociopolitical opportunities for both sides of the political spectrum.

The period under study in this book falls between two important dates of post-World War II political left history: 1968 and 1989. After 1968 the topography of the left changed. New actors on the political stage emerged, such as women, gay people and students, and the Prague Spring caused many leftists to solidify their opinions against the 'old' left and become the 'new' left. The 'old' referred to the statist, Stalinist, Leninist approach as embodied by the USSR, which expressed itself in many ways, including through the world trade union movement. The World Federation of Trade Unions (WFTU) was an institutionalised and hierarchical expression of old left trade unionism. It sat opposite the International Confederation of Free Trade Unions (ICFTU), and the two organisations represented unions on opposing sides of the Cold War.[17]

The political 'new left', in contrast, could be simply defined as a movement that expressed an alternative to the Marxist-Leninist ideology of Moscow.[18] It was, however, more complex. Peter Shipley explained the term as a 'flag of convenience ... a transmutable portmanteau, capable of changing its size and shape to accommodate all who fulfil basic qualifications of internationalism, anti-Stalinism and anti-capitalism'.[19] The new left aimed to challenge, but not

---

15 Rory Miller, *Britain and Latin America in the Nineteenth and Twentieth Centuries*, Studies in Modern History (London: Longman, 1993); Gerald Martin, 'Britain's Cultural Relations with Latin America', in *Britain and Latin America: A Changing Relationship*, ed. Victor Bulmer-Thomas (Cambridge: Cambridge University press, 1989); Ross G. Forman, 'When Britons Brave Brazil: British Imperialism and the Adventure Tale in Latin America, 1850–1918', *Victorian Studies* 42, no. 3 (1999–2000); see also Kevin Foster, 'Small Earthquakes and Major Eruptions: Anglo–Chilean Cultural Relations in the Nineteenth and Twentieth Centuries', in *Democracy in Chile: The Legacy of September 11, 1973*, ed. Sylvia Nagy-Zekmi Fernando Leiva (Brighton: Sussex Academic Press, 2005), 41–51.
16 Gavin Souter, *A Peculiar People: William Lane's Australian Utopians in Paraguay* (St Lucia, Qld: University of Queensland Press, 1991).
17 Similarly, there was a division in the world peace movement between pro-Soviet and anti-Soviet factions.
18 Willie Thompson, *The Left in History: Revolution and Reform in Twentieth-Century Politics* (London: Pluto Press, 1997), 159.
19 Peter Shipley, *Revolutionaries in Modern Britain* (London: The Bodley Hear, 1976), 207.

overthrow, the government. Accordingly, the coup in Chile shattered more than the broad front of Chilean radicals—it fuelled a firestorm of arguments over left strategy around the world.[20]

New left activists tried to insert socialist ideas at the base of the new social movements of the 1960s and 1970s.[21] As a consequence, the new left was popularised internationally and became associated with student rebellion, war protest and civil rights.[22] These causes, and the new left along with them, were linked with the growing popularity of socialist humanism—an embodiment of romantic moralism. Phrases like these are what point towards the intense emotion of the political movements of the time, including Chile solidarity.[23]

As a part of Antonio Gramsci's 'hegemonic project', the new left sought to create a lens through which reality could be perceived, and so turned towards culture as a way of establishing a socialist mentality in the populace.[24] This emphasis was prevalent in sections of the left in both Australia and Britain.[25] So while the new left may have been politically weak in the traditional sense, it had an immense cultural vitality.[26] In both Britain and Australia there were attempts to establish broad fronts, which included activists, independents, political parties, students and other groups during the 1960s and early 1970s.

The new left was, however, on the wain by the end of Allende's government. Willie Thompson has noted that the 'revolutionary potential' of the political new left had dissipated by 1974; similarly Chun lists 1978 as its final year of strength.[27] The political movement may have passed, but the concept of the broad front and the cultural legacy of the new left continued. Even though the boundaries of its influence will never be clear, it certainly affected Chile solidarity.

In Britain, the new left's legacy was embodied in the growth of the student movement and the increased appearance of single-issue campaigns.[28] In Australia the ideas of the new left were incorporated into a long history of militant behaviour, a history that should not be (according to Richard Gordon)

---

20 See, for example: Ralph Miliband, 'The Coup in Chile', *The Socialist Register 1973* (London: Merlin Press, 1974), 451–74.
21 Ibid., 190.
22 Lin Chun, *The British New Left* (Edinburgh: Edinburgh University Press, 1993), 193.
23 Ibid., 118.
24 Thompson, *The Left in History*, 184.
25 Chun, *The British New Left*, 113.
26 The Communist Party of Great Britain (CPGB) and the Socialist Party of Australia were not classified as new left, though both used some new left strategies. Michael Rustin, 'The New Left as a Social Movement', in *Out of Apathy: Voices of the New Left Thirty Years On*, eds Robin Archer, Diemut Bubeck and Hanjo Glock (London: Verso, 1989), 119.
27 Thompson, *The Left in History*, 197; Chun, *The British New Left*, 194; see also p. 118.
28 Chun, *The British New Left*, 108.

mistaken for true radicalism.²⁹ Since the split of 1968, Australia's Communist Party had been rather independent of the Soviet line; yet, it was born of the Cominform-aligned communist party, and as such, the ideas of the new left it chose to adopt were built on a continuation of the old.³⁰

How did trade unions fit into this political split between the new and the old?

Lin Chun has noted that the ideas that flowed in the 1970s are hard to catalogue as new left or non-new left, and I would argue union actions are similarly difficult to classify.³¹ Trade unions behaved like they always had: they were the product of a long history of international and extra industrial activity. In the constitutions of most unions international brotherhood and concern for society are explicit even when overt socialist rhetoric is not present and regardless of the status of union leaders of the 'old' or 'new' left. Trade unions had participated in the Spanish Civil War, the peace and disarmament movements and in actions for Indonesian independence and against the Sino–Japanese conflict.

It can be said that the solidarity movement was, in its initial stages, reactionary.

The images of the first days after the coup appeared on television screens and in newspapers around the world, burning images of the detentions and bombings into the minds of the public.³² The descriptions of the repression provoked an outcry from people and groups with an interest in democracy as well as socialism and justice. They mourned Allende and the fracture of the Chilean experiment and declared solidarity with the 'Chilean people', though often this declaration was not as inclusive as its phrasing indicated. The movement was just as much about the perception of Chile prior to the coup (the Allende years as well as a general idealisation of Latin American workers and peasants), as it was about the fate of the Chilean people during the dictatorship.

In short, the solidarity movement was as much about the perceived Chilean past as it was about its present and future. In fact, sometimes it was not about Chile at all. Peter Shipley has also noted that solidarity campaigns were 'more pertinent to revolutionary activism at home' than to events in other countries.³³ Ideological conflict in the labour movement is not often presented in 'crude

---

29   Richard Gordon and Warren Osmond Gordon, 'An Overview of the Australian New Left', in *The Australian New Left: Critical Essays and Strategy*, ed. Richard Gordon (Melbourne: Heinemann, 1970), 10.
30   Phillip Deery and Neil Redfern, 'No Lasting Peace? Labor, Communism and the Cominform: Australia and Great Britain, 1945–50', *Labour History* 88 (2005).
31   Chun, *The British New Left*, 153.
32   Alan Angell, 'The Chilean Coup of 1973—A Perspective Thirty Years Later', *El Mercurio*, 24 August 2003.
33   Shipley, *Revolutionaries in Modern Britain*, 114.

self-interested terms', but in reality unionists frequently used external issues to contest ideological themes via existing union structures.³⁴ Chile's past and present were used to aid political strategy in local internecine battles.

The coup in Chile did not cause Latin American solidarity, but it did transform the political and cultural significance of Latin American solidarity organising. The solidification of the dictatorship added a moral tone that spread the Chile issue beyond the overtly political pre-coup relationship.³⁵ Soon there were blatant human rights violations to campaign against, along with a shattered socialist dream to mourn and democracy to fight for.

The Chile solidarity movement provides a window into labour movement interaction with social movements in the 1970s. It aids understanding of how networks, ideas and key individuals affect political trade union action. It supplies examples of a single-issue movement's efforts to popularise protests around their own aims. For these reasons, and in their own right, the Chile campaigns deserve more detailed study than the casual mentions in trade union and radical histories that they have received to date, and more serious contemplation than the glorified or nostalgic memories of participants.³⁶ While there are some limited works on Chile solidarity, *this* is the most substantial work on these campaigns thus far. In this book the trade unionists of the Chile solidarity movement take centre stage.

There have previously been three works with a focus on Chile solidarity, only two of which (both masters theses) concentrate on the British Commonwealth.³⁷ Michael Wilkinson focused on British Chile and Nicaragua solidarity campaigns.³⁸ He traced their achievements as lobby groups in positive and negative lobbying environments. Gustavo Martin Montenegro, a Chilean immigrant to Australia, wrote the second study in Spanish. He amassed an impressive amount of material, but does not explain or unpack the detailed workings of Australian solidarity in the text. Both of these works recognise that trade unions played a part in solidarity but do not seek to understand the actions of organisations in more depth than a general notion of left alliance.

This is a grave oversight. Trade unions were essential to the Chilean solidarity movement: throughout the dictatorship one union or another provided the

---

34   David Plowman, 'The Victorian Trades Hall Split', in *Australian Unions: An Industrial Relations Perspective*, eds Bill Ford and David Plowman (South Melbourne: Macmillan, 1983), 304.

35   Christopher Leslie Brown, *Moral Capital: Foundations of British Abolitionism* (Oakland, NC: University of North Carolina Press, 2006), 456.

36   See, for example: Stephen Deery, 'Union Aims and Methods', in *Australian Unions: An Industrial Relations Perspective*, eds Bill Ford and David Plowman (South Melbourne: Macmillan, 1983), 75.

37   The other is: Herbert Berger, 'The Austro–Chilean Solidarity Front, 1973–1990', in *Transatlantic Relations: Austria and Latin America in the 19th and 20th Centuries*, eds Gunter Bischof and Klaus Eisterer (Innsbruck: Studienverlag, 2006).

38   Wilkinson was formerly involved in Latin American solidarity movements.

base of support for solidarity activities. Trade unionists were among the most committed individuals to the solidarity movements, and were openly courted by the Chile campaigns as likely recruits for a good cause.

This publication does not attempt to provide the reader with the history of the Chilean military regime, which eventually came to be known outside Chile as the Pinochet dictatorship.[39] Where events in Chile are referred to, it is to accomplish a more detailed understanding of the transnational nature of the solidarity movements in question, or because the event affected decision-making or strategy within the solidarity movements in some way. Furthermore, this book does not attempt to include a detailed study of the Chilean diaspora, or a comprehensive reconstruction of political or social identities in exile. Nor does it focus on the activities of personalities in exile, such as Joan Jara and Luis Figueroa, though their movements are partially tracked. This project does not claim to uncover memory of the dictatorship, or accuse governments or businesses of mismanagement or conspiracy. Finally, it is not an attempt to understand Chilean unionism, or the pressure of the dictatorship on it.[40]

What this work does do is bring together previously ignored and forgotten sources with newly collected testimonies to record a partial history of the Chile solidarity movement in Britain and Australia. A series of previously unrecorded or under-recorded case studies of trade union political action is provided. To do this, a mass of archival sources, newspapers, ephemera, artwork, music and oral history interviews has been employed. By describing trade union action in the movements under study, which previous scholarship has neglected, these activists, actions and organisations are rescued from the 'enormous condescension of posterity', as E. P. Thompson so succinctly put it in 1963.

In addition to incorporating neglected information into the historical record, this work responds to the criticism of the academic treatment of internationalism levelled by Peter Waterman and Jill Timms in 2005. 'Case studies of international solidarity actions are so rare', they wrote, 'that they tend to be repeatedly reproduced, as if the references or cases speak for themselves and do not require critical examination or reinterpretation. There are few comparative, interpretive and movement-oriented studies.'[41]

On another occasion Waterman has also noted that work on labour internationalism has been narrow, concerned with single cases and not theoretical

---

39 Most Chileans do not call it a dictatorship (*dictadura*), but 'the junta' (*junta*) or, with a slight sense of irony, the 'little junta' (*juntita*).
40 See: Guillermo Campero, *Trade Union Responses to Globalization: Chile*, report for Labour and Society Programme (Geneva: ILO, 2001).
41 Peter Waterman and Jill Timms, 'Trade Union Internationalism and a Global Civil Society in the Making', in *Global Civil Society 2004–5*, eds Helmut Anheier, Marlies Glasius and Marty Kaldor (London: Sage, 2005), 198.

in approach.⁴² John Logue is similarly disparaging of academics' explanations of international trade union activity, which, he writes, are ad-hoc collections of leaders' rationales, descriptions of events and casual linking to economic factors.⁴³ In this publication, I have attempted to deploy and extend the work of theoreticians such as Waterman through historical reconstructions. The layered international and intra-national comparative aspects as well as the exhaustive archival research contained in these pages also go some of the way to meeting these critiques.

The field of comparative labour studies continues to grow and this publication contributes an illustrative comparison by assessing many units in relation to theory.⁴⁴ Despite the fact that the labour movements of Britain and Australia vary substantially in terms of their size and depth of bureaucracy, age and geographical area, they still lend themselves to evaluation.⁴⁵ The first unions in Australia were in fact branches of their British relatives, and the definition of 'trade unions' in Australian legislation is based on the *British Trade Union Act* of 1871.⁴⁶ British radicals have looked to Australia as a new world where compulsory arbitration and the possibilities of the federal system came together in a workingman's paradise.⁴⁷ By the end of World War II, the labour movement in Australia had long outgrown any childlike need, yet it was not until 1968 that the Amalgamated Metal Workers' Union officially separated from its British parent union, the Amalgamated Engineering Union.⁴⁸ It is obvious, therefore, that growing from the strong tradition of the Tolpuddle Martyrs, the roots of Australian unionism are firmly lodged within the rich soil of British traditions.

In the 1960s and early 1970s both movements were mature and blossoming, yet the substantial divergence in the trends and styles of unionism in both countries gives life to this comparative project. The inclusion of two nations in the study also tempers the exceptionalist tendency that often plagues labour historians and trade union histories.⁴⁹ Furthermore, laying the two movements side by

---

42   Peter Waterman, *Globalization, Social Movements and the New Internationalisms* (London: Continuum, 2001), 5.
43   John Logue, *Toward a Theory of Trade Union Internationalism* (Kent: Kent Popular Press, 1980), 16.
44   Stefan Berger and Greg Patmore, 'Comparative Labour History in Britain and Australia', *Labour History*, no. 88 (2005), 10.
45   See, for example: ibid., 18; Leighton James and Raymond Markey, 'Class and Labour: The British Labour Party and the Australian Labor Party Compared', *Labour History*, no. 90 (2006), 222–9; Mark Bray, 'Democracy from the Inside: The British AUEW(ES) and the Australian AMWSU', *Industrial Relations Journal* 13, no. 4 (2007), 84–93; Andrew Scott, 'Modernising Labour: A Study of the ALP with Comparative Reference to the British Labour Party' (PhD diss., Monash University, 1999); Neville Kirk, *Labour and the Politics of Empire: Britain and Australia 1900 to Present* (Manchester: Manchester University Press, 2011).
46   Donald William Rawson, *A Handbook of Australian Trade Unions and Employees' Associations* (Canberra: Research School of Social Sciences, The Australian National University, 1973), 3; Greg Patmore and David Coates, 'Labour Parties and State in Australia and the UK', *Labour History* 88 (May 2005), 121–40.
47   Neville Kirk, 'Why Compare Labour in Australia and Britain?', *Labour History*, no. 88 (2005), 1–7.
48   Bray, 'Democracy from the Inside', 85.
49   Berger and Patmore, 'Comparative Labour History in Britain and Australia', 20.

side, including various levels of unions from workplace to peak body, enables a multilayered comparison both *intra* and *inter* national, which is very unusual and undertaken implicitly and explicitly throughout the book.

Perhaps the most well-known comparative study of Britain and Australia is Neville Kirk's *Comrades and Cousins*.[50] In it, Kirk focuses on the differences and similarities between national labour movements. The comparison contained in this publication differs substantially from that undertaken by Kirk. This work is bi-national, and it does compare the two nations broadly speaking, but is more intensely comparative in the cross-union and cross-activity spheres. This is due to a focus that includes low and mid-level decision-making and action in unions rather than solely those of the upper echelons.

The restricted period of the work, from 1973 to 1980, is not representative of the whole Chile movement in either country. There were two main phases of both movements and the transition between them occurred around 1980. In broad terms, the second half of the Chile solidarity movement moved towards a human rights campaign with an entirely different set of actors, and in Britain it had a feminist focus. In Australia, the second half of the movement was dominated by Chilean exiles. Consequently, trade union and labour involvement in the Chile movements changed substantially in the 1980s. It would be impossible to give adequate attention to the campaigns' duration in one book, and for this reason I present a partial history of the movements.[51]

It is important to note, also, that Chile actions were not just responsive activities driven by ideology, they were also influenced by the mobilising effect of rhetoric;[52] the power play between unions, unionists and political groups; pressure or inaction from the union hierarchy; opportunities for action created by social movements; genuine concern for Chilean citizens; publicity campaigns; internationalist identity; the expectation of radical engagement; and tension between 'bread and butter' issues and activism. These factors will be elucidated at length through the body of this work.

I attempt to avoid a confined political narrative by illustrating these pressures in depth. Chile solidarity was more than a narrow expression of brotherhood between two groups of the working class: it was an expression of the idealism of those who wished to change their world. Chile solidarity was not isolated from other ideological movements or historical occurrences of the time. Rather, it formed part of the cluster of radical and progressive thinking of the 1970s.

---

50   Kirk also recently published *Labour and the Politics of Empire*. The next largest publication is probably the special issue of *Labour History*, volume 88, published in 2005.
51   Due to the same restrictions on space, this work does not include every action undertaken in solidarity with Chile.
52   John Kane, *The Politics of Moral Capital* (Cambridge: Cambridge University Press, 2001), 8.

As Robert Saunders observed about Chartism in the previous century, the Chile cause was similarly bundled together with other issues and ideology in the popular consciousness, and its identity could not be separated from those issues (imperialism, multinational companies, local political party machinations and human rights, for example).[53]

The pages of this book are separated by geography into two sections. Within the sections is a series of case studies, vignettes and biographical sketches. The first chapter of each half maps the organisational space in which the solidarity movement existed, populating it with its actors: trade unionists, politicians, activists, immigrants and organisations. This helps provide a prosopographic view of those involved in the movements. It is in these two chapters that the landscapes of the Chile solidarity movements are articulated. The next three chapters provide case studies of internationalist action and synthesise a repertoire of action the labour movement would undertake for remote political gain.

These six chapters are divided by type of trade union action: indirect actions organised from without, indirect actions organised from within and the final chapter of each section attends to direct industrial action. It is, of course, immediately necessary to elaborate those categories.

Trade union politics: direct and indirect action

If we consider trade unions to be a type of sectional, interest or representative pressure group, it is reasonable to assume they would have a permanent structure established to service their organisational aims.[54] Professor of human resource management Stephen Deery notes that there are four general union objectives, the fourth of which is political. The first three are 'provision of direct services to members; improved conditions of employment; [and] organisational security'.[55] 'Political or non-industrial objectives', he writes, 'have always been regarded as a legitimate item of trade union business although few organisations have actually resorted to the use of industrial action in the pursuit of such matters'.[56]

Deery puts it very clearly: the aims of Australian unions are 'largely restricted to the negotiation of limited improvements within the framework of capitalist work relations'.[57] Bob Hawke, president of the Australian Council of Trade

---

53 Robert Saunders, 'Chartism from Above: British Elites and the Interpretation of Chartism', *Historical Research* 81, no. 213 (2008), 467.
54 Timothy May, *Trade Unions and Pressure Group Politics* (Westmead, UK: Saxon House, 1975), 3; Denis Barnes and Eileen Reid, *Governments and Trade Unions: The British Experience, 1964–79* (London: Heinemann Educational Books, 1980), 190.
55 Deery, 'Union Aims and Methods', 63.
56 Ibid., 89.
57 Ibid., 62.

Unions (ACTU) for much of the period of the Chile solidarity movement, said 'maximisation of gains for its members' social as well as material gains—is the prime objective of the union movement'.[58] A few years later, however, Hawke said:

> We have a responsibility to in fact use our own strength, our accumulated and cohesive strength in a way which will not only assist those who are directly in our ranks but also to assist those who are less fortunate and less privileged than ourselves and less able to look after their own interests.[59]

This humanitarian sentiment underpins the international actions of trade unions and works in conjunction with the socialist ideology and romantic moralism already described.

Trade union actions with extra-industrial aims fall into two main categories: 'direct' (industrial) tactics and 'indirect' (party-political) tactics.

Direct tactics include boycotts, walk-offs, sit-ins, black bans, refusals to service or go-slows. Those strategies may be aimed at goods representative of the issue (in this case, from Chile), or a general stoppage will be signalled as having a political aim through posters, press releases, meeting attendances and leafleting (indirect actions when used alone).

Indirect tactics include political lobbying, sponsorship of parliamentarians, affiliation to political parties and forwarding of resolutions.[60] Particularly pertinent to the Chile campaign is the indirect action of trade union involvement in social movements. Their attendance at meetings, demonstrations and speaking engagements, for example, contributed to political goals in an indirect manner.[61] Union (direct and indirect) action for non-industrial issues, where those actions attempted to change trade union or government policy from outside the electoral framework, could be interpreted by opposition forces as a constitutional challenge.[62] Yet the potential for disruption of internal union harmony did not stop action occurring.

---

58 Bob Hawke, in D. W. Rawson, *Unions and Unionists in Australia* (Hornsby, NSW: George Allen & Unwin, 1978), 99.
59 Bob Hawke, in Deery, 'Union Aims and Methods', 75.
60 It is hard to quantify the exact effects of sponsorship of parliamentarians due to the doctrine of parliamentary privacy. May, *Trade Unions and Pressure Group Politics*, 4, 28, 33; Deery, 'Union Aims and Methods', 87.
61 Timothy May divides indirect actions into two: constitutional actions and symbolic actions. May, *Trade Unions and Pressure Group Politics*, 99.
62 Deery, 'Union Aims and Methods', 75–6.

In order to locate union action for Chile within academic discourse it is necessary to outline the relevant abstract theoretical definitions as they have developed over time. These definitions also help to elucidate nuance in the union actions and interactions as they are revealed through the book.

I'm not going to lie: the definitions are confusing.

Over many years, historians, social scientists and theorists have laboured their points and created their own phrases. I have attempted to synthesise that below.

Internationalism: international unionism and union internationalism

The labour movement itself was conceived as internationalist in aim and construction and the concept of labour 'internationalism' first emerged from the Marxist-Leninist Internationals.[63] Internationalism, writes Waterman, a leading scholar in the area, 'is generally understood as a left-wing or democratic project for creating relations of solidarity between social classes, popular interests, and progressive identities, independently of, or in opposition to, the state or capital'.[64] As a term, it has almost universally positive connotations even though it inherently places the conception of 'nation' above any other political unit.[65]

Despite the supposed opposition to the state, the international labour movement was born out of socialist thought and socialist language and often supported an ideal type of state.[66] Peak union bodies, such as the ACTU or the Trade Union Congress (Britain), could express their internationalism through their affiliation with international organisations such as the ICFTU or WFTU, which were still divided along Cold War lines in the 1970s. These organisations, literally inter*national* unions, provided national organisations with the chance to communicate, meet and organise.[67] Such institutionalised union internationalism was easily undertaken by unions and rarely required industrial action. As already implied, it forms a part of 'trade union internationalism'; however, it is not its only expression.

---

63   Waterman and Timms, 'Trade Union Internationalism and a Global Civil Society in the Making', 179; Waterman, *Globalization, Social Movements and the New Internationalisms*, 17. Logue also asserts that internationalism in trade unions predates Marxist ideology. Logue, *Toward a Theory of Trade Union Internationalism*, 9.
64   Waterman and Timms, 'Trade Union Internationalism and a Global Civil Society in the Making', 179.
65   Perry Anderson, 'Internationalism: A Breviary', *New Left Review* 14 (March–April 2002), 1.
66   Ian Schmutte, 'International Union Activity: Politics of Scale in the Australian Labour Movement' (Master of Philosophy diss., University of Sydney, 2004), 43–4.
67   Mike Press, 'The People's Movement', in *Solidarity for Survival: The Don Thompson Reader on Trade Union Internationalism*, eds Mike Press and Don Thompson (Nottingham: Spokesman, 1989), 28.

Trade union internationalism, as a term, covers an array of activities across all levels of unionism.[68] First, there is international unionism as already discussed. Second, bilateral union relations, where unions develop direct links with their equivalent in other countries, also express internationalist sentiment.[69] Frequently, though not exclusively, bilateral relations centre on industrial issues and strategy sharing and are most often clustered around an industry similarity (such as garment makers) or a singular business (such as all employees of Toyota). Still, the relationship is based on a Marxist ideal of a brotherhood of class, and the terms 'trade union internationalism' and 'internationalist' continue to carry that connection.

The third and final, at least for our purposes, expression of trade union internationalism is the engagement in local action for non-local political gain (for example, happening in Melbourne to influence Syria). This action does not necessarily require a specific union or unionist to be the object of internationalist sentiment nor does it need an industrial aim. It may be with the aim of 'peace', for example, or 'the Chilean people'. When international action has political motives (that is: non-industrial aims), Marcel van der Linden writes, it is in general 'aimed at promoting or opposing a particular political model'.[70] Local trade union action and interaction with a social movement for non-local political gain mean this final category of internationalist expression is the most referred to in this publication.

Transnationalism

It must be said that there are more definitions in circulation, including proletarian/contemporary/labour/trade union/new labour internationalism, however, arguments towards their characterisation do not benefit this study.[71]

---

68 Ibid., 179; Jeffrey Harrod and Robert O'Brien, 'Organized Labour and the Global Political Economy', in *Global Unions? Theory and Strategies of Organized Labour in the Global Political Economy*, eds Jeffry Harrod and Robert O'Brien (London: Routledge, 2002). Van der Linden acknowledged that 'proletarian internationalism is a more multiform and less consistent phenomenon than is often supposed'. Marcel van der Linden, 'Proletarian Internationalism: A Long View and Some Speculations', in *The Modern World-System in the Longue Duree*, ed. Marcel van der Linden (Boulder, Colo.: Paradigm, 2005), 107–31.
69 Mark Anner, 'Local and Transnational Campaigns to End Sweatshop Practices', in *Transnational Cooperation among Labor Unions*, eds Michael E. Gordon and Lowell Turner (Ithaca, NY: ILR Press, 2000).
70 van der Linden, 'Proletarian Internationalism', 111; Peter Waterman, 'The New Social Unionism: A New Union Model for a New World Order', in *Labour Worldwide in the Era of Globalization: Alternative Union Models in the New World Order*, eds Ronaldo Munck and Peter Waterman (Basingstoke, UK: Macmillan, 1999), 255.
71 Trade unions did and do engage in a significant amount of international politics and political actions for the benefit of people in other nations. The actions are not restricted to workers (proletarian internationalism), are not necessarily 'new' or 'contemporary' (Waterman's version) and are not automatically moving anything but moral support or a projection of identity across borders (transnationalism). Proletarian internationalism: van der Linden, 'Proletarian Internationalism', 107. Contemporary internationalism and new labour internationalism: Waterman, Globalization, Social Movements and the New Internationalisms, 50, 52, 134;

It is necessary to mention, however, a currently fashionable term in academic history: transnationalism.[72] Transnationalism was actually formed as the academic reaction to the traditional manner of approaching international relations called 'realism'. Realism supposes that domestic and international politics are completely separate. Transnationalism argues the opposite. This idea is supported through the case studies still to come, but the term 'transnational' implies the carriage of something or someone across a border, and this restriction is one of the reasons it is not used exclusively in this book: actions may be international in intent only.[73]

Many actions discussed within these pages could be classified as transnational and many of the actors most certainly were, but 'internationalism' was the term used by those who undertook the actions and 'transnationalism' is a term imposed upon the past by academics.[74] In ideological terms, the word 'internationalism' meant something to them, just as it has a political connotation for us. For this reason, internationalism is employed in the main.

Just as you come to grips with internationalisms, I must add another layer of complexity, because international interactions involving trade unions are products *and partners* of models of union function, which are defined below.

Industrial national unionism

The structures of 'traditional' or 'old' international interaction are linked to what is called 'industrial national unionism', and adhere to a hierarchical and largely bureaucratic system focused on traditional industrial issues.[75] The industrial national framework is the national expression from which 'international unionism' springs. Where it strays outside the industrial sphere, this type of internationalism tended to follow a more paternalistic aid model, promoting a structured hierarchy in unionism and politics.[76] In general, the self-perpetuating

---

Schmutte, 'International Union Activity', 9, 53, 54; Chun, *The British New Left*, 94–5. Labour internationalism: Barry Carr, *Labor Internationalism in the Era of NAFTA: Past and Present* (Miami: Latin American Labor Studies Publications, 1995), 4.
72 Peter Willets, *Pressure Groups in the Global System: The Transnational Relations of Issue-Orientated Non-Governmental Organizations* (London: Frances Pinter, 1982), xiv.
73 Anner, 'Local and Transnational Campaigns to End Sweatshop Practices', 245.
74 Michael Hanagan, 'An Agenda for Transnational Labour History', *International Review of Social History* 49 (2004), 456.
75 Waterman and Timms, 'Trade Union Internationalism and a Global Civil Society in the Making'; Kim Moody, 'Towards an International Social-Movement Unionism', *New Left Review* i, no. 225 (1997). Or 'National/Industrial/Colonial Unionism' in Peter Waterman, 'Trade Union Internationalism in the Age of Seattle', in *Place, Space and the New Labour Internationalisms*, eds Peter Waterman and Jane Wills (Oxford: Blackwell, 2001), 9.
76 Peter Waterman, 'Trade Union Internationalism in the Age of Seattle', 11, 14; Press, 'The People's Movement', 39.

bureaucracy of these organisations tended to ensure they support activities that reflect their own forms of unionism, and their internationalism has been called 'fraternal tourism' or 'banquet internationalism'.[77] It has been prone, to use the words of Waterman's succinct chapter subtitle, to being confined to paternal 'North–South internationalism' and in the process reproduces the imagery of 'noble savages and promised lands'.[78]

In 1980, John Logue described a particular idiosyncrasy of industrial national unionism, which is perceived to be absent in the international interaction of other forms of unionism: 'international working class solidarity becomes an independent force for continued international activity … It comes, in a way, to represent a good in itself. Born of international action, it becomes a reason for international action.'[79] This is reminiscent of the well-known 'iron law of bureaucracy' outlined by the sociologist Robert Michels: the international tendency is self-replicating and self-supporting.

By the period of this study, however, industrial national unionism's self-perpetuating tendency had been placed under organisational pressure due to changes in the international nature of capital. To paraphrase van der Linden, it was challenged by the formation of trading blocs (such as the North American Free Trade Agreement, NAFTA), the proliferation and dominance of multinational (or transnational) companies and the increasing number of non-governmental organisations that took on causes that were previously on the agenda of the labour movement.[80] Industrial national unionism was aligned with the old left and was not traditionally active in seeking a broad front, yet in the new conditions and with the new left, unions began to act outside the industrial national framework, as the model does not allow for the partnership of labour with social movements or other groups. This led to the theoretical development of another model of unionism.

Social movements and new social movements

The model put forward by scholars is 'social movement unionism', but before attempting to define the paradigm, a question arises that is outside the scope of this publication but nevertheless integral to it and the types of unionism to be described: was the Chile solidarity movement a social movement at all?[81]

---

77 Ronaldo Munck, 'Labour in the Global', in *Global Social Movements*, eds Robin Cohen and Shirin Rai (London: The Athlone Press, 2000), 98.
78 Waterman, Globalization, Social Movements and the New Internationalisms, xiii.
79 Logue, Toward a Theory of Trade Union Internationalism, 35.
80 van der Linden, 'Proletarian Internationalism', 122–4.
81 Wilkinson characterises the Chile Solidarity Campaign (CSC) as a 'lobby group'. While some aspects of the CSC functioned as a political lobby group, defining it as such overlooks some rhetoric, functions and

The definition of social movements is no easy task because, again, no consensus is present in the literature. Theorist Sidney Tarrow has argued that social movements are collective challenges with common purpose, social solidarity and sustained interaction.[82] Consensus—that is, unanimity in relation to the core values of the movement—has also been noted by Frank Parkin as important to social movements,[83] though such broad statements could easily describe trade union organisation or even a football club.

Writing in 1974, John Wilson constructed a typology of social movements that included four types (transformative, reformative, redemptive and alternative). For Wilson, a social movement was a mindful, organised attempt to encourage or prevent change in society from outside its institutions.[84] He continued to thicken his description and wrote that social movements

> function to move people beyond their mundane selves to acts of bravery, savagery, and selfless charity. Animated by the injustices, sufferings, and anxieties they see around them, men and women in social movements reach beyond the customary resources of the social order to launch their own crusade against the evils of society.[85]

Wilson's model is usefully expanded if we consider the work of Jan Pakulski. Pakulski argues that social movements are 'recurrent patterns of collective activities which are partially institutionalised, value oriented and anti-systemic in their form and symbolism'.[86] The Chile movement seems to fit into these definitions, even though it did not only lobby for change to occur within its host countries.[87] Having said that, many commentators have acknowledged that

---

strategies of the CSC such as liaison with rank-and-file unionists and the use and creation of culture. Michael Wilkinson, 'The Influence of the Solidarity Lobby on British Government Policy towards Latin America: 1973–1990' (Master of Politics diss., University of Hull, 1990).
82   Sidney Tarrow, *Power in Movement: Social Movements, Collective Action and Politics* (Cambridge: Cambridge University Press, 1994), 3–4; Sidney Tarrow, *Power in Movement: Social Movements and Contentious Politics* (Cambridge: Cambridge University Press, 1998), 6.
83   Frank Parkin, *Middle Class Radicalism: The Social Bases of the British Campaign for Nuclear Disarmament* (Manchester: University of Manchester Press, 1968).
84   John Wilson, *Introduction to Social Movements* (New York: Basic Books, 1973), 8.
85   Ibid., 5.
86   Jan Pakulski, *Social Movements: The Politics of Moral Protest* (Melbourne: Longman Cheshire, 1991), xiv.
87   The beneficiaries of the 'lobbying' were meant to be Chileans within Chile. Further, another question is raised about scale: how large does an organised campaign need to be in order to be called a movement—though this question is beyond the scope of this short literature review.

the phrase 'social movement' has been used and abused by many academics, social theoreticians, activists and the general public.[88] Pakulski argues that the flexibility of its use and meaning is what makes the term attractive.[89]

As the Chile campaigns specified their aims as political solidarity and change of government in Chile, it seems they fit into the paradigm of a social movement. The question then arises: were the interactions between the Chile solidarity campaigns and trade unions a form of social movement unionism? In order to answer this question in the body of the book, it is necessary to define 'social movement unionism'.

Social movement unionism

The term social movement unionism was originally coined by Peter Waterman and later used by Kim Moody and others.[90] This 'new' unionism highlighted the social responsibility of labour and allowed trade unions to create practical relationships with community groups in order to achieve their extra-industrial goals. Social movement unions do not function in an exclusively hierarchical or vertical manner, as in industrial national unionism, but also horizontally, facilitating shopfloor alliances across borders or participating in direct contact

---

88 For example, Verity Burgmann has stated that a social movement makes demands on the state from within society rather than from within the structures of the state. While this at first seems to be a term that could fit the Chile solidarity movement, Burgmann continues that social movements are made up of imagined communities of the 'oppressed, disadvantaged or threatened'. Many of those involved in the Chile movement in the period under study were not personally oppressed. In terms of the creation of culture, I believe Burgmann fell into a trap of connecting union function paradigms (social movement unionism) and political strategies (new left cultural extension), which are not necessarily as intimately associated as could be assumed. Verity Burgmann, *Power, Profit and Protest: Australian Social Movements and Globalisation* (Crows Nest, NSW: Allen & Unwin, 2003), 4. There are also competing ideas on social movements: Byrne has noted that social movements are unpredictable (do not always arise where there is the greatest need), irrational (not motivated by self-interest), unreasonable (feel justified in their protest) and disorganised (deliberately refrain from organisation). As a definition, this is the least likely to let the Chile solidarity movement fit into its scope for reasons that are apparent through the body of this work. Paul Byrne, *Social Movements in Britain* (London: Routledge, 1997), 10–11. Cohen and Rai propose that 'human rights social movement' is an umbrella term that would take in indigenous rights, antiracism, anti-dictatorship and freedom campaigns. Robin Cohen and Shirin Rai, 'Global Social Movements: Towards a Cosmopolitan Politics', in Global Social Movements, eds Robin Cohen and Shirin Rai (London: The Athlone Press, 2000), 1–17; John Keane, *Global Civil Society?* (Cambridge: Cambridge University Press, 2003); Pakulski, *Social Movements*, xiv.
89 Its flexibility also leads to opacity and subsequently attempts to specify meaning with more and still more variations of the term, like new social movements. 'New social movements' were founded in the 1960s culture of revolution, of anger and a sense of change being possible. New social movements were thought to be those that did not pitch their arguments for or against the state, but around the state. Thompson, *The Left in History*, 193.
90 I maintain its use here, despite Waterman's change to new social unionism of 1999. He implemented this change to free the term of the Third World-ist connotations. Waterman, 'The New Social Unionism', 247–64; Kim Moody, *Workers in a Lean World: Unions in the International Economy* (London: Verso, 1997); Verity Burgmann, *Power and Protest: Movement for Change in Australian Society* (St Leonards, NSW: Allen & Unwin, 1993).

and liaison with new left or social movement groups. Social movement unions undertake lobbying of government and regulatory agencies and also the provision of practical aid, grassroots action, delegations and campaigns to raise awareness.[91]

The accepted definition of social movement unionism is 'an alliance within the class (waged/nonwaged), and/or between the class and the popular/community (workers/people, labour/nationalist)'.[92] This straightforward explanation requires, however, more detail. The theory was developed, according to Waterman, from his experiences as an activist in the 1980s and 1990s.[93] What is more, Waterman constructed the concept of social movement unionism as an interaction between theories, not as a direct explanation of the relationship between social movements and labour, as it has been popularly employed. Waterman came to construct social movement unionism by combining socialist trade union theory and new social movement theory of the late 1980s.[94] It is not my intention to take part in 'depriving' the theorem of its 'critical function', but some practicality must be considered, as this work is an attempt to actually apply the abstract theories to real case studies.[95]

Despite commonsense pointing towards social movement unionism as an adequate paradigm to explain union action in this study, it is actually interlaced with problems. First, as already mentioned, the original intent of the framework was not its application to historical events. Second, the theories and experiences from which it was constructed are from a different time period. Third, the definition Waterman used in his combination to construct social movement unionism was not 'social movements' (which, as already established, include the Chile solidarity movement), but *new* social movements'.[96]

The confusing abstract underpinning these terms weakens their possible usefulness for the application to a study of labour history.

Waterman and Timms have written that despite the proliferation of theories, the intertwined and interdependent relationship between unions and social movements does not find a theoretical expression.[97] They state that 'the growing

---

91 Carr, *Labor Internationalism in the Era of NAFTA*, 6.
92 Peter Waterman, 'Adventures of Emancipatory Labour Strategy as the New Global Movement Challenges International Unionism', *Journal of World-Systems Research* x, no. 1 (2004), 221. Further, the term social movement unionism has been consistently applied in a Third-World context, where international unions aided communities in the Third World. Waterman, 'The New Social Unionism'; Waterman, 'Adventures of Emancipatory Labour Strategy as the New Global Movement Challenges International Unionism', 247.
93 Waterman, 'Adventures of Emancipatory Labour Strategy as the New Global Movement Challenges International Unionism', 222.
94 Ibid., 220.
95 Ibid., 222.
96 Ibid., 220–1.
97 Waterman and Timms, 'Trade Union Internationalism and a Global Civil Society in the Making', 194.

presence of international unions within the global justice and solidarity movement in general ... might suggest a development in the direction of some kind of "international social movement unionism"'.[98]

But note: they specify 'international unions', not unions acting internationally and not unions expressing internationalism.

There exists much material around social movement unionism, new social movement unionism, international social movement unionism, global unionism, political unionism and various other permutations.[99] I do not intend to add to the pool of confusing acronyms. For the purposes of this study, the term social movement unionism will be used to designate an organisational form that simply allowed trade unions to create practical relationships with other community groups in order to achieve their extra-industrial goals.[100] It is popularly considered to be diametrically opposite to and mutually exclusive of the 'old' industrial national unionism. The manner in which unions moved between the two styles is an inherent focus of this research and one that is left to simple explanations of 'organic' transformation by theorists.[101] One of the principal findings of the research undertaken for this book is that the forms were not in fact discrete.

---

98 Ibid., 198.
99 Waterman asserts that old social movements were about religion and nation. 'New social unionism' implies an alliance between labour and *new alternative* social movements (one further theoretical and temporal step away from 'new social movements' and two away from 'social movements'). Waterman, 'The New Social Unionism', 247. 'Social unionism' (an opposition to traditional unionism) attempts to secure standards for workers from within the capitalist system through a three-way partnership with state and business; social unions aim for equality and justice and socially mobilise in that direction. George de Martino, 'The Future of the US Labour Movement in an Era of Global Economic Integration', in *Labour Worldwide in the Era of Globalization*: Alternative Union Models in the New World Order, eds Ronaldo Munck and Peter Waterman (Basingstoke, UK: Macmillan, 1999), 85. Political unionism is where a union allies itself with a party of the left and works to support their platforms. This, in effect, would make the union and the worker passive, and does not explain the integration into a social movement. It also offers a one-dimensional political agenda that is rare in reality. Mike Press, 'International Trade Unionism', in Press and Thompson, *Solidarity for Survival:* The Don Thompson Reader on Trade Union Internationalism, eds Mike Press and Don Thompson (Nottingham: Spokesman, 1989), 24; Moody, 'Towards an International Social-Movement Unionism', 4.
100 Waterman noted that unions had taken on their forms based on the organisation of capital, and had retained those forms, long after capital itself had changed (here Waterman is referring to the structures of industrial national unionism). Unions, he argued, were thus unable to effectively protect their constituents. New global social movements had moved away from an organisation to a network model, which more accurately matched current trends of capital and power flow. 'The old socialist and thirdworldist internationalisms are today little more than so many empty shells—a series of ideologically-defined, institutionalized and competing internationalisms of politicians and officials having little contact with workers or peoples.' Waterman, 'The New Social Unionism', 250; see also p. 55; Waterman, 'Trade Union Internationalism in the Age of Seattle'.
101 Perhaps there is a stepping-stone. The Chile campaigns began just as the new left was in fashion throughout the world. As elucidated in this volume, the strategies of the new left locked trade unions and social movement groups into a reinforcing cycle of support. The Chile movement was part of the 'new wave of non-sectarian and democratic international solidarity activities' of the 1970s that does not receive the academic attention it deserves in terms of its relationship with unions. The movements in both Australia and the United Kingdom roughly fit the ideology of the 'new left social movements' outlined in passing by Verity Burgmann. She noted that social movements harnessed the industrial language of the labour movement to succeed in changing the existing regime: it was the only language capitalists would understand and it

Having explored the abstract categories necessary for this study, it is important to recognise what has already been hinted at: the history that follows does not have an adequate explanation in the current theoretical literature. This book will record expressions of internationalism and I will attempt to place them within abstract paradigms, but theories or theoretical arguments over international social movement unions, new international unionism, social movement unionism or industrial national unionism will not obscure the actual history of the Chile campaigns. This work infers the usefulness of these theories is not in categorising union action but in helping to elucidate the politics of real people in often difficult situations.

The biggest point of confusion around the models previously defined arises when the attempt is made to align a union model with a type of internationalism, a definition of a social movement, an incarnation of left ideology and a type of trade union political action. The terms do not split neatly down the middle, aligning with 'old' and 'new', 'rigid' and 'flexible', 'industrial national' and 'social movement' or 'hierarchical' and 'grassroots'. Where the social movement unionism and industrial national paradigms serve this publication is in providing end points between which an assumed progression occurred: bookends between which I can locate historical actions.

Trade union internationalist action borrows elements of the ideology and strategy of various models without excluding others, and unions regularly slid backwards and forwards across the progressive scale. Exploring the Chile campaigns in detail dissolves the boundaries between what have been considered finite and discrete models. This book, starting with Chapter One, brings political science models to the history, but more importantly, brings this history to light.

---

was considered their only chance at success. This comment prompts an important question: was the Chile movement a new left social movement and, by default, were the unions involved new left unions? Chile solidarity was about democracy and socialism, human rights, peace, justice and solidarity and was a broad-front movement in both Britain and Australia. The title alone, however, would imply support of new left politics, not just strategies, and in this way the term loses validity for this study of Chile solidarity. Many unions, unionists and union leaders who were involved in Chile solidarity were determinedly *not* new left. While unions were incorporated into social movement function during the campaign, the Chile solidarity movement may have been more 'old' than 'new', simply because its aim was to capture nation-state power (in Chile). Waterman, *Globalization, Social Movements and the New Internationalisms*, 10, 41.

Britain

1. The 'principal priority' of the campaign: The trade union movement

On 11 September 1973 Mike Gatehouse slept through his alarm.

The twenty-seven-year-old was meant to be at work at a computer centre at the Forestry Institute in Santiago, Chile. Instead he dozed in his small flat on Ezaguirre Street. When he woke he went to the balcony at the front of the flat and looked down the street. From there he could see that the military putsch had finally come.

The Chilean Communist Party had previously issued a general instruction to its supporters to proceed to their place of work at the first sign of the imminent civil war. So Gatehouse set off. Crossing the city to the Forestry Institute in La Reina took much longer than usual as he avoided main roads. He couldn't see any fighting, but he could hear gunshots.

He arrived at the institute to find that the reality of the first hours of the perceived civil war were actually 'domestic and mundane'.[1] Those who had children and families left the institute to retrieve them from school or to check on their safety. Hours passed. A military curfew was put in place and Gatehouse found himself stuck in the institute. Later still, he recalled his escape: cleaners smuggled him out of the institute and took him to a home in a nearby shantytown.[2] Meanwhile helicopters hovered above the town, sweeping the area with random bursts of machine-gun fire.[3]

Slowly all radio stations were taken over and it became obvious that the coup had been successful. Shock descended on Santiago.[4] 'I will never forget', recalled Gatehouse, 'the press, radio and television images of the new dictatorship:

---

[1] Interview with Mike Gatehouse (Chile activist, UK), 3 August 2007 [hereinafter Gatehouse Interview, 2007], copy in possession of author. For ease of reading, disfluencies such as 'um' have been removed from all oral history quotations.
[2] The director of the institute, Federico Quilodrán, and other colleagues did not escape in time. They were arrested and taken to the National Stadium. The National Stadium is a sporting complex in Santiago. It was used as a detention centre in the first years of the dictatorship and has since been renamed the Victor Jara Stadium in honour of one of the most famous victims of the regime.
[3] Mike Gatehouse, 'Testimony: Detainee Remembers Chile 1973', *BBC News Online*, 23 October 1998, accessed 28 July 2009, <http://news.bbc.co.uk/2/hi/special_report/1998/10/98/the_pinochet_file/198743.stm>.
[4] It had previously been theorised that a coup would not be successful. It was thought that internal divisions in the military would allow trade unions and the people to rise up and oppose the coup.

the harsh robotic voice and the blank face masked by dark glasses of General Pinochet, who represents for me everything that is cruel, destructive, bigoted and philistine'.[5]

Pamphlets had been dropped all over Santiago instructing the denunciation of foreigners, and Gatehouse was at risk because of his involvement in a progressive food-allocation program set up by the Unidad Popular Government.[6] Despite warnings from friends, Gatehouse returned to his flat. He found it had been ransacked. He was there for only a short time, but long enough for a neighbour to alert the police. On his way down the stairs, he was confronted by armed police and it was claimed there had been an arsenal of weapons in the flat.

He was now a prisoner of the military government of Chile.

At the nearest police station, Gatehouse was accused of being a Cuban, despite his blonde hair, blue eyes and English accent.[7] Hours passed. Then, as part of a small group of prisoners, he was 'taken out at gunpoint and forced to lie face-down on the floor of a bus, police with sub-machine guns standing astride' the group.[8] The fear was paralysing. They moved him to the National Stadium where he became one of thousands of prisoners in the large sporting complex.[9] Armed soldiers guarded the prisoners. More soldiers with machine guns were stationed behind sandbag shelters around the stadium. The violence 'wove into a pattern of brutality, part casual and part systematic', wrote Dick Barbour-Might, another Briton interned in the stadium.[10] Gatehouse remembered that 'the "cells" into which we were herded were the team changing rooms. There were 130 prisoners in ours, and at night we were so tightly packed that we could sleep only by lining up in rows and lying down "by numbers", dovetailing heads and feet.'[11]

He recalled the food they were given. Previously, the UP Government had set up a pilot program of restaurants in one of the main parks in Santiago. There, workers could take their families and enjoy high-quality, subsidised restaurant meals. With thousands of prisoners in the stadium, the military rounded up the chefs and forced them to cook for the prisoners. The incarcerated knew the food was from the little pilot UP village in the park, and occasionally someone would

---

5   Gatehouse, 'Testimony'.
6   Ibid.; Chile Solidarity Campaign CSC, *El Arte para el Pueblo* (London: Chile Solidarity Campaign, 1974).
7   *Carabineros* are the police force of Chile. They are regarded as the fourth armed force and their leader was included in the original junta that took power from Allende.
8   Gatehouse, 'Testimony'.
9   *Gatehouse to Basnett, December 30 1976 Re: Scottish Football Team to play Chile*, CSC, CSC/1/12, LHASC, Manchester.
10 'Detained in Chile', Dick Barbour-Might, *New Statesman, September 28, 1973*, Scottish Trades Union Congress [hereinafter STUC], Scottish Trades Union Congress Archive [hereinafter STUCA], 507/2, Glasgow Caledonian University Archive [hereinafter GCUA], Glasgow.
11 Gatehouse, 'Testimony'.

come across a hunk of meat that a sympathetic chef had risked putting into the food for the prisoners. The origin of the sustenance gave them hope and buoyed their spirits, though the amount of food was pitiful.[12]

Most of Gatehouse's memories of the stadium are of a much more traumatic nature:

> The man next to me in my cell was … a Brazilian engineer, named Sergio Moraes, he had worked in a factory called Madeco …
>
> When he returned [from interrogation] he could hardly hear or speak: he had been hooded and beaten about the head and ears with a flat wooden bat. He told us that among his interrogators were Brazilian intelligence officers.
>
> I never knew what happened to him, but an Amnesty International researcher who went to Santiago some weeks later was told by a military official: 'I hope to god we killed him'.[13]

The British Embassy finally discovered Gatehouse's location in the National Stadium and negotiated with the military for his freedom. He would be released on the condition he leave the country. He had been interned for seven days.[14]

The coup in Chile changed Mike Gatehouse. He left the country reluctantly, having established a life and invested ideological and emotional energy in the UP project. The destruction of his Chilean life, his imprisonment and the death of his friends disoriented him. It was a dramatic and traumatic return to Britain. He arrived on 2 October 1973 full of pain and anger and eager to share the story of his last moments in Chile. He threw himself into the work of Chile solidarity, speaking, typing and duplicating. It was the beginning of an activist's lifestyle from which he has never fully emerged.

Writing about nineteenth-century radicals in Britain, historian David Hamer described the attributes of those he called 'faddists': 'faddists were people who were possessed of a vision and also filled with indignation and the fundamental wrongness, indeed the evil, of the existing state of affairs.'[15]

Hamer goes on to suggest that for many faddists their cause became an obsession—'the object to which their lives were consecrated'.[16] Hamer's tense is important: he clearly believes faddism was a thing of the past. In fact, he insists that 'faddism is most emphatically not a twentieth century subject' and that it

---

12 Gatehouse, in conversation with author, 2007.
13 Gatehouse, 'Testimony'.
14 *Gatehouse to Basnett, December 30 1976 Re: Scottish Football Team to play Chile.*
15 David Hamer, The Politics of Electoral Pressure: A Study in the History of Victorian Reform Agitations (Sussex: The Harvester Press, 1977), 1.
16 Ibid., 1.

had disappeared from political discourse by 1900.[17] He was wrong. Though the word itself had accumulated other connotations, the research in these pages is constructed from the historical record left by twentieth-century faddists (in the original sense). Discard the negative connotations of modern popular culture, and this word describes the people upon whose dedication the Chile cause and the Chile campaigns were built and sustained.

One of them was Mike Gatehouse. Despite his self-effacing and low-key manner, Gatehouse had a major impact on the campaign. He would become one of the most important and dedicated figures in the Chile solidarity movement in Britain.

Gatehouse's role was based firmly in the political arm of the solidarity movement embodied by the Chile Solidarity Campaign (CSC). This chapter outlines the formation and function of that organisation, arguing that CSC operation, despite its formal hierarchy and institutionalised labelling, remained the product of the idiosyncrasies of those involved.[18] The CSC is placed in the context of the British labour movement, and the interaction of political parties and trade unions with the campaign is discussed in detail. The peculiarities of British trade union politics and the interstices in the structure of the labour movement made it possible for individuals to have disproportionate influence in the left. These individuals would become the most important tactical acquisitions of single-issue campaigns such as the CSC.

Strategic individuals—only some of them modern faddists—formed webs of contacts that John Baxter termed an 'interlocking directorate'.[19] Select individuals could be more important strategically due to their bundled affiliations and acquaintances, and they might be called an interconnected node. As the political left expanded in the 1960s and 1970s to include solidarity and liberation movements, these new causes came to rely on the individuals with accumulated connections for success.

Individuals could also bring moral capital to the campaign. 'Moral capital', writes John Kane, 'is credited to political agents on the basis of the perceived merits of the values and ends they serve and of their practical fidelity in pursuing them'.[20]

---

17 Ibid., 2.
18 Other groups encompassed by the Chile solidarity movement which will be dealt with in footnotes are: CSC Cultural Committee and Chile Lucha, the Chile Committee for Human Rights (CCHR), Academics for Chile, World University Service (WUS) and the Joint Working Group (JWG) for Refugees from Chile. The arrival of more substantial numbers of immigrants caused the Centro Unica de Trabajadores (CUT, the trade unions congress of pre-coup Chile) to nominate representatives and take an office in London. The group of individuals 'Chile Lucha' was in charge of the magazine *Chile Lucha* (literally, 'Chile Fights'). In this publication, the group will be referred to as Chile Lucha and the publication as *Chile Fights*.
19 John L. Baxter, 'Early Chartism and Labour Class Struggle: South Yorkshire 1837–1840', in *Essays in the Economic and Social History of South Yorkshire*, eds Sidney Pollard and Colin Holmes (Barnsley: South Yorkshire County Council, Recreation Culture and Health Department, 1976), 139.
20 Kane, The Politics of *Moral Capital*, 20.

The need for moral capital in an organisation such as a solidarity campaign stems from the fact that rationality alone cannot be relied upon to mobilise.[21] Moral capital has a 'crucial supportive role' in public and political life that is not apparent until that capital disappears, as it legitimises persons, positions, offices and campaigns.[22] While it was imperative for solidarity organisations to attract moral capital through individuals and affiliations, the campaigns themselves could also bestow capital on participants, as will be demonstrated in the pages that follow.

This detailed description of the Chile solidarity movement provides an opportunity for preliminary assessment of the critical reasons for and against trade union political action. Ian Schmutte has argued that '[u]nions make purposive decisions about the deployment of scarce resources to achieve their goals'.[23] This is called rational choice—that is, maximum benefit for minimal loss—in internationalist actions. The unions in these pages could be called 'rational maximisers'. Regardless of ideology, the likelihood of union action for an external cause was inversely related to its potential impact on the membership.

Trade unions formed part of a web of organisations in the Chile solidarity movement, and mapping the web is no easy task: the network of organisations and individuals is daunting. Prior to the coup there had already been solidarity organisations and, naturally, these were the first to express disapproval of the coup.

Mike Gatehouse arrived from Chile to find a flurry of activity as the CSC was emerging from pre-existing organisations such as the Association for British–Chilean Friendship (ABCF) and Liberation. The association was formed during the Allende administration, and in February 1973 the group boasted 168 members including artists, academics and intellectuals such as Dick Barbour-Might, Betty Tate, Celia Bower, George Hutchinson and Pat Stocker. As a group, they professed solidarity with the UP administration and published a bulletin called *New Chile*. The group had strong rhetoric against multinational companies and published booklets on the International Telephone and Telegraph Company and information on Kennecott and their dealings in Chile.

Despite their strong international focus, they were aware of the importance of attracting the support of British trade unions. Even before the coup, at the annual general meeting in 1973, it was resolved '[t]hat the A.B.C.F. should, during the coming year, develop political support for Chile, particularly amongst British trade unionists, in order to expose the machinations of

---

21 'Reliance on moral persuasion declines in proportion as political order succeeds in accruing power and has, consequently, more and different means available for consolidating itself.' Ibid., 16.
22 Ibid., 11.
23 Schmutte, 'International Union Activity', 3.

multinational corporations'. Immediately before the coup, as the situation in Chile deteriorated, they issued a leaflet that stated in upper case: 'WE IN THE BRITISH LABOUR MOVEMENT URGENTLY CALL UPON BRITISH WORKERS TO EXPRESS THEIR SOLIDARITY WITH CHILEAN WORKERS IN THEIR STRUGGLE TO ESTABLISH DEMOCRATIC SOCIALISM.'[24]

The focus on trade unions would be inherited by the Chile Solidarity Campaign, as the main post-coup solidarity group became known, but the political emphasis would shift. The Chile campaign was a broad alliance of left groups, centralised in a small office in London. It was, as with any broad front, subject to tension within its organisation, and furthermore, the CSC was often victim of the external tensions between its affiliates, whose relationships extended beyond solidarity into the industrial sphere.[25] There were also substantial committees in both Liverpool and Scotland and the latter ran almost completely separately from the London-based committee.[26]

The first meetings of the CSC were held at the House of Commons, but soon the meetings moved to the 'wonderfully chaotic' office of Liberation in Caledonian Road, London.[27] The first letters sent from the Chile Solidarity Campaign Committee were on the Liberation letterhead. Steve Hart, secretary of Liberation

---

[24] The leaflet was signed by the following labour movement leaders and organisations: Bill Simpson; Ron Hayward; Judith Hart; Ian Mikardo; Alec Kitson; Jack Jones; Hugh Scanlon; George Smith; Alf Allen; Richard Briginshaw; Dan McGarvey; Terry Parry; Cyril Plant; Joe Craworf; Leslie Buck; Lawrence Daly; Alan Fisher; George Doughty; Charles Grieve; Alan Sapper; John Slater; Roy Grantham; Harry Urwin; BLP; TGWU; AUEW; Union of Construction, Allied Trades and Technicians (UCATT); Union of Shop, Distributive and Allied Workers (USDAW); National Society of Operative Printers, Graphical and Media Personnel; Amalgamated Society of Boilermakers, Shipwrights, Blacksmiths and Structural Workers; Inland Revenue Staff Federation; National Association of Colliery Overmen, Deputies and Shotfirers; National Union of Sheet Metal Workers, Coppersmiths, Heating and Domestic Engineers; National Union of Miners; AUEW TASS; Tobacco Workers' Union; Association of Cinematograph Television and Allied Technicians; Merchant Navy and Air Line Officers Association; Association of Professional, Executive, Clerical and Computer Staff; National Union of Public Employees. This is a prime example of an interlocking directorate. When the coup occurred, they mobilised support for the Chilean Embassy, the ambassador, Alvaro Bunster, in particular, and more generally supported the formation of a representative national solidarity committee to be formed. *Association for British Chilean Friendship, 1975*, CSC, CSC/28/2, LHASC, Manchester; *Association for British–Chilean Friendship: AGM Feb 16th. Secretary's Report, 1973*, Etheridge Papers: Longbridge Shop Stewards, MSS.202/S/J/3/2/184, MRC [hereinafter Modern Records Centre], UW [hereinafter University of Warwick], Coventry; *Hutchinson and Tate (ABCF) to TUC, 18th September 1973*, TUC, MSS.292D/980.31/1, MRC, UW, Coventry.

[25] Interview with Barry Fitzpatrick (journalist, National Society of Operative Printers and Assistants representative to the CSC), 28 July 2007 [hereinafter Fitzpatrick Interview, 2007], copy in possession of author.

[26] The Merseyside committee was extremely active and boasted a very high level of union involvement. Due to restriction of length rather than interest or importance, the focus of this chapter is the London committee. For a short history of the Merseyside CSC, please refer to: Angie Thew et al., *Commemorative Programme for the Premiere Screening of Cruel Separation* (Liverpool: Merseyside Chile Solidarity Committee, 2008). Some Scottish history is included in Chapter Four.

[27] Liberation was a small organisation that was started in the 1940s as the Movement for Colonial Freedom. At the time of the coup in 1973, it boasted prominent BLP member Stan Newens and Robert Hughes MP as its joint chairmen. Liberation served as a springboard for more specific single-issue campaigns such as the CSC. Mike Gatehouse, in Wilkinson, 'The Influence of the Solidarity Lobby on British Government Policy towards Latin America'; Gatehouse Interview, 2007; *CSC Executive Committee: Minutes of the meeting held at Liberation on February 5, 1974*, CSC, CSC/1/3, LHASC, Manchester.

and its only full-time staff member, worked with the CSC for the first year. Hart had been a member of the Communist Party of Great Britain (CPGB) at Cambridge University in the early 1970s, after which he moved to work for Liberation.[28] Hart was the youngest son of Dame Judith Hart MP, who was at the time regarded as the foremost expert on Latin America within the Parliamentary Labour Party (PLP).[29]

Soon after he arrived back from Chile, Gatehouse put his distress and culture shock aside, and contacted Amnesty International, impatient to give his testimony on the occurrences in the National Stadium.[30] He also connected with the CPGB and spoke to their branches.[31] He remembered that in December he started to attend campaign committee meetings: 'and I suppose people starting to get to know me and I was wanting to, by what ever means, to work on Chile with the whole of my consciousness. And so, in some way or another it was suggested that I become Joint Secretary' of the CSC.[32]

Working at first from the Liberation offices and soon after moving into the London Co-operative Society (LCS) building on Seven Sisters Road, Gatehouse and the twenty-two-year-old Steve Hart were joint secretaries of the CSC for the first year of its existence.[33]

Waterman has defined solidarity committees as 'voluntary organizations set up with the purpose of providing publicity, political support and financial

---

[28] He later went on to work at a Ford factory and become an officer in the Transport and General Workers' Union. Gatehouse Interview, 2007.
[29] She was a keen supporter of the Chile campaign and a member of BLP and labour movement delegations to Chile both before and after the coup. Judith Hart, 'Chile: Not the End of the Road for Socialism', *Tribune* [UK], 14 September 1973; *Chile Now: Initial Report of the Labour Movement Delegation* (London: Chile Solidarity Committee, 1984); Wilkinson, 'The Influence of the Solidarity Lobby'.
[30] Amnesty International went on to work closely with the 'non-political' Chile Committee for Human Rights (CCHR). The CCHR aimed to relieve substandard human rights within Chile. It remained as non-political as possible to enable alliance with church and other groups such as Amnesty International. It employed the energy and fame of people such as Joan Jara and Sheila Cassidy as well as testimony of refugees in order to garner support. Joan Jara was the English wife of the famous Chilean new song artist Victor Jara, who was brutally killed by the Chilean military in the first days after the coup. Sheila Cassidy was a British medical doctor detained and tortured by the military in Chile. After her release, the revelations of her treatment caused the British ambassador to be withdrawn from Chile. Wilkinson, 'The Influence of the Solidarity Lobby'.
[31] Gatehouse was, while in Chile, very close to the Chilean Communist Party. He joined the CPGB on his return. In 1974, the CPGB had just less than 30 000 members; it was a sizeable and powerful organisation. Shipley, *Revolutionaries in Modern Britain*, 219.
[32] Gatehouse Interview, 2007.
[33] The 'committee' was only tacked onto the name for the first period of the dictatorship, but was soon dropped in common conversation to simply become CSC. The LCS Education Committee let the small front office to the CSC for a minimal price. The LCS Political Committee worked with the campaign quite often and at its helm was Alf Lomas, who would go on to represent the United Kingdom in the European Parliament. The CSC office at Seven Sisters Road was happily situated close to a pub called 'The Rainbow', where the secretaries used to eat a counter meal with a pint in the evenings before returning to work in the office. Tony Gilbert, *Only One Died* (London: Kay Beauchamp, 1974), 49; Gatehouse Interview, 2007.

assistance to foreign peoples, organizations and even states'.[34] The 1970s and 1980s saw a wave of these groups, which could be semi or fully institutionalised, but even taking this into account, Waterman believes the groups were closer to social movements than to semi-state bodies.[35] They were not a part of the institutionalised labour movement and had flexibility and freedom to innovate because of that.[36] Yet their position outside the traditional hierarchy necessitated the energies of various leading personalities of the left to pull together the substantial resources and ideological impetus needed to establish a broad left campaign. It could not have been achieved by the two joint secretaries alone, despite Hart's family connections. International secretary of the CPGB, Jack Woddis, was strongly in favour of the campaign remaining a broad left conglomerate. 'And that was very important', said Gatehouse, 'because elsewhere, right across Europe, solidarity campaigns differentiated and split quite early on, because the various Trotskyist groups took the general view that Chile was the prime example of the failure of communism'.[37]

The International Marxist Group (IMG) and Socialist Workers' Party (SWP) were the two main Trotskyite groupings in Britain at the time of the coup. Ensuring the CSC was an inclusive, broad front would appease some of their criticism of both it and the UP Government with the aim of keeping the focus on solidarity. The CPGB's support for the broad front sustains the notion put forward by Shipley that the CPGB acted as a progenitor of other left enterprises, although he prefixes that with 'reluctant', which does not match Woddis's attitude towards the CSC.[38] Though the party was not known as a new left organisation, by actively encouraging a broad front, the CPGB utilised one of the new left's defining strategies. It then had a relationship with others through the united front, like Raul Sol, an expatriate Chilean journalist who was well known in British left circles.[39] The British left had learnt important lessons from a disastrous split in

---

34 Waterman, Globalization, Social Movements and the New Internationalisms, 132.
35 Ibid., 139.
36 They were, however, a 'traditional part of the democratic and socialist movement' from the early nineteenth century. Ibid., 132, 35.
37 Gatehouse Interview, 2007.
38 Shipley, *Revolutionaries in Modern Britain*, 24.
39 Raul Sol 'was, in some senses, [a] charismatic, highly intelligent very intellectual person', who held the respect of many of the Chilean and British left. Sol had established himself by taking an offer to go to the Falklands to get the 'scoop' on the invasion. According to Gatehouse, Sol 'clearly formulated the idea that we should be a unified Campaign and however much there might be disagreement among the segments within the Campaign, that there was much more to be gained for everyone by hanging together than by hanging separately'. This idea was supported by a move towards a broad left front within the National Union of Students in the 1970s. Gatehouse Interview, 2007; Interview with Mike Gatehouse (Chile activist, UK), 13 August 2008 [hereinafter Gatehouse Interview, 2008], copy in possession of author; Shipley, *Revolutionaries in Modern Britain*, 46.

the Vietnam solidarity movement, as well as from watching the splits within the French Chile solidarity movement. There was thus a predisposition to keep the movement united.[40]

Consequently, the CSC functioned as a broad left representative organisation that gathered members through an affiliation and local committee system. Trade unions were encouraged to affiliate at different levels, from national to branch, as were other groups such as political parties, student movement organisations and trades councils. Individuals were able to join too. Affiliations were sought through circulars, direct letters and speeches at demonstrations, fringe meetings and conferences.[41] For their fees, affiliates received copies of the CSC magazine, *Chile Fights*, and the bulletin *Chile Monitor*. These were both important assets of the movement, as it has been noted that communication is the nervous system of international solidarity movements.[42] Only affiliation by unions at the regional committee or national level resulted in a representative on the CSC Executive Committee.[43]

Affiliation brought both inertia and stability to the CSC. The bureaucratised nature of the relationship meant that once a union affiliated it was very likely they would remain so in the future and continue to pay affiliation fees.[44] The future was almost certain for the committee, at least in terms of funding.[45] Trade unionist Brian Nicholson said at a conference in 1982 that the CSC's strength came 'from the hundreds of party branches, trade union district committees and branches, trades councils and individual Labour Movement activists who are affiliated to the Campaign. It is they who ensure that there is *real solidarity* action with the Chilean People'[46] (my emphasis).

---

40 Having said that, it was not without its problems, especially in the early years. See, for example: *Minutes of the National Action Conference on Chile, 1974*, CSC, CSC/11/1, LHASC, Manchester; *Cal to Pat, Wednesday 10 April, 1974*, CSC, CSC/14/2, LHASC, Manchester.
41 *Gatehouse to Colleagues, July 10 1974*, CSC, CSC/4/1, LHASC, Manchester. Kitson often chaired the fringe meetings. *CSC-EC 16.10.79 Minutes*, CSC, CSC/1/5, LHASC, Manchester.
42 Waterman, Globalization, Social Movements and the New Internationalisms, 257.
43 *Affiliation to the CSC, 1974*, CSC, CSC/4/1, LHASC, Manchester.
44 Wilkinson, 'The Influence of the Solidarity Lobby', 81. Gatehouse used the same words in my interviews with him: an inertia effect of trade union affiliation. Gatehouse Interview, 2007. I found only one case where this did not occur. The Sheffield Trades Council de-affiliated in 1978, then re-affiliated within six months after a visit from Gatehouse. This was the home branch of Martin Flannery (BLP MP). *Thornes (Sheffield District Trades Council) to TUC, 21st. April, 1978*, TUC, MSS.292D/980.31/8, MRC, UW, Coventry; *Report of Meeting held on 23rd May 1978 in the House of Commons, 1978*, TUC [BLP International Department], MSS.292D/936.1/6, MRC, UW, Coventry; *CSC EC 1.8.78 Minutes*, CSC, CSC/1/5, LHASC, Manchester.
45 Other activities the CSCP undertook to raise money included merchandising, 'benefit bops', sponsored bike rides and parachute jumps. Trade unionist Barry Fitzpatrick remembered that 'it was a very enjoyable campaign, apart from the topic'. Fitzpatrick Interview, 2007.
46 *Bristol Conference, January 30 1982, Notes for Brian Nicholson*, CSC, CSC/11/15, LHASC, Manchester.

'Real solidarity' came through the implied consensus of affiliation and the funds the affiliation provided.[47] By 1976, 19 unions were affiliated to the CSC at the national level, which, estimated Gatehouse in his report to the annual general meeting, equalled a total membership of approximately 5.8 million.[48] And the campaign continued to grow. By the end of 1977 there were 30 national unions, 85 Constituency Labour Party branches, 54 trades councils, 56 student unions, 46 associations of scientific, technical and managerial staff branches, 18 Amalgamated Union of Engineering Workers (AUEW) branches and district committees, 18 branches of the Transport and General Workers' Union (TGWU), 21 National Association of Local Government Officers (NALGO) branches, eight National Graphical Association branches, 50 branches of other unions, 24 other political parties and 59 individual affiliates.[49] This created a substantial mailing list and a reasonable annual income.

The large list of affiliates yielded a 55-member CSC Executive Committee in 1977.[50] There were 22 unions represented along with seven political groups, three other groups and office holders. Average attendance was 20 across the monthly CSC Executive Committee meetings of that year.[51] Though this represents less than half of those entitled to attend, it was still a large committee taking in most sections of the labour movement and it gave authority to the CSC as a representative front.

The CSC and unions had a symbiotic relationship. By affiliating, unions could fulfil international portfolios, give substance to their solidarity and embody the rhetoric of international brotherhood with a minimum of fuss. That is,

---

47 In 1975 the CSC's affiliation rates ranged from £5.50 for individuals to £25 for national bodies. *CSC Affiliation Form, 1975*, STUC, STUCA 507/3, Glasgow Caledonian University Archives [hereinafter GCUA], Glasgow. Administrative leniency was employed, however, on various occasions to ensure that all groups who so desired could affiliate regardless of their financial status. See, for example: *Edmunds (Yeovil & District Trades Council) to CSC 1974*, CSC, CSC/4/1, LHASC, Manchester.
48 *Annual General Meeting London. February 7 1976. Secretary's Report*, CSC, CSC/1/11, LHASC, Manchester.
49 *CSC Annual Report, 1977*, CSC, CSC/1/13, LHASC, Manchester.
50 Ibid. The MPs were Andrew Bennet, Martin Flannery, John Ivenden, Jo Richardson, Judith Hart, Neil Kinnock, Eddy Loyden and Stan Newens. The political groupings were: BLP, CPGB, Youth Communist League (YCL), Liberation, IMG, SWP, Labour Party Young Socialists (LPYS). Other groups were: National Organisation of Labour Students (NOLS), London Co-operative Society Political Committee (LCS-PC), University of London Students (ULS). Trade unions: Association of Cinematograph, Television and Allied Technicians (ACTT), Associated Society of Locomotive Engineers and Firemen (ASLEF), AUEW, AUEW TASS, Civil and Public Services Association (CPSA), Furniture, Timber and Allied Trades (FTAT), NALGO, National Association of Teachers in Further and Higher Education (NATFHE), National Society of Operative Printers and Assistants (NATSOPA), National Graphical Association (NGA), NUM, NUPE, National Union of Railwaymen (NUR), National Union of Sheet Metal Workers (NUSMW), National Union of Seamen (NUS), National Union of Gold, Silver and Allied Trades (NUGSAT), National Union of Tailors and Garment Workers (NUTGW), SLADE, Society of Graphical and Allied Trades (SOGAT), TGWU, USDAW. Chile Solidarity Campaign officers and convenors and representatives of the seven CSC local committee regions also sat on the Executive Committee.
51 Chile Solidarity Campaign, *Chile Solidarity Campaign: Annual Report* (London: Chile Solidarity Campaign, 1977).

they rationally maximised their gain for use of resources.⁵² As the incentive for solidarity with Chile was remote (apart from bragging rights and fulfilment of identity), action for Chile needed almost *no* impediment for it to occur.

The ability of the campaign to be flexible and innovative due to its lack of institutional base was attractive to some unions. Ken Coates and Tony Topham have written that contrary to what opponents believe, unions are 'ill-adapted organs for the refinement of detailed political strategies, [thus] they tend to find themselves reacting to the initiatives of others, rather than assuming any overall innovative tone'.⁵³ Unions were both reactive to and exploitative of the campaign: they were opportunists when it came to internationalism.

The establishment of local committees of the CSC was not as vigorously pursued as trade union links. The local committees formed in a largely organic and haphazard manner, dependent on the efforts of local activists to set up and maintain them.⁵⁴ They were encouraged to integrate into the national campaign (which occurred to varying degrees) as well as to coordinate trade unionists at the local level and elicit the cooperation of trades councils. The functioning of local committees varied: some had complex structures complete with their own cultural committees while others were more ad hoc or seasonal.⁵⁵

Local committees and trade union affiliations provided the main routes through which information flowed to and from the regions of the United Kingdom and Ireland.⁵⁶ There was an early attempt to divide the local committees into seven regions, each with one representative on the Executive Committee;⁵⁷ however, this model did not function well due to the differing nature of the local committees, extended travel time, lack of funding and the deficiency of resources for coordination at the national office.⁵⁸ The central office in London

---

52   Schmutte, 'International Union Activity', 61.
53   Ken Coates and Tony Topham, *Trade Unions in Britain* (London: Fontana Press, 1988), 358.
54   The only case of the central CSC trying to stimulate the formation of a local committee that was found in the archives is a letter prompting Lyn Murray to organise a committee in Manchester in 1974. *Gatehouse to Murray, November 19 1974*, CSC, CSC/13/5, LHASC, Manchester.
55   Local committees included: Aberdeen, Bath, Bradford, Brighton, Birmingham, Bristol, Bury St Edmunds, Cambridge, Cardiff, Chelmsford, Colchester, Coleg Harlek, Coventry, Crawley, Cumbria, Darlington, Dundee, Dublin, Durham, East Anglia, East London, Exeter, Falkirk, Fife, Galway, Glasgow, Gloucester, Greenwich, Harlow, Hemel Hempsted, Hull, Humberside, Ilford, Kent, Lancaster, Leicester, Leigh, Lewisham, London School of Economics, Luton, Leeds, London, Manchester and Stockport, Merseyside, Mansfield, Newport, North Gloucestershire, North London, Northants, Northampton, Norwich, Nottingham, Oldham, Oxford, Portsmouth, Portsmouth Polytechnic College, Redditch, Rochdale, Sheffield, Skelmersdale, Southampton, St Albans, Strathkelvin, Sterling, Swansea, Swindon, Tyneside, West London, West Middlesex, York.
56   Affiliates and local committees received separate communications from the CSC with different tones, but largely similar information.
57   The regions were Scotland, North-East, North-West, South-West, East-Central, South-East and London. *CSC: Regional Structure, 1974*, CSC, CSC/1/3, LHASC, Manchester; *List of Local Chile Solidarity Committees, By Regions, As of May 15 1974*, CSC, CSC/1/3, LHASC, Manchester.
58   National meetings of local committees were held in an attempt to reflect the democratic nature of the CSC's structure.

did its best to keep up with regional matters, but the CSC was at best a loose federation and at worst an anarchistic and individualist alliance.[59] That's not to say that all were happy with the status quo. As early as the 1974 annual general meeting, joint secretary Gatehouse warned that the 'over-emphasis on the administrative efficiency of the Campaign, advance distribution of documents, etc, would lead to a diminution of the real solidarity work, unless substantial funding could be found for expanding the Campaign office'.[60]

From the outset the issue of internal democracy bedevilled the campaign and, by 1977, a Chile Solidarity Campaign Commission was formed to investigate the democratic processes of the CSC with a focus on the relationship between the executive and the local committees. The importance of trade union participation for the CSC (which impacted on funding and legitimacy) was evident in the commission's report. It recommended that the vexed question of the timing of the executive meetings (midweek to suit MPs and trade unionists; weekends to suit local committees) should be settled in favour of the trade union affiliates.[61] This decision was ironic, because local committees were almost always more ideologically sympathetic to the UP and Chilean politics than the trade unions, and the CSC had positioned itself as the political arm of the solidarity movement. Nevertheless, trade union and labour movement support was more valuable than the ideologically pure, but numerically few, local committees.

Harnessing the power of the labour movement was the most important strategic goal of the CSC.[62] Trade unionists were elected to public positions in the campaign (explained further below) and a concerted effort was made to include the actions of all trade unionists at all levels of the movement under the CSC banner. The national office reminded CSC local committees in 1976 that trade union councils and branches were imperative to action, especially direct action.[63] The campaign instructed its local committees to make an effort to fit in with the 'procedural' nature of trade unions. Trade union liaison had rapidly absorbed the majority of time in the CSC, though the campaign noted that 'boycotts have usually been [at] the initiative of the workers concerned, and in few, if any, cases has the Campaign had any direct influence'.[64]

---

59 A system of minute collection from the regions was not employed. Instead the national office relied on a more ad-hoc system of word of mouth and sporadic correspondence. Correspondence with Brian Anglo of the Manchester local committee can be found at: *Gatehouse to Anglo, December 13, 1975*, CSC, CSC/2/2, LHASC, Manchester.
60 *CSC: Annual General Meeting, December 14 1974, Islington South-East Library, 1974*, Coventry Trade Union Council, MSS.5/3/6, MRC, UW, Coventry.
61 *CSC Commission Final Report, 1977*, CSC, CSC/1/12, LHASC, Manchester.
62 This has been identified as an aspect of the archetypical 'new left movement'. Burgmann, *Power, Profit and Protest*, 22.
63 *Suggestions for Local Committees re: Trade Union Work, 1976*, CSC, CSC/16/2, LHASC, Manchester.
64 *CSC. Executive Committee: Analysis of Campaign Performance to Date. Discussion Document. 23/10/74*, CSC, CSC/1/4, LHASC, Manchester.

In the office itself, Mike Gatehouse and Steve Hart assiduously worked the long days of a modern faddist for a lean wage.

Sacrifice did not bring reward for Hart.

At the first annual general meeting of the CSC, Hart was pushed out of the position by groups of the 'ultra-left' who were uncomfortable with two communists in the powerful organising positions in the CSC.[65] 'But it wasn't a bad thing', said Gatehouse in 2007, 'I think Steve was pissed off at the time, but I think he was ready to move on anyway'.[66]

The departure of Hart from the campaign weakened its ties to Liberation and helped the CSC stand on its own. This was the first major administrative change but it was by no means the last. The influential position of general secretary of the campaign moved through various activists' hands over the 17 years of the CSC's existence. Each of these professional activists brought to the CSC their own political ideas and their own organising style, not to mention their own set of contacts.[67]

The work of the CSC organiser was hugely varied. They were expected to be the 'renaissance' activist: able to speak at meetings, write letters, make telephone calls, write apologies, incite emotion, paint pictures, design posters, look after public figures, cope with the secret service, counsel Chileans, organise tours, photostat, type with a minimum of mistakes (paper was especially scarce in the first years of the campaign) and, above all, raise their own salary.

The role evolved slightly over the years. As the CSC became more and more organised and entrenched in its functions and hierarchies, as well as more stable financially, the work of the secretary became less a jack-of-all-trades and more a master of the social movement. Artists could be employed to design and complete posters and companies could be enlisted to distribute them. Over the years of the campaign, the title used for this position varied—general secretary, organiser, joint secretary—but essentially the role stayed the same: these dedicated people were the organising workhorses of the CSC. They were the faddists, whose commitment to the cause superseded almost any other factor.

---

65   The vote for the unpaid post was between Steve Hart and Colin Henfrey. Henfrey won 57 votes to 29. Colin Henfrey was a Liverpool academic and a CPGB member. *CSC Annual General Meeting. December 14 1974.*
66   Gatehouse Interview, 2007. Hart returned to Liberation, where he had continued to perform duties in conjunction with his involvement in the CSC.
67   Mike Gatehouse (joint secretary), 1973–79; Steve Hart (joint secretary), 1973–75; Ken Hulme (trade union organiser), 1975–79; Colin Henfrey (joint secretary), 1977; Jerry Hughes (national organiser), 1979–81; Bill McClellan (CSC officer/national organiser), 1979–85; Quentin Given (national organiser), 1982–89; Helen Garner (CSC organiser), 1986; Carole Billinghurst (CSC organiser), 1987–89. Others who occasionally took on organising roles include Jane McKay (Glasgow), Sue Carstairs (1975), Anne Brown, Carl Blackburn (Secretary, 1991), Angela Thew (Liverpool, late 1980s), Graham Jones (1975), Gordon Hutchinson (local committees organisation), Duncan MacIntosh (distribution), Imogen Mark (publications) and Celia Bower (finance). Dates in this table are estimated from the appearance of their names in the CSC archive and other sources.

In the CSC office, during the early period, Gatehouse divided his time among three types of activities. The first was collecting and publicising information from grassroots groups and trade unions on solidarity actions occurring around the country. The second was organising and implementing endorsable (by trade unions, political parties or key individuals) actions such as tours, demonstrations or the national consumer boycott campaign. Third, the central office maintained the structure of the movement by preparing newsletters, organising meetings, writing letters and other administrative tasks. Gatehouse remembered that his hours in the office were 'frantic'. The nature of a very small office with a very large number of affiliates meant that many hours a week were spent stuffing envelopes, leaving little time for other tasks.[68] As in other organisations of the labour movement, however, the secretaries were generally more powerful than their title suggests, as every communication passed through their hands.

After Hart's departure in 1974, Gatehouse first worked beside Graham Jones. 'But', said Gatehouse, 'he couldn't cope with the ultra-left and they gradually put the squeeze on him to get him out'.[69] So, in March 1975, the CSC created a new position specifically to channel trade union support. The man who got the job of trade union organiser was Ken Hulme.[70]

Hulme was a young man of twenty-five years when he entered the CSC office. He had graduated from Warwick University where he had been active in the Trotskyite International Socialists (IS). After finishing university, he went to work on a shop floor in the motor industry in Coventry. 'I was a bit of a student revolutionary', he remembered.[71] He had been secretary of the Coventry Trades Council, a member of the district committee of the TGWU and had helped to establish the CSC local committee in that city.

In early 1975 Hulme departed Coventry and the ultra-left for some time off before beginning a masters degree at the London School of Economics. Peter Binns, one of the leaders of the IS, called Hulme to ask him to apply for the organising position on the CSC. Hulme recalled that there was an ongoing 'battle' in the broad-front CSC executive between political factions. The IS was looking for a capable organiser to contest the CPGB candidate. Hulme continued: 'I don't think they expected me to get appointed, and they tried to get me to take a tape recorder into my interview so everything could be taped.'[72]

---

68 This sort of 'mechanical' lobbying (pamphlets, newsletters and effective administration) led to many of the political ultra-left considering that the CSC was overly bureaucratised. Gatehouse insists that this criticism was mainly because they were not controlling the committee themselves. Gatehouse Interview, 2007.
69 Ibid.
70 Both Gatehouse and Hulme were paid £23 a week plus £4 travel expenses. *Annual General Meeting London. February 7 1976. Secretary's Report*.
71 Interview with Ken Hulme (Chile activist, UK), 1 September 2007 [hereinafter Hulme Interview, 2007], notes in possession of author.
72 Ibid. The panel at the interview was Brian Nicholson, George Anthony (at the time called Trade Union Convenor), Gatehouse and Colin Henfrey (Merseyside CSC). They would make a recommendation to the executive, who would ultimately decide. *CSC: Annual General Meeting, December 14 1974*.

Hulme was successful because of his trade union experience, which the CPGB candidate could not equal;[73] but as Gatehouse explained in 2007, the tactics of the IS backfired because 'unbeknownst to them [Hulme] was already in conversation with the Communist Party to become a Communist Party member, which he did very shortly after joining the Campaign, which really pissed [the IS] off big time'.[74]

When asked about the amount of pressure that was put on Hulme by his defection from the IS to the Communist Party, Gatehouse remembered that Hulme was a 'very hale hearty strong character ... [who] enjoyed provoking and taunting the ultra left'.[75] Hulme admits he had uneasy relations with the ultra-left, remembering with clarity the underlying tension between himself and co-activist Gordon Hutchinson.[76] Hulme devoted himself to organising, and his presence in the CSC ironically appeared to calm the storm of factional politics on the executive for a short time. His 'defection' also meant the CPGB had members in almost all positions in the CSC at the national level.[77] With his youth and zeal, Hulme brought organisational skills and experience. Gatehouse thought Hulme was 'splendid', a 'wonderful organiser' who 'easily spoke the trade unionists' language and was easily accepted by them'.[78]

In spite of this, the title of trade union *organiser* was perhaps misleading. Hulme was young, Gatehouse was considered an 'intellectual sort', and as both were relatively inexperienced neither was in a position to tell weathered trade unionists where and when to act.[79] Rather, the office tried to support actions that were occurring at all levels of complicated trade union organisation.[80] They publicised and encouraged activities and held campaigns that created an atmosphere of moral authority in which trade unionists could be confident to act.[81] They also pulled trade unionists into the CSC hierarchy.

---

73 The CPGB candidate was Graham Jones.
74 Gatehouse Interview, 2007. Hulme left the CSC in 1979 for a position as district organiser for South Essex CPGB. *Affiliates' Newsletter No. 32, January 6 1978*, CSC, CSC/1/23, LHASC, Manchester.
75 Ibid.
76 Local committees and refugees portfolios within the CSC. Hutchinson worked in the JWG and became very close with and involved in Chilean factional politics through the refugees. Hulme Interview, 2007. *O'Brien to Hutchinson (JWG), 30 April, 1976*, Sandy Hobbs Papers, Box untitled, GCUA, Glasgow.
77 The CPGB's influence in some trade unions, its pre-existing network of sympathisers across the United Kingdom and ability to represent the more radical sections of the BLP were positive attributes for the CSC. Non-CPGB members consistently raised concerns about CPGB domination in the campaign.
78 Gatehouse Interview, 2007.
79 Hulme Interview, 2007.
80 Ibid.
81 Wilkinson, 'The Influence of the Solidarity Lobby on British Government Policy towards Latin America', 28.

No Truck with the Chilean Junta!

Figure 1.1 Ken Hulme, third from left, and Mike Gatehouse, at right, in 1976.

Source: From right: YCL National Treasurer, Nina Temple, and YCL International Secretary, Norman Lucas, Ken Hulme and Mike Gatehouse. Ms Temple made the banner to present to the CSC on behalf of the YCL. 'A Special Gift from the Young Communist League…', *Morning Star*, 6 September 1976, 5, courtesy of the Marx Memorial Library.

The unionists at the helm of the CSC national organisation were Alex Kitson, Brian Nicholson and George Anthony. Their names dominated letterheads, their public personas were called on at rallies and they were the voice of the cause in the press. Nevertheless, the responsibility of the everyday liaison between the campaign and the labour movement fell back on campaign workers and it required an intricate web of interactions both official and personal. Many union actions were decentralised, but the records of the period were—frustratingly for a historian—created by the centre. Therefore despite trade union figurehead involvement, despite grassroots action, the story of British solidarity is funnelled through a small, underfunded office at the centre. The centre and periphery of the movement were further confused by the split structure of the British trade union movement, which was divided into two separate streams: the unions themselves and trades councils.

While all unions had different sets of rules, each union generally had district and national-level representation and one national-level office. The executive committee of a union did not generally possess policymaking power. Policy was decided by a national committee or at a national conference attended by working trade unionists as well as officials. This structure enabled delegates from all regions to resolve and vote on policies. At the national level unions could affiliate to the Trades Union Congress (TUC). National unions could also affiliate to international bodies such as the International Steel Trades Confederation.[82] The many layers of hierarchy led to an administrative distance between the rank and file and the national offices, creating internal interstices in the structure and numerous idiosyncratic relationships. This is an inherent problem in the industrial national structure of unions. Further complication ensues when parallel to union structure at the shop-floor level, (joint) shop stewards' committees existed. They comprised elected individuals who were members of distinct unions.[83] Furthermore, towns or small regions also had trades councils.

No two unions had an identical structure or ideology in the trade union movement and the confusion this creates is actually the point: the official hierarchy of parallel and different systems allowed for the politically strategic placement of individuals. For example, one local-level union member could sit on its regional and national councils at the same time as being a shop steward leader and on the local trades council (not to mention involvement in other labour movement organisations such as political parties or single-issue campaigns). By the same token, a unionist higher in the hierarchy could be a member of a TUC committee,

---

82 See, for example: *AUEW: Structure and Function of the Union, 1976*, Amalgamated Union of Engineering Workers [hereinafter AUEW], MSS.259/AEUW/6/AC/11/13, Modern Records Centre [hereinafter MRC], University of Warwick [hereinafter UW], Coventry.
83 For more information on shop stewards, refer to: Chris Wrigley, *British Trade Unions Since 1933* (Cambridge: Cambridge University Press, 2002), 37.

his own union's executive council, as well as having political party affiliation. The people who had sufficient individual experience to have varied connections through organisations *and* knowledge of each organisation's idiosyncrasies and complexities gained disproportionate influence in the political left. By courting strategic individuals, the CSC could effectively punch above its weight in political arenas.

An example of this was Alexander H. Kitson, whose strategic importance to the CSC was perhaps unparalleled. Kitson was the treasurer of the campaign from its inception. Born and raised in Edinburgh, he was president of the Scottish Commercial Motormen's Union at the time of its amalgamation into the TGWU.[84] In the 1970s Kitson was both an executive officer of the TGWU and a member of the British Labour Party (BLP) National Executive Committee and thus had a substantial amount of influence in the most powerful groups in the labour movement in Britain.

As an executive officer of the TGWU, Kitson had a close working relationship with general secretary, Jack Jones.[85] If the CSC organisers had to meet Kitson at Transport House, he almost always organised a visit with Jones as well.[86] As well as being leader of the TGWU, Jones was president of the TUC International Committee, a fortunate link for the Chile campaign, as it was the third most powerful TUC committee behind the general and finance committees.[87] Jones's own heavy involvement in the BLP led to the understanding that Kitson had freedom in his TGWU position to participate in activities of the Socialist International, which were largely concerned with BLP activities rather than TGWU business.[88]

Kitson in fact chaired the Socialist International's Chile Committee.[89] It was also widely rumoured he was linked romantically to Jenny Little of the BLP International Department and was active in the BLP's Latin American

---

84 Jack Jones, *Jack Jones: Union Man. An Autobiography* (London: William Collins & Sons, 1986), 242; Transport and General Workers Union National Executive Council, *The Story of the T.G.W.U.* (London: Transport & General Workers Union, 1977), 46.

85 Both Kitson and Jones were high-profile trade unionists in the Trade Union Section of the BLP National Executive Committee. Their closeness as political allies ebbed and flowed. Kitson's subordinate role to Jones in the TGWU meant that he gave Jones 'blind loyalty' in 1975, according to Barbara Castle. By 1976, however, Moss Evans (national organiser, TGWU) and Kitson were united against Jones over the election of Joan Maynard or Margaret Jackson to the BLP National Executive Committee. Barbara Castle, *The Castle Diaries 1974–1976* (London: Weidenfeld & Nicolson, 1980), 412; Tony Benn, *Tony Benn: Against the Tide* (London: Arrow Books, 1989), 615.

86 Gatehouse Interview, 2007.

87 Coates and Topham, *Trade Unions in Britain*, 134.

88 Gatehouse Interview, 2007. Socialist International affiliates included the Australian Labor Party, BLP and the Chilean Radical Party.

89 Trades Union Congress (TUC), 'Notes of Proceedings at a Conference on Chile held at Congress House, Great Russell Street London, on Thursday, 24th April, 1975' (England: TUC, 1975).

Subcommittees.⁹⁰ More specifically, he attended the short-lived BLP International Department's Chile Coordinating Committee, which was set up in May 1974 to ensure BLP action on Chile was coherent and coordinated. In his capacity as a member of the BLP International Committee, Kitson was expected to liaise directly with the CSC in lieu of an official BLP representation on its executive.⁹¹ Furthermore, he chaired the BLP Executive's Latin America Study Group from its inception in 1975 until 1978 and sat on the Liaison Committee of the Central Unica de Trabajadores (CUT, the trades union congress of Chile) and the BLP.⁹² This confusing array of involvements serves to demonstrate both Kitson's commitment to the Chile cause and his use of the Chile issue to establish moral authority and dominate the party and union discussion around the topic.⁹³

Ken Hulme, trade union organiser for the CSC, confirmed that 'Alex more than anybody was our "in" into the more senior positions in the labour movement'.⁹⁴ Liverpool unionists Jimmy Nolan and Antony Burke concurred that Kitson was a 'lifeline' into the upper hierarchy of the labour movement.⁹⁵ Kitson's name on the top of the CSC letterhead, his public profile and personal endorsement (almost always with the qualification 'Executive Officer TGWU' after his name) gave the CSC political credibility and the respect of the labour movement. Moreover, with such a high-profile treasurer (he was also treasurer of the Scottish Trades Union Council, STUC),⁹⁶ the CSC was above being accused of financial mismanagement.⁹⁷

---

90 Gatehouse Interview, 2007; Hulme Interview, 2007. Alan Angell, a leading Latin Americanist scholar, was also active on occasion in these committees. At the time of the coup he was at St Antony's College Oxford and he spent much of the next two years working for Academics for Chile. Academics for Chile was an organisation that helped academics in Chile gain contracts in Britain so they could escape persecution. The immense amount of work involved in organising such activities led Angell to go to the World University Service to ask for organising aid. That organisation then took over most of the running of Academics for Chile. *Academics for Chile, 1975*, Papers of Barry Carr, Melbourne; *Angell (St Antony's College Oxford) to Hart, 16 October 1973*, CSC, CSC/13/3, LHASC, Manchester; *Academics for Chile, 1975*, CSC, CSC/41/1, LHASC, Manchester; Interview with Alan Angell (Chile activist, academic, UK), 30 August 2007 [hereinafter Angell Interview, 2007], notes and recording in possession of author.
91 Having an official representative on the CSC committee would imply the BLP's unequivocal support of the CSC's actions. This way the BLP had pre-warning of the CSC's activities in exchange for the CSC's use of Kitson's reputation. *Report to meeting of Chile Co-Ordinating Committee—May 1974*, TUC [BLP International Department], MSS.292D/936.1/2, MRC, UW, Coventry.
92 *Minutes of Meeting of the Latin America Study Group (27/1/75)*, TUC [BLP International Department], MSS.292D/936.1/3, MRC, UW, Coventry; *NEC Latin American Sub Committee: Minutes of the Last Meeting held on July 25th 1978 in the House of Commons*, TUC [BLP International Department], MSS.292D/936.1/6, MRC, UW, Coventry; *Programme of Work, 1976*, TUC [BLP International Department], MSS.292D/936.1/3, MRC, UW, Coventry; Coates and Topham, *Trade Unions in Britain*, 118.
93 Kitson had in fact met Allende in Chile before the coup. TUC, 'Notes of Proceedings at a Conference on Chile held at Congress House', 15.
94 Hulme Interview, 2007.
95 Nolan Jimmy, Antony Burke, Hugo Santillar, Angela Thew and Anthony Santamera in discussion with Ann Jones, Recorded 9 August 2008.
96 *Solidarity with the People of Chile—A trade union conference organised by the CSC, 1975*, CSC, CSC/11/2, LHASC, Manchester.
97 This was not a new strategy. See: Shipley, *Revolutionaries in Modern Britain*, 47–8.

The advantages of his connections came, however, with a certain mystery. According to Mike Gatehouse, 'there was more than met the eye' to Alex Kitson. He continued:

> I went there once or twice to meet him with Chilean Trade Unionists ... and he could be very probing, prying, intrusive and sometimes on the verge of being downright rude. And you didn't [pause] it came out of the blue. You didn't understand where it was coming from, or exactly what it related to.[98]

Kitson was definitely a strong character, who pushed repeatedly for Chile resolutions and support at the BLP National Executive Committee and conferences.[99] For some, politics was thirsty work and, according to Gatehouse, Kitson 'had a big drink problem, but didn't they all?'[100] He did share this trait with many trade unionists at the time, and when Bill McClellan was in Chile preparing for the arrival of the labour movement delegation of 1984 he sent a pamphlet of the hotel where the delegation was to stay with an arrow to the mini bar and the statement 'this is for Brian [Nicholson] and Alex [Kitson]'.[101]

Nevertheless, Kitson undoubtedly felt strongly about the cause and consistently delivered good speeches and relentlessly fought for Chile. At the 1975 Trade Union Conference on Chile, he said: 'We in Britain can be proud of our role in this international solidarity movement ... We are involved in this because we know that the forces of fascism in Chile are the same ones that threaten us.'[102]

By involving strategic figures such as Kitson who could use their knowledge of labour movement quirks, the CSC had a direct liaison with some of the more powerful committees in the labour movement. The deliberate and considered choice of Kitson as treasurer illustrates a canny political selection by the CSC on two levels. First, the campaign gained respectability and true trade union connections from the outset. Second, his involvement in organisations across the left strengthened the image of the CSC as a united left campaign. His was a moderating presence in what could have been perceived as a CPGB-dominated organisation.

Alex Kitson was one among many trade unionists who figured heavily in the structure of the CSC. Labour Party MPs Ian Mikardo, Neil Kinnock, Judith Hart and Jo Richardson were all strong supporters of the Chile campaign, but despite their high public profiles, none of them was chosen as the chair. In a distinctive

---

98 Gatehouse Interview, 2007.
99 Castle, *The Castle Diaries*, 506.
100 Gatehouse Interview, 2007.
101 *Hotel Santa Lucia, 1984*, CSC, CSC/5/3, LHASC, Manchester.
102 Chile Solidarity Campaign, *Chile and the British Labour Movement: Trade Union Conference Report* (London: London Caledonian Press, 1975).

and unique move, the CSC placed two rank-and-file trade unionists in the positions of joint chairs: Brian Nicholson of the TGWU and George Anthony of the AUEW. These were the two largest unions in Britain, and as a consequence had the biggest vote in the BLP. They were also two of the best placed in terms of possible blacking or boycotting of Chilean goods.

Both men had mottled reputations; it was said you were not a fully fledged member of the CPGB until you had punched George Anthony at least once. According to Gatehouse, they were both 'notoriously and scandalously rough as chairmen and had no compunction in telling people to sod off or whatever. They were quite macho and … it gave a very distinctive flavour to the Campaign.'[103] 'George and Brian', continued Gatehouse:

> [T]he 'terrible twins' we used to call them, they were quite good at puncturing any … complacency and so on, though they were not without it themselves, but they punctured ours. And Executive Committee meetings were very 'boom boom': functional, decisive, not a lot of waffling went on, and certainly very little ideological discussion.[104]

Brian Nicholson was a member of TGWU Region One, which took in North London and the docks. He was a CPGB member who sat on the National Executive Committee of the TGWU, which was 'bankrolling' the Chile campaign.[105] This was a kind of guarantee for Nicholson's actions, and he ran campaign meetings as if they were trade union meetings. Nicholson took a slightly more prominent role in the CSC than George Anthony.[106] He visited the small CSC office regularly, according to Gatehouse, and chaired meetings and conferences for many years; but, despite his commitment of time to the collective movement, Nicholson was a 'supreme individualist': 'Brian did what Brian wanted.'[107]

Nicholson brought some extracurricular activities to the campaign office, such as coopting Gatehouse to type the *Cherry Blossom*. Cherry Blossom was a famous brand of boot polish, predominantly black in colour: the *Cherry Blossom* was a blacking list for the unofficial pickets of the docks. After Gatehouse typed and photocopied the list, Nicholson would take it down to the docks and the lorry firms listed would not be allowed through the lines on that day.[108]

---

103   Gatehouse Interview, 2007.
104   Ibid. Evidence of Anthony and Nicholson attempting to stifle an ideological discussion on the lessons of the Chilean coup for the National Action Conference can be seen at: *Minutes of the Meeting of the CSC Executive Committee—held at Cooperative centre, Sunday March 2, 11am, 1974*, CSC, CSC/1/3, LHASC, Manchester.
105   Referring to the support of Jack Jones and Alex Kitson. Interview with George Anthony (activist, unionist, UK), 22 August 2007 [hereinafter Anthony Interview, 2007], notes in possession of author.
106   The record shows that Anthony attended more Executive Committee meetings between 21 December 1973 and 16 October 1975.
107   Gatehouse Interview, 2007.
108   Ibid.

Many solidarity activists believed that both Nicholson and Anthony were involved in the CSC to further their political careers. On the other hand, they may have been 'gifted' representation on the CSC by their unions to keep them busy and away from more politically important or local issues. Yet, Gatehouse remembered that their time commitment alone would seem to refute these accusations. They were 'very key to the Campaign', according to Gatehouse: 'they were neither Labour Party officials and although they officially represented their unions, they were not high up in the union, they were not full time trade union officials. They were working trade unionists.'[109]

Accompanying Nicholson as joint chair was George Anthony, who worked in ship repairs at the Royal Albert Dock in London. He joined the Amalgamated Engineers' Union (later the AUEW) at seventeen and rejoined after his national service at twenty-one years of age. He was president of the North London District of the AUEW in 1974.[110] A member of the CPGB, Anthony was a part of the London Trades Council in 1973 from which Dr Amicia Young nominated Anthony as the delegate to the CSC.[111] Gatehouse remarked that Anthony was a 'a complex character. I mean, very difficult and he quarrelled in a big way with some of the ... younger women in the Campaign'.[112] Anthony in fact blames 'the women' for eventually forcing him out of the campaign.[113]

His confidence came through from the first. Even though Anthony was not the elected representative of the AUEW he took the liberty of representing them. 'Well, because Brian Nicholson was from the TGWU', he remembered in 2007, 'I felt it was only right, really, that the [AUEW] should have an equal status'.[114] Because of Anthony's persistent attendance, he was gradually considered to be a representative of the AUEW and managed to manoeuvre himself into a high-profile position in the solidarity movement.

---

109 Ibid. Anthony originally represented North London Trades Council at the CSC.
110 *Gatehouse to Colleagues, July 10 1974*, CSC, CSC/4/1, LHASC, Manchester.
111 Young, of the Association of Scientific Technical and Managerial Staffs (ASTMS), did this perhaps to lighten her own load—she attended the first CSC meetings along with Anthony. Her political persuasion is unclear though most probably towards the CPGB. Her husband was a commander in the Royal Navy; she was a medical doctor. The exact political reasons for Anthony's nomination for the London Trades Council are unclear. When asked about it, Anthony's response was: 'Oh yeah, well, she liked me.' *Chile Solidarity Committee: Minutes of the meeting held at the House of Commons on 17.12.73*, CSC, CSC/1/1, LHASC, Manchester; Anthony Interview, 2007. Anthony is also listed as being CSC Trade Union Convenor for a short time. *CSC Executive Committee, 1974*, CSC, CSC/1/3, LHASC, Manchester.
112 Gatehouse Interview, 2007.
113 Anthony Interview, 2007.
114 Anthony Interview, 2007.

1. The 'principal priority' of the campaign: The trade union movement

Figure 1.2 George Anthony (centre).

Source: *Untitled*, Morning Star Photograph Collection, Marx Memorial Library, London, courtesy of the Marx Memorial Library.

Although the nuances of such stories are hard to corroborate through archival sources, it is certain that Anthony and Nicholson took advantage of a niche, or an interstice, that appeared in this portion of the labour movement structure. Here they could entrench themselves in positions to further exploit the gaps and disjunctures that the broad left front threw up. The joint chairs of such a broad-front organisation raised their profile and power base to a level much higher than their actual union positions. Archival evidence suggests they quite often spoke for the largely silent masses of trade unionists affiliated to the CSC, and because there was little vocal trade union opposition, they took the liberty that they were in fact correct and justified in doing so.

Other evidence suggests Anthony was detached from the workers' understanding of the Chilean situation or their ability or desire to act. Anthony believes the presence of Nicholson and himself at meetings was enough to reassure the trade union movement that things were in good hands.[115] Considering that almost all union organised action was initiated at the periphery and not in the central CSC

---

115 'I mean, they didn't come because they didn't want to ... I suppose they felt in a way well, Brian and George are handling it, you know, there will be nothing to worry about.' Ibid.

office or national-level union offices (as demonstrated in later chapters), this seems like quite a presumption. Anthony even admitted that 'workers never complained' about him calling a boycott, 'but they never took action on' the call.[116]

Even so, Gatehouse reflected that 'both George and Brian did really [a] huge amount … in their own style. And often that style would be rather *prepotente* as they would say in Chile, and macho and sometimes difficult and sometimes quite undemocratic.'[117]

The leadership style of Anthony and Nicholson was a form of democratic centralism, but despite the potential for negative reflections of the two, Gatehouse judged that 'on the whole they were enormously important. And I don't think the Campaign would have got where it did or hung together or been what it was without them.'[118]

Kitson, Nicholson and Anthony's presence as trade unionists in the campaign, however, was not enough to entice the TUC to affiliate. In fact, the CSC and the TUC had a tense relationship.[119] The Chile campaign was not 'official enough' to be important to the council, whose political agendas ran far over the heads of the Chile activists.[120] Gatehouse thinks that

> there is a political level in the TUC international work that has absolutely bugger all to do with the individual trade unions. Many of the unions, particularly unions like the Miners were deeply critical of it, absolutely loathed the TUC international committee and regarded them as a bunch of spooks.[121]

The TUC organisation was big enough to run not only its International Committee, but also an International Department. The *New Statesman* described the TUC International Committee 'like most other parts of the TUC structure, [as] oligarchic rather than democratic, and has generally been a preserve of the Right'.[122]

---

116 Ibid.
117 Gatehouse Interview, 2007.
118 Ibid.
119 This caused the CSC to describe its membership in sneaky ways: 'Over half total membership of TUC affiliated through their unions to CSC.' Chile Solidarity Campaign, *Chile and the British Labour Movement*, 8.
120 Hulme Interview, 2007; Gatehouse Interview, 2007. This did not stop the CSC using every scrap of acknowledgment for its own means. In his introduction to the annual general meeting in 1976, Gatehouse said 'the CSC's *presence in the movement* was demonstrated by its presence in the TUC for its AGM, and by the affiliation through their unions of more than 7 million British workers'. *CSC-AGM 19.02.77 Minutes*, CSC, CSC/1/12, LHASC, Manchester.
121 Gatehouse Interview, 2007. The TUC nevertheless was a very important avenue for small lobby groups to get their ideas to government. Wilkinson, 'The Influence of the Solidarity Lobby on British Government Policy towards Latin America', 14.
122 'The TUC's "foreign policy",' New Statesman, 1981, CSC, CSC/28/19, LHASC, Manchester.

1. The 'principal priority' of the campaign: The trade union movement

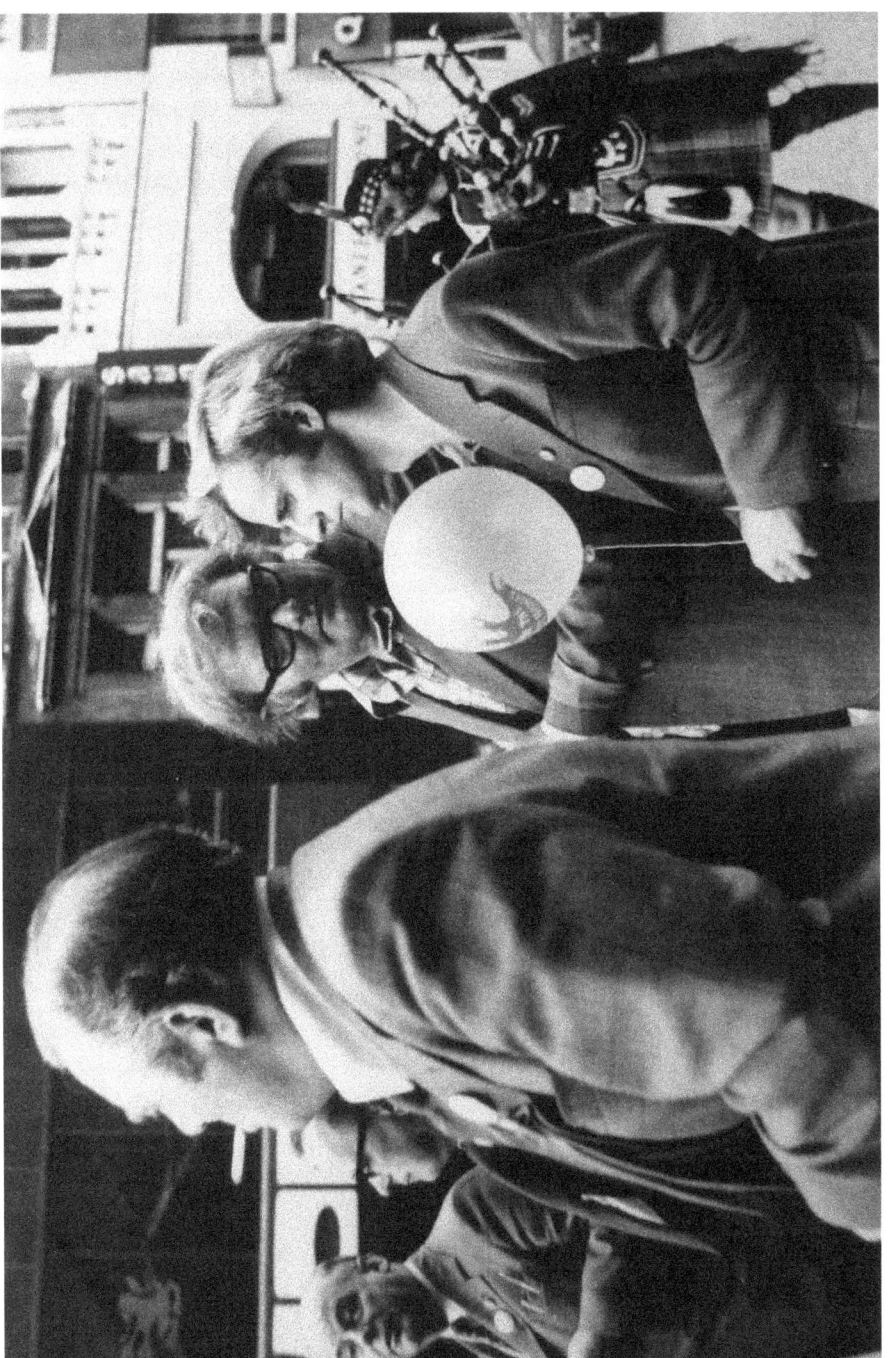

Figure 1.3 Brian Nicholson and Mike Gatehouse at a Chile demonstration, 1974.

Source: Untitled, Photo box 3, People's History Museum, LHASC, Manchester. The Deal Girl Pipers can be seen in the background of the 1974 demonstration photos.

The TUC established its own Chile Fund in October 1973.[123] They used public occasions, such as the speech of Luis Figueroa at the Trade Union Conference for Chile in May 1975, to donate large sums to this fund and urge other unionists to encourage their own executive committees to donate also.[124] The TUC also donated £1000 to the International Confederation of Free Trade Unions (ICFTU) Fund for Chilean Relief when it began in 1974.[125] By widely circulating news of this generous donation, the TUC encouraged affiliated organisations to donate to the ICFTU fund (and away from the CSC).[126] Between December 1973 and May 1974, £3928.90 was donated to 'Chile' through the TUC from 31 unions.[127] Donations varied from £10 from the Rossendale Union of Boot, Shoe and Slipper Operatives to the National Union of Public Employees (NUPE) and the TGWU, which each donated £1000.[128] By undertaking this financial administration, the TUC could not be accused of ignoring the notion of solidarity. It kept a parallel morality with the CSC with little effort and without forgoing control of their own affairs, just as the BLP had by declining affiliation to the CSC but associating with it through key individuals.

Some unions were careful with their choice of fund. For example, the Society of Lithographic Artists, Designers, Engravers and Process Workers (SLADE) instructed the General Secretary of the TUC to direct their money only to the TUC Chile Fund. They perceived the fund to be in a better position to connect directly with Chilean trade unionists than the unwieldy organisation of the ICFTU.[129] Not all were so trusting and some members of the trade union

---

123   *TUC to Stanley (POEU), December 22, 1975*, TUC, MSS.292D/980.31/5, MRC, UW, Coventry.
124   Harry Sterne, 'Chile and the TUC', *Tribune* [UK], 9 May 1975; *Record*, May 1975, 14: '*Boycott Chile Junta Call*,' Transport and General Workers [hereinafter TGWU], MSS.126/T&G/193/1/55, MRC, UW, Coventry. Donations included £25 from Westminster TUC's Branch of the Association of Professional, Executive, Clerical and Computer Staff (APEX). *Brown (APEX) to Murray (TUC), 31/10/74*, TUC, MSS.292D/980.31/4, MRC, UW, Coventry.
125   *TUC International Committee Minutes, November 27, 1973*, TUC, MSS.292D/901/6, MRC, UW, Coventry. The ICFTU also held a workshop of solidarity with Chile in Oslo, 7–8 October 1974, among many other activities. T. Jenkins attended, as an employee of the TUC International Department. It was at this conference that the recommendation for a coordination committee to direct assistance to the CUT was formed. *ICFTU Workshop of Solidarity with Chile, OSLO, October 7–8, 1974*, TUC, MSS.292D/980.31/4, MRC, UW, Coventry.
126   *TUC Circular no. 59 re: Fund for Chilean Trade Unionists, December 14, 1973*, TUC, MSS.292D/980.31/2, MRC, UW, Coventry.
127   This figure is apart from donations and affiliation fees to the CSC or CCHR. *Jenkins to Hargreaves, May 3, 1974*, TUC, MSS.292D/980.31/4, MRC, UW, Coventry.
128   *Whittaker (The Rossendale Union of Boot, Shoe and Slipper Operatives) to TUC, 16th January, 1974*, TUC, MSS.292D/980.31/4, MRC, UW, Coventry; *Fisher (NUPE) to Murray (TUC), 21st January, 1974*, TUC, MSS.292D/980.31/4, MRC, UW, Coventry. The TGWU donation was made under the auspices of Jack Jones, who was the general secretary of the TGWU as well as secretary of the TUC International Committee. *Jones (TGWU) to Murray (TUC), June 14, 1974*, TUC, MSS.292D/980.31/4, MRC, UW, Coventry. The TGWU donated a further £500 to the TUC Chile Fund. *Minutes and Record of the Statutory Meeting of the Finance and General Purposes Committee of the General Executive Council, January 10, 1974*, TGWU, MSS.126/T&G/1186/A/52, MRC, UW, Coventry.
129   SLADE donated £75 on this occasion. *Parish (Society of Lithographic Artists Designers Engravers and Process Workers) to Murray (TUC) 28th January 1974*, MSS.292D/980.31/4, MRC, UW, Coventry.

movement were still dubious about how the money was being spent.[130] These fears may have been justified, as the ICFTU and TUC started collecting funds for Chile without any clear plan or method to get the money from their European offices to trade unionists in need in junta-controlled Chile.[131]

The ICFTU only acknowledged the first £1000 sent to them from the TUC.[132] This, along with a pattern of donations from the TUC to the CSC for events and the CUT for office equipment, suggests the bulk of the almost £4000 sent to the TUC intended for Chile in the early years of the regime stayed in the kitty at the TUC and was subsequently used almost exclusively within Britain for British involvement in Chile solidarity.[133] The amount of money is not surprising. The easiest way of expressing solidarity is by donating money. Unions do this in a regular, bureaucratised and structured manner.

In terms of policy, an emergency resolution at the TUC Blackpool Congress in September 1973 congratulated the trade unions in Chile on supporting the UP Government and resisting fascist takeover.[134] At subsequent TUC conferences the Chile section of the international report spanned several pages. It detailed visits by Cyril Plant and Jack Jones to the Foreign and Commonwealth Office, delegations received and international (United Nations, International Labour Office, ICFTU) Chile resolutions, indicating the high profile of the Chile issue. Every year until 1989 there was at least one page of the report dedicated to Chile, although it was sometimes in conjunction with other Latin American countries. On top of this, resolutions of condemnation of the dictatorship were passed, accompanied by long soliloquies by the speakers listing the regime's oppressions and British trade unions' solidarity efforts.[135]

The high profile of the Chile issue at congress is not necessarily reflected in the general international policy (and certainly many actions of the International Department) of the TUC. In fact, many unions did not support the TUC's international activity. The TUC often followed the policy of the Foreign and Commonwealth Office (subsequently referred to as the Foreign Office) rather than representing the interests of trade unions within Britain. There was an

---

130 At the Trade Union Conference on Chile in 1975, Len Willet said: 'I am a little unhappy in a sense, about the support that we have been asked to give to the TUC fund, not unhappy about the support but I am unhappy about the progress or lack of it to see where the money is going. To see whether it is being spent wisely, and in the proper direction.' Len Willett, *Post Office Engineering Union National Executive Council, 1976*, CSC, CSC/11/4, LHASC, Manchester.
131 *Jenkins to Hargreaves, January 4, 1974*, TUC, MSS.292D/980.31/4, MRC, UW, Coventry.
132 Ibid.
133 *TUC to Stanley (POEU), December 22, 1975*, TUC, MSS.292D/980.31/5, MRC, UW, Coventry; *Ryder to Walsh, November 29, 1982*, TUC, MSS.292D/980.31/11, MRC, UW, Coventry.
134 *Emergency Motion, TUC Blackpool, 1973*, TUC, MSS.292D/980.31/1, MRC, UW, Coventry.
135 See, for example: George Anthony, *TUC Annual Conference Report*, 1975 (held at LHASC, Manchester), 498–9.

established practice of personnel exchange between the TUC International Department, the BLP International Department and the Foreign Office. The *New Statesmen* reported:

> The TUC ... has stood at the centre of the official structure of international unionism ever since the forties. But the official structure—still deeply penetrated by the CIA, and by the anti-ideology of the British Foreign Office—no longer represents, if it ever did, the aspiration of workers' organisations to escape from national constraints.[136]

Since 1961 the International Department of the TUC had employed Alan Hargreaves.[137] Hargreaves was disliked in the trade union movement and was, according to Patrick Wintour, 'one of the least-forthcoming and least-known officials in British unionism'.[138] He did not carry any sense of being a 'trade unionist', remembered Gatehouse, who continued: 'he was extremely hostile, difficult to deal with', and he was on occasion 'ludicrous, inappropriate, but manifestly hostile'.[139] He kept the International Department of the TUC on a tight rein, instructing his staff to keep all work confidential, even from TUC officials. His internal notes to Len Murray, general secretary of the TUC, suggested a close relationship that bypassed formal committee communications.

His 'skilful manoeuvring' within the TUC ensured he maintained control over the correspondence of the International Department with trade unions.[140] Hargreaves even went as far as discouraging trades councils from affiliating to the CSC.[141] When asked about Hargreaves and his International Department, Ken Hulme simply declared: 'they weren't nice people.'[142] A member of the BLP International Department said 'the trouble with Hargreaves [was] that he [did] not like foreigners'.[143] As noted, Hargreaves had been recruited from the

---

136 *'The TUC's "foreign policy"'*.
137 The International Department of the TUC was not the same as the International Committee. The International Department was staffed by paid workers, not elected representatives of trade union affiliates. Alan Hargreaves' initials (J. A. H.) identify his authorship of documents in the TUC archives.
138 *'The TUC's "foreign policy"'*. This article was loosely based on the articles presented in *Where Were You Brother?*, published by the War on Want. Murray, the general secretary of the TUC, said this article was 'almost certainly libellous'; however, I found it does echo sentiments conveyed in the oral history interviews completed for this project. *I.C. 5. March 5, 1979*, TUC, MMS.292D/901/14, MRC, UW, Coventry.
139 Gatehouse Interview, 2007. Hargreaves represented the TUC at the British Atlantic Committee, Royal Institute of International Affairs, Overseas Labour Consultative Committee and the UK committee for the United Nations International Children's Emergency Fund (UNICEF). *General Council Representation on Bodies Dealing with International Matters, 1975*, TUC, MSS.292D/901/9, MRC, UW, Coventry.
140 Ibid.
141 Hargreaves wrote to Mrs Burgess of the Portsmouth Trades Council: 'It is the usual practice for Trades Councils to avoid becoming involved in political activities not connected with industrial matters of more immediate interest. Such activities are best dealt with by the political wing of the Labour Movement, and it would be more appropriate for co-operation with the CSC to be carried out through the local BLP branch.' *Hargreaves (TUC) to Burgess (Portsmouth Trades Council) July 16, 1974*, TUC, MSS.292D/980.31/4, MRC, UW, Coventry.
142 Hulme Interview, 2007.
143 *'The TUC's "foreign policy"'*.

1. The 'principal priority' of the campaign: The trade union movement

Foreign Office, and he maintained relations with the office well into his term at the TUC. For example, Hargreaves learned of the 1974 delegation of Australian unionists to Chile from an unsolicited letter from the Foreign Office. This named the full delegation, their union affiliations and activities in Chile well before communications arrived from unions in Australia.[144] Mike Gatehouse's feelings on Hargreaves were clear: 'this Hargreaves character at the TUC … I felt sick to have met this bloke.'[145]

If only the attitudes of the TUC International Department were taken into account, it would seem that the Chile campaign did not have labour movement support. Fortunately for the committee, close to the top of the trade union movement in Britain was an individual who was strongly sympathetic to the cause: Jack Jones. He sat at the head of the TUC International Committee.[146] Jones was a widely known and powerful trade unionist whose international credentials stemmed from his participation in the Spanish Civil War. Together with Hugh Scanlon of the AUEW, he was known as one of the 'Tsars of the trade union movement' in Britain.[147] Gatehouse said that Jones 'was a very upright man I think, in many ways, I think probably one of the least corrupt … he was the most puritanical of the trade unionists'.

Although Gatehouse recalled that Jones did not have a 'feeling of real warmth. I think he cared a lot, but he didn't sort of display it.'[148]

Generally respected as a man of integrity, Jones was also on the BLP National Executive Committee, the Management Committee of the International Transport Workers' Federation (ITF)[149] and was the general secretary of the TGWU. A poll commissioned by the BBC in 1977 revealed that the public believed Jack Jones wielded more power than the prime minister.[150]

Apart from Jones, the CSC had few friends in the TUC International Department. The relationship between Hargreaves and Jack Jones was imperfect.[151] It was said that Jones 'had particular antipathy towards Hargreaves', but never managed to dislodge him from his position at the TUC.[152]

---

144   *Hurst (Foreign and Commonwealth Office) to Hargreaves, 25 April 1974*, TUC, MSS.292D/980.31/4, MRC, UW, Coventry.
145   Gatehouse Interview, 2007.
146   Jones, *Jack Jones*.
147   Gatehouse Interview, 2007.
148   Ibid.
149   Sterne, 'Chile and the TUC'.
150   Tony Greenland, ed. *The Campaign Guide 1977* (Westminster: Conservative & Unionist Central Office, 1977).
151   Hargreaves was technically below Jones in hierarchy, but as a full-time employee, he spent much more time at the TUC offices. He wielded much more power than his title suggests.
152   *'The TUC's "foreign policy"'*.

53

Despite the power struggle between Hargreaves and Jones and the TUC's general hostility towards the CSC, trade union support for the CSC was actually widespread. The attitude of Hargreaves and consequently the International Department of the TUC shows the ideological and organisational split between sections of the trade union movement that occurred within the industrial national model. The disjuncture between union levels allowed Hargreaves to establish himself and wield greater power than his position might otherwise allow. His actions did keep some TUC and other labour movement support from the CSC. It could be argued, however, that his attempts to block official TUC action created the space for the committee to expand its official network through the affiliation of unions dissatisfied with the representation of the TUC and who subsequently sought a more social movement-oriented internationalism.

A test of strength and organisational obedience occurred when the CSC decided to organise a demonstration for 15 September 1974.[153] It would take advantage of the visit of Salvador Allende's widow, Madame Hortensia Allende. Mme Allende was invited to Britain as a guest of the BLP,[154] the London Cooperative Society Political Committee, the STUC and the Scottish Chile Solidarity Committee.[155] Gatehouse accompanied and translated for her. He also organised her tour, even typing out in Spanish descriptions of people with whom Mme Allende was to meet in order to make her feel more comfortable.[156] Trade union empathy for and generosity towards Allende's widow was embodied in many acts of kindness—for example, Clive Jenkins of the Association of Scientific, Technical and Managerial Staffs (ASTMS) loaned his car for her exclusive use.[157] Mme Allende returned to Britain various times during her exile, including a more extended tour in 1975. Mike Gatehouse almost always accompanied her.

The Chile campaign invited the BLP, as host of Mme Allende's 1974 trip, to sponsor the demonstration. The Labour Party, in turn, invited the TUC to co-sponsor the event.[158] At the BLP International Committee in June it was informally reported that Jack Jones (strategically placed in the BLP, TUC and TGWU, as already described) had said that the TUC International Committee would co-sponsor if asked.[159] As simply as that, Jack Jones committed the

---

153 In February 1974, a national demonstration was held in Liverpool—a separate action to the one described here. The demonstration in Liverpool was organised by the London office to recognise the grassroots leadership from the docks that was occurring there. *Programme of Activity for the Campaign for 1974–5*, CSC, CSC/2/1, LHASC, Manchester. Nolan Jimmy et al., discussion with Ann Jones.
154 *Hayward (BLP) to Murray (TUC), 28 August, 1974*, TUC, MSS.292D/980.31/4, MRC, UW, Coventry.
155 *Gira en Gran Bretana. Septiembre 1974*, CSC, CSC/20/1, LHASC, Manchester.
156 'Mike Gatehouse se alojara en el hotel para asegurar el bienestar de las visitas' ['Mike Gatehouse will stay in the hotel to ensure the wellbeing of the visitors']. Ibid.
157 Ibid.
158 *Hayward (BLP) to Murray (TUC), 4th July, 1974*, TUC, MSS.292D/980.31/4, MRC, UW, Coventry.
159 *Hargreaves to Murray, July 5, 1974*, TUC, MSS.292D/980.31/4, MRC, UW, Coventry.

resources of the national trade union body of Britain. Such were the advantages of having a sympathetic person in such a strategic position in the interlocking directorate of the labour movement.

Figure 1.4 'Mrs Hortensia Allende [centre] met in London yesterday by Labour Party International Department Secretary Jenny Little and (right) Mike Gatehouse of the Chile Solidarity Campaign.'

Source: 'Junta is Terrorising the People—Chile Bishops', *Morning Star*, 11 September 1975, 1, courtesy of the Marx Memorial Library.

According to Jenny Little of the BLP International Department, only the BLP and the TUC would be listed as sponsors, despite contributions in money and effort towards organising the event from the AUEW, TGWU and other organisations.[160]

---

160   *Chile: Demonstration, 1974*, TUC, MSS.292D/980.31/4, MRC, UW, Coventry. See, for example, the AUEW Executive Council resolving to assist organisation of the 1974 demonstration: *Minutes. Meeting of Executive Council, held in General Office, on the 4th June, 1974 at 2.45 p.m.*, Amalgamated Engineering Union, MSS.259/AEU/1/1/215, MRC, UW, Coventry.

The speakers were to be Mme Allende, Neil Kinnock, Ken Gill (AUEW Technical and Administrative Staffs Section: AUEW TASS), John Gollan (secretary, CPGB), Tariq Ali (IMG) and Jack Jones.[161]

The inclusion of an IMG speaker at the expense of an IS speaker raised protests in that section of the Trotskyite left.[162] In a letter, Peter Binns (IS and also member of the CSC Executive Committee) pleaded with the CSC to change its decision.[163] Gatehouse, in a conciliatory response, pointed out that trying to construct a balanced platform of speakers from the various groupings was a difficult task: time was too short to let everyone speak.[164]

The inclusion of Ali had more extensive implications than offending the IS. The TUC International Department refused the BLP invitation to co-sponsor the demonstration because of the IMG speaker on the platform.[165] They wrote, in a conspiratorial tone, to the BLP that they *must* refuse due to 'IMG activities elsewhere in the trade union movement'.[166] The BLP International Department agreed with the peak union body's views on the IMG speaker, but as Mme Allende was a BLP guest, they could not withdraw their support for the demonstration without embarrassment.[167] In spite of this, Jenny Little talked with the CSC about withdrawing Ali from the platform, and threatened to remove sponsorship if he was not.[168] The BLP was to reconsider the support of the demonstration at their national executive committee meeting on Wednesday, 24 July.[169] The paper trail of correspondence on this subject in the archives then stops for some months.

The BLP ultimately withdrew its official support for the demonstration, 'because of the general election'.[170] Factional politics had won over international sentiment, and in the process of maintaining its broad united front, the CSC had alienated itself (further) from the TUC and the BLP, arguably the two most important labour movement groups, certainly within the industrial national structure. In practice, however, the withdrawal of support may have been an attempt at intimidation only. Gatehouse remembered that 'the threat was

---

161   *Gira en Gran Bretana*. Others included Inti Illimani and Isabel Parra.
162   This decision was passed by both the CSC Committee (6 July) and the Campaign Executive (19 July) of 1974. *Gatehouse to Binns (IS), July 20 1974*, CSC, CSC/45/2, LHASC, Manchester.
163   *Binns (IS) to CSC, July 19th 1974*, CSC, CSC/45/2, LHASC, Manchester.
164   *Gatehouse to Binns (IS), July 20 1974*.
165   *Hargreaves to Murray, July 5, 1974*.
166   *TUCIC 5.8.74: Chile*, CSC, CSC/4/1, LHASC, Manchester.
167   *Hayward (BLP) to Murray (TUC), 28 August, 1974*.
168   *Chile: Demonstration, 1974*.
169   Ibid.
170   Beatrix Campbell, 'Chile's Torturers Stand Accused', *Morning Star*, 10 September 1974.

1. The 'principal priority' of the campaign: The trade union movement

uttered but not carried through'.[171] Kitson and MPs such as Judith Hart and Martin Flannery would not have been able to continue their vocal support if the BLP disapproved so openly of the CSC.

Meanwhile, one level down the trade union hierarchy, the General Executive Council of the TGWU (of which Jack Jones was general secretary) wrote that it would 'extend the Union's fullest support and participation to all expressions of solidarity with the Chilean people being sponsored by the Labour Party, particularly the nationwide demonstrations to be held on September 15'.[172] Jones would speak at the rally on the understanding that it would be on behalf of the *TGWU only*.[173] The TUC International Committee, of which Jones was head, suggested bleakly that he refer to the TUC international policy on Chile before giving his speech. On top of this, by June 1974 the AUEW National Executive— Engineering Section, the Welsh Area National Union of Mineworkers (NUM), Scottish Area NUM, London Cooperative Society Political Committee and the National Union of Students had also pledged support for the demonstration.[174]

The protesters would gather at 1 pm at Speakers' Corner and march via Oxford Street, Regent Street and Haymarket to Trafalgar Square. Speeches would start there at 4.30 pm, from a platform on the steps of the fountain.[175] The protest was to be set out for maximum effect: at the head of the march a Chilean flag would be carried, then the platform speakers and the CSC banner, pipers and 10 more Chilean flags. After this would be trades unions and trades councils, local CSC committees, constituency Labour parties, CPGB and finally the IMG, IS and others.[176]

On the day of the demonstration, the *Morning Star*, a newspaper associated with the Communist Party,[177] reported that 'exiled Chilean folk singers, their fists clenched, pounded out revolutionary songs as nearly 12,000 rain-soaked marchers ... trooped into Trafalgar Square'.[178] The figure is more likely to have been 10 000.[179] It was the biggest Chile demonstration ever seen, according to

---

171 Mike Gatehouse, email to Ann Jones, 26 July 2009.
172 *Chile: Passed by the General Executive Council of the Transport and General Workers Union on June 7, 1974*, CSC, CSC/4/1, LHASC, Manchester.
173 *JAH re: note attached—CHILE: DEMONSTRATION*, 1974, TUC, MSS.292D/980.31/4, MRC, UW, Coventry.
174 *Local Committees Newsletter No. 4, June 25 1974*, CSC, CSC/44/1, LHASC, Manchester.
175 Ibid.
176 The division of the march thus indicated the importance of each of these groups to the CSC. It also served to keep disputing factions away from each other. *Order of March as Agreed for September 15th, 1974*, CSC, CSC/20/1, LHASC, Manchester.
177 The *Morning Star* was not the official organ of the CPGB, but functioned as if it was. There were 50–60 000 copies circulated per day in the 1970s. Shipley, *Revolutionaries in Modern Britain*, 42.
178 Ibid.
179 On top of 3000 at the Glasgow demonstration the day before. *The Times* put the total at the Trafalgar Square rally at 10 000. Peter Strafford, 'Two Worlds under Chile's Junta', *The Times*, 16 September 1974.

the *Seamen's Journal*.[180] The entire executive of the TGWU spearheaded the march, alongside Judith Hart (then Minister for Overseas Development), Martin Flannery MP (BLP), Alex Kitson (TGWU, BLP and CSC), John Gollan (CPGB) and Dai Francis and Emlyn Williams (South Wales NUM National Executive Council members, CPGB and BLP respectively).

The demonstration was an 'outstanding success', wrote Max Engelnick, district organiser of the CPGB.[181] There were at least 200 union banners present.[182] Four hundred miners travelled from Wales and 200 from Yorkshire to march. After a last-minute shuffle, the speakers included Hortensia Allende, Harald Edelstam (former Swedish ambassador to Santiago),[183] Tariq Ali (IMG) and Jack Jones.[184]

Significantly, mass participation triumphed without the official support of the two most powerful and all-encompassing groups of the labour movement: the TUC and the BLP. The great numbers of trade unionists in the street highlighted the lack of connection between the rank and file and the upper echelons in the trade union movement. The insistence on a broad front had created space for Tariq Ali to step in and purloin more power than his position warranted.

What was more telling was that one individual could override the structure and political idiosyncrasies of the labour movement: Jack Jones, by his presence alone, gave the appearance of TUC, BLP as well as TGWU endorsement, despite the behind-the-scenes machinations.

By ensuring the participation of strategic trade unionists, the CSC had benefited from more than the power of an individual. According to Kane, morally justified actions are 'legitimate'.[185] In this way, a person such as Jones with accumulated moral capital was used to access opportunities that would otherwise not be available.[186] Jones was not a faddist. He did not 'attach an exalted significance' to the Chile campaign;[187] but he was a strategic individual: an access point to and voice of the trade unions of Britain. Through the industrial national framework,

---

180 This is unlikely to be true, as the demonstrations in the German Democratic Republic (GDR: East Germany) and Cuba were on a larger scale again. 'Chilean's Charge—Appalling Brutality by Esmeralda Crew', *Seamen's Journal* 29, no. 6 (July 1974); *The GDR's Fervent Solidarity with the Courageous Chilean People* (Berlin: Panorama DDR, c. 1973).
181 *Engelnick (CPGB London District Committee) to Gatehouse, 16th September, 1974*, CSC, CSC/45/2, LHASC, Manchester.
182 There were, among this figure, 30 trades councils, 20 AUEW branches and 10 TGWU branches.
183 Edelstam was a fixture on the solidarity circuit in Europe.
184 Other speakers included Jimmy Symes (Liverpool Dockers), Ken Gill (AUEW and TUC), Bob McKluskey, (Seamen's), Alf Lomas (LCS), Neil Kinnock, Steve Parry (Students) and Peter Plouviez (British Actors Equity). Steve Parry was quite heavily involved in the CSC in the first two years. He was a CPGB member. Shipley, *Revolutionaries in Modern Britain*, 36. Jones is not listed in some reports of the demonstration—for example: *Chile Fights 8* (London: CSC [Chile Lucha], 1974). Gatehouse remembers that he was present.
185 Kane, The Politics of *Moral Capital*, 15.
186 Ibid., 11.
187 Hamer, *The Politics of Electoral Pressure*, 1.

1. The 'principal priority' of the campaign: The trade union movement

the CSC had gained the support of the TGWU, AUEW and rank-and-file levels of unions. Through horizontal movements, more akin to the relationships described in social movement unionism, they had gained Jack Jones. His status as an interconnected node gave the blessing of the whole labour movement to the Chile campaign.

The CSC continued to rely on unions. In their program of activity for 1974–75, the CSC stated: 'Our principal support has been in the trade union movement, and we must extend this much further, with an extended campaign to increase affiliations, and to provide ample stimulus for participation to our affiliates.'[188] The activities the campaign undertook in order to stimulate affiliate participation are focused on in the next chapter. In the meantime, trade union work would 'remain the principal priority of the Campaign'.[189]

---

188 *Programme of Activity for the Campaign for 1974–5*.
189 Ibid. Trade unions remained the focus of the campaign for the 1970s and into the 1980s. For example, the campaign took the side of the National Union of Journalists (NUJ) and National Graphical Association (NGA) rather than that of its own (long-term) member Imogen Mark in 1983: 'While the CSC is not a trade union, it is firmly rooted in the labour movement and can scarcely be expected to take a completely neutral attitude to serious breaches of elementary trade union discipline.' *Given to Mark, 12th January, 1984*, CSC, CSC/28/35, LHASC, Manchester.

No Truck with the Chilean Junta!

Figure 1.5 Mme Allende addresses the crowd in Trafalgar Square, September 1974.

Source: *Untitled*, Photo box 3, People's History Museum, Manchester.

1. The 'principal priority' of the campaign: The trade union movement

Figure 1.6 Judith Hart and Hortensia Allende embrace on the platform of the first anniversary march. Alf Lomas of the London Co-Operative Society Political Committee looks on.

Source: Chris Davies, 'Remember Allende', *Labour Weekly*, 20 September 1974.

2. A 'roll call' of the labour movement: Harnessing labour participation

The Chile Solidarity Campaign's strategy at the 1974 May Day rally was simple: assemble a strong contingent and move as close to the front as possible. The CSC was hoping that Lawrence Daly of the National Union of Mineworkers would mention Chile in his address, and they planned to hand out 15 000 copies of a special leaflet covering the situation of trade unions in Chile.[1]

Like participation in May Day, trade union involvement in the movement of solidarity with Chile used a range of strategies familiar to any student of democratic politics in Britain, from mass demonstrations to petitions. Union involvement in the Chile campaign was not just financial with a representative aspect as described in the previous chapter. Union actions for Chile were primarily indirect and predominantly led by groups of individuals outside the trade unions. Trade unions often relied on this particular type of indirect action in order to fulfil their internationalist obligations, and the CSC exploited the opportunistic and resource-optimising nature of British trade unions to garner support for their cause. As such, the relationship was symbiotic. Interestingly, the actions described in this chapter were taken in the style of both industrial national and social movement unionism, often at the same time.

Although the origins and machinations of the first anniversary demonstration have already been explained in the previous chapter, its essential features as a public ritual are typical of many others and are worth lingering over in detail. The establishment of artistic and cultural activities, including banner making, mural painting and the use of music are, is explored in this chapter, highlighting the blend of labour tradition with social movement and new left strategy. As well as these group expressions of solidarity, the chapter will also explore the more intimate 'adopt a prisoner' program and specially organised conferences as methods of mobilising action using existing union structures.

With the establishment of the CSC came an annual calendar of events that revolved around significant Chilean and labour movement dates. Navy Day in Chile is marked on 21 May, and is important in the relationship between Britain and Chile. Lord Cochrane, a British citizen, was the commander-in-chief of the Chilean Navy during the War of Independence in the nineteenth century and

---

1 *CSC Executive Committee: Minutes of the meeting held on Thursday April 11 1974 at Seven Sisters*, CSC, CSC/1/3, LHASC, Manchester.

it is traditional for Chilean Navy officers to travel to London to lay a wreath at the foot of his tomb in Westminster Abbey each May. This became one focus of campaigning.[2]

The anniversaries of the September coup were, however, what became most prominent in the calendar of protest. For the left in general and trade unions in particular, demonstrations and marches were a part of the existing repertoire of political action. The organisation of demonstrations was a canny move on the part of the CSC, as it required little organisational output for the unions to participate and lend mass support to the cause.[3] The CSC was part of a social movement yet it harnessed a traditional strategy of the old left and coopted unions through their industrial national structure. It is a supreme example of the manner in which abstract models of unionism were blended in practice.

On the night of Saturday, 14 September 1974, at the Trade Union Centre in Carlton Place, Glasgow, protestors gathered. At 11.30 pm, they stepped aboard a coach that travelled through the night to London. Some hours later, on another side of the country, 200 Yorkshire miners started their journey towards the capital, and about the same time a train left Liverpool full of demonstrators.[4] In Oxford, the local CSC filled two coaches of travellers. From South Wales, a train carrying 400 miners travelled through the morning, led by five members of the Merthyr AUEW and five more representatives from the Merthyr Communist Party.[5]

At 1 pm on Sunday, 15 September 1974, 10 000 people assembled at Speakers' Corner in Hyde Park.[6] This was not a motley mix of citizens churning together, but a highly choreographed, large-scale statement.[7] The CSC stewards divided the march into four sections, demonstrating the broadest support possible from the British labour movement for the people of Chile.

The speakers were at the head of the march, including the executive of the TGWU, who walked in front of the Chile Solidarity Campaign Committee banner (carried

---

2 The year after the coup the authorities at the Abbey would not let the Chilean Navy representatives enter. Instead a labour movement delegation placed wreaths at the tomb in memory of the members of the Chilean armed forces who were loyal to the constitutional government, and who had died since the coup. The delegation comprised BLP MPs Ian Mikardo, Eric Heffer, Frank Allaun, Norman Buchan, Jo Richardson and Russell Kerr. Protests continued on 21 May 1974 when the CSC picketed the evening reception held by the Chilean Navy. No official British Navy or government representative attended. *The Chile Monitor no. 6, 1974*, CSC, CSC/7/3, LHASC, Manchester; *CSC Executive Committee: Minutes of the meeting held on Thursday April 11 1974 at Seven Sisters*; *CSC Annual report, 1977*, CSC, CSC/1/13, LHASC, Manchester.
3 Further more, they made money. It cost £1577.82 to organise the parade, but the collections at the demonstration meant the profit came to £1066.49. *CSC Provisional Accounts. October 7 1974*, CSC, CSC/1/3, LHASC, Manchester.
4 'Protest at Chilean Embassy', *Morning Star*, 12 September 1974.
5 'Trade Unionists fill Demo Train', *Morning Star*, 4 September 1974.
6 Despite being in student holidays and on the eve of a general election, there was still a strong turnout. *CSC. Executive Committee: Analysis of Campaign Performance to Date*; Campbell, 'Chile's Torturers Stand Accused'.
7 *Order of March as Agreed for September 15th, 1974*.

on one side by Mike Gatehouse) and MPs Judith Hart and Martin Flannery.[8] Then there were nine Chilean flags, followed in turn by the Chile Lucha banner[9] and the London Co-Op Political Committee.[10] Policemen in overcoats and helmets in lines on each side of the protestors restrained the demonstration.[11]

More impressive than the head of the march was its body, which was made up of unionists from all over the country. The TGWU was the first of the union section, followed by the NUM contingent. Their traditional banners held aloft, the miners marched to 'the beat of a single bass drum in the prize-winning Llyd Coed brass band'.[12] Next, the AUEW marched, then the NATSOPA. Actors Equity marched with the Electrical, Electronic, Telecommunications and Plumbing Union (EETPU) and then the Post Officers along with AUEW TASS. There were then more than 30 trades council contingents with banners. Shop stewards from Rolls Royce and Leyland came as well, with their 2 metre-wide banners.[13]

The last section of the demonstration was reserved for political parties (note that this was behind the trade unions). The International Socialists' delegation held their own rally in Hyde Park, then followed on to the national demonstration, joining the final section.[14] The International Marxist Group also sent a delegation but the largest of all was the Communist Party, with more than 100 banners from constituencies all over the country. The Labour Party was represented by 50 constituency and Labour Party Young Socialists contingents, which flew

---

8 *Chile Fights 9* (London: CSC [Chile Lucha], 1974).
9 Chile Lucha was a publication group set up by the Chilean immigrant Raul Sol. He was a member of MAPU Garreton, which had different politics than MAPU (Movimiento de Acción Popular Unitario: United Popular Action Movement). He was a charismatic, very intelligent man and attracted a small group of loyal followers, of diverse backgrounds, while in Britain. He was strongly in favour of a broad front for the campaign. The group included Imogen Mark, who was vital to the success of the publication. Chile Lucha ran out of 'Boardwick Street in Soho in London … you went up the fire escape at the back and there was this little flat'. Sol had a deep effect on the campaign, because many of the people he mentored through the group became crucial in the following years to Chile and other Latin American campaigns. Those people include Sarah Trask, Gordon Hutchinson and Imogen Mark. They established the Latin America Archive, which was loosely attached to Latin American Newsletters (a commercial newsletter operation). Hugh O'Shaughnessy and Richard Gott both worked there, and their influence in newspapers of the time is perceptible (including in those used in this thesis). People from within Sol's small group went on to positions in organisations that attracted funding from the Government and other funding agencies. The groups they worked in included Oxfam, Christian Aid and War on Want. Gott became a reporter on the junta in Chile; however, he ended up working at the Military College in Santiago. Gatehouse Interviews, 2007 and 2008.
10 London Co-Op was a major supporter of the campaign, and the CSC courted it carefully for financial support. For these reasons, the London Co-op Political Committee (LCPC) was high in the order of the march.
11 *Chile Fights 9*.
12 Campbell, 'Chile's Torturers Stand Accused'.
13 'The exceptionally strong trade-union turn-out suggested that the Campaign's work with the trade union during the year had been well received.' *CSC. Executive Committee: Analysis of Campaign Performance to Date*; *Chile Fights 9*.
14 Campbell, 'Chile's Torturers Stand Accused'.

in the face of the BLP Executive's decision to not sponsor the rally. Added to this were the International Brigade and bodies of workers from Spain, Italy, Portugal and Ireland.[15]

Figure 2.1 The yearly anniversary rallies had a loyal following.

Source: This image probably shows the 1983 demonstration—it was a particularly rainy day. *Untitled*, Photo box 3, People's History Museum, Manchester.

---

15   *Chile Fights 9*.

2. A 'roll call' of the labour movement: Harnessing labour participation

Figure 2.2 Anniversary demonstration, September 1976, London.

Source: Photographer unknown, 'Great Show of Solidarity with Chile', *Morning Star*, 13 September 1974, courtesy of the Marx Memorial Library.

Martin Gostwick reported in the *Morning Star*:

> Car workers and boilermakers, vehicle builders and railwaymen, building workers and construction men, co-operators, miners, Labour Party members and Communists filed by in a seemingly endless stream.
>
> Engineers and steelworkers, blast furnacemen, farm workers, journalists and print workers—the march from Hyde Park to Trafalgar Square was like a roll call of the British labour movement.[16]

Some walked silently, some chanted. They advanced up Oxford Street, turning at Regent Street, through Haymarket before entering Trafalgar Square. The crowd streamed into the square to the sounds of Inti Illimani singing *Venceremos* (*We Will Triumph*).

The first speaker was the widow of Salvador Allende, Madame Hortensia Allende. An immaculate and glamorous woman, her crisp clothing, coiffured hair, bejewelled fingers, flawless make-up and silk scarf tied to a bow about her neck remained seemingly untouched by the rain that fell on the crowd. She thanked the trade unionists of East Kilbride, Rosyth and Liverpool.[17] Ken Gill (AUEW TASS) also spoke, stating that the Chilean experience provided a lesson to the British left when confronting fascism: they must stay united.[18] Harald Edelstam received a 'mighty ovation' in thanks for the lives of Chilean refugees he had saved in his swift actions as Swedish Ambassador to Chile after the coup.[19]

The steps on which the speakers stood were full, with the eight members of Inti Illimani, the speakers, translators and executive members of unions who felt they had the right to be represented on the platform. It was not only unionists' personal ideological commitment that compelled them to be present. It was also a manifestation of the alliance between their unions and the social movement: the presence of unionists at this rally was a typical example of their involvement in indirect political action. The rally was organised externally to the unions, but fully embraced by them. Their presence at this traditional-style event was a part of their duty as good unionists. Union delegations would continue to attend anniversary demonstrations under the obligation of their affiliation until the dictatorship fell.

---

16 Martin Gostwick, 'Solidarity with Chile's Democrats', *Morning Star*, 14 September 1974, 2.
17 Davies, 'Remember Allende'.
18 Bob McLuskey (National Union of Seamen: NUS) and Neil Kinnock (BLP) also spoke.
19 Campbell, 'Chile's Torturers Stand Accused'. Edelstam spent lots of time in Britain after the coup, and attended many rallies and presentations as well as delegations to the foreign office and so on. I believe this is because his children were attending British public schools.

Figure 2.3 'Señora Salvador Allende speaking before a mass rally in support of Chilean resistance, Trafalgar Square, London, 15 September 1974. Organised by the British Joint Labour Movement and the Chile Solidarity Campaign. In the foreground are trade union banners and in the background Chile Vencera banner by John Dugger of AFD.'

Source: Brian Nicholson can be seen in blue shirt and black jacket immediately below the image of Salvador Allende. *Arts Festival for Democracy in Chile*, CSC, CSC/12/1, LHASC, Manchester.

As Inti Illimani moved forward to sing for the final time, the crowd huddled together for warmth. The musicians sang, in front of them a sea of faces and banners, behind them on the steps was a huge strip banner. John Walker described the banner: 'Its vivid expanses of red and blue and its highly simplified figures appeared modern in comparison to the more Victorian style of the British trade union banners among the crowd.'[20]

The monumental strip banner, described as 'an anti-fascist artwork', was specially constructed for the 1974 demonstration.[21] It was called *'Chile Vencera'* (sic) ('Chile will overcome'). The banner was, according to the artist, 'a blend of Californian mural painting and traditional British trade union or Baptist Church banner making'.[22] The symbolism of its content was important because, unlike art hung in a gallery, the practice of displaying banners behind speakers meant the audience viewed the piece for a relatively long time, as rallies would often last hours.[23]

It had 10 figures: two copper miners, a fisherman, a foundry worker, two *campesinos* (farm workers), one of whom was an armed woman collecting eggs, a metal worker, a medical worker, a 'cultural worker' with a gun and a guitar modelled on Victor Jara and an education worker with a book from which the words *'Chile lucha!'* ('Chile fights!') rise.[24] The artist advised that the message told of the 'need to organise collectively to over-throw fascism and includes the principle of solidarity to those engaged in a struggle against a military fascism, namely—the dual nature of our support, "for food and guns"'.[25]

This reflects the belief that there was strong resistance in Chile (there was not), and quite possibly the radical involvement of the artist or those with whom he consulted in the drafting process.[26] The artist, John Dugger, was certainly aware of liberation struggles as well as conditions in the Third World and he also had a keen interest in the British trade union banner traditions.[27] Dugger considered

---

20   John Walker, *Left Shift: Radical Art in 1970s Britain* (London: I. B. Tauris, 2002), 124.
21   *Notes on the Big Chile Vencera Banner (Profiles and Analysis), 1976*, CSC, CSC/12/1, LHASC, Manchester.
22   Dugger in: *Banner Arts Project, Patrick Johnson, 1976*, CSC, CSC/12/2, LHASC, Manchester.
23   Walker, *Left Shift*, 205.
24   *Notes on the Big Chile Vencera Banner (Profiles and Analysis)*. *'Chile Lucha!'* can also be translated as 'Chile fight!' (a command).
25   *Banner Arts Project, Patrick Johnson, 1976*.
26   Dugger visited China in the early 1970s and was heavily influenced by Mao. Walker, *Left Shift*, 87.
27   In 1971 Dugger and Medalla had formed the Artists Liberation Front, the slogan of which was 'socialist art through socialist revolution'. Their banner consisted of the slogan with the images of Marx, Engels, Lenin, Stalin and Mao. Dugger, along with Cecilia Vicuña, Guy Brett and David Medalla, was a founding member of Artists for Democracy in Chile, which was established in the Royal College of Art in 1974. Artists for Democracy held a two-week exhibition in September 1974 in London and was able to garner high-level support such as from Judith Hart, Harold Edelstam and Alvaro Bunster. Dugger and Medalla would go on to form a banner studio. Dugger was later employed by the Greater London Council, from 1983 to 1985, as a banner maker. Lucy Lippard, 'Spinning the Common Thread', *A World of Poetry*, accessed 3 June 2008, <http://www.worldofpoetry.org/cv_t2.htm>; Walker, *Left Shift*, 86, 204; *Chile Fights 9*; 'John Dugger born

banners of this type to be a 'portable-mural-without walls'.[28] He believed murals were a cheap way to bring art to the people. The *Chile Vencera* banner was his first monumental strip banner, a form in which he would go on to specialise.[29] It was also a rich symbol of the marriage of the labour movement and trade union traditions with new innovations of the social movement.

Making the banner was a long process that started with sketches and moved through various prototype phases until finally the templates were cut out of canvas and appliquéd onto the strips. The banner was then embroidered. The strips allowed for the use of machines and industrial thread, and created a sturdy banner. The final version of the banner was 'laid out and assembled, [and] cut into 20 strips' on the first anniversary of the coup, 11 September 1974.[30] The banner alone weighed 23 kg, but with its trunk, the two 18 m rigging ropes and the 42 coloured tassels, it weighed 32 kg. It was roughly 5 m high and 7.5 m wide.

The September 1974 rally had 10 000 participants, though in his report Dugger estimated that 20 000 people viewed the banner on that day. After the 1974 demonstration it was used at the Labour Party rally in September 1975. Following this, early in 1976, the banner started its transnational journey when it was sent to the United States and used for an Inti Illimani concert in San Francisco. It then spent May Day in Berkeley at La Peña Cultural Centre.[31] The banner returned to Britain for the September 1976 rally.[32] Dugger estimated there were approximately 65 000 viewers of the banner over this time: it was a mobile monument to Chile solidarity.[33]

Pedro Cornejo (CUT) declared a different piece of art to be 'a magnificent token of solidarity with our people'. It was a mural commissioned by the AUEW.[34] Maureen Scott was the chosen artist. According to the AUEW, the mural

---

1948', Tate Gallery, accessed 3 June 2008, <http://www.tate.org.uk/servlet/ViewWork?cgroupid=999999961&workid=4042&searchid=13877&tabview=text>; John Gorman, *Banner Bright: An Illustrated History of the Banners of the British Trade Union Movement* (London: Allen Lane, 1973).

28 'John Dugger born 1948'. Nicholas Mansfield, 'Radical Banners as Sites of Memory: The National Banner Survey', in *Contested Sites: Commemoration, Memorial and Popular Politics in Nineteenth-Century Britain*, eds Paul Pickering and Alex Tyrell (Aldershot, UK: Ashgate, 2004), 81–99.

29 Dugger (in his 'Banner Arts' project phase) was later commissioned by the CSC to produce a 5 m x 3.7 m banner based on a patchwork design. It hung at the Albert Hall concert in 1978. *CSC Annual Report, 1978*, CSC, CSC/1/13, LHASC, Manchester.

30 *Banner Arts Project, Patrick Johnson, 1976*.

31 Ibid.

32 Mme Allende also spoke. Mme Allende wore a white coat in 1974. At the 1976 rally there is no Salvador Allende banner present in the foreground of the photos.

33 *Banner Arts Project, Patrick Johnson, 1976*.

34 *Cornejo (CUT) to Boyd (AUEW), August 2 1976*, CSC, CSC/32/3, LHASC, Manchester.

portrayed 'the present plight of the Chilean people and the struggle of the workers to restore democracy in their country'.[35] Scott had trained at Plymouth College of Arts and her practice focused on workers and trade unions.[36]

The style of the painting recalled that of Mexican muralists. Its rectangle was tightly packed with figures. Pinochet dominated the centre of the picture in his sunglasses and, below him, in a river of blood, flowed the bodies of his victims. At his shoulders were two figures, a skeleton in the junta uniform and a combat soldier. Allende appeared, looking older than when he passed away, bleeding in a bottom corner. Above Pinochet, a larger figure looked to the heavens, his face obscured both by the angle of this action and by the fact that the painting cut half of it off. He appeared to be straining against chains around his wrists. At the bottom of the painting, people of various races marched holding 'the flame of resistance'.[37] The whole painting seemed to be set in an amphitheatre—perhaps a reference to the stadiums that were used as holding pens for prisoners. In the background of the painting, sitting starkly against the blue sky, there were red banners, which stuck up like rocks. Upon them were union slogans.

When it was unveiled in the council chamber of the AUEW at the Peckham Road offices, the former Chilean ambassador Alvaro Bunster spoke at the event, along with Luis Pavez of the CUT.[38] Ken Hulme, trade union organiser for the CSC, was also present, along with John Boyd (who features in Chapter Four) and Hugh Scanlon, with Elaine Nicholson interpreting.[39] Pedro Cornejo of the CUT wrote to Boyd shortly after the mural was unveiled requesting permission to use the image of the mural on a postcard to raise money and to advertise solidarity.[40] Cornejo also requested a number of photos of the mural to use in pamphlets, and 'it may even be possible for us to smuggle a few copies to Chile, so that our comrades there can see direct evidence of the solidarity of British working people'.[41]

---

35 Ibid.
36 Walker, *Left Shift*, 51, 53, 71.
37 Ibid., 218.
38 Luis Pavez was a construction worker who sought exile in the United Kingdom. *'Chile's wall of resistance' Labour Weekly, 1976*, CSC, CSC/7/9, LHASC, Manchester; *Gatehouse to Roberts (AUEW), June 6 1976*, CSC, CSC/32/6, LHASC, Manchester.
39 The AUEW devoted the back page of the August 1976 edition of its journal to the unveiling of the mural (the same month the export of war frigates was granted. See Chapter 4). *CSC-Exec 26.8.76 Minutes*, CSC, CSC/1/10, LHASC, Manchester.
40 Cornejo was announced as the CUT representative in Britain. He was originally adopted when still a prisoner by NUPE Hammersmith. Chile Solidarity Campaign, *Chile and the British Labour Movement*, 14.
41 *Cornejo (CUT) to Boyd (AUEW), August 2 1976*.

Figure 2.4 The unveiling of the AUEW mural, 1977. From left to right: Ken Hulme (CSC trade union organiser), Mrs and Mr Alvaro Bunster (ambassador to Britain from the Allende Government), John Boyd, Luis Pavez (CUT), Hugh Scanlon, Elaine Nicholson (interpreter) and Maureen Scott (artist).

Source: *AUEW Journal: 'Solidarity with people of Chile,'* 1976, Amalgamated Engineering Union, MSS.259/AEU/4/6/56, MRC, UW, Coventry.

Despite this enthusiasm, art and design historian John Walker said, 'while there is no doubt about the artist's emotional sincerity, the mural's pictorial rhetoric was antiquated'.[42] Walker goes on to say that 'one of [the mural's] aims was to foster solidarity among trade unionists around the world in the hope that they would use their power to mount an international blockade of Chile's commerce'.[43] In this respect, the mural was a failure, as shortly after its unveiling it disappeared into

---

42 Walker, *Left Shift*, 218.
43 Ibid.

the museum of the AUEW.[44] It was a gesture of solidarity, dripping in symbolism and of itself very unlikely to change the situation in Chile. It was an indirect action and an expression of the internationalism of the AUEW.

Other artistic undertakings of the Chile solidarity movement included exhibitions,[45] but more prominently, music concerts. All over the world the protest music of Chile became an integral part of the Chile solidarity movement as it had been for the Allende Government. For many years a cultural committee existed within the CSC, functioning as a semi-autonomous body, while still being held underneath its rubric.[46] The Cultural Committee was unofficially affiliated with Movimiento de Izquierda Revolucionaria (MIR: Movement of the Revolutionary Left), one of the more extremist groupings in Chilean politics.[47] This occurred in part because the actors and artists who arrived in Britain as refugees were mostly *miristas*.[48] Most of the activists involved in the Chile campaign were CPGB members and the differing ideologies, along with linguistic problems, caused some tension.[49] Gatehouse, secretary of the CSC, freely admitted the importance of the cultural committee's activities, but noted there were always difficulties with them due to their extreme affiliates. 'The differences were never quite explicitly phrased, but they were apparent', he recalled.[50]

The biggest and most remembered music concerts were not organised by that committee. The group which organised the bigger concerts was formed when Joan Jara arrived back in Chile with her daughters.[51] At its centre was Peggy Kessel. She was a Hampstead intellectual,[52] involved in pre-coup solidarity with Chile through the Association for British–Chilean Friendship.[53] She had organised concerts for Vietnam and was, in 1974, working at the National Theatre. Soon after the Chile coup broke, she foresaw the need for an anniversary concert and booked Queen Elizabeth Hall.[54] Members of the high-profile Chilean groups

---

44   *Minutes. Meeting of Executive Council, held in General Office, on the 13th July, 1976 at 10.00 a.m.*, Amalgamated Engineering Union, MSS.259/AEU/1/1/224, MRC, UW, Coventry.
45   Including exhibitions of posters, photos and patchwork from within Chile, made by exiles or circulated by the international solidarity movement.
46   Sometimes called the Agit-Cultural Committee in documents (where 'agit' is short for agitation). It was established in an ad-hoc manner to organise the Chile Festival of March 1974. *Report from the Cultural Committee of the CSC to the Campaign Executive. May 9th. 1974*, CSC, CSC/1/3, LHASC, Manchester.
47   The adherents of MIR were among the only Chileans to undertake any form of armed resistance to the junta.
48   Gatehouse Interview, 2007.
49   Ibid.
50   Ibid.
51   Joan Jara was the widow of Chilean new song artist Victor Jara, who was murdered in the first days of the regime. Roger Burbach, *The Pinochet Affair: State Terrorism and Global Justice* (London: Zed Books, 2003), 57.
52   Kessel was entrenched in the Hampstead artistic and acting community (CPGB).
53   *New Chile, 3 March/April 1973 p. 8*, CSC, CSC/7/1, LHASC, Manchester; *Association for British–Chilean Friendship, 1972*, Etheridge Papers: Longbridge Shop Stewards, MSS.202/S/J/3/2/166, MRC, UW, Coventry.
54   Gatehouse Interview, 2007.

which toured, Inti Illimani and Quilapayun, were predominantly Chilean Communist Party affiliates and for that reason Kessel was a more appropriate organiser than the MIR-aligned cultural committee.[55]

Gatehouse remembered that Kessel was a 'formidable woman; she was absolutely terrifying to work for'.[56] She was so efficient she had a letterhead printed on which to write her Chile concert correspondence, and she promised the concert would be 'an evening of moving, but highly professional entertainment, such as is rarely found in London'.[57] The first large-scale concert was on 16 September 1974 and neatly coincided with Mme Allende's tour and the first anniversary demonstration.[58] Mme Allende was present along with Inti Illimani, Isabel Parra, Joan Jara and other British artists.[59] The concert was titled 'Inti Illimani Sing for Chile' and proceeds were to go to the Chile Relief Fund (connected with the CCHR).[60] Kessel gained the sponsorship of a string of church officials, as well as left personalities, such as Dame Peggy Ashcroft and Adrian Mitchell. Eight Labour MPs put their names forward as sponsors.[61]

The success of the music concerts, which produced empathy and sympathy despite the language barrier, led to various performances being held throughout the 1970s. One of the biggest was the 7 March 1978 concert, featuring Pete Seeger and Quilapayun. It was patronised by 13 Labour MPs and was supported by various personalities such as Michael Palin.[62] Behind the stage was a banner made by John Dugger's Banner Arts Project, with the words (in Spanish) 'Never give in or stray from the road'.[63] The advertising space in the program was sold to raise money. Many unions purchased space, but all were outdone by the TGWU colour advertisement that took up the whole back cover (see Figure 2.5).[64] It seems like an inconsequential detail, but by appealing for sponsorship of such easily supportable events the Chile movement harnessed labour movement power

---

55   Ibid.
56   Ibid.
57   Ibid.
58   After the concert, Mme Allende, Judith Hart, Steve Hart, Alex Kitson, Alf Lomas and George Anthony were invited to dine at the house of the Cuban ambassador. *Gira en Gran Bretana. Septiembre 1974.*
59   Ibid.
60   *Kessel re: A Concert in aid of Chile Relief Fund Inti Illimani Sing For Chile, 1974,* TUC, MSS.292D/980.31/4, MRC, UW, Coventry.
61   Ibid.
62   The concert was organised by Chilean Records for the CSC and the Chile Relief Fund. Chile Solidarity Campaign (UK), *Pete Seeger and Quilapayun: In Concert for Chile* (London: London Caledonian Press, 1978).
63   *Nunca te entregues ni te apartes del camino.* Ibid.
64   The unions included Society of Graphical and Allied Trades (SOGAT), AUEW, CPSA, NUPE, Union of Shop, Distributive and Allied Workers (USDAW), NATFHE, Iron and Steel Trades Confederation (ISTC), NGA, National Union of Dyers, Bleachers and Textile Workers (NUDBTW) and TGWU. Other concerts included: Inti Illimani and John Williams at the Dominion Theatre; Inti Illimani, Quilapayun, Isabel Parra and Patricio Castillo at Royal Albert Hall (30 September 1975; 3800 people attended); and Quilapayun and Bert Jansch, Theatre Royal (25 September 1977). CSC, *'Inti Illimani, John Williams in Concert for Chile,' (Manchester). Local Committees Newsletter No. 14, 24.9.75,* CSC, CSC/44/1, LHASC, Manchester; Chile Fights 25 (London: CSC [Chile Lucha], 1977); *Annual General Meeting London. February 7 1976. Secretary's Report.*

with comparatively little work. The symbiotic relationship was manifested as the unions also managed to fill internationalist prerogatives and sections of their journals with little effort.

Figure 2.5 The front and back pages of the Pete Seeger and Quilapayun concert program. The image on the front page is the Banner Arts banner that was suspended behind the singers. The back cover is a full-page advertisement from the TGWU.

Source: This copy of the program was signed by Pete Seeger. He wrote as a greeting *'Mayibuye Africa!'*, which was one of the rallying cries of the anti-apartheid movement. Chile Solidarity Campaign (UK), *Pete Seeger and Quilapayun*.

The strategic cultural achievements of the Chile campaign then migrated to the Nicaragua and El Salvador campaigns, which took cultural integration to new levels. Activist Diane Dixon remembered that CSC 'essentially gave birth to the other solidarity movements'.[65] Another strategy that found success in many solidarity campaigns after accomplishment with the Chile movement was the adoption of prisoners, a program that was administered by the CCHR.[66]

---

65 Interview with Diane Dixon (Chile activist, Scottish human rights campaigner, CPGB), 4 September 2007 [hereinafter Dixon Interview, 2007], copy in possession of author.
66 For a time, they also ran an adopt-a-town program, but this was not as successful. This program was separate from the 'town twinning' program that was encouraged through CSC local committees. *CSC Annual Report, 1976*; *Chile: the tide has turned Annual Report, 1983*, CSC, CSC/1/13, LHASC, Manchester.

The CCHR was a registered charity which ran out of 1 Cambridge Terrace, London.[67] Established from the Chile campaign, the CCHR focused on human rights and aimed to work with a broader range of groups than the CSC. They did this by remaining 'non-political' and attempting to harness church and human rights groups as well as labour movement support.[68] The CCHR worked (more than the CSC) closely with the Committee of Peace, followed by the Vicariate of Solidarity in Chile[69] and other human rights organisations such as Amnesty International (British Section).[70] There were times when some groups within the solidarity movement pushed for the CCHR and CSC to combine forces for more productive use of activist resources, but this was always resisted because the political nature of the CSC would have led to the loss of some CCHR supporters and vice versa.[71]

The adopt-a-prisoner program had a high level of labour movement involvement and was supported and pushed by the CSC. The Chile campaign admitted that the adoption program was 'perhaps the most important activity we engage upon for maintaining and projecting the issue of Chile into the British labour movement'.[72] Participants wrote letters to the prisoners and often to their families, offering moral and sometimes financial support, and from time to time a prisoner was offered work to help obtain a visa for Britain.[73] Chilean and British authorities were also contacted and articles were published in union journals and newspapers to keep members informed of progress.[74] Sometimes, unions were misinformed when the snippets of information that made it to Britain were pieced together incorrectly. Tom Pilford, however, of the London County Association of Trades Councils, when giving advice to unions considering adopting a prisoner, said: 'you have to keep on plodding, even if you do make a mistake.'[75]

Success in adoption could be a long process drawn out over many months and perhaps years, with multiple letters to representatives in Chile and Britain.[76] John Fairley of the Ladbroke House Branch of the National Association of Teachers described the process of making contact with a prisoner as taking

---

67 *Affiliates' Newsletter No. 21, June 12 1977*, CSC, CSC/1/12, LHASC, Manchester; *Reg Williams (CPSA) to CPSA Branches, 24 November 1978*, CSC, CSC/11/7, LHASC, Manchester.
68 The CCHR newsletter distribution list was to 10 000 people. Wilkinson, 'The Influence of the Solidarity Lobby on British Government Policy towards Latin America'.
69 *CSC Annual Report, 1976*.
70 *CSC Annual Report, 1977*.
71 *CSC-AGM 19.02.77 Minutes*.
72 *Suggestions for Local Committees re: Trade Union Work, 1976*; *CSC Annual Report, 1976*.
73 Sample letters in English and Spanish were sent to each adopting organisation by the CCHR as part of a guidelines pack drawn up with the help of Amnesty International. *Chile Committee for Human Rights: Report on Adoption Scheme, April 1976*, CSC, CSC/31/1, LHASC, Manchester.
74 *CSC Annual Report, 1976*.
75 *Tom Pilford: Chairman, Greater London Association of Trades Councils, 1976*, CSC, CSC/11/4, LHASC, Manchester.
76 Contact was not guaranteed and much of the time did not occur; see, for example: *'Avon's adopted Chilean Freed,' Public Service, April 1976*, CSC, CSC/28/9, LHASC, Manchester.

about five months. Once established, they kept up a relatively steady stream of letters with the prisoner. It was published in the journal of the National Association of Teachers in Further and Higher Education (NATFHE) that 'the first clear result of our Branch work shone through from the tone of our prisoner's letters themselves: our involvement in and concern for his case clearly boosting the prisoner's morale and giving him some hope even in his distressing circumstances'.[77]

Further, the lifting of the individual's morale had an expansive effect, for, as Pilford put it, 'the grape vine is great and it is going round the prisons that the people of England are concerned about them'.[78] In November 1976, the CCHR received news from Chile that one sole prisoner in the Osorno Penitentiary was not adopted when all his prison mates were. A member of the CCHR wrote that 'obviously, he is very sad and this confirms, how important the work of adoptions is emotionally'.[79] His adoption was quickly confirmed.

The adoption process sometimes resulted in very direct and personal contact with Chilean citizens. Receiving a letter from an incarcerated trade unionist in Chile was a moving event in a trade union meeting, and served to mobilise them further.[80] For example, a letter from Benito Sanchez Muñoz of Lota in southern Chile surely provoked such a reaction. He was a miner of only twenty-three years of age who had been general secretary of the Young Socialists in his town. He wrote to the Scottish Area NUM, which had adopted him, begging for aid: 'I fear that this letter won't reach you, but I'm taking the chance ... I beg you to see what could be done for my wife and my little girl. I do not dare to tell you all the things which has happened to us.'[81]

Pilford described how the adoption of another young prisoner led to contact with his parents, who sent the Electrical Trades Union his thumbprint, his identification cards, his photograph, his military service record, a photograph of him with Allende and a letter from the local military authorities stating that he had good behaviour while incarcerated.[82] With such stories and moments, it is easy to see how the program effectively 'personalised the issues'.[83] If an adoption such as this was ultimately successful and the prisoner made their way to Britain, the effect on the trade unionists could not 'be over-stated'.[84]

---

77 '"Adopting" a Chilean Prisoner,' NATFHE Tech Journal 2, March 1978, CSC, CSC/7/14, LHASC, Manchester.
78 Tom Pilford: Chairman, Greater London Association of Trades Councils, 1976.
79 As it turned out, he had already been adopted by the Glasgow 7/194 Branch of the TGWU. The CCHR prompted Doug Bain (Chile Human Rights Committee, Glasgow) to chase this up, and soon the prisoner's sentence was commuted. The prisoner accepted an offer to go into exile in Scotland. *Magali (CCHR) to Bain, 2 November 1976*, Sandy Hobbs Papers, TGWU, GCUA, Glasgow.
80 Suggestions for Local Committees re: Trade Union Work, 1976.
81 Mellado Torres to Jose, 27th January, 1975, Sandy Hobbs Papers, NUM, GCUA, Glasgow.
82 Tom Pilford: Chairman, Greater London Association of Trades Councils, 1976.
83 Wilkinson, 'The Influence of the Solidarity Lobby on British Government Policy towards Latin America'.
84 Suggestions for Local Committees re: Trade Union Work, 1976.

Despite the commitment of unionists and the rolling success of the program, not all adoptions were successful and in some cases the strategy backfired.[85] For example, the mother of dual citizen William Beausire, herself an ex-detainee, appealed to the CCHR to stop using the incarcerated Beausire as an example, because the publicity could be damaging to him.[86] Similarly, Sheila Cassidy noted that one of her fellow prisoners in Tres Álamos was returned for more torture in Villa Grimaldi whenever her name was mentioned in a foreign newspaper. Cassidy maintained that 'these reprisals, however, were a small price to pay for the knowledge that her death would not pass unnoticed, and ultimately the unflagging efforts of thousands of people in the free world were rewarded, for in December 1976 she was released from prison and expelled from Chile'.[87]

The Civil and Public Services Association (CPSA) was a particularly successful adopter, with all three of its adoptees freed by 1978.[88] The third of these was Jose Gonzalez Salas, who had been imprisoned without trial for three years. Salas was in his early twenties. As is the custom in Chile, all young men are required to undertake military service after finishing secondary school and his started in 1974, only three months after the coup. During this time the military intelligence attempted to bribe him to join their ranks, but he refused their advances.

---

85   The Scottish Trades Union Congress (STUC) Youth Advisory Committee sent a letter of strong resolution on their adoptee to the Chilean Embassy in 1979. The embassy replied that in terms of the disappeared persons, 'your concern is appreciated but it is doubtful that your adopting a missing person can really help with the enquiries'. The STUC Youth Committee consistently resolved very strongly for Chile. The STUC Women's Committee only did so in 1974 and 1977. *Berguno (Charge d'Affaires of Chile) to Harrison (STUC YAC), 17 May 1979*, STUC, STUCA 475, GCUA, Glasgow.
86   See, for example: Jonathon Power, *Amnesty International: The Human Rights Story* (Oxford: Pergamon Press, 2001), 34; David Cross, 'British Seek Truth on Missing Man', *The Times*, 18 November 1981; Clifford Longley, 'Prisoners of Conscience; Chile: William Beausire', *The Times*, 28 July 1978; 'MPs Call on Carter to Help Briton in Chile', *Guardian* [Manchester], 7 May 1977; Burbach, *The Pinochet Affair*, 109. Among those used to deflect attention for the Beausire case was Excequiel Ponce Vicencio, a unionist on the docks (see <http://www.memoriaviva.com> for more information on his detention) and Ricardo Lagos (who would go on to become President of Chile in the 1990s). In 1975 Susie Carstairs of the CCHR reported that they were going to attempt to move away from 'VIP' prisoners and shift the focus to lesser-known prisoners. New guidelines had been made, and all letters to Chile would be siphoned through the CCHR due to the 'risks involved'. *CCHR, July 30th 1975 circular*, Sandy Hobbs Papers, Box untitled, GCUA, Glasgow; *CSC Committee Meeting at Liverpool. 8.2.75*, CSC, CSC/1/5, LHASC, Manchester.
87   Sheila Cassidy, *Sheila Cassidy: Audacity to Believe* (London: Collins, 1977), 303.
88   *'Our sponsored Chilean prisoner released,' CPSA Red Tape 1978*, CSC, CSC/7/14, LHASC, Manchester.

No Truck with the Chilean Junta!

Figure 2.6 1979: A delegation to the Foreign Office, which sought reassurances on the safety of William Beausire. From left: Jim Richardson (NATFHE), Peter Holt (National Association of Local Government Officers), Reg Williams (Civil and Public Services Association), Gordon McLellan (CPGB), Joan Lestor (BLP), Frank Dobson (BLP), Owen O'Brien (National Society of Operative Printers and Assistants), Mike Gatehouse. They hold a petition of 11 000 signatures urging Britain to refuse the return of the Ambassador to Chile and reject arms sales to the dictatorship.

Source: 'Junta Victim May be Dead, Says Minister', *Morning Star*, 12 September 1979, 3, courtesy of the Marx Memorial Library.

One day, 50 women were arrested and taken to the base in northern Chile. Among them was Salas's girlfriend, who 'was tortured and shot before his eyes'.[89] Salas was then forced to watch the torture of the other women, but he could not. He turned his back and wept. He was taken to the Regiment Prison in Calama at gunpoint and given electric shock torture.[90] The torments that followed included starvation, with his weight falling from 60 to 45 kg, and being shot at as he was forced to run. He recalled:

> Every night guards would beat me up. Sometimes they would put me in blood-stained cells and make me clean them up. They would grab me by the hair and rub my face in my comrades blood … My limbs are scarred. I almost lost my right leg. They gave me injections of drugs to try and brainwash me.[91]

When Salas was finally released, the CPSA's journal, *Red Tape*, relayed Salas's gratitude to the union.[92] He was formally greeted by the joyous Executive Committee of the CPSA, providing a photo opportunity for the journal, which showed Salas relaxing with a drink with the committee.[93]

Both the adopt-a-prisoner program and the demonstrations made use of an efficient strategy of 'routinising' Chile into the everyday working of the trade union movement.[94] Of all the adoptions, the CCHR estimated that half were from trade union branches, and the rest by trades councils, students' and women's groups followed by church and school groups.[95] Adoption measures, primarily letter writing, were indirect actions easily undertaken within union branch structures at little organisational cost;[96] but that does not cheapen the feelings or intent of many trade unionists in this solidarity action. Adoptions made trade unionists feel as if they could alleviate the harsh conditions of those suffering in Chile, at least in part.[97]

---

89 *CPSA-Sponsored Chilean Prisoner Released, 1978*, CSC, CSC/44/4, LHASC, Manchester.
90 Jose Gonzales Salas, in ibid.
91 Ibid.
92 'Our sponsored Chilean prisoner released,' *CPSA Red Tape 1978*.
93 Ibid. Gonzalez Salas kept some sort of relationship with the union, speaking at their conferences, and so on. From Reg Williams (CPSA) to CPSA Branches, 24 November 1978, CSC, CSC/11/7, LHASC, Manchester.
94 By doing so, they perhaps used to their own benefit the tendency described by Max Weber of movements to routinise and bureaucratise. Pakulski, *Social Movements*, xvii.
95 *CSC Annual Report, 1976*. In 1975, the CSC and CCHR said there were more than 150 Chileans adopted by trade unions, trades councils, shop stewards and student unions. 'At least 4 of these prisoners have been released and are now in Britain, partly as a consequence of their adoption.' In 1976, 500 prisoners were adopted in the United Kingdom and 49 of those had been released. In April 1976, the CCHR reported that 'currently adopted through us: 521 prisoners, adopted by 354 branches of 40 different labour movement and religious organisations'. In 1978 there were 410 prisoners adopted by trade union branches and church groups throughout Britain. *Report on CSC for LCS Political Committee, 1974*, CSC, CSC/1/6, LHASC, Manchester; *Chile Committee for Human Rights: Report on Adoption Scheme, April 1976*; *CSC-AGM 19.02.77 Minutes*; *CSC Annual Report, 1978*.
96 *Suggestions for Local Committees re: Trade Union Work, 1976*.
97 Ibid.

The adoption program appealed to the unionists on a personal level. For Pilford, speaking in 1975, it was as if he could see himself:

> [L]ike most of you [I] was horrified when the news broke in '73 when Aliendi [sic] had been murdered and thousands of our comrades who were in the Trade Union movement were slaughtered and their crime, [was] being like us, being politically minded, being involved in the Trade Union movement of fighting for rights to give workers decent homes and decent living conditions and a right for the things that we do every day and fight for.[98]

Chilean trade unionists were 'just like us'. This personalisation was a similar tactic to the nineteenth-century socialist model of worker-to-worker solidarity, which implicitly emphasised the common long-term interests of class.[99] If there was any self-subordination to the victim, it was apparent in the complete moral authority conferred to the prisoners. Their innocence, cooperation and political suitability were assumed. The rewards to the victims of the regime were great when there was a success: they gained freedom. The reward to trade unions, and the solidarity movement, was a boost in moral capital and strengthening of their organisational relationship.

Above any organisational gain, the plight of an individual unionist was above political difference. Everyone concerned with human rights could agree with the adopt-a-prisoner program. Who could not be moved by stories of burnt retinas, mutilations and dogs trained to rape?[100] In this way the adoption program was a means of multiplying and solidifying solidarity.[101] The CSC acknowledged that while the adopt-a-prisoner program was not vital to the campaign's human rights work, it was 'important for building the entire campaign, as was evident at the trade union conference'.[102]

The conference referred to was organised by the CSC in 1975 and was 'the most constructive and important development yet in the trade unions on Chile'.[103] Adoption of prisoners was one focus of discussion, and after the conference 60 new prisoners were taken on.[104]

---

98   *Tom Pilford: Chairman, Greater London Association of Trades Councils, 1976.*
99   Waterman, Globalization, Social Movements and the New Internationalisms, 52.
100 Judy Maloof, *Voices of Resistance: Testimonies of Cuban and Chilean Women* (Kentucky: University Press of Kentucky, 1999), 207, 209; Carol J. Adams, 'Woman-Battering and Harm to Animals', in *Animals and Women: Feminist Theoretical Explorations*, eds Carol Adams and Josephine Donovan (Durham, NC: Duke University Press, 1999), 68, 78.
101 *CSC-AGM 19.02.77 Minutes.*
102 *CSC Executive Committee: Discussion Document, December 17 1975*, CSC, CSC/1/5, LHASC, Manchester.
103 *Shonfield (National Rank and File Organising Committee) to Gatehouse (CSC), 27 October 1975*, CSC, CSC/4/2, LHASC, Manchester. The Rank and File Organising Committee was part of the International Socialists. Shipley, *Revolutionaries in Modern Britain*, 51.
104 *Annual General Meeting London. February 7 1976. Secretary's Report.*

Figure 2.7 Flyer for the Trade Union Conference on Chile, 1975.

Source: *Solidarity with the People of Chile—A Trade Union Conference* [flyer].

The organisation of the conference stemmed from a resolution at the 1974 annual general meeting of the CSC and thus even its inception starts in a typical procedural trade union manner.[105] The conference that resulted was 'the most important activity organised during the past year' and was 'a great tribute' to the work of the executive committee.[106] Gatehouse started organising in January 1975. This period coincided with the beginning of Ken Hulme's time at the CSC, and with his enthusiasm the conference quickly moved from being affiliates only to a 444-unionist-strong conference in October.[107] The TUC also called a conference on Chile in 1975, but it did not have anywhere near the attendance of the CSC's Trade Union Conference for Chile.[108]

It appeared the CSC had out-unioned the unions.

A set of papers was produced for each delegate of the CSC conference, including a draft declaration voted on in the final moments of the conference.[109] The sheets were packed with information explaining the history and composition of the CSC, highlighting its strengths in trade union affiliations and its achievements, its current programs and available resources as well as detailed descriptions of what was currently occurring in Chile.[110] There were also instruction sheets on practical things that trade unions could do, including the adopt-a-prisoner scheme,[111] helping refugees in Britain[112] and copper and wine boycotts.[113] Harry

---

105 *Minutes of the CSC Executive Committee, 24/3/75*, CSC, CSC/1/6, LHASC, Manchester.
106 *Annual General Meeting London. February 7 1976. Secretary's Report*; *CSC Executive Cttee: 20th November—House of Commons, 1975*, CSC, CSC/1/5, LHASC, Manchester.
107 *Minutes of the CSC Executive Committee, 10/1/75, at Seven Sisters Road*, CSC, CSC/1/6, LHASC, Manchester. The TUC also grandstanded their own contributions to the CUT at this conference. TUC, 'Notes of Proceedings at a Conference on Chile held at Congress House', 36.
108 The only speaker to overlap was Alex Kitson, who was chair at the CSC conference but spoke from the floor at the TUC conference. *CSC Executive Committee Meeting held on Friday February 28 1975*, CSC, CSC/1/6, LHASC, Manchester. The TUC conference was held on a weekday, which would limit rank-and-file participation. TUC, 'Notes of Proceedings at a Conference on Chile held at Congress House'. Looking more broadly, the CSC conference drafted appeals and letters to Kurt Waldheim of the United Nations, Jim Callaghan (British foreign secretary) and the International Conference of Solidarity with Chile (Athens, 1975). *CSC Trade Union Conference Saturday October 25 1975—SPECIAL APPEALS, 1975*, CSC, CSC/11/2, LHASC, Manchester.
109 The declaration called for the British labour movement to get behind trade union boycotts, consumer boycotts as well as the adoption of prisoners. *CSC Trade Union Conference Saturday October 25 1975—DRAFT DECLARATION*, CSC, CSC/11/2, LHASC, Manchester.
110 *CSC Trade Union Conference Delegate's Briefing No 1: What is the CSC?, 1975*, CSC, CSC/11/2, LHASC, Manchester; *CSC Trade Union Conference Delegate's Briefing No 3: What is happening in Chile? 1975*, CSC, CSC/11/2, LHASC, Manchester.
111 *CSC Trade Union Conference Delegate's Briefing No 4: Adopt a Prisoner Campaign, 1975*, CSC, CSC/11/2, LHASC, Manchester.
112 *CSC Trade Union Conference Delegate's Briefing No 6: Helping Chilean refugees in Britain, 1975*, CSC, CSC/11/2, LHASC, Manchester.
113 *Briefing Document on Copper Boycott August 1975*, CSC, CSC/11/2, LHASC, Manchester; *Briefing Document on Chilean Wine July 1975*, CSC, CSC/11/2, LHASC, Manchester; *CSC Trade Union Conference Delegate's Briefing No 4*.

Smith, national organiser for AUEW TASS, urged each delegate to return to their organisation, talk about Chile and 'bring life and energy to the commitment of the approximately nine million trade unionists represented at the Conference'.[114]

Kitson and Nicholson chaired the event, and Luis Figueroa (president, CUT) also spoke in addition to 24 speakers from the floor.[115] There were 11 sponsoring unions, and the TGWU was the most notable absentee. Of course, the TGWU made it onto the flyer more prominently than the sponsorship list thanks to Alex Kitson's position.[116] Delegates were sent from 34 different unions, and of those, 17 had executive members present.[117] On top of this, there were 35 trades councils and 19 shop stewards' committees, making a total of 266 different organisations.[118] The breadth of representation indicates the success the CSC had in channelling labour movement power and attention through their affiliation system.[119]

The day was recorded and the findings published in a pamphlet called *Chile and the British Labour Movement*, and it was cheap to buy and distribute through affiliates. The CSC worked hard to gain maximum momentum from their organising.[120]

Luis Figueroa and Pedro Cornejo of the CUT used the conference as an opportunity to thank the labour movement for its solidarity, actions and adoptions. Cornejo told of his stay in prison and indicated how moved he was by the trade union conference: 'only through the kind of direct contact

---

114   *CSC Trade Union Conference Report to Delegates no. 2 Report of Proceedings, 1975*, CSC, CSC/11/2, LHASC, Manchester.
115   Tom Pilford, Alex Ferry (AUEW Glasgow), Brian Anderson (AUEW Liverpool), Jimmy Symes (Merseyside Docks Shop Stewards) and Harry Smith all spoke. *CSC Trade Union Conference Saturday October 25—AGENDA, 1975*, CSC, CSC/11/2, LHASC, Manchester; *Annual General Meeting London. February 7 1976. Secretary's Report*. For a list of all speakers, see: *CSC Trade Union Conference Report to Delegates no. 1 Attendance, 1975*, CSC, CSC/11/2, LHASC, Manchester.
116   The sponsoring unions were Association of Cinematograph, Television and Allied Technicians (ACTT), Associated Society of Locomotive Engineers and Firemen (ASLEF), Association of Teachers in Technical Institutes (ATTI), AUEW, AUEW TASS, NALGO, National Society of Operative Printers and Assistants (NATSOPA), NUPE, NUM, SLADE and SOGAT. *Solidarity with the People of Chile—A Trade Union Conference* [flyer].
117   ACTT, ATTI, AUEW, AUEW TASS, CPSA, Musicians' Union, NALGO, NATSOPA, NUGSAT, NUM, NUPE, NUR, NUS, Post Office Engineers Union (POEU), SLADE, SOGAT and Tobacco Workers' Union.
118   *Annual General Meeting London. February 7 1976. Secretary's Report*. NALGO sent the most delegates, with sixty-eight. Kitson said at the time that it was 'something really new for a white collar union to be in the forefront in a cause such as this'. NALGO also made adoption official union policy. AUEW sent 56 delegates, AUEW TASS 17, TGWU 54, and ASTMS and ATTI sent 28 each. *CSC Trade Union Conference Report to Delegates no. 1 Attendance*; Chile Solidarity Campaign, *Chile and the British Labour Movement*; *Tom Pilford: Chairman, Greater London Association of Trades Councils, 1976*.
119   More than £300 was collected at the conference and each delegate was charged a £1 fee.
120   Chile Solidarity Campaign, *Chile and the British Labour Movement*; *From Gatehouse to Editors, Trade Union Journals & Labour Movement press re: Chile and the British Labour Movement*, CSC, CSC/11/2, LHASC, Manchester; *Trade Union Conference Report, 1975*, CSC, CSC/11/2, LHASC, Manchester. The success of the conference led to various others being organised by the CSC, the most prominent of which was 'Bread, Work, Freedom' (1979).

afforded by this conference can one get to know a class beyond the boundaries of nation, flag and language, and perceive the true nature of the international workers' movement.'[121]

The internationalist rhetoric of the speeches temporarily united the attendees despite their local political differences.

The conference encompassed a range of ideological and strategic opinions among the trade unions. Some focused on socialism, while others openly admitted the reason for their involvement was a commitment to Christian values.[122] For example, on the one hand Kitson said the job of the British trade unionists was limited to pressuring Jim Callaghan, the British Labour Prime Minister, to change government policy. On the other hand, some unionists wanted to fight fascism directly and bring the junta down.[123] The conference was used as a way of airing ideological differences and managing that conflict without endangering or involving the industrial aims of the unions. The unifying internationalist rhetoric provided an umbrella that protected unions against the factionalist storm.

The organisation of the conference by the CSC repeated the strategy of routinising the Chile issue.[124] Support and attendance were easy, resource-sensible actions for trades councils and unions to undertake. If international activity of unions is contingent on the sum of incentives, capacities and impediments to action, as Schmutte has said, the CSC was extremely successful in promoting action.[125] They provided activities, such as this conference, that negated most impediments (lack of finance, lack of organising hours, lack of leadership) and made expressions of union internationalism easy. Conferences were a way of life for the trade union movement. After the unions agreed to the consensus of affiliation by joining the campaign, it was merely good trade unionism to send along delegates, just as the TGWU would send delegates to ITF congresses. The conference was an indirect action using a strategy of industrial national style, yet it was organised by a social movement that mimicked deep traditions. It exposes the overlap of the abstract models when applied to real-life examples of union–social movement interactions. Nothing is clear-cut.

---

121 *CSC Trade Union Conference: Concluding speech of Luis Figueroa, President of the Central Unica de Trabajadores (CUT), the Chilean TUC, to the conference, 1975*, CSC, CSC/11/2, LHASC, Manchester; *Hand Written notes—Trade Union Conference 1976*, CSC, CSC/11/4, LHASC, Manchester.
122 *Hand Written notes—Trade Union Conference 1976*.
123 Ibid.
124 The campaign also did this with trade union publications. They took a very organised approach to ensuring that Chile was covered in trade union journals. See, for evidence: *Chile in the Union journals, c1978*, CSC, CSC/28/15, LHASC, Manchester.
125 Schmutte, 'International Union Activity', 65.

The conference, and the other activities described in this chapter, fits neither the industrial national unionism nor the social movement unionism paradigms. Almost all Chile solidarity activities were organised, promoted and run externally to the trade unions by a social movement group. The CSC exploited the hierarchical, official, stratified and ingrained structures, procedures and habits of the trade unions in order to achieve its own goals. The actions in this chapter demonstrated the flexibility of the internationalist sentiment of trade unions. In contrast to the rigidity of the theoretical models of trade union action contained in scholarly descriptions, real events were capricious.

The next chapter discusses another institutionalised trade union action: the delegation. The industrial national nature of this delegation's organisation did not mean it was independent of the social movement, but it did not mean it dominated the Chile discourse at the time. The rigid organisation of the delegation is contrasted with the efforts of one rogue individual. This individual had sufficient moral capital to act outside the hierarchy of the traditional labour movement.

Figure 2.8 Jack Jones presents Luis Figueroa (CUT) with a TGWU mini banner.

Source: *Chile Fights: Chile—Trade Unions and the Resistance 11* (London: CSC [Chile Lucha], 1975), 2.

3. 'Unique solidarity'? The mineworkers' delegation, 1977

The delegation had arrived in Chile just in time for May Day.[1] Protests on the streets were banned and the junta refused permission for official unions to celebrate the radical holiday; but they could not ban a mass for the feast of St Joseph, the Worker. Three British miners donned their jackets and joined a procession of Chilean trade unionists into the cathedral. They 'witnessed the scenes of enthusiasm and defiance as the crowd chanted freedom slogans under the eyes of the military'.[2]

It was the National Union of Mineworkers (NUM) which sent the delegation to Chile in 1977 and it was unusual in that the idea came from within the upper ranks of the union.[3] The NUM was not integrated into the Chile Solidarity Campaign as much as other unions, yet the delegation represented a very significant act of British–Chilean solidarity. By attempting to avoid what theorists would retrospectively call social movement unionism and sticking with a more stringent (yet not unaltered) industrial national idea of internationalism, the miners actually strengthened the social movement from which they were trying to remain independent. Ironically, despite loyalty to the industrial national structure, the effect of the delegation within the upper reaches of the Trades Union Congress (TUC) or International Confederation of Free Trade Unions (ICFTU), for example, was limited. The NUM was unable to move the TUC to take substantial action, yet inversely, their action buoyed the solidarity campaign.

Another British citizen who travelled to Chile was Jack Jones. His status and his knowledge of the idiosyncrasies of all levels of trade unions allowed him to use his (very short) time in Chile in a very different manner to the NUM. His position at the top of labour movement organisations in Britain and in the world, as well as the moral authority gained from his career since the Spanish Civil War, enabled him to use the names of organisations within his reach without being bogged down by their organisational bureaucracy. This chapter compares the two delegations: industrial national versus a strategic individual.

In 1974 the CSC embarked on a scouting mission for affiliations, but the NUM reaction towards the new solidarity organisation was far from confident.[4] While

---
1   *Gatehouse to Bynger, October 25 1977*, CSC, CSC/28/12, LHASC, Manchester.
2   *CSC Annual Report, 1977*.
3   It was not the only type of action undertaken by the NUM, the members of which were also enthusiastic adopters of prisoners and hosts to Chilean unionists.
4   *CSC Executive Committee: Minutes of the Meeting held on Friday March 15 1974 at Seven Sisters*, CSC, CSC/1/3, LHASC, Manchester.

preparing for May Day, the CSC was still not sure that NUM president Lawrence Daly would even mention Chile in his address at the rally in Trafalgar Square.[5] Months later, in October of the same year, the CSC was still persistently seeking NUM affiliations at both the national and the area levels.[6]

In strategy akin to peer pressure, a list of prominent unions which had already signed up to sponsor the CSC's Trade Union Conference on Chile was sent to the NUM, and the CSC's coercion led to the NUM's national-level affiliation in July 1975.[7] This did not, however, herald their loving commitment to the group. In fact, further evidence of the NUM detachment from the CSC structure was shown in the CSC annual general meeting for the year immediately before the delegation in 1976. Only one NUM representative attended the meeting. Other unions had sent full delegations;[8] however, the NUM did have a permanent representative on the executive committee of the campaign. His name was Jack Collins.[9]

Collins was a 'lovely man', according to Mike Gatehouse, and he was a member of the Communist Party.[10] Collins was the NUM National Executive Committee representative from the Kent coalfields.[11]

It is not clear why Collins was nominated to attend the CSC, but possible reasons may have included his willingness or giving the responsibility for a peripheral campaign to a small and less important region. Or it may simply have been due to Collins' communist sympathies. Regardless of the reason, Collins attended the CSC regularly, and 'he kept Chile on the agenda at the Mineworkers all the way through', said Gatehouse.[12]

And agendas were fairly vigorously argued at the NUM. Their nominal support of solidarity did not bring a wave of enthusiasm that overcame their reticence to be involved in a social movement. Their desire to remain separate is only understood by taking a snapshot of the union's organisation and the main players within it.

It was essentially an industrial union, representing the majority of manual workers in a single industry. The NUM was organised by areas, within which

---

5 *CSC Executive Committee: Minutes of the meeting held on Thursday April 11 1974 at Seven Sisters.*
6 *CSC. Executive Committee: Analysis of Campaign Performance to Date. Discussion Document. 23/10/74.*
7 In June 1975, Jack Collins attended the CSC Executive Committee as a delegate, indicating that affiliation went through. *Minutes of the CSC Executive Committee meeting, held on 26th June 1976 at the House of Commons*, CSC, CSC/1/5, LHASC, Manchester; National Union of Mineworkers (UK), *NUM Annual Conference, 1975* (Scarborough: NUM, 1975).
8 Through 1975–76 the unions with the most visible support at the CSC were NATSOPA, ASTMS, SOGAT, NGA, AUEW and TGWU. *CSC Annual General meeting for 1976*, CSC, CSC/1/12, LHASC, Manchester.
9 *Minutes CCS-EC 27.04.76*, CSC, CSC/1/5, LHASC, Manchester.
10 Gatehouse Interview, 2007.
11 At the time, Collins was one of six communists on the NUM National Executive Committee. Kent was a relatively isolated area in the NUM. Joe Gormley, *Battered Cherub* (London: Hamish Hamilton, 1982), 138.
12 Ibid.

were lodges and branches, which were almost all based on place of work: pits or collieries. Each area's distinct history, their different-sized mines and divergent working and economic conditions led to a diverse political make-up and some inter-area rivalry. In 1975 there were 20 structural units: 14 regions and six industrial groups.[13] Areas had considerable political and administrative autonomy from the national leadership.[14] While the industrial activities of areas were the responsibility of the national union, the areas kept most of the union fees, and essentially carried out the day-to-day administration of the union.[15]

Sitting on the NUM National Executive were 20 area officials, all with the same formal power. Full-time officials were elected and those posts were permanent. The NUM National Executive Committee members elected from the regions could in theory be working, rank-and-file miners, but due to reputation and the local profile necessary for electoral success, overwhelmingly full-time officials were the ones selected.[16] While the selection of annual national conference delegations and other ballots were conducted at the pithead, ensuring very high participation, there was no set method of electing the executive members.[17] This was a relatively undemocratic method of electing what was, in practice, the day-to-day controlling body of the union.[18] It was also the body from which the miners who travelled to Chile were selected.

As with many unions, an annual conference was held, with the idea that it safeguarded the democratic nature of the organisation. The annual national conference brought together area delegations whose interests and votes were mandated by previously held area conferences;[19] but the rules were extremely restrictive.

Emergency resolutions could only be submitted with the consent of 75 per cent of delegates present. No more than three resolutions and two amendments per area were allowed.[20] Submission of resolutions was required at least 14 weeks

---

13 The white-collar section (previously Colliery Officials and Staffs Association) had approximately 31 000 voting members in 1960. That section was in competition with the Association of Professional, Executive, Clerical and Computer Staff (APEX). There were also two groups within the union which held joint affiliations to other unions (TGWU and General and Municipal Workers Union). David Edelstein and Malcolm Warner, *Comparative Union Democracy: Organisation and Opposition in British and American Unions* (Westmead, UK: Gower, 1975), 210, 211–12.
14 The federal structure of the original amalgamation in 1945 still influenced the union into the 1970s. Several areas were themselves federations before the 1945 amalgamation. Ibid., 235.
15 Arthur Marsh, *Trade Union Handbook: A Guide and Directory to the Structure, Membership, Policy and Personnel of the British Trade Unions* (Westmead, UK: Gower, 1980), 245.
16 Edelstein and Warner, *Comparative Union Democracy*, 268; Stephen Milligan, *The New Barons: Union Power in the 1970s* (London: Temple Smith, 1976), 115.
17 Pithead ballots employed small, private voting booths that members had to pass through to enter the mine. They would thus turn out between 60 and 80 per cent of members—much higher than postal or branch ballots. Milligan, *The New Barons*, 115.
18 Ibid.
19 Sometimes instructed by the area council rather than the conference.
20 With this in mind, resolutions had to be palatable to the politically diverse union. Academic Martin Harrison wrote that 'militant Areas like Scotland often try to word resolutions so innocently that they will command wide, and unsuspecting, support in the coalfields'. Harrison, in Edelstein and Warner, *Comparative Union Democracy*, 234.

prior to the conference and amendments at least six weeks in advance. These rules meant that many issues were decided before the conference. Deceptively, the actual control of the proceedings of the conference was not with the caucus of area delegations. Resolutions on economic control, or other topics that the NUM National Executive believed to be impractical, could be remitted to their own meetings. Thus the potential to launch the union into action was dependent on the politics and whim of the National Executive. This included any international action. The oscillations in the area versus national power swing wildly through the structure of union business, not least because often the amount of power relied on the character of those in leadership.[21]

At the head of the NUM were the president and general secretary, both full-time positions and roughly equal in stature and power.[22] While the president was technically above the general secretary, the power balance could swing due to personality.[23]

The leaders of the union in the 1970s were Lawrence Daly and Joe Gormley. Daly had been active in the CPGB until 1956, when he left over the party's support for the Soviet Union. He was then a founding member of the Fife Socialists League, a socialist/humanist grouping associated with the *New Left Review*. Under that banner, he was elected Fife County Councillor in 1958. When the organisation dissolved, he joined the Labour Party, which he had previously regarded as bureaucratic and 'over orthodox'.[24] Concurrently, Daly moved up the ranks of the NUM, starting in the Youth Committee of the Scottish Area followed by an election to the area's rank-and-file council. His first full-time NUM post was in 1964 as a mineworkers' agent for Fife, Clackmannan and Stirlingshire. To obtain that position, he defeated the communist candidate and had the support of the anti-communists (individuals and groups) of the area. One year later he was secretary of the Scottish Area, the first non-communist to hold the position for almost 20 years.

In 1968 Daly ran for NUM General Secretary against Joe Gormley. Daly was a man of charisma—so much so that he once recorded a selection of Robert Burns' love songs for television—and this quality was no doubt put to effective use to win the election.[25] He ran a roughly organised campaign,

---

21 Ibid.
22 Ibid., 214; Milligan, *The New Barons*, 83.
23 Edelstein and Warner, *Comparative Union Democracy*, 215; Gormley, *Battered Cherub*, 78. Both of these full-time officials along with the vice-president were *ex officio* on the executive committee: they held no vote, except in the case of a tie, when the president held the casting vote. The president and general secretary were elected by pithead ballot, but the vice-president was elected at the annual conference. Milligan, *The New Barons*, 115.
24 Edelstein and Warner, *Comparative Union Democracy*, 247; David Howell, *The Politics of the NUM: A Lancashire View* (Manchester: Manchester University Press, 1989), 20.
25 Milligan, *The New Barons*, 118.

utilising various left press outlets, whereas Gormley had almost no coverage at all. The largely communist-dominated regions supported Daly against the relatively right-wing Gormley, despite the former's previous relationship with anti-communist organisations.[26]

Not to be held back by this defeat and in fact learning from it, Gormley ran in the 1971 presidential election against prominent Scottish communist Mick McGahey. His area executive donated £8000 towards canvassing for his election—an unheard of tactic in the NUM. And it worked. Gormley was a right-winger or 'moderate' (though he thought of himself as a 'progressive') who fought many battles, elections and otherwise, against communists at all levels of the NUM organisation.[27] He sat on the BLP National Executive Committee and was the secretary of the NUM North Western Area. He was a self-proclaimed socialist by 'gut belief' and also pronounced himself as a strong internationalist.[28] Gormley was also a BLP International Sub Committee member for 10 years, and would go on to become the vice-president of the Miners' International Federation.[29] One commentator said Gormley was 'a reassuring personality. He lacked panache, but [could] be refreshingly blunt.'[30] Mike Gatehouse remembered contradictions:

> Ah Joe Gormley! Joe Gormley was a complex man, I mean he was right wing in his politics, but he was a genuine miner and it was said of him that when he went on delegations abroad, everyone else sort of boozed up in the hotels and Joe Gormley went round the mines.[31]

The leadership of the NUM was split between these two politically disparate men. Though Daly was said to have been a much stronger orator than Gormley, a prolonged illness in the 1970s kept him at the sidelines of the union. According to Stephen Milligan, Daly was eclipsed at conferences by McGahey (vice-president from 1972) and later by Arthur Scargill, who was a non-CPGB, hardline Marxist.[32]

---

26 Edelstein and Warner, *Comparative Union Democracy*, 249–50.
27 Gormley, *Battered Cherub*, 161; Milligan, *The New Barons*, 116–17.
28 Gormley, *Battered Cherub*, 47, 118.
29 Ibid., 118, 188.
30 Ibid., 118.
31 Gatehouse Interview, 2007.
32 Scargill made a visit to the United States in 1979 to the Rouge plant in Detroit to attend a rally supported by the United Auto Workers; at this rally, he urged the US trade union movement to boycott all Chilean trade. He was, however, not overly concerned with the CSC or solidarity at all. 'There were also, I think, sections within the trade union movement who regarded the whole stuff about Chile as a bit of a diversion, and a digression. I always thought Arthur Scargill was one of those people, because although the miners as a whole were sort of supportive, Scargill, who was supposed to be on the left, actually he never said anything against but he just wasn't particularly interested and you would have expected him to be. But maybe he wasn't because Mick McGahey … [was] also the right wing within the miners union, notably, Joe Gormley who was a horrible man, God he was horrible, who was General Secretary of the NUM.' Gatehouse Interview, 2007; *Scargill (NUM) to Gatehouse (CSC) 16th February, 1979*, CSC, CSC/11/10, LHASC, Manchester; Michael Crick, *Scargill and the Miners* (Middlesex: Penguin Books, 1985).

The NUM organisation was large enough that it ran its own International Department, in which Vernon Jones was employed.[33] Gormley claimed responsibility for the establishment of the department.[34] Much of the union's own international activity was based on Rule 3(b) of the NUM, which stated that an objective of the union was to 'federate with and assist associations that have the same or similar objects in view'. Keeping this in mind, it is useful to note that the NUM, in many ways, did not help Chilean miners in a direct manner, but tried to prop up the Federación Industrial Nacional Minera (FINM: Chilean Mineworkers' Federation). This approach was obviously welcomed by Chileans involved with that organisation. Hernán Cofre told the 1978 NUM conference that '[t]he situation of our workers is difficult. Even more difficult, perhaps, is the situation of the organisations of workers. Our Federation is virtually in chaos as far as its finances go.'[35]

The NUM's first act of Chile solidarity started well before their affiliation to the CSC with a resolution at the NUM National Executive on 13 September 1973, just two days after the coup. It was agreed that the NUM support the TUC and BLP condemnation of the coup and the Chilean ambassador be contacted.[36] The 1974 NUM Conference in Llandudno, north Wales, voted 280–92 in support of a resolution calling on the British Government to sever diplomatic relations with Chile, and calling on the TUC to lend all possible support to the restoration of democracy.[37]

In addition to resolutions, by February 1975 a proposal to send a Scottish Area NUM delegation to Chile was in circulation, supported by the NUM South Wales Area.[38] Consistent reports thereafter emerged of NUM plans to send a delegation to Chile.[39] The Kent, South Wales and Scottish areas of the NUM were the most consistent and vocal in their support of the CSC and also the most radical politically.[40]

The solidarity demonstrated within the NUM and the union's interaction with the CSC were distinct from the AUEW and the TGWU. The latter unions regarded their involvement and funding of the CSC to be vital parts of their overall

---

33 *Gatehouse to Vernon Jones, December 27 1978*, CSC, CSC/28/19, LHASC, Manchester.
34 Gormley, *Battered Cherub*, 188.
35 Hernan Cofre, *NUM Annual Conference, 1978* (Torquay: NUM, 1978), 566.
36 National Union of Mineworkers (UK), *Annual Report and Proceedings for the Year 1973* (England: NUM, 1973).
37 National Union of Mineworkers (UK), *NUM Annual Conference, 1974* (Llandudno: NUM, 1974). The next resolution at a NUM conference (though discussions and passing of reports always occurred every year) was in 1978, with a long resolution of support for Chile and a call for a boycott of all companies who traded with Chile. National Union of Mineworkers (UK), *NUM Annual Conference, 1978* (Torquay: NUM, 1978).
38 *CSC Executive Committee Meeting held on Friday February 28 1975*. NUM South Wales strongly supported the CSC.
39 *Minutes of the CSC Executive Committee, 24/3/75*, CSC, CSC/1/6, LHASC, Manchester.
40 *Gatehouse to General Secretaries and CSC Executive delegates of affiliated Unions and Conference co-sponsors. September 30 1975*, CSC, CSC/1/6, LHASC, Manchester.

approach to Chile solidarity and to internationalism. NUM solidarity, on the other hand, was dominated by independent actions framed as largely unaffected (though not uninfluenced) by the CSC or the solidarity movement. The Chile campaign encouraged the NUM's independent action in any way it could.[41]

The NUM gained enough momentum from the CUT visit in 1975 to put a proposal to the TUC, but, given the attitude of the TUC International Department as described in Chapter One, they received a reply that a British representative should go as part of an international delegation.[42]

The wind seemed to have been expelled from the NUM delegation's sails.

In the case of the miners, the CSC had to satisfy itself with riding the waves of enthusiasm. Gatehouse wrote in a letter to Dick Barbour-Might, long-term friend of, and activist in, the CSC:

> I'm convinced that if we tout the idea [of the delegation] around for long enough, we will persuade someone to take it up, and that if a good job of preparation and reporting-back is done, a delegation could have as big a mobilising effect for solidarity as say the trade union conference last year, or the [prisoner] adoption scheme.[43]

And Gatehouse was confident that despite the relatively right-wing leadership of the NUM at the time, 'there was some real feeling' towards Chile solidarity.[44]

At the 1976 NUM Conference on the Isle of Man, Pedro Cornejo, CUT representative in Britain, was given a standing ovation. The CSC was deeply intertwined with the London offices of the CUT at that time and in that capacity Gatehouse had accompanied Cornejo to the conference. In this way, the CSC overcame its exclusion from formal NUM business and was able to promote the idea of a delegation. In fact, in his speech, Cornejo asked the NUM to send a delegation to investigate mines in Chile, and with this direct request, the delegation began to solidify.[45] It was the culmination of gentle, extra-organisational pressure to massage just the right sort of action.

The NUM delegation was an initiative taken outside the influence, and without the blessing, of the TUC. It was also a 'risky' and 'daring' thing to do, Mike Gatehouse explained:

---

41 See, for example, the CSC discussion about the NUM delegation: *CSC Executive Committee: Minutes of the meeting held on Friday May 2 1975 at Seven Sisters Road*, CSC, CSC/1/3, LHASC, Manchester.
42 Keeping in mind the conservative forces controlling much of the TUC and the TUC International Department in particular makes this reaction unsurprising. *CSC Executive Committee: Meeting of October 16 1975 at the House of Commons*, CSC, CSC/1/5, LHASC, Manchester.
43 *Gatehouse to Barbour-Might, July 18 1976*, CSC, CSC/15/1, LHASC, Manchester.
44 Gatehouse Interview, 2007.
45 *Delegation from the NUM to Chile and Bolivia 21st April – 7th May 1977*[draft?], TUC, MSS.292D/980.31/7, MRC, UW, Coventry.

Delegations are quite high risk ... you are going somewhere where you don't know, where you don't speak the language ... there are absolutely no guarantees as to who you'll meet, whether it's official or not, let alone in conditions of dictatorship.

So it wasn't an un-enterprising thing for the Miners to do.[46]

While planning the delegation, the NUM invited a speaker to the executive meeting: Julian Filochowski of the Catholic Institute for International Relations. Filochowski had recently been to Bolivia and Chile. He reported what he saw there and brought a message from the FINM: they would welcome the delegation, which would be very important to their program to make contact with other mining unions. The federation suggested 'arrangements should be outside official Chilean channels'.[47] It was a 'secret' delegation, according to Wilkinson,[48] or, as David Jones called it, a 'cloak-and-dagger mission'.[49]

The executive immediately agreed to send a donation to the FINM through a trustworthy channel,[50] and furthermore that arrangements would go ahead for a delegation to Bolivia and Chile.[51] No explicit aims were dictated to the delegation in the NUM executive meeting minutes. In the Finances and General Purposes Committee, the delegation was charged with the responsibility to investigate the efficacy of giving the requested larger sums of money to FINM.[52]

The delegation left in 1977 and represented a 'considerable achievement' for the campaign and the culmination of two years' efforts.[53] Four members of the National Executive Committee were to go (though three went in the end), and it was specified that these members were not to be from the foreign delegation rota.[54] Journalist David Jones stated that Joe Gormley chose the

---

46 Gatehouse Interview, 2007.
47 National Union of Mineworkers (UK), *Annual Report and Proceedings for the Year 1977* (England: NUM, 1977), 62.
48 Michael Wilkinson, 'The Chile Solidarity Campaign and British Government Policy towards Chile, 1973-1990', *European Review of Latin American and Caribbean Studies* 52 (June 1992), 58.
49 David Jones, 'When You Look into the Eyes of a Mother Who has Lost a Son, You Can Tell Who is Telling the Truth and Who is Not', *Daily Post*, 12 November 1998, 18.
50 The Finances and General Purposes Committee put this into action, donating £1000 each to the Bolivian and Chilean miners' federations. National Union of Mineworkers (UK), *Annual Report and Proceedings for the Year 1977*, 116.
51 It appears that the Catholic Institute for International Relations may have been involved in the organisation of the delegation. McKay later said the trip was organised by the Catholic Church. 'Former Miner Tells of Pinochet Horror', *Mail*, 21 December 2006.
52 National Union of Mineworkers (UK), *Annual Report and Proceedings for the Year 1977*, 116.
53 Jones, 'When You Look into the Eyes of a Mother'; *CSCC 14.05.77 Minutes, 1977*, CSC, CSC/1/5, LHASC, Manchester.
54 Nomination for appropriate members of the delegation from appropriate committees took the form of a rota system. This functioned at national and area levels, and it meant delegations were always viewed favourably by members. Edelstein and Warner, *Comparative Union Democracy*, 246–7.

three delegates.⁵⁵ Gatehouse confirmed: 'I think largely through Gormley's agency they hand picked two of the most right wing regional secretaries or regional figures to go.'⁵⁶

Gatehouse was referring to Ted McKay and Ken Toon.⁵⁷ Despite the relatively conservative tendencies of these two, the Chilean coup had caused genuine revulsion through the whole political spectrum of the labour movement:

> Ken Toone [sic] was on the right of the Party and associated with right-wing trade unionists … Nevertheless he was profoundly affected by his visit to Chile and did an enormous amount of work on behalf of the Chilean miners on his return to Britain, despite his knowledge that many of the Chilean miners he met and their leadership were Communists.⁵⁸

Jack Collins was not chosen to go to Chile despite his time representing the union on the CSC Executive Committee. Gatehouse remembered that he was 'pissed off', but he maintained his commitment to the CSC for years afterwards.⁵⁹ Further, it was not Gormley's 'style', said Gatehouse, to allow the CSC to have involvement in the organisation of the delegation and perhaps less to allow an 'anti' (someone who consistently voted negatively at NUM National Executive Committee meetings) to enjoy a delegation. Incidentally, Gormley's 'antis' were always communists; he indicated in his autobiography that Collins clearly fell into this category.⁶⁰ Gormley also wrote: 'perhaps I'm a bit of a bully.'⁶¹

Despite this setback, the CSC was present in the delegation in another capacity. The interpreter and organiser sent to accompany the miners was an Irish woman named Ann Browne. Gatehouse said she was 'one of our people'. She was a blessing for the Chile cause, acknowledged Gatehouse, 'because there is a whole art to being the accompanier of a delegation, keeping them together in one place, making sure they don't get pissed, making sure they don't behave badly, making sure they get to the right places on time, all of that'.⁶²

The delegation of 1977 was Browne's first trip to Chile, but she had extensive organising experience and was educated in the Chilean situation through her

---

55 Jones, 'When You Look into the Eyes of a Mother', 18.
56 Gatehouse Interview, 2007.
57 'The NUM sort of put forward what the left of the Communist Party said was right wingers for the … miners delegation to Chile: they were bloody terrific.' Hulme Interview, 2007.
58 Gatehouse, in Wilkinson, 'The Influence of the Solidarity Lobby on British Government Policy towards Latin America'.
59 Gatehouse Interview, 2007.
60 Gormley, *Battered Cherub*, 150.
61 Ibid., 78.
62 Ibid.

involvement as secretary of the Joint Working Group for Refugees from Chile in Britain, which was run out of Uxbridge Road, London.[63] Again, the organised Chile solidarity movement played a tangential but influential role.

The conditions under which Browne worked in Chile were very trying. On top of chaperoning duties, she also understood in more depth what was occurring in Chile. 'She was extraordinary', said Gatehouse.[64]

The NUM first applied to enter Chile officially as a union delegation, but the junta refused permission, just as they had refused entry to the Ad Hoc Working Group of the United Nations Human Rights Council (UNHRC) since 1975.[65] As a CSC report heroically proclaimed: 'But NUM was not to be put off, and determined to send its delegation with or without Pinochet's permission.'[66]

While the military government would not authorise the delegation, remarkably, visas were not required to enter Chile. So the miners entered '"privately" rather than secretly and without asking permission from anyone', wrote Gatehouse in 1977.[67] There was a possibility they would be turned away at the border or deported if the nature of their mission became publicly known. The miners were not put off, despite the fact they risked more than their own safety.

The delegation spent 16 days in Latin America; six of those were in Chile.[68] They first travelled in Bolivia and met tin miners,[69] and then spent a short time in Peru

---

63 The Joint Working Group (JWG) was formed in 1974 as a group for refugees from Chile, and was less overtly political than the CSC. The JWG later broadened its focus to include refugees from all Latin American countries. It attracted government funding for the settlement of refugees. It ran a boarding house in London. In 1980–81, its funding was cut by the conservative government. Chile Solidarity Campaign, *Chile and the British Labour Movement*; T. Kushner and K. Knox, 'Refugees from Chile: A Gesture of International Solidarity', in *Refugees in an Age of Genocide: Global, National and Local Perspectives during the Twentieth Century*, eds K. Knox and T. Kushner (London: Frank Cass, 1999), 289–305; Imogen Mark, 'Ann Browne', *Guardian News and Media Limited*, 2000, accessed 9 January 2009, <http://www.guardian.co.uk/news/2000/feb/15/guardianobituaries2>; *CSC Trade Union Conference Delegate's Briefing No 1*.
64 After the JWG was disbanded, Browne went on to work for the International Federation of Miners (MIF) in 1982 in Brussels, and was instrumental in forming that organisation's links with Latin American mineworkers' unions. Gatehouse believes she was 'very beloved by miners from all over the world because she was so good and dedicated'. Despite this, in the 1970s, Browne was referred to in NUM documents as 'our interpreter' rather than identified by her name. See, for example, when Ted McKay paid tribute to the interpreter in his address to the NUM 1977 Conference. ICEM, 'Ann Browne: A Tribute', in *ICEM News Release No. 8/2000*, 2000, accessed 22 August 2008, <http://www.icem.org/en/5-Mining-DGOJP/437-Ann-Browne:-A-Tribute>; Gatehouse Interview, 2007; National Union of Mineworkers (UK), *NUM Annual Conference, 1977* (Tynemouth: NUM, 1977), 467; 'Saved Chileans to be Allowed Here: Success for Mrs Hart', *Morning Star*, 16 September 1975, 5.
65 Gatehouse to Bynger, October 25 1977.
66 *CSC Annual Report, 1977*.
67 Gatehouse to Bynger, October 25 1977.
68 *Report of the 109th Annual Trades Union Congress* (Enfield: Trades Union Congress, 1977), 510; *CSCC 14.05.77 Minutes, 1977*.
69 Bolivia was ruled by dictator General Banzer at the time. His reign included high economic growth and human rights abuses.

in order to gain entry to Chile.[70] Throughout the trip they posed as tourists and then mining engineers, mining equipment salesmen or industrial archaeologists studying the old mining equipment in Chile.[71] From Peru, they travelled the long road through the Atacama Desert. The *Mail* reported that 'at one stage they had to be hidden among rocks on a beach next to the Pacific' Ocean to avoid an army patrol.[72]

On 30 April 1977, the NUM delegation arrived in Santiago and immediately set out to contact the FINM.[73] Their first impression of the streets in the capital was 'of apparent calm and order. However … We were never taken directly to meet union officials for fear of being followed, and we never arrived until it was established that we had not been.'[74]

Meetings were never held in any public space and people were too scared to hold them in their houses. Ken Toon reported that 'people we spoke to were at great personal risk of arrest if they were caught talking to us'.[75] Thus, 'contact was difficult and sometimes failed'.[76] Meetings and visits to the coalmines were often in the middle of the night, described Lawrence Daly, and the men constantly had to deal with 'security forces and all the rest of it'.[77] They never stayed in one safe house more than a few hours and Ted McKay wrote simply: 'I often wonder what would have happened to us had we been caught.'[78]

The delegation passed within 32 km of mines they wanted to see, but turned back because it had become too dangerous due to road checks.[79] They witnessed 'gross violation of trade union and human rights', according to Ken Toon: 'A physical, social, political and economic repression was being rigidly enforced.'[80] There still existed a curfew on activities.[81]

---

70 Chile Solidarity Campaign, *Chile Solidarity Campaign: Annual Report*, 1977. It was 'frightening' in the mining area in Bolivia, said McKie, as the military had an overt armed presence. National Union of Mineworkers (UK), *NUM Annual Conference*, 1977, 469, 70.
71 '"Stop Aid" Demand as NUM Men Visit Bolivia and Chile', *Miner*, May–June 1977, 1; Jones, 'When You Look into the Eyes of a Mother', 18.
72 'Former Miner Tells of Pinochet Horror'.
73 They also met representatives of the Federation of Building Workers (FIEMC), textile workers, bakers, pensioners, metallurgical workers and peasants. None of the officials they met in these unions was recognised as official by the junta. National Union of Mineworkers (UK), 'Trade Union and Human Rights in Chile & Bolivia', in *Report of the National Union of Mineworkers Delegation* (England: NUM, 1978); 'Chile, Bolivia: "Their problems should be our problems … their achievements will be our achievements"', *Miner*, June–July 1977.
74 'Chile, Bolivia: "Their problems should be our problems"'.
75 Toon, in *Report of the 109th Annual Trades Union Congress*, 511.
76 'Chile, Bolivia: "Their problems should be our problems"'.
77 National Union of Mineworkers (UK), *NUM Annual Conference*, 1977, 467.
78 Jones, 'When You Look into the Eyes of a Mother', 18.
79 'Former Miner Tells of Pinochet Horror'.
80 *Report of the 109th Annual Trades Union Congress*, 511.
81 *Delegation from the NUM to Chile and Bolivia 21st April – 7th May 1977*[draft?].

Toon reported that the only place where Decree 198, which severely limited trade union activity, could not be enforced was in a place of worship.[82] While there was a ban on protest in the street, the junta dared not ban a Catholic service. So, Cardinal Silva invited Chilean trade unionists to celebrate a mass for the feast of St Joseph, the Worker.[83] The main cathedral in the centre of Santiago was a cavernous construction, and on 1 May 1977, more than 100 unionists gathered at one of its side entrances. The NUM members were invited to participate, despite the obvious dangers of such a meeting.[84] 'We were so moved by the mood of the people that we couldn't just stand by and watch', they said in their report, so they joined the unionists.[85]

After a cue, the unionists moved to walk into the cathedral. Inside were well more than 2000 people, a crowd so large it overflowed into the square outside. When the unionists, with the NUM delegation among them, entered the cathedral, the whole crowd burst into 'loud and continuous' applause.[86] They walked up the centre of the cathedral and sat in rows behind the altar. The priests blocked their view of the congregation, but also blocked the unionists from view. It was reported that they were 'watched by Chilean secret police, the DINA. Outside, the cathedral was surrounded by machine-gun carrying police.'[87]

The homily of Cardinal Silva was a pertinent and rousing speech on the importance of participatory democracy.[88] As the Eucharist ended, the cathedral erupted, reveals the report, into a mass protest meeting. 'The Cathedral resounded with shouts of "Freedom" as everyone joined in loud protest regardless of the armed police who stood at the main entrance.'[89] The delegation members recalled that it was 'an experience we won't easily forget ... We felt that we were truly hearing the voice of the people of Chile, and there could be no doubt as to whom they recognised as their leaders'.[90] Toon later said that May Day in the Chilean cathedral was the highlight of the trip. Yet, it was not without intense anxiety. Ted McKay recalled: 'When we came out onto the steps, there were troops with machine guns and tanks and I felt I could not move. There was a fear I could not describe and, at that moment, I thought we were going to get shot.'[91]

---

82 *Report of the 109th Annual Trades Union Congress*, 511.
83 Chile Solidarity Campaign, *Chile Solidarity Campaign: Annual Report*, 1977.
84 *CSCC 14.05.77 Minutes*, 1977.
85 *Delegation from the NUM to Chile and Bolivia 21st April – 7th May 1977*[draft?].
86 Ibid.
87 Stephen Kelly, 'Chile: NUM Sees Repression and Union Solidarity at First Hand', *Tribune* [UK], 13 May 1977, 16.
88 Cardinal Silva Henriquez, in *Delegation from the NUM to Chile and Bolivia 21st April – 7th May 1977* [draft?].
89 National Union of Mineworkers (UK), 'Trade Union and Human Rights in Chile & Bolivia', 21.
90 *Delegation from the NUM to Chile and Bolivia 21st April – 7th May 1977*[draft?].
91 Jones, 'When You Look into the Eyes of a Mother', 18.

Later, he wrote in a letter: 'That experience in the Cathedral on May Day 1977 will stay with me for the rest of my life.'[92]

The delegation quickly established that the junta regarded the organised labour movement as a major hurdle to the implementation of its economic regime, and that it had thus set about cleansing the movement entirely. The Government did this in a physical manner and also through laws and decrees. The NUM delegation found that workers were banned from holding meetings without a permit issued by the military, and even then, there would be a member of the military or police present. Unions were not even able to draw up rules, collect dues or collectively bargain, let alone strike or undertake more militant activities.[93] The delegation reported that the ruling military had institutionalised the repression to such an extent that mass arrests and executions were no longer necessary.[94]

The members of the NUM delegation educated themselves about Decree 198, which severely limited trade union activity in Chile, monitoring even their elections at factory level. But the delegation found:

> [D]espite the devastating brutality, mass imprisonment and executions perpetrated immediately after the coup, and the subsequent permanent intimidation and 'disappearance' of prominent trade-unionists, some individual unions have been strong enough to survive and some union leaders strong enough to maintain their positions, though not recognised legally.[95]

The delegation reported on the clandestine union activity they found. Small amounts of money had been collected and the occasional illegal bulletin was printed to make its way through the workplaces. Indeed, at some moments, the report of the delegation even sounded hopeful: 'The unions dissolved or not recognised by the military are gradually imposing their presence ... the fact that they were able to receive our delegation and arrange an extensive programme of activities was itself a major achievement.'[96]

The implementation of junta policies had, however, severely altered the landscape of the Chilean labour movement. Some unions had Christian Democrats (the opposition when Allende was in power) placed at the head of their organisations as part of a puppet union structure set up by the junta.

---

92 Ted McKay, Letter to Ann Jones, 1 November 2007, copy in possession of author.
93 Toon, in *Report of the 109th Annual Trades Union Congress*, 511.
94 'Chile, Bolivia: "Their problems should be our problems"'.
95 Ibid.
96 Ibid.

There were 10 of these, unimaginatively called the 'Group of Ten'. By mid 1976, the delegation members believed that even the Group of Ten was being more openly critical of the junta.[97]

The report gave an account of general statistics on inflation, wages, unemployment and other information gained through churches, rather than any in-depth discussion of actual conditions in the pit. The conditions of miners were referred to specifically only on one page of the section on Chile.

The delegation was able to visit two coalmining towns, both of which were within the Región del Bío Bío, the eighth administrative region of Chile.[98] Arauco Province of Bío Bío was an established coalmining area and the British delegates visited the towns of Lebu and Lota.[99] There they witnessed first hand the people's reluctance to talk to foreigners for fear of persecution.[100] The report describes the scene of arrival: 'When we arrived in Lota heavy, torrential rain was falling. The following morning mud from the hills was flowing like rivers through the streets. Barefoot children ploughed through it on their way to school.'[101]

Most of the workers lived in wooden shacks, and had no means or money to build further rooms or purchase more substantial dwellings. The shacks in Lebu consisted of one room for parents and up to 10 children.[102] They received what Hernán Cofre would later call 'wages of misery': enough to barely stay alive.

The delegation described the extremely high rate of inflation and the unequal rise of wages. In their report, they noted that 'as we walked through the streets we were struck by the number of children who went barefoot and the number of men and women selling only 2 or 3 articles of very little value'.[103]

What the delegates spent on a meal, the workers in Chile would not earn in a month.[104] In their report, they indicated that their informants admitted to never

---

97 The report noted that the Chilean Group of Ten was 'faced with the serious deterioration in the economic situation of their membership, they found themselves more and more forced to reflect the demands coming from the grass roots'. The state was quick to discipline miscreants. The Copper Miners' Federation, for example, was a 'tame cat' union, recognised by the junta. Even so, when the Copper Miners' Federation raised its voice against the junta, its whole executive was dismissed. It was not a member of the Group of Ten, and did not have a connection with the FINM (which was completely clandestine and unofficial) with whom the NUM expressed their most steadfast solidarity. The FINM claimed to represent approximately 54 000 members. National Union of Mineworkers (UK), 'Trade Union and Human Rights in Chile & Bolivia', 18, 19.
98 Chile Solidarity Campaign, *Chile Solidarity Campaign: Annual Report*, 1977.
99 President of the Lebu Coalminers' Union, Victor Echevaria, travelled to the United Kingdom in 1978. National Union of Mineworkers (UK), *NUM Annual Conference*, 1978, 564. It was later discovered that British company Gullick Dobson was trading mining equipment with the Chilean junta. The NUM subsequently protested. Ibid., 563.
100 Toon, in *Report of the 109th Annual Trades Union Congress*, 511.
101 National Union of Mineworkers (UK), 'Trade Union and Human Rights in Chile & Bolivia', 20.
102 *Delegation from the NUM to Chile and Bolivia 21st April – 7th May 1977* [draft?].
103 *Delegation from the NUM to Chile and Bolivia 21st April – 7th May 1977*[draft?].
104 'Chile, Bolivia: "Their problems should be our problems"'.

seeing so much poverty. It was noted that 'they can no longer feed their own children'.[105] Women started soup kitchens serving one meal a day to children whose parents were unemployed, detained or disappeared. It was reported that in Santiago 30 000 children were subsisting on this service alone.[106] Even with family and rent allowances, a miner would use all his income buying two sacks of flour and 900 g of sugar.[107]

Further, it was noted that the education system was 'user pays', and most people thus could not afford the correct equipment for primary school let alone university. But, said the NUM delegation report, the miners were proud that they were collectively supporting a workmate at university. In the future, the report described, he would say 'all I have, all I am, I owe to the miners of Lebu'.[108]

While in Lebu the delegates attended the funeral of a miner who had died in an accident two days previously. The number of accidents had risen due to a cut of one-third of the workforce with no reduction of production levels.[109]

'Men, women and children walked behind the coffin which was laid in a wooden cart. The miner's workmates pulled it towards the graveyard.'[110]

The mineworkers collected stories of the oppression on their travels, including the murders and the military trials followed by executions. They learned of the imprisonment immediately after the coup of the Chilean miners' leader, who told them of his torture while strung up by his thumbs.[111]

They spoke to a woman whose miner husband was one of six taken by the police to a prison in the next town one month after the coup. The wives of the miners travelled to the prison but were refused permission to visit. The delegation's report in the NUM newspaper told its readers how all six miners were transferred the next day, with their hands cuffed behind their heads, to a prison in Valparaiso.[112] The wives travelled to the large port city of Valparaiso and spent a day asking after their husbands. They were told eventually that the men were in another, smaller town. The women travelled there and approached the police, who sent them to the military, who, in turn, told them to go to the hospital. Their husbands' names were registered. A doctor told them their husbands had been executed.

---

105   National Union of Mineworkers (UK), 'Trade Union and Human Rights in Chile & Bolivia', 18; *Delegation from the NUM to Chile and Bolivia 21st April – 7th May 1977* [draft?].
106   *Delegation from the NUM to Chile and Bolivia 21st April – 7th May 1977* [draft?].
107   Ibid.
108   National Union of Mineworkers (UK), 'Trade Union and Human Rights in Chile & Bolivia', 20.
109   *Delegation from the NUM to Chile and Bolivia 21st April – 7th May 1977* [draft?].
110   National Union of Mineworkers (UK), 'Trade Union and Human Rights in Chile & Bolivia', 20.
111   Jones, 'When You Look into the Eyes of a Mother', 18.
112   'Chile, Bolivia: "Their problems should be our problems"'.

The women did not believe the story.

They thought their husbands were alive and being tortured, so they asked to see the bodies: 'They were taken to the morgue where the bodies lay riddled with bullets. There was no explanation.'[113]

In a sense, these women were lucky: their husbands had not simply been disappeared, or buried in a mass grave. They at least knew their husbands' fates.

The British unionists concluded: 'For us it has been a great privilege to meet with so many people of courage and determination. Their problems should be our problems, their achievement will be our achievements.'[114]

Additionally, the NUM should be proud of itself, declared the report, because it was the first union anywhere in the world to send a delegation independent of other organisations.[115] Jack Collins, the NUM representative to the CSC, said that in his opinion, the visit 'was probably the most important delegation that has ever gone out from this Union of ours to a foreign country'.[116] Gatehouse was more restrained, but he concurred years later when he said it 'was a brave delegation ... they did it and succeeded and did a good job'.[117]

The men were clearly affected by their time in Chile. Ted McKay more recently remembered: 'I'm now in my mid 70s so time dims the detail but there are some feelings and emotions that will stay with me always one was leaving those brave men and women behind.'[118]

The mineworkers' sprang into action on their return, after first being welcomed back at a NUM Executive meeting on 12 May 1977.[119] By the June NUM Executive meeting, the full report of the delegation was received, and the extensive recommendations were adopted in full. They included publicising the findings of the delegation, press conferences and interviews. Further, it was recommended that the NUM make formal submissions to the TUC, and through that organisation, to the appropriate international organisations.[120] These submissions would deal with the findings of the delegation and also raise the

---

113 Ibid.
114 'Chile, Bolivia: "Their problems should be our problems"'.
115 This fact is unconfirmed. National Union of Mineworkers (UK), 'Trade Union and Human Rights in Chile & Bolivia', 14; Kelly, 'Chile', 541.
116 Collins, in National Union of Mineworkers (UK), *NUM Annual Conference*, 1977, 470.
117 Gatehouse Interview, 2007.
118 Ted McKay, Letter to Ann Jones, c. 21 July 2008, copy in possession of author.
119 National Union of Mineworkers (UK), *Annual Report and Proceedings for the Year 1977* (England: NUM, 1977), 128. The first and immediate effect of the delegation was of course the moral boost to Chilean unionists. 'The trade unionists we talked to were most encouraged by the unique solidarity shown by British trade unions', said the delegates. Kelly, 'Chile', 16.
120 ILO, European Trade Union Council (ETUC), ICFTU and MIF. For a full list of recommendations, see: *Delegation from the NUM to Chile and Bolivia 21st April – 7th May 1977* [draft?].

issue of puppet Chilean representatives at the international trade union level. It was recommended that contact be kept and strengthened with the FINM by inviting representatives to Britain. Money would be sent to the FINM. At length, they passed resolutions on the isolation of the junta and encouraged other unions to follow the example of the NUM in making direct contact with unions in Chile.[121]

The NUM considered the publication of the reports as a part of their commitment to the Chilean people.[122] McKie said the report was compiled from the 'sad material, the horrid material' that the mineworkers had brought back from their journey. At the time, McKie said the editor of the *Miner* and the head of the Miners International Department had written the report, whereas Gatehouse remembered that Ann Browne was the author of much of it.[123] Ted McKay confirmed Gatehouse's recollections about Ann Browne in 2008: 'now, we took all the praise after we got home, but it was Ann Brown [sic] who was the main stay of the delegation. She was also very knowledgeable about everything, although we took credit it was Ann who wrote our report.'[124]

Lawrence Daly sent a letter to Lionel Murray, the general secretary of the TUC, requesting that a copy of the booklet-like report be distributed to all affiliated unions, with instructions to order in bulk through the NUM headquarters.[125] Orders of 10 or more would carry a 50 per cent discount. The NUM sent 700 copies of the report to the 1977 TGWU congress, because, said Daly, 'we want everybody to read it'.[126] They gave 1000 free copies to the CSC.[127] More than 20 000 were distributed at the heavily subsidised price of 20 pence.[128] The Miners International sent copies to all its English-speaking affiliates, and it was hoped that translations would be made for others. The Miners Parliamentary Group (BLP) circulated the report to ministers and the TUC International Committee discussed its findings.[129]

Lawrence Daly considered it to be 'beautifully produced' and 'one of the most excellent reports that has ever been produced by a delegation of the National Union of Mineworkers'.[130] The report was, of course, part of the educational drive of industrial national internationalism. It was an indirect action in an

---

121 National Union of Mineworkers (UK), *Annual Report and Proceedings for the Year 1977*, 168–9.
122 *CSCC 14.05.77 Minutes, 1977*. 'With its delegation, NUM contracted a long-term obligation and commitment which it has fulfilled magnificently.' Chile Solidarity Campaign, *Chile Solidarity Campaign: Annual Report*, 1977.
123 National Union of Mineworkers (UK), *NUM Annual Conference, 1977*, 469.
124 Ted McKay, Letter to Ann Jones, c. 21 July 2008.
125 *Daly (NUM) to Murray (CUT), 18th July 1977*, TUC, MSS.292D/980.31/7, MRC, UW, Coventry.
126 National Union of Mineworkers (UK), *NUM Annual Conference, 1977*.
127 Chile Solidarity Campaign, *Chile Solidarity Campaign: Annual Report*, 1977.
128 Ibid.
129 National Union of Mineworkers (UK), *NUM Annual Conference, 1977*, 467.
130 Ibid.

attempt to influence the political outcome in Britain, Chile and in other countries around the world. Gatehouse concurred with Daly, saying it was a decent and influential report. He continued: 'It wasn't greatly political but you know, it was fine. And in fact, curiously because' the delegation members 'were so right wing within the [NUM] they could sort of carry the whole union with them, although some of the left were very snooty about it'.[131]

Ken Hulme confirmed this view in his interview: 'I have the highest regard for the commitment and work of the left of the trade unions but frankly it was far more effective to see people who were regarded as ordinary non-political trade unionists or right-wingers getting really angry about things. And that … was very effective.'[132]

To further harness the momentum, CSC affiliates were encouraged to invite the NUM delegation members to speak at their meetings or rallies.[133] The delegation members received so many invitations to speak around the country that the NUM Executive agreed that all requests for them to speak should be handled through the head office to relieve the administrative pressure on the individuals and branches.[134] McKay reported to the 1978 national conference that they had told the story of the delegation all over Britain. He said:

> I, for example, have retold my story to meetings of what would be called the extreme left, extreme left students that were so far left they made Stalin look like Enoch Powell. I have also been across the spectrum of the left … when I retold the story from a pulpit in an Anglican church.[135]

Even further afield, Ken Toon travelled to Geneva to give evidence at the UN Commission on Human Rights Ad-Hoc Working Group.[136] McKay went to Algiers to give testimony to the Commission of Enquiry into the Crimes of the Military Junta in Chile.[137] The three men were sent by the NUM to a conference

---

131 Gatehouse Interview, 2007.
132 Hulme Interview, 2007.
133 *CSCC 14.05.77 Minutes*; Gatehouse Interview, 2007.
134 National Union of Mineworkers (UK), *Annual Report and Proceedings for the Year 1977*, 733. See, for example, Ken Toon speaking alongside Martin Flannery at a Joint Labour Movement event in Camden. 'Report from Chile', *Tribune* [UK], 17 June 1977, 11.
135 National Union of Mineworkers (UK), *NUM Annual Conference, 1978*, 560.
136 'Toon to Testify on Chile to UN Group', *Miner*, July–August 1977, 1; National Union of Mineworkers (UK), *Annual Report and Proceedings for the Year 1977*, 706.
137 In January 1978, at the fifth session of the Investigating Committee of the Crimes of the Military Junta of Chile, evidence was given. National Union of Mineworkers (UK), *NUM Annual Conference, 1978*, 307; Chile Solidarity Campaign, *Chile Solidarity Campaign: Annual Report*, 1977; 'Former Miner Tells of Pinochet Horror'.

in November 1978 in Madrid.[138] Ken Toon spoke at the trade union session there, calling on unions to 'imitate NUM and establish relations with their equivalent unions in Chile'.[139]

The participation of these three men in the delegation enabled them to step above their actual place in the solidarity movement. They would otherwise have played a very peripheral role in Chile or international issues; but genuine belief or feeling and even direct experience did not grant them power within the labour movement structures. The TUC's reaction to the NUM delegation, which it had barely encouraged in the beginning, was tepid. In 1977, Ken Toon moved a resolution on Chile and Bolivia at the TUC Congress, as was recommended by the delegation report. He called for an examination of trade, the credentials of the Chilean representatives at the International Labour Office (ILO), the development of stronger links with Chilean unions and lobbying for aid for Bolivian miners.[140] A similar resolution was submitted to the BLP conference.[141]

The correspondence about the delegation that was received by the TUC International Committee was summarised down to three sentences in the minutes.[142] Action on the suspect ILO credentials of Chilean and Bolivian representatives would be 'pursued as opportunity offered'.[143] Inquiries were made and by the 5 December 1977 International Committee meeting, it was reported that the TUC was not 'able to submit a formal complaint to the ILO against the government of an ILO member state other than the UK'.[144] Such a complaint would have to come from the Chilean delegation. The best thing the TUC could come up with as a consolation was the fact that the ICFTU and the ILO were considering the information contained with in the NUM's report for use in new or existing complaints against Chile and Bolivia.[145] The TUC was not willing to push the NUM delegation's results.[146] The NUM's fidelity to the

---

138   Chile Solidarity Campaign, *Chile Solidarity Campaign: Annual Report* (London: Chile Solidarity Campaign, 1978); *World Conference of Solidarity with Chile: Madrid, Nov 9–11, 1978*, CSC, CSC/11/7, LHASC, Manchester.
139   *World Conference of Solidarity with Chile*.
140   Toon, in *Report of the 109th Annual Trades Union Congress*, 1977, 510–11.
141   *Resolution submitted to the 1977 T.U.C. Congress by the National Union of Mineworkers*, CSC, CSC/28/2, LHASC, Manchester. Further, Ken Toon appeared at the CSC fringe meeting held at the Old Ship Hotel, Brighton, that year, beside Norman Buchan (MP) and Carlos Parra (Chilean Radical Party). 'CSC', *Tribune* [UK], 30 September 1977.
142   *Gormley (NUM) to Murray (TUC), 29th July 1977*, TUC, MSS.292D/980.31/7, MRC, UW, Coventry.
143   *TUC International Committee Minutes, June 28, 1977*, TUC [BLP International Department], MSS.292D/901/11, MRC, UW, Coventry.
144   *TUC International Committee Minutes, December 5, 1977*, TUC [BLP International Department], MSS.292D/901/12, MRC, UW, Coventry; *Report of the 111th Annual Trades Union Congress*, 1978.
145   *TUC International Committee Minutes, December 5, 1977*.
146   A further outcome credited to the NUM delegation was opening Chile to other delegations. By breaking ground, it was argued, it made it much easier for delegations to enter and openly tour Chile. Indeed the delegation occurred immediately before a small burst of open opposition to the junta. In 1978 some brave workers celebrated May Day on the streets away from the protection of the Church, witnessed by Enoch Humphries of the STUC. National Union of Mineworkers (UK), *NUM Annual Conference*, 1978, 565.

industrial national model, their refusal to let the social movement run their internationalist activism, their willing output of resources and efforts were not rewarded by the upper hierarchy of the international structures.

The NUM continued its 'exemplary work' in follow-up for many years after the delegation returned, which included maintaining contact with the FINM.[147] There commenced a series of reciprocal delegations. In November 1977, Alamiro Guzman, president of the FINM, visited Britain as a guest of the NUM.[148] Guzman returned to Chile and became the first Chilean unionist elected before the coup to travel abroad and return safely.[149] Guzman was followed by Carlos Pozo, who was the seventy-one-year-old treasurer of the FINM in 1978. He had been imprisoned during the repression of the 1950s in Chile. He was a nitrate miner and his wife died on a hunger strike demanding his release while he was imprisoned.[150] Gatehouse wrote that he was a 'wizened old comrade with an amazing sense of humour'.[151] The NUM put money towards Pozo's medical expenses when he travelled to Hungary for treatment.[152] After this he described himself as 'a new man' and continued on to Britain.[153] He visited Wrexham as a guest of Ted McKay, as they had met when the delegation was in Chile. Pozo confided in McKay that he had a sense of foreboding about returning to Chile. 'He said we might never meet again. He feared the arrests might happen', McKay told the *Evening Leader*.[154] Pozo was right to be frightened: he disappeared when the offices of the FINM were raided on 20 October 1978.[155] McKay travelled to the Chilean Embassy in London to inquire after Pozo. Soon after, McKay went as part of the British delegation to the Conference of Solidarity with the Chilean People in Madrid, where he vowed to bring up Pozo's disappearance.[156]

Around the same time, the FINM announced that Hector Troncoso was to be their representative in Britain. The NUM reported that he was a refugee who had 'lived through the beating that he received at the hands of this regime'.[157] Hernán Cofre flew from Santiago to join Troncoso and visited Nottingham, South Derbyshire and Kent.

---

147 Chile Solidarity Campaign, *Chile Solidarity Campaign: Annual Report*, 1978.
148 National Union of Mineworkers (UK), *NUM Annual Conference*, 1978, 307.
149 Chile Solidarity Campaign, *Chile Solidarity Campaign: Annual Report*, 1977.
150 *Gatehouse to Collins, June 29 1979*, CSC, CSC/28/19, LHASC, Manchester.
151 Ibid.
152 It is unclear exactly what Pozo was being treated for. Chile Solidarity Campaign, *Chile Solidarity Campaign: Annual Report*, 1978.
153 Pozo's journey was paid for by the CSC, NUM and the Hungarian Solidarity Campaign (SZOT). *Gatehouse to SZOT, February 24th 1979*, CSC, CSC/28/19, LHASC, Manchester.
154 'Miners' hero is missing in Chile,' *Evening Leader, November 9, 1978*, CSC, CSC/28/19, LHASC, Manchester.
155 Ibid. There is a handwritten note on the photostat of this article in the archives that says 'Mike not maybe 100% true'.
156 Ibid.
157 National Union of Mineworkers (UK), *NUM Annual Conference*, 1978, 567.

Cofre's suitcase went missing on the journey and he spent his time in Britain wearing the clothes of CSC campaigners and generous miners.[158] He spoke at the NUM conference with Gatehouse translating: 'Thank you, comrades, for listening to me and for the reception you have given me. It is really emotional for me ... Thank you for giving two modest Chilean workers the opportunity to ... join in fraternity with the workers of your country here.'[159]

Figure 3.1 Ted McKay, Ken Toon, Hernán Cofre, Hector Troncoso and Mike Gatehouse at the NUM Annual Conference, 1978.

Source: *'Standing ovation at Torquay for Chilean miners,' Miner, July/August 1978*, CSC, CSC/7/14, LHASC, Manchester.

The NUM produced a pro-solidarity badge and sent thousands of FINM badges to Chile.[160] It was even rumoured that Joe Gormley would visit Chile.[161] In 1978 Hector Troncoso attended the Scottish Mineworkers' Gala. 'As usual', reveals the CSC annual report of the Scottish gala, 'a float was provided for the Chilean refugees to decorate, and a tent set aside for the Scottish Chile Defence Committee to mount an exhibition'.[162]

---

158 National Union of Mineworkers (UK), *NUM Annual Conference*, 1978.
159 Ibid., 567; *'Standing ovation at Torquay for Chilean miners'*.
160 Chile Solidarity Campaign, *Chile Solidarity Campaign: Annual Report*, 1978.
161 *CSC EC 1.8.78 Minutes*. Cofre and Troncoso of the FINM invited him to come, but this time 'via the front door'. *'Standing ovation at Torquay for Chilean miners'*; National Union of Mineworkers (UK), *NUM Annual Conference*, 1978.
162 Chile Solidarity Campaign, *Chile Solidarity Campaign: Annual Report*, 1978. Gatehouse said that 'many people like [McGahey] were extraordinary and did a huge amount for ... the Chile Movement'. McGahey was a 'severe' man and a member of the CPGB Political Committee, and he was a strong supporter of Chile Solidarity, though was hardly ever directly involved with the London office of the CSC. Troncoso's journey was the third time the Scottish Area NUM had invited a Chilean representative to their gala. Luis Corvalan was to attend the NUM gala in 1977, after they had hosted Cornejo in July 1976. They went on to host Rene Plaza in 1979. Milligan, *The New Barons*, 118–19; Gatehouse Interview, 2007.

The generosity of the NUM, and their ongoing relationship with Chile, was aimed at the FINM and its members, and as such, could be classified as bilateral internationalism. The FINM influence in Chile, on politics or working conditions was (during the 1970s) very weak, and thus NUM solidarity with them had little effect on the dictatorship or positive results for the Chilean people. The NUM delegation and their relationship with Chile were restricted by their form of organisation—that is, by the old forms of internationalism based on industrial national conceptions. They expressed their solidarity with their equivalent organisation rather than with the people or with a social movement. Even so, the delegation and the ongoing relationship with the FINM were substantial symbolic actions.[163] The CSC noted the NUM's ability to establish their own contacts with Chile as a 'gesture of defiance to the dictatorships which want them completely isolated'.[164]

Figure 3.2 Hector Troncoso, Mike Gatehouse and Mick McGahey at the head of the Scottish Miners' Gala March.

Source: 'Miners on the March', Miner, July–August, 1978, 11, courtesy of South Wales Area NUM.

Ted McKay was immensely proud and believed the whole union was behind the delegation: 'When the NUM joined, with one voice, to face the common enemy of fascism ... we showed the world what the Union stands for.'[165] Gormley listed the Chile delegation and subsequent interactions with Chilean miners as the high points of NUM internationalism in his time with the union.[166] Daly

---

163 Given the standing ovations, and glowing reports of the NUM in the left press, it would be easy to assume that there was no opposition to the delegation. This was not so. See, for example: 'What Were We Doing in Latin America?', Miner, September–October 1977.
164 Chile Solidarity Campaign, *Chile Solidarity Campaign: Annual Report*, 1977.
165 Ted McKay, 'NCB warned—No help for Junta', Miner, July/August 1978, CSC, CSC/7/14, LHASC, Manchester.
166 Gormley, *Battered Cherub*, 189.

articulated similarly: 'it is another expression of the British Miners Union's belief in international solidarity'.[167] And that expression was confined to and limited by the industrial national framework.

Of course, the NUM was not the only union which believed in internationalist rhetoric. Jack Jones said in 1975: 'As democrats, we cannot rest while the inhuman regime in Chile continues its policy of imprisonment, of maiming, of killing those who it perceives as a threat, and while democracy is denied to the people of Chile.'[168]

Jones travelled to Chile on two occasions, first in 1974 and subsequently in 1975. Jones's moral authority stemmed from his long history of fighting fascism, including in the Spanish Civil War, and his years of solid leadership of the TGWU.[169] The first trip was as part of an International Transport Workers' Federation (ITF) mission that comprised Jones (then vice-president of the ITF) and four other members of the executive board.[170]

The men set out from London on a British Caledonian flight, arriving at Santiago on 25 November 1974.[171] They were escorted off the plane and told they would be taken directly to the office of Air Force General Diaz. As they walked across the tarmac and into the airport, they walked below the area where the public could view arrivals. Someone above shouted 'Jack Jones!', and as he looked up a note floated down.[172] It was the name and address of a British Embassy official. The unionists were put into a limousine with air force officers accompanying them and escorts in front and behind.

The general told the delegates the mission would not be allowed to enter Chile to make investigations because it would interfere with the ILO Committee for Investigation and Conciliation on Matters of Trade Union Freedom which would soon arrive.[173] The dates proposed and the interference by the ITF mission

---

167 Daly, in National Union of Mineworkers (UK), *NUM Annual Conference*, 1977, 467.
168 TUC, 'Notes of Proceedings at a Conference on Chile held at Congress House'.
169 Jones was president of the International Brigade Memorial Trust. Jones, *Jack Jones*.
170 H. Aasarød (president, Norwegian Sailors' Union), J. Post (vice-president, Transport Workers' Union of Holland), D. Seacord (president, Canadian Brotherhood of Railway, Transport and General Workers' Union), H. Lewis (assistant general secretary of the ITF). The men were accompanied by Ms J. Goodin, who served as an interpreter. *To Jack Jones from Diaz Estrada, 26 November 1974*, CSC, CSC/8/6, LHASC, Manchester; *ITF Representatives refused permission to carry out mission in Chile, 1975*, CSC, CSC/8/6, LHASC, Manchester.
171 Jones, *Jack Jones*, 290.
172 Ibid., 290.
173 There was a British member of that ILO delegation whose last name was Kirkaldy. He does not appear to have had any further engagement with Chile and was a relatively right-wing individual within the TUC. *Diaz Estrada to Jack Jones, 26 November 1974*, CSC, CSC/8/6, LHASC, Manchester; *ILO commission sets date for Visit to Chile, 1974*, TUC, MSS.292D/980.31/4, MRC, UW, Coventry; *Duff to Murray (TUC), 21st April 1974*, TUC, MSS.292D/980.31/4, MRC, UW, Coventry; *Free Chile (September 1975)*, Papers of Gustavo Martin Montenegro [hereinafter Papers of GMM], Canberra.

'would constitute an obvious undermining of [the Chilean] national dignity'.[174] The ITF mission was invited to return on or after 20 December, after the ILO mission was successfully disposed of.[175]

Jones only briefly described the meeting in his autobiography, but the reader gets the sense of the tension and mood of the general as he flipped between anger and placatory behaviour.[176] At the end of the meeting, after the general had spent time defending the anti-labour movement actions of the junta, he was handed a list of disappeared transport workers. He did not react kindly. Jones persevered, and mentioned the names of two men he believed had been killed. While the general promised to investigate each of the men personally and report his findings to the ITF, Jones recalled that 'the atmosphere became heated towards the end and his final words were that we must leave on the next plane'.[177]

Jones thought they would be taken back to the airport, but the interpreter explained that the next plane would be in two days. They were accompanied to a hotel.[178] Jones contacted the British Embassy official who had thrown down his details at the airport and they went into the centre of Santiago to meet the Interdenominational Peace Committee. Jones was moved by the people he met there;[179] but it seems that this small foray onto the streets of Santiago was enough for the Chilean Government to find a plane on which to deport the unionists in less than two days. So, barely 24 hours into a five-day visit, the ITF delegation was sent on its way. 'It was frustrating, but not entirely pointless', Jones was reported as saying.[180]

At the BLP conference just days after his return to Britain, he emphasised the need for the labour movement to unite behind the Chilean people; 'Jack received an ovation'.[181] The TGWU General Executive Council fully supported Jones's part in the mission and gave him permission to return if another mission was organised.[182] Jones spoke of his short time in Chile on various platforms, including the TUC-organised conference on Chile in April 1975. Pulling at the

---

174 *Diaz Estrada to Jack Jones, 26 November 1974.*
175 The general's ministrations were useless in this sense. The delegation left Chile and went directly to Lima (Peru), where they met the chairman of the ILO mission and told him what had occurred in Chile. Ibid.
176 Jones, Jack Jones, 291.
177 Ibid., 391. Lists appear in the archives (though it is unclear if this is a copy of the list Jones gave the general or a different one he obtained from the Peace Committee, or if these were one and the same). *The attached refers to 205 Chilean trade unionists who were arrested, 1975*, CSC, CSC/8/6, LHASC, Manchester; *Jones (TGWU) to Murray (TUC), 15 January 1975*, TUC, MSS.292D/980.31/3, MRC, UW, Coventry.
178 The final member of the delegation was Gleason from Canada. Gleason was, according to Jones, a close friend of George Meany, whose absence showed the lack of real support of the American Federation of Labor (AFL) and Congress of Industrial Organizations (CIO) for the Chile cause.
179 Jones, *Jack Jones*, 292.
180 'Chile Bars Jack Jones', *Observer*, 1 December 1975.
181 *Record, January 1975, p3: 'Chilean workers are not alone'*,TGWU, MSS.126/T&G/193/1/55, MRC, UW, Coventry.
182 *Minutes and Record of the General Executive Council, June 3, 1975*, TGWU, MSS.126/T&G/1186/A/53, MRC, UW, Coventry.

conscience and provoking the outrage of his audience, Jones listed unionists executed in the first days of the coup. He said: 'they will not regain their freedom, but there are hundreds here on this list who with our help and the help of the world trade union movement can yet regain their freedom.'[183]

Jones's second visit to Chile, in 1975, was as part of an ICFTU delegation, and lasted only nine hours. At the conference in Mexico City, Jones insisted that an ICFTU delegation visit Chile and demonstrate their solidarity with the oppressed labour movement. Though the congress voted for Jones to lead the delegation, he was adamant that Otto Kersten, general secretary of the ICFTU, lead the party. The delegates left from Mexico City to travel to Chile. After getting off the plane, Jones guided the delegation straight to the Peace Committee to renew his acquaintances there. This time, he was successfully able to meet with Cardinal Silva. Jones remembered in his autobiography: 'It was a serious yet happy occasion, and I was proud to pin the badge of the International on his robe.'[184] Jones continued:

> We were under close observation during the whole of our day in Santiago but that did not stop us passing and receiving messages to or from brave people who were operating illicitly and who were encouraged by our visit ... It was at the airport, when we were going to catch our return flight, that the secret police showed their hand.[185]

As they passed through customs, the delegation members were surrounded by armed guards. They were manhandled into a room on the side of the customs area. They separated off Jones and let the rest of the men go. It was still not clear what was going on and Jones's colleagues started to create a ruckus outside the room. A Canadian diplomat who came to farewell the delegation started to make representations on his behalf.

The guards shuffled through Jones's papers and then confiscated them. Jones was absolutely indignant, and as he was led out to the open area to rejoin his delegation, he shouted: 'This is what the Fascists do to a visitor from a friendly country. They are thieves. They have taken my property!'[186] The police were no doubt happy to get rid of the delegation and Jones's papers were returned three months later through the Foreign Office. Jones was reported as saying that the ICFTU delegation had 'helped to identify the international trade union movement with the fight of Chilean workers and with the humanitarian efforts being made by the peace committee to help the wives and families of detainees'.[187]

---

183 TUC, 'Notes of Proceedings at a Conference on Chile held at Congress House'.
184 Jones, *Jack Jones*, 293.
185 Ibid.
186 Ibid., 239.
187 *'Fight Chilean Fascism'*, Record, November 1975, 6, TGWU, MSS.126/T&G/193/1/55, MRC, UW, Coventry.

As Jones reported to the Finance and General Purposes Committee of the TGWU upon his return: 'During the Mission's visit he had been personally subjected to the Junta's fascist activities, including having personal papers (since returned), taken from him.'[188]

Despite Jones's irritation at the abuse of his freedom, it does seem an exaggerated assumption to liken his experience to the oppression suffered by the Chilean left. Although his trips to Chile may have been bold international gestures, the lack of time and profound contact with the Chilean movement renders them as just that: gestures.

These gestures, however, seemingly simple and bureaucratically loose, had consequences that extended beyond Jones as an individual. One outcome of Jones's travels to Chile stems from the confiscation of his papers. The abuse of his freedom was used as a reason by the ITF to call on all its affiliates to boost the harassment of Chilean transport from 1 January 1976.[189] This gave fuel and support to boycott actions all over the world, including that which occurred in Australia (see Chapter Eight).[190] Jones's personal experiences ensured that the TUC was unable to ignore the Chile issue.

While the mineworkers were motivated by feelings against fascism and injustice, as well as feelings of working-class and trade union solidarity, Jack Jones sought to express his solidarity with the 'Chilean people'.[191] The NUM delegation was daring in some ways but exhibited limited flexibility to act outside structural and ideological restrictions. 'It is', said Jack Collins, 'our *working class duty* to make sure that the nightmare that is now taking place in Chile and Bolivia, the nightmare that these people are living through, is ended forthwith in order that we can also share in the victory of that nightmare being brought to an end' (emphasis added).[192]

The NUM's practical solidarity was, however, directed at an organisation rather than at miners or a class. They did not target solidarity with the workers or the 'Chilean people' in general, but with a select group of mostly incapacitated unionists. As Waterman suggests, solidarity committees often identify with

---

188 *Minutes of the Statutory Meeting of the Finance and General Purposes Committee of the General Executive Council, November 5, 1975*, TGWU, MSS.126/T&G/1186/A/53, MRC, UW, Coventry. Jones always seemed to report verbally to his executive committee on Chilean matters. See, for example, *The General Secretary's Twenty-First Quarterly Report, 1974*, TGWU, MSS.126/TG/385/A/2, MRC, UW, Coventry.
189 'Harassment planned for Chile Junta', *Record*, January 1976, 6, TGWU, MSS.126/T&G/193/1/56, MRC, UW, Coventry.
190 WWFA, *Memo Re; ITF – Chile and ITF Circular, December 18 1975*, Waterside Workers' Federation of Australia [hereinafter WWFA]: Federal Office, N114/932, Noel Butlin Archive Centre, The Australian National University [hereinafter NBAC: ANU], Canberra; *International Transport Workers' Federation Circular no. 11/S.6/D.1, 76/1/29, 1976*, WWFA: Federal Office, N114/942 ITF Circulars 1975 vol. 3, NBAC: ANU, Canberra.
191 'Standing ovation at Torquay for Chilean miners'.
192 Collins, in National Union of Mineworkers (UK), *NUM Annual Conference*, 1977, 470–1.

3. 'Unique solidarity'? The mineworkers' delegation, 1977

particular leadership claiming to be representative of workers rather than the real workers of the recipient country, and in this case, so did the union.[193] The problem with this was the fact that the national-level FINM organisation was at that point largely redundant. They were persecuted, restricted and impoverished. Despite the international aid received, they remained so for some time.

The limitations of the NUM delegation were also in evidence when the TUC, its own trade union peak body, did not enthusiastically support it. The lacklustre adoption of the recommended courses of action is the case in point, and there was an uninspiring carriage through to international-level industrial national organisations. Their lack of a strategic individual in the TUC and faithfulness to the hierarchy of industrial national unionism hampered the overall influence of the delegation.

The CSC, a committee with little of the institutionalised power of the TUC, but with links to the most powerful labour movement groups in the country, ensured that the small NUM delegation enjoyed flexibility and fame beyond the borders of their own union. Travelling to give evidence on the international stage, interviewed about their experiences for years after, the three NUM members selected by Gormley achieved prominence above and beyond their union positions. As Gatehouse wrote: 'we regard the work of NUM and of yourselves in particular as being an example to the whole of the rest of the trade union movement.'[194]

In contrast, the relatively minor forays of Jack Jones to Chile had ramifications that outweighed their planning and implementation purely because of Jones's stature. His union and political positions were what allowed him to act in this manner. Logue has noted: 'In general, we can expect that the incidence of "parasitic elite activity" will be inversely related to the degree of democracy prevailing in the organisation.'[195] Jones, who was elected for life, could partake in his international delegations with impunity: he was in a position that did not require him to account for his actions. His interest in Chile was not only backed by the name of the TUC and the ability to circumvent its oppressive committee structures and hostile employees, but also drew with it the ITF and the ICFTU. Amidst the abstract models of trade union international activity, historians and political scientists have often overlooked the role of the individual.

The NUM delegation, perhaps guided by their union's own rule book, judged that the FINM would be the appropriate gateway through which their compassion and financial aid might be channelled. They pursued this vigorously and attempted to keep it distinct from any action of the CSC. In a different strategy,

---

193 Waterman, Globalization, Social Movements and the New Internationalisms, 135.
194 *Gatehouse (CSC) to McKie (NUM), February 4th 1979*, CSC, CSC/11/10, LHASC, Manchester.
195 Logue, *Toward a Theory of Trade Union Internationalism*, 29.

Jones spent little time in Chile, but went straight to the heart of a Chilean-run organisation. The Peace Committee, of course, benefited from solidarity and funds, but it was not a direct result of them. In judging where aid and publicity would be most useful in resistance to the regime, Jack Jones chose the reality of a social movement organisation. The NUM members and their union chose to prop up a relic of the industrial national structure.

The real winner, in terms of organisational gain, was the CSC, which benefited with little effort from newsworthy events and capable speakers. The CSC did not begrudge the separation that the NUM felt necessary from the CSC. In fact, as the Glasgow Free Chile Committee had previously done with the East Kilbride boycott (Chapter Four), the CSC encouraged the activities of the unionists, who could be presented as nonpartisan and morally upright to a politically sensitive audience. Though Gormley had attempted to swing control away from the left in his choice of delegates, he actually helped the broad front of the CSC more than a left-wing delegation could have hoped.

It was very soon after his final trip to Chile that Jack Jones retired. At the function that the union held in honour of the occasion, Chilean band Mayapi provided the entertainment. Jones wrote to the CSC to thank them. Gatehouse replied that it was a 'unique opportunity' for the band, as they could play and pay tribute to the international work of Jones. It was a 'very small way of saying thankyou for the tremendous contribution you have made to the struggle of the people of Chile'. Gatehouse continued that he hoped that during his retirement, Jones could return to Chile but under very different circumstances, and where there will be no DINA, but a 'crowd of welcoming trade unionists to meet you at the airport'.[196]

---

[196] *Gatehouse to Jones, March 4 1976*, CSC, CSC/1/16, LHASC, Manchester.

4. Pinochet's jets and Rolls Royce East Kilbride

Figure 4.1 Arms sales were a consistent issue throughout the 1970s and 1980s.

Source: *CSC, 'No arms sales to Chile,'* Box 2 Posters and exhibition graphics, People's History Museum, LHASC, Manchester.

The helmet looked too big for his head. It sat awkwardly askew, falling backwards, and the man beneath looked up and out through thick-rimmed glasses. One hand grasped a machine gun, but his jacket still held its pocket square and remained buttoned up over his patterned jumper. He looked like a grandfatherly academic pulled away from his desk to defend the country. It was 11 September 1973 and these were the last hours of President Salvador Allende's life. Planes roared over the Chilean capital. The whine of their engines reverberated off the old buildings and cobbled streets in the centre of the city.

The military coup was in full swing.

Jets strafed the palace, coming within metres of the edifice. They fired their rockets with accuracy. One pilot is said to have aimed for the windows, later boasting that he could land a rocket in a tin of condensed milk. With each hit an explosion of dust appeared, so thick it looked solid as it hung in the air. Deafening blasts filled the atmosphere as the bulky stone of the palace was blown apart and windows shattered, reducing sections of its fine facade to rubble. Flame, smoke and dust flowed in the wind away from the palace. And still the jets came.

These were Hawker Hunter jets, the main offensive aeroplane of the Chilean military.

Some time later, the ground forces had pushed their way into the palace shielded by tanks and President Allende lay dead in his office.

On the other side of the world 3000 men worked in a Rolls Royce factory in East Kilbride, just outside Glasgow. For a couple of days after the coup the factory routines went on as normal. The working week wore on, and on the third morning at 7.45 in the factory canteen, the scheduled shop stewards' meeting opened. Peter Lowe was acting convenor and began proceedings with usual union business. Wage claims and finances were discussed and nothing was amiss or unusual.[1] Towards the end, Bob Somerville raised his hand. He moved a resolution against the military takeover of the Chilean Government.[2] Somerville was a Communist Party of Great Britain (CPGB) member and he later admitted that it was 'a political move on my part'.[3] While there was nothing unusual or even unpredictable about that, what was unexpected was that an Amalgamated

---

1 The previous convenor, McCulloch, was undergoing a major operation. Lowe would soon be elected to the role.
2 *Minute of the Shop Stewards' Meeting held in the main canteen on Friday 14th September 1973*, Rolls Royce East Kilbride Shop Stewards Papers, Rolls Royce Factory, East Kilbride [hereinafter RREKSS]. *Fighting bloody hand of Chile's fascists by Jim Tait, 1974*, RREKSS.
3 Interview with Bob Somerville (Chile activist, UK), 27 July 2007 [hereinafter Somerville Interview, 2007], notes in possession of author.

Union of Engineering Workers (AUEW) delegate with openly right leanings named John Burn seconded the resolution. Bob Somerville remembered that this left–right alliance 'jelled the workforce'.[4]

The boycott had started.

It was a small resolution at the time—a gesture of revulsion against fascism— but it became, to borrow Bob Somerville's words, 'one of the greatest episodes in the history of Scottish socialism'.[5]

The gesture grew legs and a heart and became an action that moved under the influence of many masters. It would be wrong to think of it as isolated in the factory, or even within Scotland, without external influence. There were three main arenas that affected the boycott and each had their own tensions and politics: the factory at East Kilbride, the national-level leadership of unions and the parliamentary Labour Party. Each interacted to shape the skirmish between Chile and the workers at Rolls Royce East Kilbride. This chapter will draw together the threads from each arena in an attempt to understand the anatomy of such a boycott, and the effect of the different puppetmasters. The shipbuilding yards on the Firth of Clyde were under the same pressures, but there ideology and action intersected with a very different outcome.

The British unions with the most strategic industrial locations in terms of trade with Chile were the AUEW (due to their involvement in arms and shipbuilding),[6] the Transport and General Workers' Union (TGWU: docks and road transport) and the National Union of Seamen (NUS). The East Kilbride action involved the first two of those unions. What follows from here is a detailed reconstruction of the inter and intra-union politics of the AUEW and TGWU. It's a laborious task, but one necessary to truly understand how a boycott for remote political gain unfolds.

The Rolls Royce aero-engine factory in East Kilbride was divided into four large sheds, labelled Blocks A–D. The factory primarily engaged in 'servicing', which is the repair and reconstruction of older engines, and Rolls Royce (1971) Limited held long-term service contracts with civil airlines and military forces around the globe.[7] In the early 1970s maintenance on an aero-engine involved stripping and cleaning, with each component placed into an engine tray. Inspectors would use a pile of cards to check each piece no matter how small for its serial numbers and the quality of the work.[8] It was tactile labour. Bob Somerville remembered

---
4 GCUA, 'Chile and Scotland: 30 Years On', Paper presented at the Witness Seminar and Open Forum Series (No. 3), Saltire Centre, Glasgow Caledonian University, Saturday, 29 November 2003.
5 Neil MacKay, 'The Scot Who Humbled Pinochet Tells His Story', *Sunday Herald*, 2002, RR East Kilbride Witness Seminar and Open Forum, GCUA, Glasgow.
6 *The Chile Monitor no. 6, 1974*.
7 Rolls Royce Heritage Trust did not respond to any letters I sent about this project. Rolls Royce (1971) Limited is hereinafter referred to as Rolls Royce.
8 Somerville Interview, 2007.

'you had a hand on every bit of that engine, booking it in'.[9] The Avon 207 engine, which powered jets such as the Hawker Hunter, was a very successful industrial engine for Rolls Royce;[10] however, the engine could not be 'taken down' in sections. It had to be totally 'stripped', which meant a significant amount of skilled work.[11]

Somerville was an aero-engine inspector in the subassembly section in B Block. He applied for a job at Rolls Royce because his wife's cousin had alerted him to the company's need for tradesmen.[12] He was an active community man and a CPGB member, and had joined the AUEW when he was fifteen. He ended up serving for 50 years.[13] When the Chilean coup occurred he was a senior steward and the Rolls Royce factory was particularly well organised.[14] In fact, the whole factory was unionised. Somerville recalled: 'You didn't-a get started at Rolls Royce unless you joined a union ... So it was always a hundred percent [on] the shop floor.'[15]

There were about 3000 workers in the factory in 1973. These workers were divided into sections within the blocks and each section elected shop stewards. The Rolls Royce East Kilbride (RREK) Shop Stewards' Committee comprised about 100 men.[16] Sitting above the shop stewards was a Rolls Royce East Kilbride Works Committee (RREKWC, or the Works Committee) of seven members.[17] Each member of the RREKWC was elected annually from factory level, with a high level of re-election.

The AUEW held at least four positions on the Works Committee, in line with its predominance within the factory. The rest of the RREKWC consisted of one or more TGWU members and at least one allied trades (welders, sheetmetal workers, and so on) member.[18] Scholars Coates and Topham have noted: 'At plant

---

9 'Book in' refers to the process of writing down the 'make' (identification such as serial number) of every component of the engine. To 'work' an engine refers to the process of working on an engine. Ibid.
10 Commonly called the 'Hawker Hunter boycott' because the Avon engines were for Hawker Hunter fighters.
11 The ability to take an engine apart ('take down') in sections was a design function to make it easier and more cost effective to repair or replace parts. 'Totally stripped' means the engine was completely disassembled, cleaned, repaired and put back together. Somerville Interview, 2007.
12 Ibid. Somerville did his apprenticeship making mining equipment at Anderson Mavors—another militant workplace. Anderson Mavors was also involved in a (separate) Chile boycott.
13 In 2001 he received an MBE for his 16 years on the Motherwell College Board, 25 years on the Community Council, 25 years of youth work in judo and at the football club and 50 years as a trade union member and activist. Somerville to MacKay (Home Affairs Editor, *Sunday Herald*), 27.5.02, Robert Somerville, Rolls Royce East Kilbride Witness Seminar and Open Forum, GCUA, Glasgow.
14 Somerville Interview, 2007.
15 Ibid.
16 Ibid.
17 Ibid. In 1973 the RREKWC comprised Peter Lowe (convenor, AUEW), Dugald 'Dougie' Gilles (sub-convenor, AUEW), John Keenan and Robert 'Bob/Bobby' Somerville (both senior shop stewards and AUEW), Wally McKluskie (AUEW), Gavin Gordon (Allied Trades) and Jimmy Douglas (TGWU), who was soon after replaced with Danny Doorman.
18 Ibid.

level, multi-union steward organization is frequently of a more developed and hierarchical character than in the single-plant union; union heterogeneity seems to encourage stronger steward organization, which in turn makes inter-union co-operation more manageable.'[19]

The Rolls Royce East Kilbride organisation supports this assertion. The stewards were highly organised, and highly effective.[20] The ordered and consistently managed structure of the unions in the factory ensured that news of action could be relayed among the 3000 workers quickly and effectively. Every action was reported from shop steward to section to committee where it was endorsed or rejected.

When interviewed in 2007, Somerville was coy about the political affiliations within the Works Committee. He did say that of the seven-man works committee, two were members of the BLP (John Keenan was one of them). As a CPGB member, Somerville was politically close to Gavin Gordon, who was of the left. Somerville remembered that the workforce was particularly militant, and estimated that 80 per cent of shop stewards were members of political parties, not always of the left, but predominantly so. Within the factory, there was an industrial branch of the CPGB and wide distribution of its newspaper, the Morning Star.[21]

Outside the factory in the same period, the town of East Kilbride was home to particularly well-organised community and worker groups. East Kilbride's strong Labour/left organisation was a microcosm of the Scottish movement. The Scottish sections of national unions were generally regarded as radical and extremely well organised, as well as strong-headed and rebellious. All of this pointed towards action.

Shortly after the original resolution, Bob Somerville came in to the factory to start a shift, when he was called into the convenor's office. According to Somerville, the convenor informed him that one of the stewards in his section had refused to work an engine for Chile. That steward was Bob Foulton. Somerville was surprised, because Bob was a church elder and not known to be a political man. As it turns out, he had refused to work the engine as a Christian on humanitarian grounds.[22] With this first action, the RREKWC realised there

---

19 Coates and Topham, *Trade Unions in Britain*, 162.
20 Furthermore, the RREK example supports Peetz and Pocock, who note that if confidence, training, support and proper delegation of authority occur within a workplace, there will be greater union power. David Peetz and Barbara Pocock, 'An Analysis of Workplace Representatives, Union Power and Democracy in Australia', *British Journal of Industrial Relations* 47 (2009), 26.
21 'I've got to pay special thanks to Jimmy Milne, who stood solidly behind us. The *Morning Star*, who I was continuously … I was the sort of liaison between anything that happened in the factory, the *Morning Star*, Jim Tate, Andrew Clark whoever was available "this is happening"—Bang. It's flashed to the rest of the country. Tremendous support, tremendous support.' Somerville, GCUA, 'Chile and Scotland: 30 Years On'.
22 Somerville Interview, 2007.

were Chilean engines in the factory. Somerville went to investigate and then reported details of the stoppage back to the convenor. The RREKWC accepted the action as legitimate in light of the previous resolution and officially blacked the engines. Out of courtesy, the committee contacted management, and also the AUEW National Executive Committee, asking them to endorse the action in line with the policy and previous resolutions of the union.[23] Peter Lowe, RREK convenor, also sent a telegram to Tony Benn, Trade and Industry Minister, stating: 'Inform you we are refusing to work on Avon 207 engines used in the Hawker Hunter fighter/bomber in for overhaul for the Chilean Air Force.'[24]

The reaction of management to the boycott was remarkably calm. The good relationship that existed between the shop stewards and the company had much to do with this. The management persistently asked the stewards to get their labourers to work the engines. They did so politely, though with veiled threats. Catherine Curruthers of Rolls Royce wrote to the workers:

> I must emphasise to you the serious position that would prevail if the Company is sued for non-performance of these legal obligations, and the further adverse effect which the attendant publicity would have on our order book and the future level of employment and prosperity among your members.[25]

Although management tried to persuade the unionists to work on the engines,[26] in hindsight, Somerville felt that it was very awkward for them: 'some of them we knew accepted that what we were doing was the right thing.'[27] The workers did not lose hours or receive penalties for their stance.

When the boycott at RREK began Somerville 'took a wee step back' from its public leadership in the factory. He was on the Scottish committee of the CPGB at the time and it was important to the success of the boycott, and the Chile movement, that the action was not seen as a communist plot.[28] The Glasgow Chile Defence Committee also kept a distance, respecting the public relations value of an 'un-tampered' worker-led boycott.[29] A Works Committee, rank-and-file-led boycott held firm moral high ground.

Convenor Lowe was not politically minded, according to Somerville, but this worked in favour of the boycott. Having a nonpartisan public leader meant

---

23 *Lowe to 'sir and bro', 25th March 1974*, RREKSS.
24 *Telegram from Lowe to the Hon. A. Benn, M.P., 22/3/74*, RREKSS.
25 *Situation Report, 12 noon: Tuesday 2nd July 1974: Chilean Engines*, RREKSS.
26 It was thought the maintenance contract would be taken up by Rolls Royce Motors, a wholly owned subsidiary in Brazil. 'Rolls-Royce Nears Deal on "Blacked" Chile Jets', *Telegraph*, 1 September 1974.
27 Somerville Interview, 2007.
28 Ibid.
29 The Glasgow Chile Defence Committee (GCDC) recognised that 'the working class character of the campaign has put it in the forefront of the international solidarity movement from the start'. Chile Defence Committee, 'Resolution to Glasgow Chile Defence Committee A.G.M' (Glasgow: 1974).

it could not be easily attacked as a biased plot. Lowe was invited to speak at various conferences and rallies.[30] Even after the boycott was lifted, he was invited to speak at the trade union conference on Chile, 'Bread, Work and Freedom', in March 1979, because the Rolls Royce action was regarded by the Chile Solidarity Campaign in London as 'an outstanding example to the whole trade union movement'.[31] He did so much travel for 'Chile business' that the shop stewards put money towards a new briefcase for him.

That briefcase was to be the centre of an event that underlined the seriousness of the boycott for the Scottish unionists. Somerville recalled that Lowe travelled south 'to do a TV programme and [when he] went to his hotel he put his briefcase down as all Scotsmen do, and went for a wee bevvy just to settle his nerves'.

When he returned, the briefcase was gone. He reported it to the police, but they just said he must have misplaced it. Later, when he arrived home, he heard a noise outside his house. Somerville continued:

> [A]nd he went out, and here was these bundles of paper that had been pushed through the door. It was his papers that had been in the briefcase. So Peter being Peter [he] quickly ran to the window which looked up the main road, and there, lo and behold, was a policeman running out and into a car and driving off.[32]

Despite Lowe's non-political background, his leadership of the East Kilbride boycott had brought him to the attention of some authorities. It also brought him prominence within the progressive labour movement. One episode could colour a whole career, overshadowing years of leadership on industrial issues.[33] On Lowe's retirement from Rolls Royce, the Rolls Royce Hillington Shop Stewards' Committee wrote:

> [Y]our Committee at East Kilbride with Peter at the helm will be remembered in working class history for your persistent refusal to release the Avon engines intended to power the very Hawker Hunter Aircraft which were used by the Fascist Junta in Chile to straff [sic] the Presidential Palace and people of that country who were defending democracy.[34]

---

30 For example: *Dobbie (CSC Tyneside) to RRSSEK* [Rolls Royce Shop Stewards East Kilbride], *5th September 1978*, RREKSS. *Lowe's Speech: I would like to take this opportunity and thank the Chile Solidarity Committee, 1978*, RREKSS; *Keenan invited to Bristol for trade union conference: Comite Chileno to Keenan (RRSSEK), 1978*, RREKSS; *General request for speaker Manchester CSC Committee, 22nd. July 1974*, RREKSS.
31 *Gatehouse (CSC) to Lowe (Shop-Stewards Rolls Royce East Kilbride), February 4th 1979*, CSC, CSC/11/10, LHASC, Manchester.
32 GCUA, 'Chile and Scotland'.
33 This is also true in part of John Keenan. His concern for workers' safety and other industrial issues took most of his union organising time rather than internationalism. John Keenan, Interview with Ann Jones, 8 September 2008, copy in possession of author.
34 *McCormack (Rolls Royce Ltd, Hillington Shop Stewards Committee) to Rolls Royce East Kilbride Shop Stewards Committee 1st June 1983*, RREKSS.

Without meaning to, Lowe and the RREK workers became known for what was initially a gut reaction to the coup, a mere resolution passed at a breakfast meeting.[35]

Despite its eventual prominence, at first, the boycott continued for some months without official AUEW support. The majority of RREK workers were members of the AUEW, and in order to understand the representative quality of the boycott, it is necessary to discuss that union's democratic practice. The AUEW's structure at the time was complex, overlapping and exceedingly confusing, but also very important to understand so that individual actions and reactions can be appreciated in their correct context. The AUEW was one of the two largest unions in Britain: in 1975 it had 1 204 934 members, of which 133 425 were in Scotland.[36] In 1976 the membership was broken into four sections: Engineering (the largest section by far); Construction Engineering; Foundry Workers; and Technical, Administrative and Supervisory Section (TASS).[37] Its structure was complicated and its constitution based on that of the United States, with an elected parliament, an executive and a judiciary. The AUEW's founding members had constructed the voting system to ensure that the rank and file had control of union business but, as John Higgins argued, 'this admirable desire also gives rise to a very large rule book and the feeling that procedures are such as to prevent anyone from doing anything'.[38]

The title of the union was also misleading, since there was never a full amalgamation.[39] Various mergers had strengthened the union's numbers, but also led to its hopelessly fractured structure. Each section enforced its own rules and had its own constituent body (the national committees). Representatives of the sections came together to form the National Executive.[40] The president and general secretary of the Engineering Section were always the president and general secretary of the AUEW as a whole, reflecting the domination of the union structure by the engineers. The 52 representatives of the Engineering Section National Committee met once a year with the foundry representatives (seven), TASS (seven) and Construction Section (three representatives). Together, this

---

35 Somerville's other community involvement and activist career were also over shadowed by his involvement in the Chile boycott.
36 The Engineering Section had 214 members in Gibraltar, USA, Canada and New Zealand in 1975. *AUEW: Structure and Function of the Union.*
37 The sections' memberships were: Engineering (1.2 million members); Construction Engineering (30 000); Foundry Workers (50 000); and Technical, Administrative and Supervisory Section (TASS) (130 000). The AUEW Engineering Section is explained in more detail than the other sections here because it is that section which is most highly represented in the action at East Kilbride. It is also the biggest and most influential. Jim Higgins, 'Amalgamating the Engineers', *Spectator*, 1976; Milligan, *The New Barons*.
38 Higgins, 'Amalgamating the Engineers'.
39 Due to an apparent loss of votes that the Engineering Section would suffer.
40 The National Council of seven men governed or administered the Engineering Section in line with the policies of the National Committee. If the national councilmen did not agree with the decisions of the National Committee they could take it to the appeal court, which also consisted of rank-and-file members. In this manner, the union was constructed to ensure that its lay members were theoretically in control of the union.

body was the AUEW National Conference.[41] The National Conference decided on matters of joint policy affecting the union as a whole and was very obviously dominated by the Engineering Section. The AUEW structure was cumbersome, but democratic in that almost all of its posts were elected, not appointed.[42]

Yet still further detail of the structure of the union is needed in order to understand the correct organisational context of the interaction between national-level leadership and rank-and-file activists at East Kilbride. There were 2740 branches. These branches met every two weeks. They were grouped into 234 districts, which were grouped into 26 organising divisions, which, in turn, were grouped into seven executive council divisions.[43] The structure, however, had blurry boundaries. For example: 'Parts of one organising division may be in more than one E.C. Division but no district is split in this way. Thus, two Districts and their branches may vote for the same Divisional Organiser, but, in [s]ome cases, for two different Executive Councilmen.'[44]

One of the consequences of this complex, confusing structure was to give local committees more power. Higgins wrote that 'the divisions and districts of the AUEW operate very much its independent fiefdoms', and the president, Hugh Scanlon, tried to run the union like 'an oversized shop stewards committee'.[45] Indeed, Scanlon said that a divisional organiser was 'king' in his own area and held more power there than the regional officer.[46]

The Executive Council[47] (distinct from the National Conference or national committees) of the AUEW first discussed the coup in September 1973. There

---

41 Each divisional committee elected two delegates for a total of 52 representatives on the National Committee of the Engineering Section. The National Committee met once a year and was the primary policymaking body of the Engineering Section. The president of the union chaired this meeting, and the general secretary and National Council members were present but were not able to vote. *AUEW: Structure and Function of the Union*.
42 The 186 full-time officials (president, National Executive Committee members, general secretary and various levels of organisers) and part-time branch officials were all elected. With the incorporation of TASS into the structure, a postal ballot was introduced. The postal vote system was expensive and the varied election times across the organisation made elections messy. The change in voting practice led to the right wing making a steady comeback against the left wing at a national level. In 1975 John Boyd (right wing) was to take the general secretary position from Bob Wright (left wing). Jim Higgins, 'Trade Unions: Democracy at the Top', *Spectator*, 1975; Milligan, *The New Barons*, 127–8; see also p. 23; *AUEW: Structure and Function of the Union*; Jim Higgins, 'AUEW: Decline of a Union', *Spectator*, 1975.
43 *AUEW: Structure and Function of the Union*.
44 Ibid.
45 Higgins, 'AUEW'.
46 Edelstein and Warner, *Comparative Union Democracy*, 310.
47 The AUEW National Executive Committee was constructed of the Engineering Section National Council, with two representatives of each of the foundry and TASS and one or two representing the Construction Section. The AUEW National Executive Committee was thus made up of 12 or 13 persons, plus the president and general secretary, who, as mentioned previously, were always from the Engineering Section.

was no resolution, but it was decided that the Ambassador of Chile should be contacted and the British Government urged not to recognise the junta.[48] This halfway approach reflected the attitude of the president, Hugh Scanlon.

Scanlon was a democrat,[49] yet his support for Chile action appeared to wax and wane. In his capacity as a member of the executive of the Trades Union Congress (TUC), Scanlon put his name to various publications and was listed as an individual sponsor of the CSC, but he never committed completely to the cause.[50] Nevertheless Scanlon's international credentials were significant: he was nominated by the European Metal Workers' Federation to go to Chile to secure the release of prisoners.[51] Furthermore, in 1977 Scanlon agreed to raise the abuses of trade union rights in Chile at an International Metal Workers Federation conference in Munich.[52] But his approach was scattergun. Scanlon did not seem to have anything personally against the CSC, or solidarity with Chile in general, but his, and subsequently the AUEW's, interest in Chile did not match that of Jack Jones of the TGWU.[53]

By 1974 Scanlon and Jones were not as close personally or politically as many perceived. In relation to another issue, Scanlon scathingly said at the 1974 TUC Brighton Conference that 'I do not care if Jack Jones is Jesus Christ, and he thinks he is, but he will not change the AUEW's decisions'.[54] By that time, however, Scanlon appeared tired, and at the TUC congress, Ken Gill (communist leader of the AUEW TASS) seemed to be doing the talking for the AUEW.[55] The decline of Scanlon in the eyes of the public continued with the right-wing swing in the AUEW elections of 1975.[56] This fact is important to remember in the context of the boycott, along with the confusing structure with its various interstices and the personal politics of the leaders.

---

48 The AUEW also put their name on many publications for the CSC and lent official support to marches. *Gatehouse to Local Committees, May 15 1974*, CSC, CSC/44/1, LHASC, Manchester; *AUEW Journal October 1973: Abstract Report of Council Proceedings*, Amalgamated Engineering Union, MSS.259/AEU/4/6/53, MRC, UW, Coventry.
49 Higgins, 'AUEW'.
50 *To Callaghan (Secretary of State), October 9, 1974*, STUC, STUCA 531/4, GCUA, Glasgow; *Press Release from the TGWU, October 9, 1974*, STUC, STUCA 531/4, GCUA, Glasgow; *CSC (pamphlet), 1974*, CSC, CSC/7/2, LHASC, Manchester.
51 He was president of this organisation. He was also vice-president of the International Metal Workers' Federation (1969–78). *Minutes. Meeting of Executive Council, held in General Office, on the 26th February, 1974 at 10.00 am*, Amalgamated Engineering Union, MSS.259/AEU/1/1/214, MRC, UW, Coventry; Terry Pattinson, 'Lord Scanlon: Charismatic Trade-Union Leader', *Independent*, 28 January 2004.
52 *Meneses and Navarro to Scanlon, October 6 1977*, CSC, CSC/28/12, LHASC, Manchester. He did, however, leave the congress before any resolution on it was passed. *Scanlon to Gatehouse, 2nd November, 1977*, CSC, CSC/28/12, LHASC, Manchester.
53 Moody has argued that passivity is a product of bureaucracy, and perhaps this was so in the case of Scanlon. Moody, 'Towards an International Social-Movement Unionism', 6.
54 This was the same conference at which the RREKWC representatives were summoned to break the boycott. Higgins, 'AUEW'.
55 Ibid. TASS always strongly supported the RREK boycott.
56 Scanlon was succeeded by Terrence Duffy as president of the AUEW in 1978 and in 1979 was elevated to the House of Lords, becoming Baron Scanlon of Davyhulme. He had sworn previously to never accept a peerage and this caused embarrassment and some ill feeling towards him. Pattinson, 'Lord Scanlon'.

Born in 1913 in Australia, Scanlon immigrated to Britain with his widowed mother at the age of two. He joined the CPGB in 1937, and separately worked his way up from the shop floor to become president of the AUEW (1968–78).[57] A small, wiry, charismatic man, he was known for his scruples and quick-witted humour.[58] Pattinson wrote in Scanlon's obituary that his militancy influenced both Labour and Tory government relations with unions. His ascendance in that field was, in part, due to the nature of the industries in which his workers were employed.[59] His union was involved in almost all facets of the arms industry in Britain.

On 27 April 1974, the Engineering Section of the union passed a motion to stop delivery of warships and submarines and to pressure MPs.[60] It did not mention other arms or spares. On 1 May 1974, the AUEW TASS released a statement that called for the immediate cancellation of all military equipment orders for Chile.[61] TASS was more direct with demands and rhetoric because its members were not likely to be involved in trade with Chile, and therefore had little chance to black. At East Kilbride the AUEW (mostly the Engineering Section) workers continued to boycott the engines without National Executive Committee approval.

After the RREK boycott had begun on 12 May, the AUEW Executive (where Scanlon still held a casting vote, making a left majority) sanctioned the terms of the boycott. They sent circulars to their 2700 branches instructing members to not work any 'ships, vehicles, aircraft, or any other weapons which could be used against our brothers and sisters in Chile'.[62] The original resolution of the AUEW Engineering Section had focused on ships and submarines, but it was challenged by the East Kilbride action. The AUEW Executive had been forced to extend the resolution to include aircraft. The rank-and-file action and the ideological support from the TASS had forced the hand of the AUEW National Executive and the new circular gave strength to the East Kilbride blacking.[63]

---

57 He was a CPGB member until 1955. Ibid.; '"The Walrus", Hugh Scanlon: From Awkward to Ermine', *Socialist Worker Online*, accessed 7 February 2004, <http://www.socialistworker.co.uk/art.php?id=622>.
58 Pattinson, 'Lord Scanlon'.
59 Ibid.
60 Rolls Royce had already written to the AUEW (W. Aitkin, divisional organiser) asking for clarification on the union's position by 25 March 1974. *McCollum (Rolls Royce ltd) to Aitkin (AUEW ES Paisley), 25th March, 1974*, RREKSS. During 1974 Scanlon openly supported the boycott on Chile armaments, specifically frigates and submarines. 'Chile: Scanlon Acts', *Tribune* [UK], 10 May 1974.
61 Gill, leader of TASS, was a member of the CPGB. TASS had a CPGB-dominated leadership. *The Chile Monitor no. 6, 1974*. The AUEW TASS Executive Committee sent a letter expressing their support and admiration of the East Kilbride Shop Stewards. *Gill (AUEW) to Lowe, 21st May, 1974*, RREKSS.
62 Scanlon later said that the black ban of jet engines and warships may widen to involve components. Raymond Perman, 'Ban on Work for Chile may be Widened', *The Times*, 15 May 1974; *The Chile Monitor no. 6, 1974*.
63 *A trade unionist's guide to the Chile issue: Does your firm trade in Torture?c1974*, CSC, CSC/16/2, LHASC, Manchester. It was sent to 2700 branches and more than 200 district committees. Perman, 'Ban on Work for Chile may be Widened'.

The Glasgow Chile Defence Committee succinctly summarised events up to this point: 'ROLLS ROYCE workers' action inspired the national AUEW to call on its members to black all arms going to Chile. The AUEW action, in turn, sparked off a debate within the Labour Party on the need for greater solidarity with the struggle in Chile.'[64]

The AUEW blacking at Rolls Royce caused, according to the CSC, the British Government to cancel the Rolls Royce service contract with the Chilean Air Force.[65] The contract was worth £70 000 a year to Rolls Royce—a very small portion of their overall business. The Glasgow Herald reported that the engines were invaluable because they were among the first Avons ever made. Of course, they were also invaluable to the Chilean Armed Forces for a different reason, and provided political ammunition for all sides of British politics.[66]

Britain held 18 per cent of the South American arms market, and the Ministry of Defence and the Treasury both considered arms sales economically essential. Given an estimated 170 000 people were employed in the arms industry, fears of mass unemployment were easily conjured to allay planned boycotts. Private manufacturers of arms benefited from taxpayer-funded research, so from their point of view movement towards banning arms trade with any country set a dangerous precedent. The ministries and private companies unsurprisingly pressured the prime minister to maintain trade with Chile.[67]

The politics of selling arms to Chile was haunting the newly elected Labour Government. The BLP conference had passed a resolution immediately after the coup calling on the Government to withhold all aid loans and credit;[68] however, as Barbara Castle noted in her diaries, 'relations between the Government and the National Executive' of the BLP 'remained sensitive. Trouble was likely to flare up at any time. It did so over the question of Chile.'[69]

On 28 March 1974, the Defence and Overseas Policy Committee of the Parliamentary Labour Party (PLP) decided that no new arms contracts with Chile would be entered into. Existing naval and arms contracts posed a problem though, and the Labour Government was embarrassed by its previous strong moral stand in opposition.[70] There were outstanding contracts worth £50 million

---

64 Chile Defence Committee…, *Glasgow Chile Bulletin Number One* (Glasgow: 1974).
65 Chile Solidarity Campaign, *Chile and the British Labour Movement*, 8, 9.
66 *Move to End Chile ban*, Glasgow Herald, 19/8/76, CSC, CSC/15/1, LHASC, Manchester.
67 Wilkinson, 'The Influence of the Solidarity Lobby on British Government Policy towards Latin America'.
68 'Conference Decisions: Chile', *Tribune* [UK], 12 October 1973.
69 Castle, *The Castle Diaries*, 63.
70 On 23 November 1973, the PLP had called on the Conservative Government to prevent arms sales and Judith Hart made the mistake of stating that *none* of the ships should go there and that the trade unions were taking 'effective steps' in the matter. Ibid., 64.

for two Leander Class frigates, two Oberon submarines (at Yarrows and Scott's respectively, both situated on the Clyde) and the refitting of a destroyer, as well as smaller projects such as the Rolls Royce engines.[71]

Cabinet decided that the difficulties of cancellation of the contracts were too great and would be deemed illegal.[72] They argued that Chile might cut off its copper supply to Britain (compromising 30 per cent of the nation's imported copper) if the contracts were not fulfilled, and that future military contracts would be lost.[73] As Castle confided to her diary, however, this was a vexed moral and political question: 'Even more important than our sales to Latin America (which Mason had said would be at risk) was to stick to the view that we took in opposition. That was paramount. Otherwise we lost credibility.'[74]

On the first day of April 1974, the chancellor, Jim Callaghan, told the House that contracts would be fulfilled. The Tribune scathingly made fun of his 'honour' and his decision to 'honour' the contracts.[75] Resolutions from constituency branches of the party flooded in, calling for the decision to be reconsidered.[76] A week later Cabinet was still in moral turmoil in determining the appropriate attitude to take towards Chile.[77] In a single meeting it was decided on one hand to invite Madame Allende to visit Britain in solidarity with the plight of Chileans, but on the other Callaghan stood firm on the fulfilment of armament contracts and sending warships to Chile.[78]

The decision by the Government was taken as an affront by trade unionists.[79]

It was easy for the left to construe the Rolls Royce workers as heroes: the men gamely standing up to the Chilean and British Governments. There was some truth in this. As one commentator put it, 'it was only the determination of [Rolls Royce]

---

71 Ibid., 57; 'Chile will get Warships', *The Times*, 9 April 1974.
72 The BLP, through a letter from Ted Rowlands to the CSC in November 1975, justified its shipment of arms to Chile, stating that it was illegal to back out of a contract and citing protection of Britain's trading reputation. It assured the CSC again that no new contracts would be entered into.
73 Castle, *The Castle Diaries*, 76–7. General Arturo Yovanne proposed to the junta that the copper be suspended. Florencia Varas, 'Chile Threat to Stop Copper Sales to Britain', *The Times*, 30 March 1974.
74 Castle, *The Castle Diaries*, 77.
75 'Frigates for Chilean Junta: Why the Government Must Think Again', *Tribune* [UK], 19 April 1974.
76 *Resolutions Received from Constituency Labour Parties and Trade Unions, 1974*, TUC [BLP International Department], MSS.292D/936.1/2, MRC, UW, Coventry.
77 This was increased when junior minister Eric Heffer violated the code of collective responsibility and spoke out against the decision. *Heffer wins for the Left, 1974*, Labour Party—Eric Heffer Papers, LP/ESH/10/30, LHASC, Manchester; *Heffer to Wilson, 12th April, 1974*, Labour Party—Eric Heffer Papers, LP/ESH/10/32, LHASC, Manchester; *Wilson set for a Showdown over Speech, Times*, 15 April 1974, Labour Party—Eric Heffer Papers, LP/ESH/10/30, LHASC, Manchester; *Extract from a speech made by Eric S Heffer MP, Minister of State for Industry, at the Pirrie Labour Club, Walton, Liverpool, on Saturday, April 13, 1974, at 8.30PM*, Labour Party—Eric Heffer Papers, LP/ESH/10/32, LHASC, Manchester; *Heffer guns for Harold, Daily Express, 19 April 1974*, Labour Party—Eric Heffer Papers, LP/ESH/10/30, LHASC, Manchester; John Groser, 'Mr Heffer to Face Wilson Rebuke over Chile', *The Times*, 15 April 1974; Michael Hatfield, 'Callaghan Rebuke over Warships', *The Times*, 2 May 1974.
78 Michael Hatfield, 'No Policy Reversal on Ships for Chile', *The Times*, 25 April 1974.
79 Just after this the AUEW national resolution was extended to include spares.

workers which kept the grounded Hawker Hunter engines in Britain'.[80] The conception of the East Kilbride workers as morally superior to the parliamentarians added to the loss of credibility in the BLP, which grew steadily into a maelstrom over the next six weeks. On 19 April, Ron Hayward, general secretary of the BLP, criticised the decision to fulfil the contracts at the Scottish Trades Union Congress (STUC).[81] Despite an attempt by Callaghan to calm the Chile storm at the party's National Executive, the radical left thought he was 'pussyfooting'.[82]

One commentator observed that 'the Government and the party have decided to go their separate ways'.[83] The Cabinet and the Government seemed to separate too: more than 100 BLP MPs had signed the motion against delivery of vessels.[84] The Times noted: 'Some ministers say frankly that differences within the Administration, the Parliamentary Labour Party, and the trade union movement over supplying Chile with arms are creating the most serious difficulties since Mr Wilson formed his Government.'[85]

By 2 May, the tension within the PLP was taut, Wilson was receiving pressure in Parliament from the Tory leader, Edward Heath, and embattled Chancellor Callaghan lashed out at various MPs in the left-wing Tribune Group, accusing them of muttering and smirking at him while he spoke.[86] On 6 May thousands of 'banner waving demonstrators' walked from Hyde Park to Downing Street demanding the cancellation of contracts. Stan Newens MP spoke against the Government's decision at the rally.[87] Three days later, Tony Benn, Secretary of State for Industry, along with Judith Hart, Ian Mikardo, Michael Foot and Joan Lestor, added their voices to the dissent surrounding the Government's decision at an International Committee meeting.[88]

---

80   Chile Defence Committee, *Glasgow Chile Bulletin Number One*.
81   The feeling at the BLP, which ran out of offices in Transport House (owned by TGWU), was not friendly towards the PLP. Hayward said that the BLP 'would do well to remember whence it came and where a great deal of its support lay: namely, in the trade union movement'. Alan Hamilton, 'Mr Hayward Rebukes Cabinet on Chile Ships', *The Times*, 19 April 1974.
82   Chile Defence Committee, *Glasgow Chile Bulletin Number One*. In reply, on 24 April 1974, Callaghan asked for leave of the seat of chairman at the BLP National Executive Committee to address the meeting. He was 'very mild' about Chile, but Castle believed he calmed the trade union contingent and the left on the National Executive Committee. Castle, *The Castle Diaries*, 87.
83   This was particularly bad news for the CSC, whose influence on the PLP was much weaker than within the BLP. 'Ministers Accused of Retreat on Chile', *The Times*, 23 May 1974.
84   Kinnock and Flannery gathered 160 signatures on their early day motion against the export licences. It came to light immediately after the announcement that the engine repairs had still not been paid. *CSC Annual Report, 1978*. Stated as 140 signatures in: *Affiliates' Newsletter no. 29, July 23rd 1978*, CSC, CSC/1/21, LHASC, Manchester.
85   'Blocking of Arms for Chile Beset by Legal Difficulties', *The Times*, 17 May 1974. See also: Castle, *The Castle Diaries*, 86.
86   Heath and Wilson exchanged words in Parliament in May 1974 over the East Kilbride issue. 'Heath Accused Wilson of a "further capitulation to his left wing", and Wilson retaliated by saying that Heath had a "lickspittle attitude" to the Pinochet regime.' MacKay, 'The Scot Who Humbled Pinochet Tells His Story'; Hatfield, 'Callaghan Rebuke over Warships'.
87   Staff Reporter, 'Marchers Protest over Arms Sale to Chile', *The Times*, 6 May 1974.
88   Our Political Staff, 'Mr Benn Joins Attack on Sale of Warships', *The Times*, 9 May 1974.

Despite all of the turmoil, dissent and temper tantrums that further undermined the unity of the party, Wilson and Callaghan stuck to the decision: the contracts would be fulfilled, but no new contracts entered into. By enforcing the execution of the contracts, the Government had opened itself up to attack internally and externally. The CSC's campaign on violence in Chile and the importance of cutting arms and aid had created such a climate of moral authority that the BLP's wellbeing was endangered. Work on the frigates and submarines would take several years to complete. In one sense, every minute of those years represented a failure of the labour movement and a 'betrayal of the Chilean people', as well as of the BLP.[89] Despite this, Barbara Castle was confident of government support on the Hawker Hunter boycott as distinct from the frigates and submarines, because the RREK was a grassroots action.[90]

Figure 4.2 Michael Foot, Joan Lestor and Tony Benn chase down Callaghan with the Chile football.

Source: Nicholas Garland, *Daily Telegraph*, 17 May 1974, © Telegraph Media Group Limited 1974, The British Cartoon Archive, University of Kent, <www.cartoons.ac.uk>.

It was not to be so. The Government asked the AUEW leaders to work the engines (despite it being directly contrary to the TUC and BLP conference resolutions) because the engines were the property of the Chilean Government. Having them in the factory apparently delayed the cancellation of the maintenance contract,

---

89 Bill Spiers, 'Frigates Deal a "Betrayal" of Chilean People', *Tribune* [UK], 19 April 1974.
90 Castle, *The Castle Diaries*, 86.

and the Government wanted to rid itself of further political embarrassment.[91] With this sort of attitude from the Government, Rolls Royce was then able to put pressure on the AUEW to lift the ban.[92] Scanlon received various well-argued letters from Sir William Nield, deputy chairman of Rolls Royce, doing just this. Nield also forwarded the letters to John Boyd for his attention.

Boyd was a right-wing member of the AUEW Executive and pivotal at some stages of the boycott.[93] He was a prominent teetotaller, a 'tuba playing' Salvation Army member, who, at that point, was the AUEW National Executive Committee member for Scotland.[94] Boyd's involvement at this critical juncture of the East Kilbride Chile boycott policy was indicative of both a swing towards the right wing of the union (it was immediately before a right-wing swing in the 1975 AUEW elections when Scanlon was looking ill) and apathy on this issue within the hierarchy. Boyd undoubtedly had a large impact on the events that followed.[95] Boyd himself was not openly against Chile solidarity, but perhaps was against direct industrial action for external political causes such as that taken at Rolls Royce East Kilbride.

At a meeting in early September 1974, the AUEW Executive decided to consider ways to settle the 'dispute' only months after agreeing to support the boycott (after the Government had asked the AUEW to work the engines).[96] Here the structure and rules of the unions played a crucial role. 'The executive may run into some trouble', commented the Telegraph's industrial correspondent, 'for East Kilbride workers had operated the ban unofficially for two months before getting official backing'.[97] The backlash from members and solidarity interests came quickly.

---

91 Angela Singer, 'RAF Denies any Involvement in Removal of Chile Aero-Engines', *Guardian* [Manchester], 29 August 1978, 24.
92 *Situation Report, 12 noon: Tuesday 2nd July 1974*. The threat by Rolls Royce to the union was that reductions in orders would lead to layoffs. MacKay, 'The Scot Who Humbled Pinochet Tells His Story'.
93 He would go on to become the general secretary in the late 1970s. Marsh, *Trade Union Handbook*, 168. Nield sent the same letter to Jones of the TGWU, but did not provoke a jump to action. Nield had said that 'the Company's goodwill with its customers, and so its capacity to maintain employment, are bound to be damaged'. *Nield (Rolls Royce Ltd) to Scanlon (AUEW), 5th August, 1975*, RREKSS.
94 Boyd had been selected as the right-wing successor to Bill Carron, who retired as president of the AUEW in 1968; but Boyd was defeated at election by the left-wing Scanlon. The total poll included only 130 030 of 1 129 000 members. Scanlon won with 68 022 to Boyd's 62 008. Scanlon's re-election in 1970 was by an even larger margin. Thus there were deep ideological and personal differences between the two. In lieu of president, Boyd turned to the position of general secretary, ousting the pillar of the broad left caucus, Bob Wright, who was touted as Scanlon's successor. Milligan, *The New Barons*, 123; Edelstein and Warner, *Comparative Union Democracy*, 311; Jim Higgins, 'AUEW Election', *Spectator*, 1975; Shipley, *Revolutionaries in Modern Britain*, 55.
95 *Nield (Rolls Royce Ltd) to Scanlon (AUEW), 22nd August, 1974*, RREKSS; *Minutes. Meeting of Executive Council, held in General Office, on the 31st August, 1974 at 12.45 p.m.*, Amalgamated Engineering Union, MSS.259/AEU/1/1/216, MRC, UW, Coventry.
96 As early as September 1974, Scanlon wrote that the AUEW Executive Council could see no reason why the members should not work to facilitate the service of civilian aircraft for Chile: *Scanlon to Milligan, 10th September, 1974*, RREKSS.
97 'Rolls-Royce Nears Deal on "Blacked" Chile Jets'.

The AUEW Executive Committee met on 1 October 1974 to discuss the correspondence from branches which were concerned about the expected decision to withdraw support for the boycott.[98] Significantly, all the branches were in support of continuing the boycott. Further, in the interim, Chilean trade unionists in exile Luis Figueroa, Humberto Elgueta and Anibal Palma had met with the AUEW Executive, which had expressed its sympathy with the Chilean cause. But their feelings of sympathy or solidarity did not override the politics at play within, and perhaps the economic imperatives of, the executive. Trying to fathom interactions in the spartan and opaque executive minutes is difficult, but it is obvious that John Boyd stamped his authority on the situation, splitting the committee to his favour with a four–two majority. The engines were to be worked. The International Marxist Group (IMG) reacted with its usual vigour: 'the labour movement, and its' leaders, allowed John Boyd and his placemen in the AUEW to isolate and cut down the Rolls Royce, East Kilbride, black on aircraft engines, the most important blacking action in Europe, without raising a hand to defend it.'[99]

Boyd was the only protagonist in this situation whose influence and personal contact spanned all levels of the movement, from national to local. He secured the decision to work on the engines by summoning RREK convenors Lowe and Gillies, accompanied by Milligan (Mid Lanark district secretary), to Brighton on 3 September 1974.[100] The RREK shop stewards were chastised in retrospect for informing the press of the boycott before the AUEW National Executive had the chance to communicate with the District Committee and shop stewards. It was reiterated that the resolution at the 1974 National Committee was much narrower, and the interpretation had to be broadened in concession to the East Kilbride action. Boyd told the convenors how the decision to expand the resolution was unacceptable to other sections within the union executive as well as members such as those working on submarines and warships (whose boycott actions we will come to shortly).[101] Boyd highlighted the executive's own ministrations with the Government, which led to the prime minister's statement in Parliament on 21 May 1974, as if this ought to be enough of an effort for Chile solidarity.[102] Boyd further emphasised the goodwill of the Rolls Royce company.

---

98 The AUEW National Executive Committee's solidarity did not, however, extend to boycotts, and few, if any, of the requests in the letter were taken seriously. *Gatehouse to Les Dixon (AUEW), October 19 1975*, CSC, CSC/4/2, LHASC, Manchester.
99 IMG—Scotland produced this pamphlet. *Chile Solidarity—Build and Defend the Blackings, 1974*, STUC, Tony Southall Collection, GCUA, Glasgow.
100 Probably while at the TUC congress in Blackpool. Ironically, Madame Allende attended that very Brighton conference; see Figure 2.3. *Fighting bloody hand of Chile's fascists by Jim Tait*, RREKSS; Chile Defence Committee, *Glasgow Chile Bulletin Number One*.
101 *Scanlon (AUEW) to Milligan (AUEW District Sec Mid Lanark), 4th September, 1974*, RREKSS.
102 This statement included the recommendation to Rolls Royce that it give three months' notice to the Chilean Government of termination of contract. Rolls Royce received written confirmation of this from Tony Benn. *Statement to East Kilbride Works Committee: Chilean Air Force Engines, 1974*, RREKSS; *Fighting bloody hand of Chile's fascists by Jim Tait*; For Rolls Royce action on the termination see: *D McLean, 2 July 1974*, RREKSS.

With that, the AUEW Executive ordered its East Kilbride members to complete the overhauls, 'under the arrangements and conditions as contained in the letter received from Sir W. Nield'—the very one forwarded to Boyd.[103]

The Glasgow Free Chile Committee said in its newsletter that the 'Rolls Royce shop stewards were not impressed'.[104] Lowe and Gillies refused to lift the ban, stating that if the AUEW wanted to rescind on their instruction to black the engines, they would have to issue another instruction to the whole union.[105] When the unionists returned to the factory, a letter directly instructing them to work the engines was waiting.[106] As Somerville recalls: 'The message from the executive of the [AUEW was] "Work on them" ... It was a directive. If we'd said "no", they [could just take] our shop stewards credentials off us.'[107]

The disparate attitudes to Chile solidarity between the upper hierarchy of the union, or at least one man who spanned the echelons of the union (Boyd), and the rank and file reflect the endemic disconnection between the various levels of such a large union. Somerville continued:

> The work force: oh! We had a battle with the workforce. [But] we said OK, we'll do them, but they'll never get out of the factory ... Although a lot of people just refused point blank ... And the lad who initiated [it] just refused point blank ever to work on an engine [from Chile].[108]

Somerville said the AUEW directive 'was a terrible letdown',[109] and even more so because of its timing. It was the week of the first anniversary of the coup, when workers from the Rolls Royce factories at East Kilbride and Hillington travelled to London for the huge demonstration. Solidarity was otherwise at a peak.

The engines were put together with bolts untightened and placed into crates (without corrosion protection) then moved into the expansive yard that surrounded RREK.[110] Workmen painted 'Chile' in white on the side of the crates so that drivers could make no mistake, and the overseer of the yard kept watch.[111] Dougal Gillies also kept an eye on them, as he could see the crates from

---

103 *Scanlon (AUEW) to Milligan (AUEW District Sec Mid Lanark), 4th September, 1974*; *Fighting bloody hand of Chile's fascists by Jim Tait*.
104 Chile Defence Committee, *Glasgow Chile Bulletin Number One*.
105 Somerville said to him: 'But you're a Salvation Army man, you're a Christian, why are you telling us to do something!?' Somerville Interview, 2007; *Fighting bloody hand of Chile's fascists by Jim Tait*. Keenan tells a similar tale. Keenan Interview, 2008.
106 Though Scanlon signed this letter, I believe it was probably written by Boyd, who was given Nield's letter to 'deal with'.
107 Somerville Interview, 2007.
108 Ibid.
109 Somerville, in MacKay, 'The Scot Who Humbled Pinochet Tells His Story'.
110 Somerville Interview, 2007.
111 Ibid.; *Move to End Chile ban, Glasgow Herald, 19/8/76*, CSC, CSC/15/1, LHASC, Manchester.

his house across a field.¹¹² The 'bitter disappointment and disgust' experienced by the workforce at East Kilbride were felt across the country and many wrote to the shop stewards about this.¹¹³ A supporter wrote: 'if General Pinochet does get his engines back I hope they are so rusty as to be useless.'¹¹⁴

The AUEW leadership was happy to wipe its hands of the affair, stating that it was now a problem that concerned the TGWU and Rolls Royce.¹¹⁵ In its correspondence with affiliates and local committees, the CSC did not mention the pressure applied by the AUEW on the rank and file at East Kilbride. They dared not interfere with union politics directly, and could not afford to lose the support of the AUEW at the national level.¹¹⁶ The CSC had courted the AUEW at all its levels: nationally for the political stability and money, and at the grassroots level, where direct action could take place. Despite these efforts, the CSC could do nothing to control the internal policy and politicking of regime and procedure change such as that which occurred in the AUEW in 1975. The CSC never had high-level personal support in the AUEW as it did in the TGWU (with Kitson and Jones among others). Moreover, the CSC could not rely on broad left/right voting groups in the AUEW Executive Committee. Such partisan splits did not necessarily always function along the obvious dividing lines. As Higgins said, 'like most other spheres of endeavour, our union hierarchs are often motivated by personal rivalry and antipathy as much as ideological differences'.¹¹⁷ Even if Scanlon had wished to continue the boycott, his power was limited and was, it seemed, diminishing.

Paradoxically, despite previously pressuring the AUEW to work the engines, the Government withdrew the export licences in 1975 using further atrocities in Chile as a justification.¹¹⁸ The inconsistencies within the PLP/BLP decisions were symptomatic of a split leadership between its sections and the sheer bulk of its organisation. Immediately after the engine export licences were withdrawn, four of the engines were secretly moved and taken to a warehouse in Paisley.¹¹⁹ It took three weeks for activists to find them despite their proximity to East Kilbride. The agents of the Chilean junta were Kuehne & Nagle of Hayes, Middlesex.¹²⁰ The TGWU sprang into action, as reported by Alex Kitson in 1975:

---

112   GCUA, 'Chile and Scotland'.
113   *Chile Fights*29 (London: CSC [Chile Lucha], 1978); *Howden (AUEW Glasgow) to RRSSEK, 5-2-75*, RREKSS.
114   *Francis to RRSSEK, 6th August 1978*, RREKSS.
115   *Milligan (AUEW ES District Secretary) to Lowe, 13th August, 1975*, RREKSS.
116   See, for example, the unspecific language: 'Eventually such pressure was exerted that the men were forced to carry out the repair work for which the engines had been sent.' *Affiliates' Newsletter no. 29, July 23rd 1978*, CSC, CSC/1/21, LHASC, Manchester. Furthermore, the CPGB, which had representatives in most organising positions of the CSC, was very wary of using industrial tactics. Shipley, *Revolutionaries in Modern Britain*, 55.
117   Higgins, 'AUEW Election'.
118   *Fighting bloody hand of Chile's fascists by Jim Tait*.
119   Ibid. Beckett says they were taken to a 'less squeamish plant in Paisley'. Andy Beckett, *Pinochet in Piccadilly: Britain and Chile's Hidden History* (London: Faber & Faber, 2002), 151–2.
120   *Lowe to McIntyre (Rosyth Dockyard Workers), 29.3.76*, RREKSS; *Nield (Rolls Royce Ltd) to Scanlon (AUEW), 5th August, 1975*.

We have told the haulier who had them that if he attempts to move them from that warehouse then we will take the necessary action against him in other spheres to ensure that it interferes with his business, and these engines will lie there until they rot and they will not be worth anything by the time they are released.[121]

Despite the threat, the 'four engines got away, and eventually reached Chile'.[122] Four remained in the RREK factory.

The crates sat in the yard at RREK, exposed to the inclement Scottish weather, while in London, Conservative MP Edward Taylor, whose seat was in Glasgow, called on the Government to stop its 'conspiracy of silence' on the Rolls Royce matter. In a sarcastic tone, he endeavoured to embarrass the Foreign Secretary, Tony Crosland, into convincing Jack Jones to lift the ban. He said, 'as Mr Jones is always so anxious to tell the Government how to run the country the Government ought now to ask him if anything can be done'.[123] Before this comment, in long and rousing speeches at the TUC-organised conference for Chile in 1975, Jones had committed himself and the TUC to Chile solidarity. He said, 'if we all stand together we shall win in this great cause'.[124] It was clear Jack Jones thought something could be done, even if it was not what Taylor had in mind.

All the while, the engines sat in their crates in the yard next to the workers who ran past during their informal lunchtime soccer matches. In 1977 management asked the workers to take the engines back into the factory to work them after the indicators showed severe corrosion.[125] The workers refused. They were mostly AUEW members.[126] For the most part, however, the maintenance of the boycott now rested in the hands of the TGWU workers, and their union had taken an entirely different tack with Chile solidarity.

The TGWU was the biggest union in the United Kingdom, with more than two million members in the mid 1970s.[127] The TGWU was similar to the AUEW in that its founding principle was to allow lay members to decide policy and elect those

---

121 TUC, 'Notes of Proceedings at a Conference on Chile held at Congress House', 17.
122 *Scottish Chile Defence Committee: Rolls Royce Engines for the Chilean Air-Force, 1978*, RREKSS.
123 *Statement to East Kilbride Works Committee: Chilean Air Force Engines; Move to End Chile Ban*.
124 Jack Jones, in TUC, 'Notes of Proceedings at a Conference on Chile held at Congress House'.
125 *Rolls Royce Engines Snatched for Chilean Junta*, Oxford Chile Joint Committee, MSS.21/1279, MRC, UW, Coventry.
126 MacKay, 'The Scot Who Humbled Pinochet Tells His Story'; *Fighting bloody hand of Chile's fascists by Jim Tait*; Singer, 'RAF Denies any Involvement in Removal of Chile Aero-Engines', 24.
127 The TGWU was divided into 11 sections: General Workers; Docks and Waterways; Commercial Services; Passenger Services; Public Services and Civil Air Transport; Vehicle Building and Automotive; Power and Engineering; Chemical, Rubber and Oil Refining; Food, Drink and Tobacco; Building, Construction and Civil Engineering; Administration, Clerical, Technical and Supervisory.

who implemented it.[128] The character of the TGWU was dual: representatives on its general executive council were elected partially on a geographic basis and partially according to industry group affiliation.[129] Branches were the base unit of the union and below them shop stewards in each workplace dealt with the everyday wellbeing of members.[130]

The 35-member TGWU General Executive Council (TGWU GEC) was the highest governing body of the union. It reflected the two organisational groups of the union in that geographical representatives were elected by ballot of the membership of the regions, and there was one representative from each national trade group committee.[131]

The TGWU GEC members were all part-time voluntary officeholders who appointed the paid national and local officers.[132] The appointment, rather than election, of these senior officials meant the TGWU could be conceived as being less democratic than the AUEW. What is more, the general secretary was elected by ballot of all members of the union. Once elected, however, the general secretary held the office for life. The autocratic nature of the union was thus played out. Stephen Milligan has emphasised that this tendency was exacerbated by low member participation and high turnover of members.[133] The general secretary was an extremely powerful position, further enhanced by the personal connections of Jack Jones to the BLP (see Chapter One), but this did not necessarily translate to control over the rank and file.

In some sectors (notably the docks and waterways) the general secretary and the Executive Council had very limited influence because of the strong grassroots leadership.[134] The sheer size and oligarchic tendencies within the branch

---

128 The Biennial Delegate Conference decided on policy. Delegates were nominated from branches and voted on by regional trade groups. This is a democratic process but very low attendance at branch meetings meant that elections (and branches in general) were generally controlled by an inner circle, or oligarchy. Those elected were nominated from or by this inner circle. As with most unions, the TGWU claimed its structure was 'designed to give members on the shop floor a voice in policy-making and decision-taking'. Milligan, *The New Barons*, 216–17; Marsh, *Trade Union Handbook*, 347; Transport and General Workers Union National Executive Committee, *The Story of the T.G.W.U.*, 7.
129 Marsh, *Trade Union Handbook*, 347–8.
130 In the 1970s there was a gradual shift towards more single-workplace branches (rather than multi-shop branches). Jack Jones saw the shift to single-shop branches occurring and tried to accelerate the process to decision-making at a shop steward level. He met with limited success as branch oligarchs controlled all communication and the shift was a threat to the power of some branch officials who had benefited from low voting attendance at multi-factory branch meetings. 'Only a small percentage of union members ever attended trade union meetings. This meant that a small number of members, such as communists, could effectively take control.' Keith Laybourn, *A History of Trade Unionism c. 1770–1990* (Phoenix Mill, UK: Alan Sutton, 1992), 177; Milligan, *The New Barons*, 95.
131 In 1975 'roughly half a dozen' members of the Executive Council (39 members) were communists. Milligan, *The New Barons*, 95.
132 Ibid., 94.
133 Ibid., 95.
134 Ibid.

structure meant that the TGWU, despite its large staff and (it was generally agreed) honest leadership from Jones, was a union with a potential disjuncture between its hierarchy and its lay members, its leaders and its led.

Immediately following the coup, the TGWU GEC resolved to support Allende's widow, and, distinct from the AUEW, planned to lobby unions in the United States to press their own government on the Chile issue.[135] At a meeting on 5 December, the TGWU GEC noted their commitment to a unilateral boycott (the TGWU only) of the Chilean junta if no other sort could be achieved.[136] On 7 June 1974, a lengthier resolution was passed calling on all TGWU members to support the boycott campaign on all aircraft, warships and other equipment that could be used by the junta against the Chilean workers.[137] Early in 1976, the TGWU took to using the phrase 'harassment of Chilean transport' as was employed in the ITF resolutions, and this embodied the degradation of ferocity of the official position of the union.[138] As the junta in Chile solidified its grasp on power, the TGWU progressively softened its stance, though it never completely withdrew support for direct action.

The TGWU GEC minutes show that Chile, and Jones's activities to do with Chile, were constantly discussed over many years. According to the sums listed in the minutes, the TGWU effectively bankrolled the CSC and Chile solidarity in general. Yet, in those same minutes, the RREK boycott was never specifically discussed. It seems that despite the organisational possibility of autocracy, the TGWU members at East Kilbride were free to boycott Chile as they saw fit.

It would soon be out of their hands.

The Hamilton Sherriff Court (Scotland) ruled an injunction on the engines in favour of the Chileans in August 1978, stating clearly that the junta was the rightful owner of the boycotted engines.[139] While this may not have said anything new, it did start things moving in favour of the junta. Rolls Royce

---

135 An immediate deputation from the TGWU General Executive Committee was sent to the Foreign Secretary. *Minutes and Record of the two-hundred and fifth statutory meeting of the general executive council held at transport house: First day, September 17, 1973*, TGWU, MSS.126/T&G/1186/A/51, MRC, UW, Coventry.
136 *Minutes and Record of the General Executive Committee, December 5, 1973*, TGWU, MSS.126/T&G/1186/A/51, MRC, UW, Coventry.
137 *Minutes and Record of the General Executive Council, Fifth Day, June 7, 1974*, TGWU, MSS.126/T&G/1186/A/52, MRC, UW, Coventry.
138 This seemed to be so that they would avoid legal problems. *Minutes of the General Executive Council, March 4, 1976*, TGWU, MSS.126/T&G/1186/A/54, MRC, UW, Coventry.
139 'Rolls-Royce Workers Free Aero-Engines Overhauled for Chile', *The Times*, 19 August 1978, 3; Singer, 'RAF Denies any Involvement in Removal of Chile Aero-Engines'; Ronald Faux, 'Docks Watch by Workers for Chilean Engines', *The Times*, 29 August 1978, 2; *Fighting bloody hand of Chile's fascists by Jim Tait*.

declared its intention to cooperate with the Chileans, who had the legal right to their engines.[140] They posted notices around the factory stating the company's legal position.[141]

A general election was looming at the time of the injunction.[142] It became obvious that the export licences were the last major legal barrier to the junta's repossession of the engines.[143] The CSC recorded that the junta and their 'friends' ran a 'carefully orchestrated' campaign 'designed to modify British Government policy with regard to Chile'.[144] Robert Adley (a Conservative MP representing Christchurch and Lymington)[145] suggested the Government was holding the engines at the 'instigation' of the East Kilbride Shop Stewards, implying that the Government was run by rank-and-file trade unionists.[146] Adley said the issue was not the situation in Chile, but 'nothing less than international banditry by the Government'.[147] General Gustavo Leigh of the Chilean Air Force accused the Government of obstructing the return of the engines through bureaucratic means,[148] and the less than progressive (according to the CSC) Scottish press and the Daily Telegraph pressured the shop stewards to give up the boycott.[149]

At the factory in East Kilbride, the shop stewards received letters that melodramatically linked the boycott to the 'red takeover' and moral decay of the United Kingdom.[150] Some were threatening, such as an anonymous and very poorly written note to 'Peter Low': 'we are now taking steps to shut) you up) about Chillie also you talk about the (IRA) we will be getting your Black Specks off so that you will be able to see to work so a Warning (Shut Up Low).'[151]

The CSC was slow to respond to the crusade for the release of the engines. They were preoccupied with a wave of hunger strikes and a highly choreographed demonstration on 9 July 1978.[152] The CSC did manage to encourage a letter-writing campaign, aiming to stop the engines from leaving the country and halt further

---

140 *Chilean Air Force Engines, 1982*, RREKSS.
141 'Rolls-Royce Workers Free Aero-Engines Overhauled for Chile'.
142 MacKay, 'The Scot Who Humbled Pinochet Tells His Story'.
143 *CSC Annual Report*, 1978.
144 Ibid.
145 Adley and others were labelled 'Tory backwoodsmen' by the CSC. Adley had his suggestion for an emergency debate on the export licences rejected by the speaker. *To: CSC Local cttee secs Re: March for the 2,500—Sunday July 9th London, 1978*, CSC, CSC/1/20, LHASC, Manchester; Benedict Birnberg, 'Government Accused of International Banditry', *The Times*, 14 June 1978, 14.
146 Birnberg, 'Government Accused of International Banditry', 14.
147 Ibid.
148 'Trade Union Stops Return of Jet Engines to Chile', *The Times*, 10 June 1978, 2.
149 *To: CSC Local cttee secs Re: March for the 2,500; Affiliates' Newsletter no. 29, July 23rd 1978*.
150 Robert Leckie wrote: 'It is trade Unions that has brought this Country to its knees.' *Leckie to RRSSEK, 29-8-78*, RREKSS.
151 *Peter Lowe. We are now taking steps to shut) you up)*, 1978, RREKSS.
152 *CSC Annual Report*, 1978. The march for the 2500 missing people in Chile was silent, accompanied by the beat of a single drum. It aimed to have one white carnation for each missing person in Chile. *To: CSC Local cttee secs Re: March for the 2,500*.

softening of the British Government's position on Chile.[153] The inaction of the CSC during the attack on the boycott could point to overwork of the staff in the office. It might also be evidence of their confidence in the unbreakable strength of the boycott, which had become a symbol of the worker-based nature of the solidarity movement. On the other hand, perhaps the campaign could not afford to become embroiled in union business.

In London, facing pressure from the left and the right, Callaghan had turned to his legal counsel to solve the problem. Rolls Royce was the only case of unfulfilled work since the ban of arms to Chile was first laid down in 1974.[154] Consequently, Edmund Dell, Secretary of State for Trade, adhered to a cabinet subcommittee decision and the export licences were granted on 20 July 1978.[155] Rumours circulated that there would be state collusion in the removal of the engines, including a mobilisation of the Army.[156] *The Times* speculated that a 'lightning raid' to repossess the engines would occur.[157] Callaghan simply said he hoped no subterfuge would prevent their removal.[158]

The fact that the Labour Government which withdrew their ambassador after British citizen Sheila Cassidy was incarcerated and tortured had now granted export licences for the engines caused disbelief and further disillusionment within the left in Britain.[159] It was, said Peter Lowe, an 'immoral act'.[160] Support from unionists, union branches and individuals flowed to East Kilbride, some urging continuation of the boycott, and some supporting the workforce decision, whatever it be. Notable by its absence was national-level support from the TUC,

---

153　*Affiliates' Newsletter no. 29, July 23rd 1978.*
154　'R-R Engines Can Go to Chile', *The Times*, 21 July 1978, 2.
155　Ibid.; *Fighting bloody hand of Chile's fascists by Jim Tait*. The Cabinet had been advised that they were legally obliged to do so after the injunction by the Scottish court. Callaghan said the engines needed to be returned to Chile and it was a purely commercial matter that the Government had no part in. Faux, 'Docks Watch by Workers for Chilean Engines', 2; 'Removal of Aero Engines a Commercial Matter', *The Times*, 28 July 1978, 4.
156　*TheTimes* reported that Bruce Millan (Secretary of State for Scotland) in the Cabinet Defence and Overseas Policy Committee meeting had suggested the use of troops to remove the engines while the workforce was away. Frederick Mulley (Secretary of State for Defence) opposed the plan, saying it would be an inappropriate use of the armed service. It was from this suggestion that a rumour grew of state collusion in the removal of the engines. Rolls Royce advised against the use of troops. MacKay, 'The Scot Who Humbled Pinochet Tells His Story'; Peter Hennessy, 'Government Will Issue Export Licences for "Blacked" Engines Soon', *The Times*, 19 July 1978, 4.
157　*Rolls Royce Engines Snatched for Chilean Junta.*
158　'Removal of Aero Engines a Commercial Matter', 5.
159　Sheila Cassidy was a British citizen who had been detained because she helped an insurgent with medical treatment. *Docks and Waterway's National Committee Minutes, 20th October, 1977*, TGWU, MSS.126/TG/820/1/4, MRC, UW, Coventry; Patrick Keatley, 'Stronger Line on Chile Demanded', *Guardian* [Manchester], 6 January 1976. A full description of Cassidy's life in Chile, her arrest and imprisonment can be found in: Cassidy, Sheila Cassidy. *Solly (Putney BLP) to Owen (MP) 3rd August 1978*, RREKSS; *Geleit (Epsom & Ewell Advisory Committee NGA) to RRSSEK October 9th 1978*, RRSSEK; *Jackson and Brooks (SOGAT Waterlow & Sons ltd 'Radio Times' Warehouse Chapel) to RRSSEK, 5th Aug. 1978*, RREKSS.
160　Faux, 'Docks Watch by Workers for Chilean Engines'.

although the STUC was strong in its encouragement.[161] The TGWU leadership commented through Alex Kitson that the boycott was in line with the TGWU's policy of 'hostility' to the Chilean Government and the union supported its rank-and-file members.[162]

Unionists and others offered to guard or sabotage the engines. Scottish Area NUM general secretary, Eric Clarke, wrote to the shop stewards saying: 'You are not alone—keep up the resistance and if there is anything we can do, morally or physically to help, please do not hesitate to ask.'[163]

'The final hurdle' in relation to the repossession of the engines was in the hands of the rank and file in East Kilbride.[164] The pressure caused the RREK Shop Stewards to seek legal advice from solicitor Peter T. McCann and the learned senior counsel Charles MacArthur QC.[165] Any picket, the advice argued, could be viewed as criticism of the Hamilton court and therefore could be counted as contempt.[166] Refusing to obey an order could end in dismissal, but contempt of court could mean a jail sentence.[167]

---

[161] It is very likely the Glasgow Chile Defence Committee's persistence, along with its connections within the communist party, had an affect on STUC attention to Chile. The Scottish unions were led by the Scottish Trades Union Council (STUC), which consistently passed strong anti-junta resolutions. Large sections of the STUC annual report were dedicated to Chile. Scottish solidarity was perhaps the strongest of all in Britain. One of the largest campaigns was over soccer. Chile Defence Committee, 'Resolution to Glasgow Chile Defence Committee A.G.M'; *Scottish Trades Union Congress Seventy Eighth Annual Report (1975)*, STUC Annual Reports, GCUA, Glasgow; *Milne (STUC) circular, 16 January 1976*, STUC, STUCA 507/1, GCUA, Glasgow; *Don't Play Ball with the fascists!, 1977*, CSC, CSC/1/12, LHASC, Manchester; *Petition to: The Scottish Football Association concerning: The Scotland–Chile Match, 1977*, CSC, CSC/1/12, LHASC, Manchester; *McLean (NUM Scottish Area) Circular re Chile, 12th August 1977*, RREKSS Chile; *McLean (NUM) to RRSSEK, 1st September 1977*, RREKSS; *Scotland v Chile June 15th 1977* [flyer], STUC, STUCA 516, GCUA, Glasgow; *Minutes of the Statutory Meeting of the Finance and General Purposes Committee of the General Executive Council, March 31, 1977*, TGWU, MSS.126/T&G/1186/A/55, MRC, UW, Coventry.
[162] 'Trade Union Stops Return of Jet Engines to Chile', 2. John Henry, deputy general secretary of the STUC, was asked if the boycott would continue after the grant of export licences. He deferred to the authority of the rank and file at the East Kilbride Factory. '[T]hat will be a decision taken by the Rols-Royce workers. I imagine that the blacking would still stand', he said. Hennessy, 'Government Will Issue Export Licences for "Blacked" Engines Soon', 4. Jimmy Milne, STUC general secretary, echoed this view: 'in the end it is the decision of the workforce that matters.' Moss Evans, general secretary of the TGWU, told the CSC: 'We can assure you that our members will maintain their spontaneous act of solidarity on this issue.' *Affiliates' Newsletter no. 29, July 23rd 1978*. Jimmy Milne (STUC) said, 'there is no way any of our members will get those damned engines out of Britain. If scab labour is brought in, they will not get past the front door.' Milne, in MacKay, 'The Scot Who Humbled Pinochet Tells His Story'. The TGWU 'enlisted' the support of local haulage firms to ensure the engines would stay where they were. The Road Haulage Association said it feared for the safety of its members and their property. *'Blacked Engines "Too Hot to Handle"', Sunday Express, 20 October 1978*, RREKSS.
[163] *Clarke (NUM Scottish Area) to RRSSEK, 20th July 1978*, RREKSS. Leeds Trades Council also offered to help in such a manner. *Huffinley (Leeds Trades Council) to RRSSEK, 31st August, 1978*, RREKSS.
[164] Faux, 'Docks Watch by Workers for Chilean Engines', 2.
[165] *McCann (solicitor) to Lowe (RRSS), 15th August, 1978*, RREKSS.
[166] This also included a round-the-clock watch, which some workers in the factory were keen to man. *Fighting bloody hand of Chile's fascists by Jim Tait*; Somerville Interview, 2007.
[167] 'If any members of the Union who are employed by Rolls Royce took active steps physically to try and stop the departure of the engines then he would be in serious trouble … It is, however, a wholly different matter if an employee of Rolls Royce is asked to shift an engine and refuses to do so.' *Note by Senior Council for T.&G.W. Union, 1978*, RREKSS.

In August 1978 a 75-minute meeting of 1500 workers from RREK decided they would not impede the removal of the engines.[168] They unanimously passed the resolution that 'we refuse to co-operate in the removal of the Chile engines from the factory'.[169] Dougald Gillies and Peter Lowe, the convenors, said the men would not break the law. If they did so they would be 'reducing [themselves] to the level of the thugs in Chile'.[170] A handwritten note on the back of the solicitor's advice revealed a two-part contingency plan:

1) Refuse to cooperate in the removal of the Chile engines from the factory

2) [In] the event of anyone attempting to remove the Chile engines from the factory, we call an immediate stoppage of work and a protest demonstration.[171]

The workers at East Kilbride were never able to put the plan into action.

As was customary at the time, all the factory workers would take their annual three-week holiday at one time. The whole place was basically deserted. John Keenan, shop steward, along with maintenance staff were the only ones who remained on duty during the period.

But they were at home in bed when at 4 am on Saturday, 26 August 1978, two lorries accompanied by the sheriff signed in at the gate of the East Kilbride Rolls Royce Factory.[172] Management representatives were woken up and called to the factory to check the documents. It took two hours to load the engines onto the lorries, as together the engines weighed 6 t and required special equipment and skills to manoeuvre.[173] The lorries had false numberplates and fictitious names painted on their sides: 'Harvey's Ltd'.[174] After they drove off into the early dawn of summer, all that remained was a 'neatly swept' gap where the Chilean engines had stood for years.

---

168 The Chilean authorities had been negotiating to get the engines for at least a year before this. They also renegotiated the contract with Rolls Royce, releasing the company from obligations to deliver the engines. 'Rolls-Royce Workers Free Aero-Engines Overhauled for Chile', 3; Singer, 'RAF Denies any Involvement in Removal of Chile Aero-Engines'; Faux, 'Docks Watch by Workers for Chilean Engines', 2; *Fighting bloody hand of Chile's fascists by Jim Tait*.
169 *Lowe to McCann, 1978*, RREKSS.
170 'Rolls-Royce Workers Free Aero-Engines Overhauled for Chile'.
171 *1. Refuse to cooperate …1978*, RREKSS.
172 *McCann (solicitor) to Chief Constable, Strathclyde Police, 26th September, 1978*, RREKSS.
173 *Fighting bloody hand of Chile's fascists by Jim Tait*; Angela Singer, 'Mystery Clouds Movement of Chile Engines', *Guardian* [Manchester], 28 August 1978, 2; Faux, 'Docks Watch by Workers for Chilean Engines'.
174 The numberplates were: DKT 33 K, MON 681 G, VCS 937 S. The inquiries by the committee found that none of the vehicles registered under those numberplates could bear the weight of the engines nor had been equipped with a crane. *McCann (solicitor) to Chief Constable, Strathclyde Police, 26th September, 1978*; *CSC Annual Report*, 1978.

4. Pinochet's jets and Rolls Royce East Kilbride

Figure 4.3 Oxford Joint Chile Committee campaign flyer.

Source: *Rolls Royce Engines Snatched for Chilean Junta*.

Union officials were furious.[175] Lowe bitterly complained that 'there is nothing we can do now that the engines have already left the factory. We can only hope that our fellow trade unionists everywhere else will take up the cudgels on behalf of the people of Chile.'[176]

With the engines off Rolls Royce property, the company (like the national union leaders) washed its hands of the whole affair.[177] The removal was conducted within the law, while any agreement on the use of union labour within the factory was suspended in the presence of a sheriff with a court order.[178]

After the boycott ended, the shop stewards received waves of grateful letters and commiserations.[179] Cornejo, CUT representative in Britain, wrote to the Rolls Royce East Kilbride Joint Shop Stewards' Committee, on behalf of the trade union movement of Chile:

> You[r] actions have become one of the most powerful symbols of the International Solidarity Movement and all Chilean Trade Unionists both inside Chile and in exile, salute you.
>
> We look forward to the day when we can greet your representatives in a free Chile.[180]

---

175 Faux, 'Docks Watch by Workers for Chilean Engines', 2; Chile Solidarity Campaign, *Chile Solidarity Campaign: Annual Report*, 1978; *Affiliates' Newsletter no. 29, July 23rd 1978*; *Reg. numbers of Lorries ... 1978*, RREKSS.
176 *Affiliates' Newsletter 57, December, 1982*, CSC, CSC/44/6, LHASC, Manchester. Also quoted in Singer, 'RAF Denies any Involvement in Removal of Chile Aero-Engines'. Martin Flannery, MP for Sheffield Hillsborough and Secretary of the PLP Chile Group, said the disappearance of the engines was 'moonlight smuggling' and he hoped the Government played no part in it. Glasgow Provost, Peter McKennar, aided the investigation of where the engines went. One engine was rumoured to have appeared in Hillingdon in the south. Empty crates similar to those that housed the engines were found in the Princes Dock in Glasgow. Dugald Gillies theorised that they were dropped into the Atlantic Ocean. Accusations that the engines were taken to the Brize Norton Base of the RAF were dismissed by RAF representatives. Gatehouse noted that if they were taken to a RAF base it would indicate that the Chilean Air Force had been granted landing permission to pick them up. McCann, on behalf of the RREKSS, lodged a complaint with Strathclyde Police about the use of false numberplates, which would be in breach of the road traffic act. Their first inquiries were politely rebuffed by the police, and McCann had to insist on the illegal nature of the false numberplates for them to investigate further. His inquiries continued, until finally hitting a wall (despite having Neil Kinnock making inquiries as well). The Crown Agent replied that there was no evidence of any offence. Singer, 'RAF Denies any Involvement in Removal of Chile Aero-Engines', 24; Chile Solidarity Campaign, *Chile Solidarity Campaign: Annual Report*, 1978; 'Chile Engine Crates Found', *Morning Star*, 16 August 1974; Somerville Interview, 2007; *Hamill (Chief Constable Strathclyde Police) to McCann (Solicitor) 13 September 1978*, RREKSS; *O'Donnell (Crown Agent) to McCann (Solicitors) 10 April 1979*, RREKSS; Singer, 'Mystery Clouds Movement of Chile Engines'; *Sill (Strathclyde Police) to RRSSC, 23 March 1979*, RREKSS; *To the Chief Constable Strathclyde Police, 6th September, 1978*, RREKSS.
177 'Chileans Reclaim "Blacked" Rolls-Royce Engines', *The Times*, 28 August 1978, 2.
178 Faux, 'Docks Watch by Workers for Chilean Engines'; *Affiliates' Newsletter no. 29, July 23rd 1978*.
179 The Chilean Committee of Norwich wrote to the 'courageous union': 'Chilean unionists and workers will never forget your solidarity.' *Chilean committee of Norwich to RRSSEK, 6 Sept 78*, RREKSS.
180 *Cornejo (CUT) to RRSSEK, 18.8.78*, RREKSS.

4. Pinochet's jets and Rolls Royce East Kilbride

Figure 4.4 Rolls Royce East Kilbride Joint Shop Stewards march in the anniversary demonstration of 1978 in London, just days after the engines were taken from the factory.

Source: 'Remembering Chile's Brave Fight', *Morning Star*, 11 September 1978, 3, courtesy of the Marx Memorial Library.

It was acutely obvious that the engines had become an emblem for the cause. Jim Tait expressed it thus:

> The length the Chile regime went to has more to do with capturing world-wide prestige than four corroded jet engines.
>
> It is an indication of how important these machines are, not as hunks of metal but as symbols of the struggle of progress against fascism in Chile itself.[181]

One leaflet stated that 'by allowing the engines to be moved the Labour Government has sold the trades unionists down the river'.[182]

It did so in more ways than one.

As has already been noted, the Labour Government successfully stopped new contracts for a time, but it soon fell to trade unions to stop the delivery of the warships for Chile. Most of the vessels had been ordered well before Allende was elected, but were to be delivered into the arms of the new military government.[183]

As already observed, in 1974 the AUEW had resolved to stop frigates and submarines for Chile.[184] Jimmy McCallum of AUEW TASS[185] had argued that '[t]he only time frigates have been used was when they bombarded the port of Valparaiso'—the first city to fall in the coup. 'The ships have been used since then as prisons and floating torture chambers for trade unionists.'[186]

It was noted furthermore by the TUC that 'a substantial proportion' of Chile's population lived within range of the guns on these ships; it gave the 'Chilean navy an unusual internal security capability'.[187] A CSC brief further confirmed the nature of Chile and Britain's military equipment trading relationship: 'The Chilean Navy and Air Force are seriously dependent upon Britain for their continuing capacity to wage both internal and external war.'[188]

And yet, how the vessels were put to use was not necessarily the strongest factor for or against a boycott.

---

181 *Fighting bloody hand of Chile's fascists by Jim Tait*. 'Nevertheless, we did our bit. The blacking lit a beacon of international solidarity for the people of Chile.' Somerville, in MacKay, 'The Scot Who Humbled Pinochet Tells His Story'.
182 *Rolls Royce Engines Snatched for Chilean Junta*.
183 'Open File', *Guardian* [Manchester], 3 October 1973.
184 *AUEW Journal December 1973: Abstract Report of Council Proceedings*, Amalgamated Engineering Union, MSS.259/AEU/4/6/53, MRC, UW, Coventry.
185 McCallum was the TASS office convenor at John Brown Engineering, Clydebank.
186 *A trade unionist's guide to the Chile issue*.
187 *Arms for Chile 1974*, TUC [BLP International Department], MSS.292D/936.1/2, MRC, UW, Coventry.
188 *Brief (29 April 1974) Britain and Chile*, CSC, CSC/15/1, LHASC, Manchester.

Figure 4.5 A CSC poster on the submarines Hyatt and O'Brien.

Source: *Poster: The Chilean people ask Stop the Subs, 1976*, CSC, CSC/44/1, LHASC, Manchester.

Take the example of two submarines called *O'Brien* and *Hyatt* that were being built at Scott Lithgow on the Clyde.[189] These submarines were due to be handed over to the Chileans in April and October 1974. On 26 September 1973, the wife of the Chilean naval attaché, who had just evicted Ambassador Alvaro Bunster from the Embassy in London, travelled to Scott Lithgow's Cartsburn Yard (Greenock) to launch the vessels.[190] Inside the yard, trade unionists boycotted the launch and outside there was a demonstration organised by local labour councillors.[191]

Would their initial reaction translate into sustained action?

The shipbuilding industry has vastly different work practices than the engine factory. Workers have one vessel to work on for a very long period (months at least, often years). Stopping work on that ship for political reasons would mean stopping work indefinitely. The editor of the Guardian commented in 1973 that 'union leaders are now faced with the bitter dilemma of not wanting to work on ships for the Junta but also not wanting to deprive their lads of the needed employment'.[192]

After the initial, symbolic protest, AUEW members continued to work on the submarines.[193] In fact, in May 1974 the 500 engineers at Scott Lithgow voted to go *against* the AUEW EC decision to stop work on warships to Chile.[194] They would work the ships.

John Teegan, shop steward at the yard, said the decision was reached unanimously, partly because of loyalty to the firm, but also because blacking the submarines would put 'hundreds of men out of work'.[195] It would directly impact the industrial conditions of the unionists.[196] The CSC office released a statement: 'The workers obviously thought blacking the two submarines being built would lead to redundancies. As a similar decision on Tyneside proved, many workers share this fear.'[197]

---

189 Also on the Clyde, two Leander Class Frigates called *Condell* and *Lynch* were being built at Yarrows. These were armed with Seacat missiles and helicopters. The frigates were due to be delivered in December 1973–January 1974. 'Open File'.
190 For further information on the submarines: John McKinlay, 'Chile Pays Debts to Get Clyde Sub', *Glasgow Herald*, 27 August 1976; John McKinlay, 'Chile Wants More Ships from Britain', *Glasgow Herald*, 28 August 1976.
191 'Chile Winds', *Guardian* [Manchester], 15 November 1973.
192 'Chile Waves', *Guardian* [Manchester], 4 October 1973.
193 'Engineers Stop Work on Frigate for Chile', *The Times*, 14 May 1974, 1.
194 'Engineers Defy Call to Stop Work on Chile Warships', *The Times*, 16 May 1974.
195 Ibid.
196 Despite Gavin Laird and Ian McKee (district secretary) talking to the men, they still decided to ignore the AUEW Executive Committee's decision. Gavin Laird, the Scottish regional officer of the AUEW, said there was no real chance of the men facing discipline for not following the AUEW Executive Committee order. Ibid. The NUS made similar statements about the men who disobeyed the National Executive Committee order.
197 *A trade unionist's guide to the Chile issue*.

On the Tyne at Swan Hunter's Wallsend dry-dock, a destroyer called *Almirante Williams* was undergoing a refit.[198] AUEW workers continued working on her also, despite the black-ban directive of their union's leadership. After she was launched, however, she soon appeared at Rosyth to load ammunition and stores. While there, she was blacked by TGWU workers, who eventually gave in and loaded minimal stores and water. They then warned other TGWU port workers that she would surely berth looking to load ammunition. *Almirante Williams* later appeared for trials in Portsmouth, where she was blacked by the AUEW. The AUEW Portsmouth district secretary, Rory McCarthy, was reported as saying that 'the feeling among his members was so strong that they had felt like sinking the ship, which was, after all, what they had done to the fascists' ships during the Second World War'.[199]

So, why do some unionists boycott, and others do not?[200]

The factor with the strongest influence is economics. Certainly, as Julian Amery MP put it, if Britain failed to supply the frigates and submarines the Government would be responsible for £50 million and the private firms would lose £10 million. More pertinently, he said the naval vessels ordered from Britain over the next two years were primarily from the Latin American market, and 'there would be serious repercussions from other countries if we failed to fulfil the Chilean contract affecting future employment'.[201] The prospect of job losses in the present and the future was of high importance when deciding whether to take action. Where action occurred it stemmed from radical individuals or groups in workplaces and almost exclusively where the sustainability of jobs and working conditions was not negatively impacted.

There is an exception to this: the pinnacle of the NUS exhibition of solidarity, when 600 unemployed seamen in Liverpool refused to sign on to Pacific Steam Navigation Company ships in 1975–76. It was not a perfect seal, stopping trade through the port as other NUS members and seamen sailed other ships to Chile in this time. Moreover, the men eventually sailed with the company when economic pressure became too great;[202] but regardless of its faults, this truly is an exception to the rule.

---

198 Another destroyer, *Almirante Riveros*, was there along with it.
199 *The Chile Monitor no. 3, 1974*, CSC, CSC/7/3, LHASC, Manchester.
200 Other actions on Chilean vessels include: 18 engineers walking off the frigate *Lynch* at Yarrows, 13 May 1974; a TGWU black at Rosyth in February 1974; Weirs Pumps in Glasgow blacked pumps for warships; and in 1976 the workers at Yarrow (Clydeside) blacked propeller shafts for Chilean vessels. The management at the firm then moved the shafts across Scotland to Rosyth, where TGWU workers promptly blacked them. *CSC Executive Committee: Minutes of the meeting held at Liberation on February 5, 1974*; 'Engineers Stop Work on Frigate for Chile', *The Times*, 14 May 1974; Chile Solidarity Campaign, *Chile and the British Labour Movement*; *CSC-Exec 26.8.76 Minutes*, CSC, CSC/1/10, LHASC, Manchester.
201 *Minutes of Executive Council. 7th February, 1974*, Confederation of Shipbuilding and Engineering Unions, MSS.259/CSEU/1/1/10, MRC, UW, Coventry.
202 *To All British Seamen: Support your Executive Council, 1975*, CSC, CSC/28/6, LHASC, Manchester.

The boycott or lack of boycott against Chilean interests in Scotland enables various conclusions to be drawn. The implementation of direct action for remote political gain is dependent on a number of factors. The first is opportunity. Boycotts are opportunistic in the sense that a product must be present for the action to occur. While Brian Nicholson may have had influence on the London docks, without any Chilean trade passing through, he would only be able to spout rhetoric. Second, for some, ideology or morality was an obvious motivation: these ideas could bind a multifaceted political workforce in a coherent manner, leading to worker action. Third, union democracy and union structure could affect the chance of direct action occurring. The attitude of the union leadership towards rank-and-file actions and the penalties implicit in disobeying the union's rules influenced the use of direct action. Decisions taken at a national level often highlighted the disconnection between the rank and file and the national office due to the cumbersome structures of unions. Fourth, individuals who had the ability to exploit opportunities, such as John Boyd of the AUEW, could affect the course of boycotts. Activists at ground level were powerless to stop his political manipulation at the national level.[203]

But when all other factors are stripped away, the final and most important factor influencing direct action for political gain has already been outlined: the economic wellbeing of members. The direct economic impact on those who had tools in their hands influenced their action. Ian Schmutte has stated: 'unions choose these activities, and indeed often choose not to act at the international scale for their own particular strategic and tactical reasons.'[204] That is, international action can be contingent on other pressures on union resources and risk to other union aims.

The RREK workers found themselves in a unique situation: they had a legitimate material to boycott and, in doing so, they would not cause major economic strife for themselves, their company or the nation. The blacking of the eight engines posed no threat to jobs at the factory. The loss of the Chilean contract alone would not produce substantial economic stress to Rolls Royce or the nation or even the loss of hours for the workers. On the other hand, the work (or perhaps the failure to stop work) of the engineers on the boats and submarines indicated that the economic loss to workers overrode ideology or moral commitment to cause.

---

203 It has been difficult to reconstruct in any detail what occurred in terms of the submarine and frigate boycott. Even Scottish activists at the time do not know the exact details. For example, Diane Dixon said 'despite the fact [it was in the] east of Scotland, I couldn't say I ever knew what the origins of it were ... I don't know, and I'd be making it up if I tried to tell you'. Diane Dixon, Interview by Ann Jones, 4 September 2007 [hereinafter Dixon Interview, 2007].
204 Schmutte, 'International Union Activity', 10.

Not surprisingly, for direct action to occur in support of a remote political motive, the 'bread and butter' of unionists must not be threatened.

Figure 4.6 Thatcher and Pinochet discuss fighter jets.

Source: *Untitled*, Chile Solidarity Photo box 3, People's History Museum, Manchester.

Australia

5. Opening doors for Chile: Strategic individuals and networks

Steve Cooper doesn't fit the present-day image of a man involved in radical politics.

He didn't in 1973 either.

He was forty-five years old with a gentle disposition and gentlemanly manners. A full moustache offset a receding hairline, and conservative clothes didn't give away his passionate interest in workers' democracy.

It was that interest which led him to Chile in 1973.[1] Chilean political parties, Cooper reasoned, were free and the Allende Government was extending workers' democracy and participation.[2] What was going on in Chile was a 'revolution in democracy', said Cooper, and he thought that if the situation remained untampered with, 'it could possibly lead to a more socialist type of society'.[3] He took a break from work and used money he had recently inherited to travel to Chile. While there he attended an international conference on multinational companies as an observer for the Amalgamated Metal Workers' Union (AMWU) of Australia as well as the World Federation of Trade Unions (WFTU) collective of unions of Sydney. He stayed in Chile for three months, moving around Santiago and getting to know workers and the situation on the ground.[4]

Steve Cooper was concerned about imperialism, which was one of the dominant themes at the time in the Australian left—a concern that was part of a tradition of conspiracy theories in the Australian labour movement.[5] In a report on the conference published in the *Tribune*, Cooper wrote that 'three of the most formidable forces in the world, the sovereign national state, the trade union movement, and the international socialist movement', were the natural enemies of imperialism and multinationals.[6] The way to combat multinationals, he continued,

---

1 Interview with Steve Cooper (Chile activist, Australia), 12 October 2005 [hereinafter Cooper Interview, 2005], copy in possession of author.
2 Cooper had researched a sort of 'anatomy' of transnational companies in Australia (1972). An excerpt of this work is: Communist Party of Australia, 'Fighting Multinationals', *Tribune* [Australia], 4–10 September 1973. This was a popular theme in the left at the time. See, for example: Tom O'Lincoln, *Into the Mainstream: The Decline of Australian Communism* (Sydney: Stained Wattle Press, 1985), 141–2.
3 The nationalisation of copper mines also contributed to his interest.
4 'International Report (Meeting C.C. 4.5.73)', (AMWU), photocopied in the notes attached to Julius Roe, 'Notes for Speech: 30th Anniversary', 2003, unpublished ms, copy in possession of author; Jim Baird, 'After the Coup: The Trade Union Delegation to Chile', 2004, unpublished ms.
5 Tom Bramble, *Trade Unionism in Australia: A History from Flood to Ebb Tide* (Melbourne: Cambridge University Press, 2008), 86.
6 Steve Cooper, 'Fighting the Transnational Companies', *Tribune* [Australia], 24–30 July 1973.

was through workers' control. International workers of the world should control international organisations; Cooper called them 'transnational socialist enterprises', which would challenge multinationals.[7]

Also attending the conference on multinationals in Chile was Glen Moorhead, federal secretary of the Australian Federated Union of Locomotive Enginemen (AFULE).[8] Moorhead came from within the Socialist Party's sphere of influence and spoke with the confidence of someone who believed he was the true representative of the Australian working class. On one occasion he told delegates: 'Although Australia is in the same hemisphere as Chile and together with New Zealand, Chile is our nearest eastern neighbour, there is no contact between the trade unions of our two countries. That situation is rectified from this moment.'[9]

The rhetoric of solidarity among workers, united across borders, against multinationals and imperialism, dominated the discussion at the conference in 1973. This sort of rhetoric was the most common of the expressions of leftist internationalist sentiment in Australia. It appears, however, Moorhead did not know about, or didn't want to acknowledge, the contact that had occurred with unionists aligned with the Communist Party of Australia (CPA) over the previous years.

The two Australian participants were from different camps: Moorhead was aligned with the Socialist Party of Australia (SPA); Cooper was an Australian Labor Party (ALP) member, though his sympathies lay further to the left. The Cold War lingered and the conference suffered the usual problems of tension between the International Confederation of Free Trade Unions (ICFTU) and the WFTU. The ICFTU did not send delegates, because they refused to be on the same platform as anyone from the WFTU.[10] Similarly, politics got in the way of a British delegation as the only invitation sent was to the (relatively conservative) TUC, which of course declined, resulting in no participation from that country. The summit was like a microcosm of the problems of the solidarity movement that it preceded: it was grand on rhetoric, rife with factional tensions and, often as not, peopled by faddists.

Despite the conference's shortcomings, when Steve Cooper returned to Australia, he immediately started agitating for Chile solidarity.[11]

More than the liberation movements elsewhere, the Chilean case was particularly pertinent to Australians due to the similarities between the countries. Chile

---

7   Ibid.
8   'Australian Speaks at Santiago', *SPA*, June 1973.
9   Ibid.
10 They did, however, send representatives from their trade sections. Cooper, 'Fighting the Transnational Companies'.
11 He continued agitating for many years: *AMWU St George Branch to CSCP, 26-5-1975*, Papers of GMM; Hamer, *The Politics of Electoral Pressure*.

and Australia both had long parliamentary and democratic traditions, were not recently colonised and their economies were dominated by mining and primary production. Most importantly, Allende and his UP Government had been democratically elected.[12]

When the coup occurred in September 1973, the reaction of the left in Australia was immediate and incredulous. Even though, as Mavis Robertson remembered, the Australian Government 'never really, even at the worst of times, felt comfortable with the Junta',[13] in October 1973, the Whitlam Government recognised the new Government of Chile.[14] Senator Arthur Gietzelt (a member of the ALP with a close relationship to the CPA) publicly declared on the television program *This Day Tonight* that he would use a petition through the Labor caucus to reverse the recognition of Chile.[15] Whitlam ordered that no minister put his name to it. Steve Cooper remembered that Whitlam's attitude was unhelpfully blunt: 'the Chinese have recognised it Comrade.'[16]

Politicians responded to their conscience, or as a result of their support for socialist internationalism, or both. Well-known MP Tom Uren was one of the ministers who contravened Whitlam's order and wrote to the prime minister to explain: 'There are times when I must act as an individual and this is one of those occasions.'[17] Fifty-seven members of the ALP caucus signed the petition.[18]

The Deputy Prime Minister, Lance Barnard, said the Australian Government's recognition of the military government of Chile did not imply approval of their policies. On this flimsy premise, the Australian Government did not withdraw its

---

12 Interview with Andrew Hewett (Chile, peace and student activist, Australia), 23 September 2005 [hereinafter Hewett Interview, 2005], Notes in possession of author.
13 Interview with Mavis Robertson (feminist, peace, anti-Vietnam War, Chile and CPA activist, Australia), 6 February 2009 [hereinafter Robertson Interview, 2009], copy in possession of author.
14 This occurred in spite of the ALP's affiliation to the Socialist International, of which the Chilean Radical Party was also a member. In hindsight the recognition was ironic, as in 1975 the Whitlam Government was ousted by a constitutional coup. Even before that, many people were comparing Allende and Whitlam. 'Libs Look to Junta: The Chilean Connection', *Tribune* [Australia], 3 December 1975.
15 Forty-four members of the Labor caucus, including eight cabinet ministers, sent a telegram to the Chilean Ambassador in Australia, revealing their commitment to help the Chilean people regain their freedom from the illegal new government. Other ministers, such as Tom Uren, were also very public in their condemnation of the military coup. Tom Uren, *Straight Left* (Milsons Point, NSW: Random House Australia, 1994), 230; Rt Hon. Billy Snedden, 'Whitlam Government: Want of Confidence Motion: 23 October 1973', in *Hansard Parliamentary Debates (House of Representatives)*, vol. 86 (1973), 2482–8; Bramble, *Trade Unionism in Australia*, 21.
16 Steve Cooper, Notes from a conversation with Ann Jones, Billy Martin (AMWU organiser, Chile activist 1980s) and Pat Johnson (AMWU organiser of the present), 21 May 2007 [hereinafter Cooper et al. Conversation, 2007], notes in possession of author.
17 Uren, *Straight Left*, 230. The ALP NSW State Council also denounced the decision. This was possibly Mulvihill's influence. 'Govt. Told: "Don't Recognise Chile"', *Tribune* [Australia], 9–15 October 1973.
18 'Action Against Chile is Urged', *The Australian*, 11 October 1973, 10; Hon. William Charles Wentworth et al., 'Adjournment: National Anthem—Health Insurance Scheme—Decentralisation—Land Transactions—Political Parties, 25 October 1973', in *Hansard Parliamentary Debates (House of Representatives)*, vol. 86 (1973), 2767; *Prime Minister's press conference, 16 October 1973*, 000010358, Whitlam Institute, University of Western Sydney, Sydney.

acknowledgment of the junta despite Whitlam's condemnation of the coup in the House of Representatives.[19] The ALP leader in the Senate, Lionel Murphy, said soon after the coup, 'all we can do is hope that democracy is speedily restored'.[20]

Prime Minister Whitlam was 'saddened' as a democrat and a socialist by the coup, but in government it was business as usual.[21] The 'que sera, sera' attitude was not shared by the workers of Australia. The Australian Railways Union (ARU), Miners Federation, Waterside Workers' Federation of Australia (WWFA), AMWU and Plumbers and Gasfitters Employees' Union all condemned the 'bloody-handed military Junta',[22] and the Australian Government's recognition of it, via telegrams sent directly to Whitlam. This is the first hint of the reservoir of goodwill, informed partially through ideological and humanitarian concerns, that could be and was accessed by the Chile solidarity cause.

In the early 1970s the left in Australia was coming to terms with a freshly split communist party. Those more faithful to the line of the Soviet Union had split off to form the Socialist Party of Australia (SPA) in 1971. Those left behind retained the title 'CPA' and found themselves able to express and explore a new, self-determinist ideology. The alternative ideology that emerged was labelled 'eurocommunism' and it was closely intertwined with the idea of extending political action to support social movements (such as that opposed to the Vietnam War). Political pluralism and the renunciation of the Leninist party state were central characteristics of eurocommunism but it was the adherence of eurocommunists to the democratic process of the bourgeois state that was an obvious departure from other socialist strategies.[23] Eurocommunists in particular believed in a broad-front approach and were attentive to the UP experience in Chile for that reason, as well as its attempt to travel the peaceful or parliamentary road.[24]

---

19 The decision, he went on to say, was based on whether the Government was in full control of the country's territories. 'Chile Recognised but not Approved', *The Australian*, 12 October 1973, 10.
20 Gustavo Martin Montenegro, 'La Campaña de Solidaridad con Chile en Australia 1973–1990: Un estudio histórico sobre el movimiento de solidaridad australiano durante la dictadura militar en Chile' (Masters diss., University of New South Wales, 1994), 107.
21 *Minister of Foreign Affairs to Scott (AMWU South Australian Branch Secretary), 21 November 1973*, AMWU: South Australian State Council, N131/211, NBAC: ANU, Canberra; *Recent events in Chile*, 000010659, Whitlam Institute, University of Western Sydney, Sydney.
22 'Govt. Told: "Don't Recognise Chile"'.
23 Eurocommunism did spring, of course, from a Leninist tradition. Thompson, *The Left in History*, 159.
24 Ibid., 182; Chun, *The British New Left*, 114. It has been observed by Peter Shipley that revolutionaries are routinely guided by examples in other countries as well as by historical traditions, and this in part explains the fascination with Chile. Shipley, *Revolutionaries in Modern Britain*, 17.

The tactic of broad alliance meant that eurocommunists moved their focus outward from the organised labour movement, though as we shall see, never forgot them.[25] The communist split meant the CPA was able to push to the forefront in many trade unions and concurrently express its ideology of the new left.[26]

The 1960s and 1970s saw radical left trade unions in Australia starting to defy what the Burgmanns called the 'caricatures of trade unions as bastions of homophobia, machismo, racism, ethnocentrism and ecological irresponsibility' as the new left ideas permeated their ranks.[27] Steve Cooper's journey to Chile and subsequent actions are perhaps a case in point. The radical unions embraced new left concerns and became centres of activism on social issues from Aboriginal rights to the environmental impact of development.[28] The growth in social activism outside the industrial sphere of the unions, and outside the orthodox objectives of a Marxist party by the CPA, locked radical unions and the party into a mutually reinforcing relationship.[29] Union support of the Chile movement in the 1970s came from all sectors of the left, but consistent support for the Chile solidarity *committees*, for much of the early 1970s at least, came from the self-determinist sector of the left including the unions. The solidarity committees formed the core of the movement.

That is not to say, however, that the SPA and Socialist Workers' Party or others ignored the plight of Chileans. While many felt that the downfall of Allende justified their positions on non-cooperation with social democrats and their commitment to armed struggle, no-one rejoiced at the brutal military coup d'état. Almost all political parties of the left played some part in events over the history of the solidarity movement. Andrew Ferguson, an activist involved in the movement, remembered that 'the interests of political parties did on occasions create tension. But with good will and focus on the incredible task of building solidarity, we would just overcome the tensions (that some personalities were probably more focused on than others).'[30]

In reality, this happened to differing degrees. The incompatible ideological positions of the CPA and SPA provided competition for ownership of issues and

---

25 Chun, *The British New Left*, 108. This occurred in the first wave of the new left in Britain, according to Chun, as they believed trade unions were not revolutionary. Ibid., 73.
26 Ibid., 26.
27 Meredith Burgmann and Verity Burgmann, *Green Bans, Red Union: Environmental Activism and the New South Wales Builders Labourers' Federation* (Sydney: UNSW Press, 1994), 121–2.
28 It is important to remember, however, that most Australians joined trade unions not because of this, but for the protection and improvement of their working and economic conditions. Deery, 'Union Aims and Methods', 62.
29 Burgmann and Burgmann, *Green Bans, Red Union*, 26.
30 Interview with Andrew Ferguson (student, Chile activist, unionist, Australia), 27 February 2009 [hereinafter Ferguson Interview, 2009], copy in possession of author.

also drove the participation of key activists. The SPA was dismissive of new left radicalism at first, which left the door ajar for CPA influence in some unions as well as in social movements.[31] As we shall see, however, this was rapidly contested.

The Australian political arena was small in the 1970s, and the diminutive size of groups caused them to be less cohesive.[32] There were less political party and union employees than in Britain and there was also a history of less reliance on manifestos in political parties. As Albert Metin noted of Australian labour in 1901: it was *le socialisme sans doctrines*.[33] Furthermore, there was less official communication between organisations and sometimes between members of separate organisations, instead replaced with friendly networks. Size meant that members were more flexible and less likely to stick loyally to their particular party line. Rather, they tended to act according to their consciences, as demonstrated by the previously described actions of Tom Uren. As Walker noted in 1952, Australian socialism was not revolutionary or ruthless, but motivated more by the 'good sense and goodwill of men', a notion supported in this research: political parties engaged in more political squabbling than in planning for a transition to socialism, but individuals found ways to work together notwithstanding.[34] Stephen Deery concurred with these observations, stating that Australian socialists, especially those within the trade union movement, represented 'more a moral dynamic and a set of ideals rather than a blueprint for a new economic and social order'.[35] Prominent activist in the Chilean movement Mavis Robertson remembered that Australians 'did things because they knew they were right, they didn't do things because they were told to do them'.[36] It could be said the collectivist convictions of the left fuelled actions based on goodwill.

The steadfast support from select trade unions formed the base of the Australian solidarity movement. The beginning of the Chilean dictatorship coincided with growth in participatory democracy and mass meetings as well as rank-and-file political activity in Australian unions.[37] For many unions, the Chile movement was not their first or their only involvement with international causes at the time, and in this regard Chile solidarity followed precedents set by previous

---

31 Bramble, *Trade Unionism in Australia*, 53.
32 Observation of Mavis Robertson.
33 As quoted in Kenneth Walker, 'Australia', in *Comparative Labor Movements*, ed. Walter Galenson (New York: Prentice-Hall, 1952), 232.
34 Ibid., 235. E. V. Elliot of the SUA confirmed this view when he wrote 'sometimes we have as many quarrels among the left-wing as we do with the right-wing'. Political parties also fought for dominance in unions through the union elections, yet ironically in doing so they were actually fighting the apolitical nature of the majority of Australian workers rather than taking steps towards revolution. E. V. Elliott, 'Chile: No Trade with Junta: Support the Resistance', *Seamen's Journal* (July–August 1977).
35 Deery, 'Union Aims and Methods', 62. This is supported by Bramble, *Trade Unionism in Australia*, 86, 87.
36 Robertson Interview, 2009.
37 Bramble, *Trade Unionism in Australia*, 38, 47, 49.

international campaigns.³⁸ Unions had previously been involved in the solidarity drive for the Indonesian War of Independence, the Spanish Civil War, and against apartheid, the Greek military junta and the Vietnam War. The involvement in these campaigns was manifested in a manner similar to some actions for Chile: demonstrations, resolutions, boycotts and donations. The Chile solidarity movement was, however, the first sustained Australian union involvement in a Latin American campaign, and would go on to be one of the longest union commitments to an international solidarity movement.

Despite the small number of activists on the Australian left, there was no shortage of solidarity groups with official-sounding names that formed in the years following the coup.³⁹ The movement across Australia was constructed of overlapping and sometimes conflicting groups. The acronym list quickly becomes unmanageable, and the visual map an immense organogram or an 'alphabet soup', as activist Barry Carr put it.⁴⁰ The multiplication of groups in the movement was partly due to the scattered cities across the Australian continent, each tending to function independently of the others, and the distance between them meant there was no national united front as in Britain.

It is perhaps easy to envisage the movement as movements at a State level, because the States functioned differently and worked separately for much of the time. In some ways, this mirrors the political structure of Australia: the States function separately, but within a federation. It was also true more generally of left political parties, whose regional factions and internal coups were legendary.

One further layer of complication of the Chile solidarity committees in Australia was their transient nature. Many committees and groupings did not survive the duration of the dictatorship, and most committees went through squalls and lulls in activity. Moreover, many changed their name, or were not clear at any one time exactly what their name was let alone its correct translation. The written record that was left in the wake of the multiple committees can be misleading. Some committees may have had a membership of fewer than 10, with little political influence and less mobilising power. If, however, they had access to a photocopier or a connection to the media, their influence may be overestimated. It is also important to keep in mind that while the map of

---

38 For example, the maritime boycott of goods to and from Chile was preceded by a boycott of the export of pig iron to Japan. Margo Beasley, *Wharfies: A History of the WWFA* (Sydney: Hallstead Press, 1996); Brian Fitzpatrick and Rowan Cahill, *Seamen's Union of Australia, 1872–1972: A History* (Sydney: Seamen's Union of Australia, 1981); Rupert Lockwood, *Black Armada* (Sydney: Australasian Book Society, 1975).

39 There was also no shortage of union members. In 1975, 58 per cent of the Australian workforce was unionised. Jim Hagan, 'The Australian Trade Union Movement: Context and Perspective, 1850–1980', in *Australian Unions: An Industrial Relations Perspective*, eds Bill Ford and David Plowman (Melbourne: Macmillan, 1983), 51. In 1980, 63 per cent of unionists were in unions affiliated to the ALP. Deery, 'Union Aims and Methods', 88.

40 Interview with Barry Carr (Chile activist, academic, Australia), 5 March 2009 [hereinafter Carr Interview, 2009], copy in possession of author.

committees is complex, some participants confess to knowing only of their own committee. Within each city there were sometimes multiple committees, each drawing on their own idiosyncratic support network.[41]

The archival sources available for the reconstruction of Chile solidarity are inconsistent; often the only hints at the existence of committees in some places are a couple of publications or mentions of protests in newspapers.[42] Tracking each group's complete history would be almost impossible. This chapter, then, gives an impression of the character of the Australian Chile solidarity movement, by way of a more in-depth description of some of the groups and individuals who played an important part in the events of subsequent chapters. These are all focused on Sydney.[43]

This does not suggest a scale of importance, interest or complexity. The choice of emphasis on Sydney is due to four factors. First, the committee which was established in Sydney was more embedded in trade unions than in other Australian cities and thus has yielded more complex relations to be explored. Second, the trade union which gave it most support in the period 1973–78, the AMWU, kept excellent records that are now available to researchers. Third, the location of the AMWU, Seamen's Union of Australia (SUA) and WWFA national offices in Sydney influenced formal union involvement in the Committee for Solidarity with the Chilean People (CSCP) (Sydney), which, due to the nature of the archived collections, is more quantifiable than in other cities. Finally, the green bans of the NSW Builders Labourers' Federation (NSWBLF) had been running for some years by the time of the coup in Chile, which promoted an atmosphere of social participation in many Sydney-based unions.[44] This impetus and ambience contributed to the pool of goodwill and led to strong cross-institutional involvement in the Chile movement.

The reservoir of goodwill that existed towards humanitarian and left issues was created in part from ideology. It was accessed by the Chile movement in Australia not only via organisational links, but by personal networks that

---

41　While the State and local structures functioned quite separately, they did not exist in a vacuum: they often corresponded with each other, and received news from all over the world via travellers, friends, circulars and radical press. They each produced and reproduced pamphlets that made their way around the country and they also cooperated on some of the major events (Chapter Six). In the late 1970s there were attempts at a more assimilated approach to national solidarity. Notwithstanding efforts and intents, national-level integration remained generally cooperative but mostly symbolic. *Solidarity with Chile, June/July Newsletter, 1979*, Papers of GMM; *Robertson to 'friends' re: Inti illimani, Chile Solidarity (1976–1978)*, Papers of Barry Carr; 'Stepping Up Chile Solidarity', *Socialist*, 20 July 1977; Robertson Interview, 2009; *Solidarity with Chile, Information Bulletin, December, 1978*, Papers of GMM.
42　Montenegro reported that a fire at Casa Chile led to lost records. Montenegro, 'La Campaña de Solidaridad con Chile en Australia 1973–1990', 211. The CSCP records were accidentally disposed of by a family member of an activist.
43　A decision almost entirely based on source availability.
44　Burgmann and Burgmann, *Green Bans, Red Union*, 124, 125.

5. Opening doors for Chile: Strategic individuals and networks

crossed ideological lines and party loyalties. Strategic individuals with access to multiple organisations and levels of the labour movement were the ones who enabled the movement to function as it did. The reservoir of goodwill was not bottomless, however, and this chapter demonstrates how the factionalisation of the Chilean arrivals contributed negatively to the continuation of the movement.

In Sydney the post-coup Chile solidarity movement started with a stroke of luck. By chance, and thanks in part to the work of Steve Cooper, the CPA Sydney District Committee had already resolved to sponsor a demonstration in solidarity with Chile.[45] It happened to be the day the Chilean coup occurred. Within hours of the military action in Chile, Sydney activists were on the street. After hearing the news while in a meeting, various members of the WWFA executive attended.[46] Ominously, while there, WWFA organiser Tasnor Bull got into a fight with some Maoists who were, he wrote in his autobiography, already partaking in the dissection of the failings of the UP Government and blaming Allende's death and the coup on the UP's inability to arm the people.[47] Hundreds of activists attended the demonstration, and with the workers' delegates present, the *Tribune* said the crowd was representative of hundreds of thousands of Australians.

The speakers included many prominent union officials and radical activists: Laurie Aarons (CPA), Laurie Carmichael (AMWU), Leo Lenane (WWFA), Joe Owens (Builders Labourers), Frank O'Sullivan (Building Workers' Industrial Union: BWIU), Brian McGahen (Young Communist Movement), Bill Brown (SPA), Malcolm Price (Communist League) and Mike Jones (Socialist Youth Alliance).[48] It was a broad front, and they were united in their shock and anger.

Directly after this protest a group of interested people went to the old boiler makers' building in Castlereagh Street and formed an ad-hoc committee.[49] This was the first of a string of gatherings that spanned the months after the coup, leading to the establishment of the official committee. There was much to discuss at these meetings: solidarity, the pros and cons of the peaceful road and possible support for the resistance. Accordingly, attendance was high. Soon after the initial gathering, 300 people attended a meeting at the Trades Hall in Goulburn Street, Sydney.[50] The meeting was supported and arranged by members of the Association for International Cooperation and Disarmament, whose encouragement of Chile solidarity was unwavering and extremely important in

---

45 For example: Cooper, 'Fighting the Transnational Companies'; 'Solidarity with Chile', *Tribune* [Australia], 4–10 September 1973.
46 Tas Bull, *Tas Bull, An Autobiography: Life on the Waterfront* (Sydney: Harper Collins, 1998), 147.
47 Ibid.
48 Speakers also included: Denis Freney (CPA), Pierina Pirisi (CPA), Jack Cambourn (Engine Drivers and Firemen). 'Action against U.S. over Chile', *Tribune* [Australia], 18–24 September 1973, 3. Maoists persisted in being a difficult presence on the movement front. 'Chile Export Ban Stays', *Socialist*, 4 June 1975.
49 Robertson Interview, 2009.
50 'Solidarity Meetings with Chilean Workers', *Tribune* [Australia], 2–8 October 1973.

the early stages of post-coup solidarity.[51] Professor Ted Wheelwright, a member of the faculty at Sydney University, spoke, and joining him was Tas Bull of the WWFA and Steve Cooper.[52]

Two days after the meeting sponsored by the Association for International Cooperation and Disarmament (AICD), 60 people attended a meeting at which David Holmes of the Socialist Workers' League (SWL) and Denis Freney of the Sydney District Committee CPA debated the lessons of the coup.[53] Holmes said the failure of the Chilean experiment was due to Stalinist betrayal. He blamed Allende and the UP for keeping the working class in the capitalist framework. Freney was more delicate, but did note that the only thing that was certain was that a neutral military never stayed neutral when workers won control.

The debate embodied a delineation in the Chile movement, which occurred from the very first protest with Tas Bull's fisticuffs. It is a dangerous simplification to divide the Australian left between pro and contra armed struggle, or pro-Soviet as opposed to pro-eurocommunism. The division was fuzzy in reality, but the difference in analysis of the Chilean situation nevertheless exacerbated tension within the committee as it attempted to sustain a broad front. From the very first an obvious pattern emerged: many Australian activists used the Chilean situation as a pawn in the wider internecine struggle. Activists could selectively adopt facts to support their arguments for or against a popular front, for or against a revolutionary strategy. Chile could be used to garner local political capital.

Ownership of the Chile issue, and perhaps by proxy the campaign committee, certainly influenced the actions of factionalised individuals; but it was not the only motivation: much of the time, key individuals just got on with the business of solidarity.

The Committee of Solidarity with the Chilean People (CSCP)[54] was formed at a meeting on 18 October 1973 that had been called to discuss solidarity options.[55]

---

51 The building that the Association for International Cooperation and Disarmament (AICD) was based in was actually owned by the AMWU, which had absorbed the building after their recent amalgamation with the Boilermakers. It was on Castlereagh Street in Sydney and was a nucleus of solidarity and peace organisations. The organisations were all roughly aligned underneath the CPA eurocommunist line. In this way, the AMWU provided immediate infrastructure, space and photocopying to the Chile movement, and more specifically to one of the committees that emerged out of it.
52 Wheelwright was also involved in the AICD. See: Association for International Co-operation and Disarmament (Sydney), *The Asian Revolution and Australia* (Sydney: Times Press, 1969); Interview with James Levy (academic, Chile activist), 12 March 2009 [hereinafter Levy Interview, 2009], copy in possession of author; 'Solidarity with the Chilean People', *Tribune* [Australia], 18–24 September 1973, 12; Shane Bentley, 'Tas Bull (1932–2003)', *Green Left*, 18 June 2003. Professor Wheelwright had been in Chile before the coup as well as Steve Cooper. Robertson Interview, 2009.
53 'Solidarity Meetings with Chilean Workers'.
54 CSCP refers to the Sydney committee unless otherwise noted. Reported in the *Tribune* as 'Sydney Committee for Chilean Democracy'. 'Sydney Committee for Chile', *Tribune* [Australia], 23–29 October 1973, 2.
55 Other organisations which aided, or formed around, Chile solidarity included the Latin America Centre and Antorcha in Sydney.

The CSCP philosophy was summed up in the sentence: 'We will support the Chilean people by all means at our disposal, until democracy is once more restored and the monstrous Junta has answered for its bloody crimes.'[56]

This was a statement that, in theory at least, the whole Australian left could embrace. There were 30 unionists present and of the six people elected to the steering committee, four had a primary affiliation to a union. The committee included Dr James Levy, a Latin American studies specialist from the University of New South Wales; Ken McLeod of the AICD; Laurie Steen of the SUA; Jack Baker of the Postal Clerks and Telegraphists' Union; and the AMWU had two prominent members on the committee, James Baird and Greg Harrison.[57]

A demonstration was proposed for 5 November, which was close to the third anniversary of Allende's inauguration as president; however, the unionists on the committee voted against it. They argued that stop-work meetings and other union meetings were more productive than a demonstration.[58] The domination of trade union representatives in the Chile solidarity movement could initially be perceived as controlling and powerful.

This was, however, not necessarily the case as ongoing individual trade unionist involvement was mostly of an ad-hoc nature and sometimes in an unofficial capacity. The committee elected at that first meeting was intended to appear representative, and for that reason included several strategic representatives of unions and/or political parties. There was an understanding, however, that a working group (mostly different people to those on the official committee in the initial months) would undertake the day-to-day decisions and work.[59] Those in that key group of workers were predominantly CPA sympathisers for the first five years of the campaign.

It is possible to divide the main activities of the CSCP into categories: publications, protests, government and parliamentary lobbying, aid to refugees, music concerts and cultural activities.[60] This range of activities was undertaken in a fairly impromptu manner (not planned long term), with the aim of keeping Chile in the minds of Australians and prolonging the consensus of the moral superiority of opposition to the dictatorship that appeared after the coup.

---

56 'Sydney: Slogans in English and Spanish …', *Tribune* [Australia], 18–24 December 1973, 3. Though they later had much more explicit aims. Montenegro, 'La Campaña de Solidaridad con Chile en Australia 1973–1990', 47–8.
57 *NSW Committee for Solidarity with the Chilean People, November 1 1973*, WWFA: Federal Office, N114/932, NBAC: ANU, Canberra; 'Sydney Committee for Chile'.
58 They also argued that the demonstration would be wasted as media attention would be on the Melbourne Cup and the Watergate scandal. It is also possible that the date was offensive to any Maoists or SPA party members who may have been on the committee as they thought Allende or his broad front was the cause of Chile's problems. *NSW Committee for Solidarity with the Chilean People, November 1 1973*.
59 Robertson Interview, 2009.
60 These activities are explored in more detail in the next chapter.

The mobilisation of a united front for Chile was a delicate affair. It involved the activation of networks based around political affiliation or acquaintance. The CPA/independent left bias of the activists in the working group enabled the CSCP to draw on the support of unions/unionists aligned to a similar view. But even across factional differences, activists on the CSCP did not have to try to motivate unionists, because, as Mavis Robertson said, people knew it was right to support solidarity. Letters were sent to trade unions, and most unions responded positively to requests for money or notional support. Robertson's network of CPA and peace contacts facilitated more substantial union support in the form of attendance at events, speakers or delegates' support. Unions were opportunistic, and would express solidarity when provided with an opportunity to do so.

Unions within the SPA sphere of influence, such as sections of the WWFA, SUA, BWIU and Firemen and Deckhands, were utilised by the campaign to a lesser extent in the first years. Men such as Tas Bull within the WWFA would be more naturally sympathetic to approaches from CPA activists. By contrast, Don Henderson's SPA-based network enabled him to mobilise within the Firemen and Deckhands, the BWIU or the SUA. The SPA-aligned unions did take actions separate from the CSCP, and also sent their own representatives to international conferences as a none-too-subtle political gesture. Unions such as the NSWBLF, with its predominantly Maoist leadership and tendency to follow the Beijing line (anti-Allende), were even less likely to cooperate with the CSCP.

It is important in the following chapters, then, to make a distinction between actions initiated by the committee, actions affiliated loosely to the committee and actions completely separate from the committee. As was the case with British solidarity, the Sydney committee did not control or have a hand in all solidarity activities. Certainly, many activities stemmed from the progressive trade unions. What impact the committee did have was due mainly to two factors: first, the moral consensus and pool of goodwill based in the ideology of left politics in Australia, and second, the mobilising power of strategic individuals from within the committee or connected to it.

One of the most important activists in Sydney was Mavis Robertson. Robertson was in Moscow at the time of the coup, at a conference of the World Congress of Peace Forces. When she returned, she very quickly took stock of what was occurring in the CPA regarding Chile and she publicly challenged the oversimplification of the situation facing the Chilean left.[61] She was immediately a leading voice of solidarity.

---

61 Mavis Robertson, 'Protest on Chile Claim', *Tribune* [Australia], 27 November – 3 December 1973, 10. The Chilean Communist Party was 'orthodox' and followed the Moscow line faithfully. Alan Angell, *Politics and the Labour Movement in Chile* (London: Oxford University Press, 1972), 86, 89.

Figure 5.1 Mavis Robertson, 1975.

Source: Photograph from: *Chile Democrático (organo oficial de la izquierda chilena en el exterior Sydney)* 3, Marzo de 1977, from the papers of Gustavo Martin Montenegro, Canberra.

Robertson was born in 1930 and her Irish mother was undoubtedly an influence on her development.[62] She attributed the founding of her desire to support the underdog to her mother, who always 'had her eye on all the little countries'.[63] After joining the Eureka Youth League as a young woman, Robertson soon started writing for the CPA. It was through this organisation that she collected pencils for Cuba in 1960–61, her first engagement with activism with a Latin American theme.[64]

---

62 Her maiden name was Moten.
63 Interview with Mavis Robertson (feminist, peace, CPA and Chile activist, Australia), 31 January 2005 [hereinafter Robertson Interview, 2005], copy in possession of author.
64 'Wanted: A Million Pencils for Cuba', *Tribune* [Australia], 12 July 1961.

Robertson had always been against violence. She believed that any result born of violence was negative, as the act of violence itself distorted the outcome. In the split of the CPA in 1971, Robertson was firmly within the democratic strand of the party, which retained the title CPA.[65] An active feminist, Robertson worked many hours for that cause and she was also involved in the anti-apartheid campaign, Vietnam solidarity and the peace and disarmament movements. She was a vocal and prominent member of the CPA until it disbanded.

By the time of her involvement with the Sydney Chile movement, Robertson was a mature woman, married with two children. Her husband, Alex Robertson, was also a CPA member and was editor of the *Tribune* for 12 years.[66] The long involvement of Robertson and her husband with peace and disarmament was also shared by many prominent left activists such as Laurie Aarons, Bob Gould, Jim Cairns, Denis Freney, Don Hewett and Ken McLeod. The network of peace activists which stretched from business owners to parliamentarians was an invaluable resource for Robertson's career in activism and as a strategic individual in the Chile movement. Her husband's early death in 1974 caused the only gap in Robertson's participation in the campaign before she moved on to other single-issue campaigns in the 1980s.[67]

The peace movement was a common denominator between Steve Cooper and Robertson as well as their involvement in the Eureka Youth League as youngsters.[68] Both were interested in a peaceful transition to socialism, and they had undoubtedly crossed paths at many meetings over the years. Robertson credits Cooper with the initiative of setting up the pre-coup solidarity organisation, which stemmed from his trip to Chile in early 1973. His experience in Chile and his absolute commitment to the cause gave him standing as a Chile expert in the early years of solidarity. Cooper was an ALP member in the 1970s, but his sympathies lay further to the left than the mainstream party.[69] He published articles in the *Tribune* and talked at many CPA meetings, including a special one-day conference called 'The Politics of the Chilean Revolution'.[70] His passion, however, didn't equal bravado. He was a 'quiet, self effacing figure', remembered Mavis Robertson.[71]

---

65 She remained a member of the CPA until 1980.
66 Mavis Robertson, 'Expressing Thanks', *Tribune* [Australia], 16–22 April 1974.
67 The published record left in his wake centres on writing on Papua New Guinea, and he was, along with his wife, heavily involved in the peace movement. Alec Robertson, 'A Communist's New Guinea. "Essentially the Same ... as Vietnam"', *New Guinea and Australia, The Pacific and South-East Asia* 6, no. 2 (1971). Mavis Robertson also presented a paper at the conference: '*The Australian Anti-War Movement and the International Movement*', a paper presented to the National Anti-War Conference by Mavis Robertson, 1971, 1988.0048.0128, Elsie Gare Collection No. 1, National Museum of Australia, Canberra.
68 *The War Lovers, Steve Cooper*, 1988.0048.0046, Elsie Gare Collection No. 1, National Museum of Australia, Canberra; Robertson Interview, 2005.
69 Cooper Interview, 2005.
70 'Australian Communists Look at Chile Events', *Tribune* [Australia], 6–12 November 1973.
71 Robertson Interview, 2005.

While Cooper was writing, organising and agitating behind the scenes and Robertson was pulling on her network of contacts, the campaign's figurehead was Senator Anthony Mulvihill.[72] Mulvihill was a life member of the Australian Railways Union, who had started his career as a shop steward at the Chullora railway yards. In the 1960s he was assistant general secretary of the NSW branch of the ALP, where he became known for representing the centre-aligned Catholics.[73] Ron Dyer, in Mulvihill's obituary in 2001, described his position within the ALP: 'Mulvihill was always regarded as a member of the right wing of the ALP, now known as Centre Unity, but he described himself as a progressive centre liner.'[74]

A keen environmentalist, Mulvihill was involved in conservation campaigns and in the green movement that fought for responsible planning in Sydney. Moreover, Mulvihill was committed to immigrant workers and immigrant issues and his interest and advocacy for Chilean immigrants started immediately after the coup.[75] He promised to help clear up Chilean issues if he secured the chairmanship of the Commonwealth Immigration Advisory Council.[76]

Mulvihill brought this experience and an extensive network as well as the resources and legitimacy that came with the title of senator along with him when he acted for the CSCP. Using Mulvihill as a figurehead was a similar ploy to that used by the British Chile Solidarity Campaign with high-profile unionist Alex Kitson. He may not have been a chief organiser, but having a senator's name on the top of the campaign letterhead certainly did no harm. In practical terms, the association meant that Mulvihill was automatically receptive and active when the CSCP approached him on specific issues. For example, the senator issued various requests for explanation to the Government in 1975 about the issue of immigration. On top of this, Mulvihill's centre-right alignment within the ALP suggested the Sydney committee was a coalition rather than a cause dominated by radicals. It gave authority to the campaign's assertions of being a broad front. This perception made it easier and more acceptable for less politically radical people to participate in the movement.[77] Senator Mulvihill's relative alignment to the right was not a problem for the working group.[78] Robertson had a history of working in united fronts on single issues.[79] Robertson remembered that she

---

72 *Solidaridad con Chile: Committee for Solidarity with the Chilean People*, September 20, 1979; *The Trades and Labour Council of the ACT*, Z147 box 57, NBAC: ANU, Canberra.
73 Nonetheless, he was not always steadfastly centre. Uren, *Straight Left*, 83, 98.
74 Ron Dyer, 'Death of Former Senator James Anthony Mulvihill', *NSW Parliament Legislative Council* (8 March 2001), 12449.
75 'Govt. Told: "Don't Recognise Chile"', 2.
76 *Letter from J. A. Mulvihill to C. Fitzgibbon, August 1975*, WWFA: Federal Office, N114/932, NBAC: ANU, Canberra.
77 This was a similar effect as the NUM delegation report from Britain, whose less-radical delegation members reinforced the more radical movement.
78 Robertson Interview, 2009.
79 Cooper et al. Conversation, 2007.

and Mulvihill 'had worked in the past and we worked again in other things, and he knew that I was of the left and I knew that he was of the right, but we were interested in an issue and we worked together'.[80]

Not all political differences resulted in such peaceful working conditions. Chileans entering Australia found it hard to understand how such a man could lead the campaign.[81] They were themselves heavily divided and with their arrival the sectarian spectrum in Sydney became confusing and crowded.

Despite the interest on the part of Australian political parties to 'secure a presence amongst the immigrant community',[82] any dissection of the UP Government or 'programmatic debate' that was raised was hastily put aside, for fear of damaging the real aim of the campaign, which was to express unified solidarity.[83] In fact, the debate 'would inevitably be brought up again and again', said Barry Carr, 'partly through Chileans, but … that was a particularly sensitive issue'.[84]

The Chileans did not initially understand that there were two Marxist parties in Australia. Describing divergent political views worked against the ethos of the unified solidarity movement. This realisation created 'some awkwardness', remembered Barry Carr.[85] The dominant groups within the Chilean community, the communists and socialists, could not sit easily with the principal party which was active and supportive of the committee, the CPA, whose eurocommunist identity was seen as a betrayal of Moscow.[86] According to Carr, it was a 'permanent source of tension in Melbourne'[87] and this awkwardness was expressed through creation of the committees whose memberships were closed to anyone but Chileans.[88]

In October 1974 the Comite Chileno de Liberación (Free Chile Committee Sydney) was established with two of the three Martin Montenegro brothers on its executive. It was a Chilean immigrant committee, which focused, according to Gustavo Martin Montenegro, on the needs of the Chilean community;[89] but not all Chileans joined it. Many overflowed into the CSCP or joined both. In

---

80 Robertson Interview, 2009.
81 Ibid.
82 Carr Interview, 2009.
83 *Against political exclusionism: For a United Front Against the Repression in Chile—Spartacist League*, Plumbers and Gasfitters Employees Union of Australia: Federal Office, N133/158, NBAC: ANU, Canberra.
84 Carr Interview, 2009.
85 Ibid.
86 Ibid.
87 Ibid.
88 While committees closed to anyone but Chileans were created in Sydney also, they were not as long lasting as the Melbourne committees. The Free Chile Committee (Melbourne) and the Support Committee for the Chilean Resistance were groups for Chileans only. *To the workers, students and people of Australia*, Papers of GMM.
89 The division between 'Australian' and 'Chilean', or perhaps 'local' and 'expat', committees also happened in Melbourne. Montenegro, 'La Campaña de Solidaridad con Chile en Australia 1973–1990', 88, 89.

Sydney the separation between local and expatriate communities definitely contributed to the growing complexity of the solidarity situation, possibly to the detriment of the campaign. In fact, sectarian behaviour in the political scene around the CSCP increased as Chileans continued to arrive.

The separate Chilean committee exemplified an emerging problem within the Chile movement: the separate aims of the Australians and the Chileans. Chilean arrivals in Australia had a difficult time separating their own internal political objectives and ambitions from the Australian Chile solidarity movement. They could not imagine that the solidarity movement was a movement for the expression of Australian sentiments. The CSCP became property over which Chilean political groupings tried to maintain authority. Robertson concluded: 'They came as a highly politicised grouping with their own political loyalties, expressed in the formation in Australia of party groups.'[90] Additionally, the collapse of the popular front in Chile made many of them feel they would never be able to work together again despite visiting Chilean leaders imploring them to do so.[91] The expatriate Chilean attitude collided with the push of CPA activists for broad-front solidarity.

This disjuncture between the nationalities had a profound long-term effect on the movement. Whereas the stated aim of many Australians was to support a 'free Chile' (and later to agitate on human rights issues), Chileans agitated for a *particular type* of free Chile, with a particular type of ruling party or political system. Often, in practice, they agitated to gain control of the committee or privileged positions in exile to the detriment of the movement.

The establishment of Chilean political groups in exile occurred all over the world, and Australia was no exception. An Australia-wide UP network was set up, with the national office in Sydney; but the UP itself was made up of separate parties and within them came the sectarian politics that were always strong in Chile, and perhaps enhanced by the traumatic coup and dictatorship.[92]

The UP's constituent units caused trouble due to the lack of clear organisation and cooperation between individuals on the ground in Australia. But the lack of UP control over the constituent groups in Australia did not mean the Chilean

---

90 Carr Interview, 2009.
91 Robertson Interview, 2009; *Programme Results—Chilean Trade Union Delegation to Australia, 11–20 September 1975*, Amalgamated Metal Workers' and Shipwrights Union (Aust.) (AMWSU), E262/137, NBAC: ANU, Canberra.
92 For more information on the effect of exile on Chilean politics, see: Alan Angell and Susan Carstairs, 'The Exile Question in Chilean Politics', *Third World Quarterly* 9, no. 1 (1987), 148–67; Diana Kay, *Chileans in Exile* (Wolfeboro, NH: Longwood Academic, 1987); T. Kushner and K. Knox, 'Refugees from Chile'; Alan Angell, 'International Support for the Chilean Opposition 1973–1989: Political Parties and the Role of Exiles', in *The International Dimensions of Democratization*, ed. Lawrence Whitehead (Oxford: Oxford University Press, 2001), 175–201; Patria-Roman Velazquez, 'Latin Americans in London and the Dynamics of Diasporic Identities', in *Comparing Postcolonial Diasporas*, eds Michelle Keown, David Murphy and James Procter (London: Palgrave Macmillan, 2009).

population was disorganised. Robertson explains: 'Amongst that small band of disorganised Chileans, if you have a small core that is organised, it is pretty clear that they start to get their own way, and that was starting to be reflected in the committee.'[93]

The organised group to which she referred was the Chilean Communist Party. Support for the Soviet Union was ingrained in the party and Chilean communists could simply not understand the new left's rejection of the Soviet Union.[94] Many Chilean Communist Party members were shocked to find the CPA's eurocommunist agenda, and felt a natural alignment with members of the SPA. Some Chilean communists accused CPA members of not being 'true communists'.[95] The Chilean Communist Party did not suffer as many splits as other Chilean parties in exile. It was always an orthodox party, and many of its leaders were exiled to the USSR. The party benefited from this consistent relationship.[96]

Other political groupings had more trouble finding partnerships with Australian parties. The Chilean political party Movimiento de Izquierda Revolucionaria (MIR: Movement of the Revolutionary Left) also established itself, but had trouble finding mass support due to their insistence on armed struggle, which ruled out potential support from the CPA, ALP and any moderate groupings.[97] The MIR was always an awkward force in Australia, remembered Barry Carr, because it had a small number of the very active Chileans affiliated to it so suffered from strong vocal chords in a weak body.[98]

The Chilean socialists also formed in Australia, despite their international organisation moving in and out of alignment with the UP in exile and suffering internal splits.[99] Factional politics within the Chilean community ran deep and were sometimes bitter. As Andrew Ferguson remembered, 'they replicated the divisions and tendencies from Chile in the solidarity movement. So it was a polemical, tedious exercise.'[100]

Robertson remembered being conscious of the unrelated aims of the Chileans and Australians:

---

93   Robertson Interview, 2009.
94   Angell, *Politics and the Labour Movement in Chile*; Robertson Interview, 2005.
95   Robertson Interview, 2005.
96   Angell and Carstairs, 'The Exile Question in Chilean Politics', 164.
97   This is noted by Montenegro ('La Campaña de Solidaridad con Chile en Australia 1973–1990', 42), and also in anecdotal conversations with Chilean community members with the author.
98   Carr Interview, 2009.
99   Angell and Carstairs, 'The Exile Question in Chilean Politics', 165.
100 Ferguson Interview, 2009.

> Basically, it did not interest me as to the stance that they were going to take on various things. What really interested me was that we didn't get so imbedded in what they wanted to do to the detriment of what we were capable of doing as Australians in Australia.[101]

It was hard for Australians to understand the different groups, the differences between groups as well as the differences within groups. Robertson remembered trying

> to work out where the MIR stood, where the Socialist Party [of Chile] in its various computations stood, where [stood] the communists in their various computations, never mind the little radicals this that and the other and the Christian something or others, the smaller your group was, the less likely it was to be cohesive anyway.

She continued: 'And every one of the Chilean political factions, you could only meet in a telephone box. I mean there is not enough time in life, actually, to get to the bottom of all these things.'[102]

Steve Cooper even remembered a group in Chile which believed that life existed on other planets, and that a solidarity connection should be made with them. 'Intergalactic solidarity', he called it, laughing.[103]

Australians found the strength of Chilean party loyalty very unusual.[104] Chileans stuck to '*la linea*' (the party line) so strongly it was cause for tired ridicule among Australian activists. Here we strike at the fundamental problem: the political sensibilities of Australian and Chilean activists differed. Chileans were often found publishing and reciting party manifestos (which were in a constant state of flux themselves). The Australian left saw the passive yet passionate party discipline of the Chileans as being archaic and a cause for paralysis.[105] The loyalty and dependence on *la linea* were exacerbated by the fact that they adhered quite strictly to the formal hierarchy of their chosen political parties, most now re-formed in exile with leaders in France, Italy, Russia or East Germany.[106]

When a Chilean Communist Party member was charged with what was considered official party business, they expected the Australian political party they were approaching would respect the formal and official nature of their approach and

---

101 Robertson Interview, 2009.
102 Ibid.
103 Cooper et al. Conversation, 2007.
104 Carr Interview, 2009.
105 Ibid.
106 Ibid. Writing in 1994, Montenegro blamed many of the problems and infighting of the Chilean exiled left which arrived in Australia on the Chilean Communist Party, whose adherence to internal party hierarchical structure frustrated other groups. Montenegro was of course not a communist party member but a member of the Christian left. His brother, Guillermo, was a UP committee member. How much of the adherence was due to political culture specifically in the Chilean Communist Party or generally in the Chilean left is unclear. Montenegro, 'La Campaña de Solidaridad con Chile en Australia 1973–1990', 90.

their representative legitimacy.[107] In such an 'official' capacity, Chileans desired direct access to the upper hierarchy of the Australian left, despite their lack of individual connections or public profile.

Chileans did not acknowledge that much of the time solidarity functioned without any deep action from, or explicit approval of, the Australian political elite. As already described, activism in Australia operated through networks of friends and acquaintances and political allies at a grassroots level. Those who had the amount of time necessary to organise in Chile solidarity were very rarely from the upper hierarchy of the labour movement. Chileans did not understand the Australian political reality—'and why should they?' asked Robertson.[108] She continued: 'some of them wanted to do things in the political processes that were quite inappropriate and, basically, what we tried to do was to find solutions.'[109]

The result of the clashes of political repertoire was a range of mutual misunderstandings. For example: meetings were long. At the beginning of the 1970s they were conducted in English.[110] Even so, Chileans used them as opportunities to air political manifestos and engage in combat with other factions within the expatriate left. Robertson remembered: 'We would have meetings and they would behave badly, then afterwards they would say "we behaved badly and we shouldn't have done that" and you know. Because they knew that people were getting frustrated about these sorts of meetings.'[111]

Soon, Chilean factions were assembling before solidarity meetings to discuss tactics. Australians activists were so uncomfortable with the politicking and inability to focus on the 'big issue' that, one by one, they gradually ceased attending meetings. Andrew Ferguson said: 'most Anglos wouldn't put up with it.'[112]

By 1978, meetings were hours long and often conducted in Spanish, which indicates that very few Australians were present.[113] Ferguson remembered meetings of this period went for three or four hours and there were 'lots of long

---

107 Further, Chileans often wanted to speak directly with parliamentary or union secretaries. Australian activists only wanted to take the high-profile Chileans to meet figures such as Bob Hawke as a constant stream of Chilean refugees was just as likely to erode goodwill as to enhance it. The ACTU was in fact engaged in a sort of rearguard action trying to support the Whitlam Government and the ALP in this period and was as such distracted. Robertson Interview, 2009.
108 Ibid.
109 Ibid.
110 Levy Interview, 2009.
111 Robertson Interview, 2009.
112 Ferguson Interview, 2009.
113 The meetings were '[o]verwhelmingly Chileans, with a few people from the Latin American left, and a couple of people from a non Latin American background that were there for political parties on the left in Australia'. Ibid.

5. Opening doors for Chile: Strategic individuals and networks

winded polemics'.[114] He was not fluent in Spanish, and at first at the meetings he recalled that he 'understood virtually nothing in terms of the political discussion, except an occasional word, the thumping of the table sort of things … and the movement in the room, and then at some point somebody would summarise what was going on, and you'd have a feel for it'.[115]

There were very few Australians who had the patience for this: Chilean politics had 'worn people down'.[116] The problem of the meetings demonstrates the imperfect fit of the two political repertoires.

The integration of Chileans into the Australian political left was minimal, and very troubled. Many groups could not find an Australian group of similar ideology with whom to integrate, and they found it hard to translate their political vocabulary to suit the Australian political reality. In short, the Chile solidarity movement suffered under the effects of the two sets of disparate sectarian tensions (both the Australian and the Chilean), each pulling internally and between each other.

As a result of these tensions, major change came to the CSCP Sydney organisation in 1978.

It had started as a united-front (though CPA-piloted) organisation, and gradually Chileans (mostly Chilean Communist Party members) started to direct meetings. Soon, those Australians still involved were predominantly aligned with the SPA, and friendly to the Soviet-aligned Chileans.

Steve Cooper, who had worked with the campaign since its inception, recalls that it was around 1978 when the SPA started to take renewed interest in the CSCP. They wished to oppose the revisionists or eurocommunists (such as Robertson), and in turn, support the growing strength of certain Chileans with whom their political alliances had matured.[117] In doing so they scored morality points; they were the 'owners' of solidarity against the dictatorship. Though Robertson did not think there were any problems within the committee that were made worse by the return of SPA interest, their loose alliance with the Communist Party of Chile would influence events to come.[118]

'Suddenly', remembered Robertson, 'there was some woman put on the committee whom no one had ever heard of before, and the next thing you know she's going to some overseas conference'.[119]

---

114 Ibid.
115 Ibid.
116 Robertson Interview, 2009.
117 See, for example: 'Stepping up Chile Solidarity', which is the first time the SPA newspaper spoke of the CSCP activities in such a manner.
118 Robertson Interview, 2009.
119 Ibid.

The activists of the first five years were being pushed out.

Those Australians who left early avoided more personal attacks. Perhaps the most scurrilous of the sectarian interactions were those towards the end of the 1970s, which surrounded Cooper's exit from the committee.[120] There was a rumour circulated that Cooper was in fact an agent of the Australian Secret Intelligence Service (ASIS) or the Central Intelligence Agency (CIA).[121] This rumour almost certainly came from Chileans from within the Chilean Communist Party. In 2009, Andrew Ferguson said he could not remember 'any public discussion at any meeting about Steve being associated with ASIO [Australian Security Intelligence Organisation] or anything like that ... I heard suggestions and innuendo about that from some individuals, and I can't remember who they are, but [that was] when Steve stopped his involvement'.[122]

The rumour made it impossible for Cooper to continue to work on the committee. He remembered that it was not quite a crude block vote, but he was voted off.[123] Mavis Robertson recalled a slightly different story: that Cooper just left the committee with no vote being taken. 'Because why would you stay with people who hate you?'.[124]

This overt piece of factional warfare was a turning point. Almost all the people who had devoted their time to the committee for the first five years left over the next few months.[125] Robertson was appalled that such an attack would occur on a fellow activist. Even though she was perhaps the most prominent CPA adherent of all of those involved in the CSCP Sydney, she said she was not attacked because 'I'm tougher. It is perfectly obvious that I am well connected. And, no one would believe rumours like that'.[126]

Her strategic importance and profile also protected her. Robertson was the general secretary of the CPA and had been working for the Federated Engine Drivers and Firemen's Association of Australia, yet she was more powerful because of her network of acquaintances.[127] Her relationship (through the peace movement) with parliamentarians elevated the level of her influence in the hierarchy of the left in Australia. Robertson thought that the rumour

---

120   Cooper et al. Conversation, 2007.
121   The same thing happened to academic James Levy, who was accused of working for the CIA. He was unable to continue to work with those who would make such offensive remarks.
122   Ferguson Interview, 2009.
123   Cooper et al. Conversation, 2007.
124   Robertson Interview, 2009.
125   Ibid.
126   Ibid.
127   *Chile Democrático (no. 3 Sydney, Marzo de 1977)*, Papers of GMM.

> was one of those things that made me realise that I needed to start moving on, if that is just what you get for all the things that Steve Cooper did, then I don't want to be involved with all these people. After all, they are all safe now, they are in Australia.[128]

While these Australian activists left the committee (though never stopped supporting the movement), another entered, who would be just as influential. Andrew Ferguson had been a member of the ALP since he was fifteen years old. Ferguson's political pedigree was impeccable. His father was deputy premier of New South Wales and his elder brothers would later become a federal minister and national secretary of the Australian Council of Trade Unions (ACTU) respectively. When he went to university he became active in student politics, and at a rally in Hyde Park in Sydney in about 1977 he met a man called Tito, who handed him a leaflet on the atrocities occurring in Chile. Ferguson already had an interest in the revolutionary politics of Latin America, particularly those of the more militant left, so the two men had a short conversation. Shortly after, Ferguson visited Tito, whose real name was Hector Perez, at his house in western Sydney.[129] While Tito may have started with the objective of recruiting for solidarity work, the two were soon firm friends. It was this friendship that was the deciding factor for Ferguson to become involved in the CSCP.[130] He started to attend solidarity meetings.

Soon, with the exit of other Australian activists, Ferguson was taking on more and more work for the campaign. He took over its administration, typing newsletters, making bookings and phone calls and chasing unions for funding. 'I spent perhaps ten hours a week doing solidarity work', Ferguson remembered, 'maybe fifteen. And also, it was a part of my social life, friendships, girlfriends and so on. So it was all involved in the same thing.'[131] At a time when many Australian activists were leaving, Ferguson thought he stayed on because his 'tolerant and patient personality' enabled him to deal more effectively with the Chileans and their political actions.[132] But more than this, the relationships he had struck up were what protected and motivated him, at least in part.

Ferguson's admiration for and friendship with Tito were coupled with political alignment. While Ferguson had been a member of the ALP since he was a young man, he admitted he was 'more a member of the [ALP] out of a tactical consideration than a philosophical commitment, and very much from the left'.[133]

---

128 Robertson Interview, 2009.
129 'Tito' was an affectionate name, also used to protect himself and his acquaintances from persecution. Perez was involved in the CUT (Central Unica de Trabajadores, the trades union congress of Chile) organisation in Australia, and was the representative of that organisation in Australia for many years.
130 Ferguson Interview, 2009.
131 Ibid. Ferguson would in fact go on to marry one of the Chilean women.
132 Ibid.
133 Ibid.

After finishing his first university degree, he went to work with the BWIU, which had a long history of communist leaders and during that period was an SPA-aligned union. This meant that Ferguson and Tito (Chilean Communist Party) had an ideological alliance. The fact that Chilean communists propagated the relationship with the SPA, while most Chilean groupings were unable to make such a link with an Australian faction, 'helped to really give a form to the Chilean communists', and facilitate their dominance of the committee.[134] Solidarity committees, according to theorist Peter Waterman, often identify with a particular leadership claiming to be representative of workers rather than the real workers of the recipient country, and the adoption of the Chilean communists in Sydney in the late 1970s is a case in point.[135]

The fact that Ferguson professed to be 'more motivated by the agenda of the radical left, than by humanitarianism' also suited the aims of the political Chileans. Ferguson was not 'captive to the political tendency in [his] union',[136] and said that though he was sympathetic to the SPA line, he also understood eurocommunism and had a productive relationship with self-determinists such as Mavis Robertson.

Ferguson was a strategic individual in more ways than just his political beliefs and ability as an interlocutor. Being a Ferguson opened doors. One activist remembered that 'people would have been very mindful that he was a member of this famous family'. The political pedigree of this individual gave him access to levels within the labour movement higher than his actual standing (when first involved with the CSCP, he was in student politics). Ferguson also created what he called a 'new front of solidarity work' by taking the Chile issue up inside the Young Labor Party, where he remembered that few people were interested in internationalism.[137] Further, his rapidly ascending path within the union made him increasingly useful to the campaign. His involvement also pleased the union hierarchy as it interfaced neatly with the new social focus of the BWIU. Ferguson's positions in the union and in the CSCP were mutually reinforcing.

Key individuals, such as Ferguson and Robertson, sustained the Chile movement in Sydney. Without their networks the movement would have faded, as Chilean exiles were unable to create the opportunities necessary to harness trade union support and activity. Ferguson admitted: 'I could open doors into a union that, people who couldn't speak English could struggle with … they just couldn't get through the bureaucracy. Mavis could, or I could.'[138]

---

134   Robertson Interview, 2009.
135   Waterman, *Globalization, Social Movements and the New Internationalisms*, 135.
136   Ferguson Interview, 2009.
137   Ibid.
138   Ibid.

The local factional activity did affect the path of the CSCP in Sydney, but only became explosively destructive when combined with Chilean exile factional activity. The reservoir of goodwill for the newly exiled could not be drawn on indefinitely. Solidarity committees have been prone to 'self-subordination to the victim'—that is, local activists subordinate their own standards and judgments to those of the victims, as their very victimhood bestows moral authority upon them.[139] Perhaps for this reason, Chilean parties in exile in Australia got away with so much. It is difficult to theorise and easy to judge the actions of the exiles in this situation. It is important to remember that their disruptiveness may have been an expression of their unease. Their efforts and desires may have been to make what had occurred in Chile mean *something*: to not let the terror in and the destruction of 'their Chile' be forgotten. The Chileans fell into a community of consideration in Australia, although it was not inexhaustible. Despite problems within the campaign, trade union internationalist sentiment being played out through the Chile issue (though often ad hoc and sometimes opportunist) remained quite consistent for the duration of the solidarity movement.

---

139 Waterman, Globalization, Social Movements and the New Internationalisms, 134.

6. 'Chile is not alone': Actions for resource-sensible organisations

For a grouping formed on the run, the Sydney May Day Committee was ambitious: for the first May Day after the Chilean coup, they invited Madame Allende to Australia.

At best the committee was a loose amalgam of interested parties, most of whom were members or representatives of the SPA. While their invitation was not accepted, they were visited by Aída Insunza and Luis Muñoz.[1] Insunza had been a professor of labour law at the University of Chile, and the wife of the former minister for justice.[2] She was a woman of 'small build but considerable presence', reported the *Tribune*.[3] Muñoz was a CUT member and a journalist.[4]

Insunza and Muñoz were representatives of the Chilean Anti-Fascist Solidarity Committee, which operated out of Berlin.[5] Their visit cost $4000 and that money was collected by a wide range of political and trade union organisations including, for example, $73.43 from a reception put on by nine unions at the Carlton Bowls Club in Melbourne.[6] The visitors led the May Day procession in Brisbane as well as in Sydney.[7] At an associated talk in Sydney, where Insunza spoke in English and Muñoz spoke through an interpreter, there were many questions about arming the people in Chile and the failings of the UP Government, as would be expected from an SPA-dominated audience. Eric Aarons concluded that despite the need for analysis, 'the main thing for the audience there, I sensed, was solidarity and warmth with all fighting for Chile's liberation'.[8]

While this may have been the case on the surface, beneath the facade, sectarian disquiet burbled. But just how much did social movement infighting effect

---

1   This visitor should not be confused with Jorge Muñoz, missing person in the later 1970s, or Mario Muñoz, over whom there was a considerable campaign and squabbling in 1976. 'Trotskyists Profit from Munoz Campaign', *Socialist*, 15 September 1976.
2   Her husband, Sergio Insunza, also spoke at the Stalinist-organised May Day rally in Sydney in 1974. He was welcomed on the front page of the SPA organ, the *Socialist*. 'Editorial: May Day—Internationalism', *Socialist*, May 1974, 3; 'Welcome to Sergio Insunza!', *Socialist*, May 1974, 1; *From the Chilean Underground, April 1974*, AMWSU, E262/137, NBAC: ANU, Canberra; 'Chile One Year After', *Workers News*, 19 September 1974, 2. Jim Baird followed up with Insunza while he was in Geneva later in 1974. Jim Baird, 'Chilean Junta on Trial before I.L.O.', *Tribune* [Australia], 12 November 1974.
3   Eric Aarons, 'Chile Resistance Fighters' Visit', *Tribune* [Australia], 7–13 May 1974.
4   'Chilean Guests' Appeal! "Keep up the Fight, Venceremos!"', *SPA*, June 1974; Aarons, 'Chile Resistance Fighters' Visit'.
5   WWFA (Syd.), SUA and Firemen and Deckhands union carried most of the cost of their visit. This makes sense due to high-level SPA participation in those unions. *Sydney May Day Committee, May 2 1974*, PGEUA: Federal Office, N133/203, 'International Matters' 1973–1975, NBAC: ANU, Canberra.
6   Ibid.
7   J. Steele, 'Big Success of Brisbane May Day Commemoration', *Seamen's Journal* (May 1974).
8   Aarons, 'Chile Resistance Fighters' Visit'.

trade union support for the movement as a whole? This chapter accompanies the discussion of Britain by focusing on indirect actions organised externally to trade unions but completely reliant on them for support. The activities include demonstrations, international conferences, tours of Chileans to Australia and cultural events. The CSCP's reliance on trade unions for support in these activities was not parasitic. The relationship between the CSCP (and other committees around the country) and trade unions was symbiotic. Trade unions' use of the campaign was a 'resource-light' method of expressing internationalist sentiment.

The tension between political factions had erupted by the first anniversary of the coup.[9] Activists from the Communist League and the Spartacist League involved in the organisation of the Melbourne rally came to fisticuffs over the failure of the Communist League to photocopy a rally pamphlet. In Sydney a protest was to be organised by the CSCP along with the Chile Action Committee (Socialist Workers League, Communist League, Socialist Youth Alliance and Spartacists).[10] The *Socialist* called people to the rally: 'The bonfires of books in Hitler's Germany 40 years ago have been re-lit in the suffering republic of Chile. She needs your help.'[11]

How much help the 11 September anniversary demonstration would offer the Chilean nation was unclear, especially since much energy in the lead-up to the event was used in internecine struggles. The separate committees did not have different aims: both wanted the junta to end and for repression to cease in Chile. Where they differed was in their interpretations of revolutionary strategy: the CSCP generally supported Allende's actions, and the Chile Action Committee believed Allende had failed the Chilean people. This situation was complicated by a power struggle within the CSCP group, as SPA activists tried to gain control of the high-profile first anniversary march, before retreating for some time.

The CSCP would not let any Chile Action Committee members speak on its platform. As a consequence, the Spartacists alleged the CSCP was dominated by the SPA and that the CSCP only recognised unions, not minority political parties.[12] In *Direct Action* (printed by the Socialist Youth Alliance), David Holmes wrote that the CSCP was in fact anti-unification and anti-broad front as it ignored a cross-partisan meeting that was being organised and just called the demonstration 'on its own and demanded that everyone join the [CSCP] and work for it. This set the pattern for the behaviour of the [CSCP] and its Stalinist supporters from then on in.'[13]

---

9   *Open Letter to the Communist League, from Marie Hotschilt, Spartacist League*, Plumbers and Gasfitters Employees Union of Australia: Federal Office, N133/158, NBAC: ANU, Canberra.
10 The Chile Action Committee sometimes called themselves the September 11 Chile Action Committee. 'Solidarity with Chile on September 11th', *Socialist*, September 1974, 1.
11 Ibid.
12 *Against Political Exclusionism*.
13 'Actions Protest Repression in Chile', *Direct Action: A Socialist Fortnightly*, no. 70, (20 September 1974), 6.

These sort of comments indicate that there were various SPA members active within the CSCP at the time, as the CPA was pro-broad front and eurocommunist and was implementing new left strategies of engaging with social movements.

By way of compromise, the Chile Action Committee and the CSCP came to an informal agreement that the CSCP would hold one rally, and following that, the Chile Action Committee would lead on to theirs.[14]

The rally was to start outside the Lan Chile offices at 5 Elizabeth Street at 4.30 pm on 11 September 1974.[15] Senator Arthur Gietzelt, Jim Baird of the AMWU, Bob Bolger of the WWFA and Chilean refugees would address the gathered crowd outside Lan Chile. Nineteen trade unions had their names listed on the accompanying pamphlet. At 5.30 pm the demonstrators would march via the US Consulate to Martin Place, where the Chile Action Committee's rally would establish what they called an 'open platform' (in an implied contrast to the CSCP's platform).[16] Only one trade unionist put their name to the Chile Action Committee platform: Bob Pringle of the NSW Builders' Labourers Federation.[17]

The CSCP organised the Lan Chile platform under a pro-Allende pamphlet and the Chile Action Committee (CAC) advertised for that demonstration as well as another in Martin Place under the understanding that there would be joint publicity for the rallies. The Chile Action Committee distributed more than 12 000 leaflets and undertook an 'energetic paste up drive' around the city in the weeks before the demonstration.[18] The CSCP did not feel the need to do similar work because their union connections would assure them of a good crowd to their section of the march and would undertake the printing on their behalf.[19]

Tension was building and then a report aligned with the Chile Action Committee noted that the SPA (mentioned specifically, not the CSCP) tried to sabotage the agreement and wreck the second rally by speaking over time.[20]

The Spartacists weighed into the fight. They published an eight-page denouncement of the 'reformists' and 'Stalinists' in the CSCP. It accused the CSCP of favouring the return of a UP government to power in Chile rather than returning to democracy.[21] The Spartacists argued that the Chile Action Committee did not try to push a line like the CSCP did with their pro-Allende

---

14 Ibid.
15 'Chile Inflation and Repression Hit all Sectors', *Tribune* [Australia], 3 September 1974.
16 Ernest Mandel was to speak on that platform. David Homes, 'CPA, SPA Sectarianism in Chile Defence', *Direct Action*, 2 September 1974.
17 Though the CAC-organised platform did have a large amount of student support (as demonstrated in the *Tharkuna*). 'Actions Protest Repression in Chile'.
18 Ibid.
19 'Chile: Solidarity Expressed in Aust. Meetings', *Tribune* [Australia], 30 July 1974.
20 'Actions Protest Repression in Chile'; *Against Political Exclusionism*.
21 *Against Political Exclusionism*.

pamphlets.²² Yet, the Spartacists burnt their bridges by then attacking the Chile Action Committee and its Socialist Workers League and Communist League constituents. They accused them of capitulating to the CSCP and called them 'pseudo-Trotskyist'. Slashing and burning their way through the labour movement, they turned their attention to trade unions, accusing them of being weak and conceding to the dominant pro-Allende sentiment of the rally. The Spartacists would go to the Lan Chile rally, and support their own open platform, separate from the two already organised. Besides the Spartacists, who would attend such a platform was unclear. They suspected it would be shut down by the CSCP supporters anyway.²³ The fact there were three rallies in the same place in support of the same cause brings to mind the old adage: the left divides, the right rules.

But really, the internecine battle that surrounded the first demonstration emphasises the competition that occurred for the political ownership of the Chile issue. Demonstrations such as those on the anniversaries were part of the regular strategies in the repertoire of trade union political tactics and were straightforward to support from the point of view of unions. At the time, one commentator said: 'international protests have a definite impact on the behaviour of the Chilean Junta.'²⁴ But like many activities in the repertoire of solidarity actions undertaken, they were indirect—that is, non-industrial—*and* organised from outside trade unions *yet* reliant upon them for success. Political factionalism played a role through the whole solidarity movement, both in and out of unions, including Australian participation in international solidarity events.

Australians started travelling almost immediately after the coup and the first trip was to Helsinki for a conference under the title of 'International Conference of Solidarity with the Chilean People'.²⁵ Bernie Taft, Mavis Robertson and Laurie Aarons were in Moscow for talks with the Soviet Communist Party before the World Congress of Peace Forces.²⁶ Taft and Robertson were contacted with the request to travel to Helsinki. Robertson remembered that 'we just left the talks, which were not very useful anyway (with the Communist Party it was like talking to a brick wall) and we went by train' to Helsinki.²⁷ Samuel Goldbloom from Victoria and Senator George Georges (ALP Queensland) also attended the first Helsinki event. Goldbloom was an official of the Campaign for International Cooperation and Disarmament in Victoria and Georges was

---

22 Ibid.
23 Ibid.
24 'Actions Protest Repression in Chile'.
25 'World Conference on Chilean Fascism: Call to Isolate the Military Junta', *Building Worker*, October 1973.
26 The Peace Forces event ran from 25 to 31 October. Mavis Robertson, 'Moscow World Peace Congress', *Tribune* [Australia], 13–19 November 1973. Taft had been involved in the anti-Vietnam War movement, and he returned to Melbourne to spread his new-found knowledge of Chile solidarity via meetings organised by the CPA. 'Chile Analysed', *Tribune* [Australia], 23–29 Octpber 1973, 10.
27 Robertson Interview, 2009.

one of the vice-presidents of the World Peace Council. Georges actually chaired sections of the Solidarity Conference.[28] All of the Australian activists were well known to Robertson, who remembered that 'George and I go back a really long time, but he was also somebody with strong pro-Soviet tendencies, so he kind of sat in the middle between the non-aligned peace movement and the World Peace Council'.[29]

These prominent peace activists joined representatives from 49 other countries for the meeting, which was held on 29–30 September 1973.[30] It was organised by a Finnish committee set up for the task, headed by that country's education minister.[31] Unidad Popular politicians already in exile were given a platform and a sympathetic audience to which they proposed a broad-front organisation to organise action against the military junta. This was not passed, however, as it was 'too binding' for 'Western socialists'.[32] Isabel Allende, daughter of the deceased Chilean president, also spoke. She said: 'We now know that the violence of reaction must be met with the violence of revolution.'[33] As it seemed that most who attended were from peace, anti-war and nonviolence movements, it was possible her rhetoric missed the mark.

Despite these tensions, congresses under the title of 'International Conference of Solidarity with the Chilean People' would go on to be held in Lisbon (1974),[34] Athens (1975, 1982), Helsinki (1973, 1976, 1979), Paris (1976), Madrid (1978) and Rome (1980). It was also the start of a pattern of international conference participation by Australians.

The International Labour Organisation ILO provided another international forum for Australian representatives. Jim Baird, for example, was invited by Chilean unionist Luis Figueroa to appear before the ILO's Commission of Inquiry on Chile Trade Unions in Geneva in October 1974.[35] He was one of 19 witnesses called to present information on the violation of trade union rights in Chile. The ILO was assessing whether the Chilean Government was breaking ILO directives and whether they should be entitled to ongoing representation in the organisation. Baird's trip was endorsed and paid for by the AMWU Commonwealth Committee, the ICFTU and the WFTU and was as a result of his

---

28 'CHILE: World Campaign of Solidarity Launched', *Tribune* [Australia], 9–15 October 1973; Bernie Taft, 'Chile and Mass Consciousness', *Tribune* [Australia], 16–22 October 1973, 8.
29 Robertson Interview, 2009.
30 'World Conference on Chilean Fascism'; 'Govt. Told: "Don't Recognise Chile"'; 'CHILE: World Campaign of Solidarity Launched'.
31 'World Conference on Chilean Fascism'.
32 Reuters, '50 Nations in Movement to Oust Chile Junta', *The Times*, 1 October 1973.
33 'CHILE: World Campaign of Solidarity Launched'.
34 Henderson attended this conference. 'Solidarity with Chile on September 11th'.
35 Baird, 'Chilean Junta on Trial before I.L.O.'; *Amalgamated Metal Workers Union, Commonwealth Council re: International work of the Amalgamated Metal Workers Union, 1974*, AMWSU: National Office, N24/560, NBAC: ANU, Canberra.

firsthand experience in Chile as a part of the delegation of 1974 (Chapter Seven). Baird was one of only six trade union witnesses at the event, and he spent a week waiting to be called to give evidence.[36] The documents he supplied were cross-examined by the ICFTU, WFTU and CUT as well as junta representatives.[37]

Baird's high-profile ILO visit and the Madrid conference in 1978 were pinnacles of internationalist participation. Yet the series of conferences that received the most consistent patronage by Australians was the freshly created 'International Commission of Enquiry into the Crimes of the Military Junta in Chile' (referred to as the commission and not to be confused with the International Conference of Solidarity with the Chilean People). The commission held its first session in Helsinki from 21 to 24 March 1974, just six months after the coup,[38] proclaiming that it was 'one of the most important non-Government bodies dealing with continued violations of human rights in Chile'.[39] The liaison committee sent letters to prominent citizens all over the world, with invitations to join the commission. Its body was intended to be populated 'by international recognized political figures, jurists, men of science and culture, particularly from those countries not yet represented'.[40]

The commission essentially heard witnesses and brought material about the repression in Chile together. They then took it upon themselves to spread the word about the wrongdoings of the junta, and the international interference in the affairs of Chile leading up to the coup. The public positions of the commission's members were used to give subsequent activities authority. By inviting high-profile, internationally recognised members, the commission sought to surround itself with persons of unshakeable moral authority in the eyes of the public. They gave press conferences, published proceedings, supported documentaries and sent delegations to the United Nations, ILO, the United Nations Educational, Scientific and Cultural Organisation (UNESCO) and the World Health Organisation. After the first session in Helsinki, the commission, or its subcommittees, met in Copenhagen, Lisbon, Mexico City, Athens, Berlin, Algiers and finally returned to Helsinki in 1983.

---

36 Baird, 'Chilean Junta on Trial before I.L.O.'; *Australian Metal Workers' Union Commonwealth Council, to CAC members from Baird re: Visit to Europe, Re: ILO Chile, November 8 1974*, AMWSU, E262/137, NBAC: ANU, Canberra; *The Commission of Enquiry, 1974*, AMWSU, E262/137, NBAC: ANU, Canberra.
37 *Baird to Cameron M. Re: I.L.O. Inquiry on Chile Trade Unions, 4th October 1974*, AMWSU, E262/137, NBAC: ANU, Canberra.
38 'Chilean Report', *Harbour News*, April 1975. The commission's headquarters were in Helsinki. 'Call for World Trade Union Action against Chile Junta', *Seamen's Journal* 30, no. 3 (March 1975).
39 It was formed by the same Finnish liaison committee that started the Conference of Solidarity in Helsinki a year previously, but was distinct from that and separate to the ICFTU and WFTU conferences. *First Session of the International Commission of Enquiry into the Crimes of the Military Junta in Chile, Dipoli, Finland, March 21–24, 1974*, STUC, STUCA 531/2, GCUA, Glasgow; Amalgamated Metalworkers and Shipwrights Union (Australia), *Chile! A Report from the International Commission into the Crimes of the Military Junta in Chile, held in Algiers in January, 1978* (Sydney: The Harbour Press, 1978).
40 *Concluding Statements*, STUC, STUCA 531/2, GCUA, Glasgow.

Yet as time went on, in the case of Australia, delegates became less and less well known and more politically factionalised. Among the 55 members of the commission at its first sitting was George Georges, the ALP senator from Queensland.[41] At the same session from Britain was Arthur Booth, a Quaker and vice-president of the International Peace Bureau. By the third sitting, little-known unionist Don Henderson was among the Australian delegates, and his ascension makes an interesting case study that will reveal itself in the coming pages.

The commission's third session, from 18 to 21 February 1975, in Mexico City was opened at the Palace of Arts in Mexico City by Luis Echeverría, the populist Mexican president, who had been a supporter and 'great friend' of President Allende.[42] The Chilean regime had recently commuted various life sentences to exile in an attempt to change its international reputation, and this contributed to the higher number of Chileans present for what was the first meeting of the commission in Latin America. Many ex-prisoners who were exiled to countries all over the world met up for the first time at this session.[43]

Don Henderson of the Firemen and Deckhands of New South Wales attended the Mexico session. His union was a very small niche union including those who worked on the ferries of Sydney Harbour. He was there representing his own union, the SUA and the SPA, and also along from Australia was Henry McCarthy of the Amalgamated Metal Workers' and Shipwrights Union (AMWSU). Henderson was elected at the Mexico City meeting to be one of the 30 members of the commission. McCarthy had already been elected at the Copenhagen session in 1974.[44] Interestingly, the only countries which had trade unionists as representatives on the commission were Australia and the USSR.[45] The other members were in the main representatives of political parties, lawyers, academics and jurists.[46]

It was at the Mexico City session that the decision was taken to seek the 'active support' of the trade union internationals, and the idea was put forward to the commission in a letter by Don Henderson. Though this seems very late—a full year and a half after the coup—it must be said that it had been assumed that the military government would not last long. Furthermore, Henderson's

---

41 Ibid.
42 Rose Styron, 'Chile: The Spain of Our Generation', *Honi Soit* (1975), 12.
43 'The affection with which they greeted each other as fellow survivors … gave all of us at the Conference an air of hope.' Ibid., 12.
44 'Chilean Report'. McCarthy continued to attend the commission sessions up to at least 1983: *Amalgamated Metal workers and Shipwrights Union—Memo to the NAC, 22 August 1983*, AMWU: National Office, Z109 Box 19 Package 1, NBAC: ANU, Canberra; Amalgamated Metal Workers Union, *Commonwealth Council re: International work of the Amalgamated Metal Workers Union*.
45 'Call for World Trade Union Action against Chile Junta'. Trade unionists from Costa Rica, the United States, Chile, Mexico, the USSR and Australia were present at the congress. 'Chilean Report'.
46 There were no trade unionists from Britain represented at the commission. Ibid.

union outlook, his 'prolier than thou'[47] attitude, gave him a point of difference to the rest of the commission members, even to McCarthy, who was much more experienced in this form of international non-governmental diplomacy.

When Don Henderson spoke to the conference he first identified the groups he was representing and brought greetings from the BWIU, WWFA (Sydney Branch), NSW Fire Brigade Employees Union, and the Australian Federated Union of Locomotive Enginemen (AFULE).[48] These were all unions and branches that had substantial SPA member involvement. When he spoke to the conference he said there was no doubt that 'unionism died in Chile on September 11, 1973' and that Australians believed the world trade union movement had a responsibility to the Chilean working class.[49] It was ironic that he was talking for Australians, for even counting the backing of the BWIU and WWFA, SUA and Firemen and Deckhands Union, he did not represent as many people as McCarthy did as a spokesman of the AMWU (let alone with the backing of the ICFTU and WFTU unions of Australia and the world). Though his speech was admirable in sentiment, it may have been slightly misdirected, given that relatively few representatives of the world trade union movement were present. Still, he finished off his speech with the rallying cry: 'Long live International Friendship, Solidarity and Peace. Long live the Democratic Forces of Chile.'[50]

Upon his return to Australia, Henderson wrote of the growing support for the conference by comparing the 19 attending countries in Copenhagen with the 33 in Mexico City.[51] He did not take into account that Copenhagen was an extraordinary session and it had been organised on a limited time frame with little chance for gathering of funds or forming travel plans.[52] Henderson also ensured that the readers of *Harbour News*, the newsletter of the Firemen and Deckhands, were not misled as to who the *real* Australian unionist involved was: 'Whilst Henry [McCarthy] is listed as an Australian Trade Union leader, in fact he is, as you know, a journalist responsible for the publishing of the A.M.W.U. Trade Union paper.'[53] Finishing his union report on the Mexican session of the commission in the *Harbour News*, he wrote: 'Every victory of the

---

47 Burgmann and Burgmann, *Green Bans, Red Union*, 54.
48 'Wider Bans on Chile Junta', *Modern Unionist* [Australia] (1975).
49 'Call for World Trade Union Action against Chile Junta'.
50 'Wider Bans on Chile Junta', 67.
51 Representatives of 32 countries attended the Mexico City session of the commission. 'Call for World Trade Union Action against Chile Junta'.
52 Still, the 30 members met in Copenhagen in order to draw attention to the military trial of UP leaders that was occurring in Chile in March 1975. 'Commission Calls on Chile to Halt Political Reprisals', *The Times*, 29 June 1974.
53 Concurrently, Henderson appeared to have fallen into the trap of misspelling many of the Chilean names and words: 'Latelier', 'Venezuala', 'Clodimero'. 'Chilean Report'.

working class wherever it may be, is another step towards the sort of society that Marx, Engels and Lenin believed in—the sort of society that I believe in and continue to strive for.'[54]

Figure 6.1 Luis Figueroa, Don Henderson and Luis Alberto Corvalan at the Mexico Commission of Enquiry.

Source: Photo from 'Solidarity Call to World Trade Union Movement', *Socialist*, April 1975, 3.

Henderson's platform oratory, however, was not a reliable measure of his influence.

McCarthy's connections and experience were actually what led to the visit of former Chilean minister of labour Luis Figueroa to Australia, and subsequently one of the most substantial gestures of Chile solidarity that the ACTU mustered during the dictatorship.[55]

Figueroa's relationship with Australian unionists began prior to the coup when Tas and Carmen Bull passed through Chile in 1971.[56] Post coup, Figueroa had spent weeks fighting in the underground;[57] but when the military junta put out a reward for his capture, it was decided that he would be better off leaving Chile and strengthening the anti-dictatorship cause from without.[58] The only time Henry McCarthy had met Figueroa was when the latter was seeking

---

54 Ibid.
55 *Press Statement of the AMWU—7/2/74: What is the Chilean Junta Up To?*, WWFA: Federal Office, N114/932, NBAC: ANU, Canberra; Julius Roe, 'Notes for Speech: 30th Anniversary', unpublished ms, 2003.
56 *Letter to President Salvador Allende from WWF of Australia, 4 August 1972*, WWFA: Federal Office, N114/932, NBAC: ANU, Canberra; *Central Unica de Trabajadores de Chile, November 3 1971*, WWFA: Federal Office, N114/932, NBAC: ANU, Canberra.
57 'Aid to Chile Struggle', *Maritime Worker*, 14 May 1974.
58 'Chilean Thanks for Australian Help', *Maritime Worker*, September 1975.

asylum in an embassy in Santiago, and there were still grave fears for his safety at that time (see Chapter 7).[59] So, McCarthy was pleased to greet Figueroa at the Mexican session of the Enquiry into the Crimes of the Military Junta and he extended an invitation to Figueroa to visit Australia as the guest of the AMWU Commonwealth Council. As Figueroa was president of the CUT in exile, McCarthy suggested he also attend the ACTU congress.[60]

In the role of president, Figueroa had travelled all over the world attending conferences, sessions and congresses; and in September 1975, he visited Australia. He addressed the 1975 anniversary rally in Martin Place, Sydney, where more than 600 people had gathered.[61] The crowd had shrunk since the first anniversary, but even so, Figueroa pronounced that 'there has been no greater concrete example of working class solidarity than that initiated by the Australian unions'. It surprised Chileans, he continued, 'as we did not realise how deeply the Australian trade union movement felt about the international solidarity of trade unionists and of working people'.[62]

He also said he thought the days of military rule were numbered.

Figueroa's relatively high-profile position as president of the CUT in exile, and as minister of labour in Allende's cabinet, allowed him to meet high-profile Australians such as the secretaries and presidents of unions.[63] He also met at the AMWU research office with David McKerlie, Brian McGahen and Steve Cooper, all three of whom were involved in the CSCP organisation.[64] Cooper recalled that they took Figueroa and his companion Luis Meneses down to the wharves just as the men instigated a half-day strike for Chile.[65] The Chileans were pleased to see that sort of action occurring.[66]

---

59 Steve Cooper, 'Journey to Chile. 1974', unpublished ms, 1974. Though it was an important meeting, McCarthy still spelt his name 'Vigueroa'. *The Commission of Enquiry, 1974*; Steve Cooper and Henry McCarthy, 'Chile—Internal Strife—Solidarity', *Tribune* [Australia], 16 July 1974.
60 The AMWU paid for Figueroa's domestic transport and accommodation. *Atkins to Figueroa, June 24 1975*, AMWSU, E262/137, NBAC: ANU, Canberra; *Cable: August 6 1975*, AMWSU, E262/137, NBAC: ANU, Canberra.
61 *Programme Results—Chilean Trade Union Delegation to Australia, 11–20 September 1975*, Amalgamated Metal Workers' and Shipwrights' Union, E262/137, NBAC: ANU, Canberra; 'Chile Venceremos', *Tribune* [Australia], 16 September 1975.
62 'Chile Venceremos'.
63 'Support Chilean Workers in their Struggle to Free their Country from Fascism', *Tribune* [Australia], 16 September 1975.
64 The existence of the research office was also imperative to the AMWU's ability to take part in extra-industrial activities. *Programme Results—Chilean Trade Union Delegation to Australia, 11–20 September 1975*; Deery, 'Union Aims and Methods', 77.
65 Luis Meneses was the CUT secretary, and he visited Australia in 1975 with Figueroa and again in 1977. Meneses was to return in May 1977 to impress upon Australian trade unions the importance of maintaining boycotts. *Baird (AMWU) to Robertson (CSCP), 11th May 1977*, Papers of GMM; *Central Unica the Trabajadores de Chile: Comision Exterior Paris, May 1 1977*, AMWSU, E262/137, NBAC: ANU, Canberra.
66 Cooper et al. Conversation, 2007; *Programme Results—Chilean Trade Union Delegation to Australia, 11–20 September 1975*.

Both Meneses and Figueroa travelled to Melbourne for the ACTU congress on 16-17 September 1975. It was probably their most important action in Australia.[67] In Figueroa's statement to the ACTU congress, he congratulated and thanked Australian unions for their solidarity. He urged the ACTU to protest through the ILO and follow the five points of action that were passed at the ILO conference in June 1975.[68] Bob Hawke, president of the ACTU at that time, declared that the ACTU would support the ILO measures. One hundred and fifty trade unionists present signed the petition to free Luis Corvalan and all prisoners, which had been circulated by Pat Clancy (Building Workers Industrial Union/SPA), Dick Scott of the AMWU and Taylor of the ARU.[69]

Figueroa spanned the hierarchy as a symbol of solidarity, from grassroots to international industrial national organisations. Any investment from social movement or unions in him could reap huge internationalist brownie points. This sort of tour could also be conducted with minimal resource output from trade unions: ideological internationalist obligations were completed without imperilling the interests of the members.

Just less than one year after his Australian trip, on 8 September 1976, Figueroa died in Stockholm after an illness.[70] Don Henderson wrote in the *Seamen's Journal* that his death far away from his homeland served to remind the world that the 'fight was not over'.[71]

---

67 *Programme Results—Chilean Trade Union Delegation to Australia, 11–20 September 1975*.
68 These were: 1) stop arms sales to Chile; 2) economic isolation; 3) moral and financial solidarity with unionists in Chile; 4) 11 September as an international day of solidarity with Chile; and 5) send a boat with food to Chile. *Statement by L. Figueroa and L. Meneses to the Delegates of the ACTU Congress, September 17 1975*, AMWSU, E262/137, NBAC: ANU, Canberra.
69 He had met with the Chileans twice as SPA member during their visit. 'Strengthen Solidarity', *Socialist*, 8 October 1975. Scott was from the AMWU SA and was an ACTU executive member. *Baird (AMWU) to Robertson (CSCP), 11th May 1977*; 'The ACTU Stands for United Action', *World Trade Union Movement (Review of the WFTU)*, no. 1 (January 1976); 'Figueroa Speaks', *Socialist*, 24 September 1975.
70 'Chilean Workers' Leader Dies in Sweden', *Tribune* [Australia], 15 September 1976; 'Sad Untimely Loss—Death of Luis Figueroa Reminder Chile Struggle Still to be Won', *Seamen's Journal* 31, no. 11 (November 1976). In 1975, Figueroa had toured both Australia and Britain.
71 'Sad Untimely Loss'. Previous to Figueroa and Meneses' visit, an alliance of the left brought another high-profile Chilean to Australian shores: Anselmo Sule. Rather than being initiated from within trade unions, the earlier visit was an indirect action organised from within the ALP as part of their obligation as a member of the Socialist International. There is an enormous web of political backwards and forwards and organisation around his visit, which was for a meeting of the Socialist International in Adelaide. For more information, see the following archival folders: AMWSU, E262/137, NBAC: ANU, Canberra; N131/211—Politics—Foreign Affairs, NBAC: ANU, Canberra; The AMWU: South Australian State Council, N131/190—General Correspondence, NBAC: ANU, Canberra; WWFA: Federal Office, N114/932, NBAC: ANU, Canberra; WWFA: Federal Office, N113/932, NBAC: ANU, Canberra; Amalgamated Metal Workers' and Shipwrights Union (Aust.) [hereinafter AMWSU]: National Office, Z26 box 5, NBAC: ANU, Canberra. Also, the following sources provide more background on Sule: 'Chilean MP Tells of Torture after Allende Overthrow', *The Times*, 3 September 1975; 'Stop Repression in Chile—Sept 11th', *Tharkuna* 21, no. 21 (1975); Angell and Carstairs, 'The Exile Question in Chilean Politics', 165; *Memo re: Appeal from ALP for finance to bring ex-Senator Sule to Australia*, Waterside Workers' Federation of Australia: Federal Office, N114/932, NBAC: ANU, Canberra; 'Chilean Terror', Maritime Worker, 27 May 1975, 6.

To continue the fight for solidarity, the CSCP used films, tours and other cultural activities to widen the understanding of the situation of Chile in the Australian community. These activities had the added benefit of raising funds. There were always accounts of torture and detention emerging from Chile as well as stories such as the banning of music that 'make people mad', and music tours reinforced and extended the support, but their organisation was a big undertaking given Australia's distance from Europe and also the distance between towns.[72]

Two of Chile's most famous folk groups were outside the country when the coup occurred, so they immediately started their exile and found sympathetic homes and audiences all over the world. Both groups were part of the Chilean new song movement that had emerged, according to a concert program from Britain, 'out of a deep-rooted need to rediscover and revive Chile's genuine popular music'.[73] New song, wrote Maurice Rosenbaum in 1978, used the 'basic instruments of Latin America' such as guitars, zamponas, drums, tambourines, woodblocks and Andean flutes. It was acknowledged in the *Socialist* at the time that 'the New Chilean Song has thrived and spread in exile and has become a powerful weapon in the Chilean people's struggle'.[74] Notwithstanding, Jill Sykes noted in her review of a Sydney new song concert in the *Sydney Morning Herald* that they could sing songs with political points without resorting to polemics.[75]

The first major tour organised was of the seven musicians of the group Quilapayun, who were based in Paris.[76] '*Quilapayun*' literally means 'three bearded men', as the band had started with three hairy university students.[77] Their musical director had been Victor Jara, the most famous new song protagonist, who was killed in the stadium in Santiago in the days immediately following the coup.[78]

In fact, it was because of the friendly relationship between Joan Jara and Mavis Robertson that the tour happened at all. The tour was presented by the CSCP in conjunction with New Chile Song Productions and with Mavis Robertson as the main organiser with the help of David McKerlie in Sydney and Philip Herington in Melbourne.[79] While the bulk of organisation fell to Mavis Robertson, there was also considerable strain placed on the Association for International

---

72 Robertson Interview, 2009.
73 Chile Solidarity Campaign (UK), *Pete Seeger and Quilapayun*.
74 'Chilean Folk Artists to Visit', *Socialist*, 18 February 1977.
75 Though how Sykes could interpret the intricacies of the lyrics through the language barrier is unknown. Jill Sykes, 'Inti Illimani's Poetic Message', *Sydney Morning Herald*, 26 February 1977.
76 They negotiated the terms of their tour to Australia through Juan Carlos Valenzuela at the Discoteca del Cantar Popular in Paris. Chile Solidarity Campaign (UK), *Pete Seeger and Quilapayun*.
77 Ibid.
78 *Quilapayun: Ambassadors without a Country, Rob Fruchtman, Chile 1975*, Papers of Barry Carr.
79 *Quilapayun*, Papers of GMM; *Final Report of Quilapayun Tour*, Papers of GMM; *Quilapayun and Jeannie Lewis: Party Bookings now open*, Papers of GMM. New Chile Song Promotions was the company set up by Joan Jara, widow of Victor Jara. Robertson Interview, 2009.

Cooperation and Disarmament (AICD), as the Chile campaign still used their offices.[80] Robertson also knew popular folk singer Jeannie Lewis, who was tactically selected to ensure an audience for the locally unknown Quilapayun.

Furthermore, Robertson was acquainted with Kevin Jacobsen, entertainment company owner and tour organiser. He was on the left of the ALP, and a very experienced promoter. Robertson approached him for advice and he gave her a plan and a sheet that would help her organise what would turn out to be a very successful music tour. For example, he suggested that activists and groups sold tickets, because 10 people selling 10 tickets each was 100 seats sold. This strategy meant a reduction in advertising costs and little chance of failure. Each trade union connection within the reach of the committee was contacted to sell tickets and there was not a progressive union in Sydney without such contact.[81]

As soon as Quilapayun stepped off the plane, they were put to work at a press conference. When Robertson wrote to them before their departure for Australia she had requested that they 'please make sure that the group come off the plane wearing their dramatic ponchos'.[82] Despite this level of detail in organisation, very little appeared in the mainstream press before the concerts in Melbourne and Sydney, although there was more success in other cities. This was put down to the fact that 'all too little is known yet about "Quilapayun"'.[83] The band's tour proved very popular with radio stations, with various features being played across the nation as well as 2JJ recording the Canberra concert to make a radio feature.[84]

Joan Jara came to Australia at the same time as the band and spoke at the beginning of each concert on the tour, which included Sydney, Melbourne, Brisbane, Wollongong, Adelaide and Canberra.[85] Jeannie Lewis supported at all concerts and Lucia Abarca explained things between songs.[86] The concerts had a deep effect on those present. When the lights went up on stage, there were the seven men and Joan Jara. Jara gave the introduction. She told of the killings and the oppression in Chile and called for concrete actions. She said 'Chile is not alone', and continued: 'We are not here tonight to weep. We bring you music prohibited in Chile today but it is the music of living Chile.'[87]

The concert in Sydney went very well, despite the poor acoustics at the Town Hall.[88] While no Quilapayun record was available, interested persons could buy

---

80   *Final Report of Quilapayun Tour*, Papers of GMM.
81   Robertson Interview, 2009.
82   *Robertson (CSCP—Syd) to Valenzuela, 13th June, 1975*, Papers of GMM.
83   *Robertson (CSCP—Syd) to Valenzuela, May 7th, 1975*, Papers of GMM.
84   *Final Report of Quilapayun Tour*, Papers of GMM.
85   Della Elliott, 'Special Supplement: Quilapayun Singers in Australia—The True Voice of Chile', *Seamen's Journal* 30, no. 7 (July 1975), 165–8.
86   Robertson Interview, 2009.
87   Elliott, 'Special Supplement'.
88   *Final Report of Quilapayun Tour*, Papers of GMM.

Victor Jara's *Manifesto* from Don Henderson at the Firemen and Deckhands for only $5.[89] The commercial opportunity was not lost for long, as after the tour EMI decided to release two of the band's records into the Australian market.[90]

While in New South Wales, the band played for students and visited workers on the South Coast, and in Newcastle and they visited the Chullora workshops as the guests of the shop committee and the AMWU.[91] Not everything was a popular success, and everyday work pulled unionists in the opposite direction. On a visit to the Sydney waterfront, it had originally been hoped that Jara would speak at a stop-work meeting but the union failed to establish a quorum. Instead, Jara and the band visited some ships and were hosted by the WWFA for a function.[92] One of the members of the band delivered a speech in which he said: 'Our people will win. Our people will defeat the Junta. Our people will triumph for Chile and also for all the democratic movement all over the world.'[93]

Afterwards, the SUA journal proclaimed that Quilapayun were 'the true voice of Chile'. The fact that the band had not lived in or visited junta-controlled Chile was ignored in this judgment.[94]

The Chilean community of Sydney wanted to meet the band members, and so did many of the Spanish-speaking community; but it was decided that the Chileans would have exclusive time together first. Robertson wrote to the group stating that the reason behind the decision of exclusivity was that 'some Latin American[s] are in the "armchair revolutionary class" and were therefore critical of the Chilean left'.[95]

On top of that, tension was developing among the Chileans resident in Australia as to whom, or where, the money from the tour would be going. Some Chileans suspected that the Chilean Communist Party controlled the international solidarity movement and that all the money was going towards their political dominance. While Robertson remembered that at the start of that first tour she was 'singularly unaware' of the sectarian tensions behind the use of musical bands in solidarity, by the end, it was very clear. Despite this and the normal difficulties of organising such a large tour, Robertson remembered that '[i]n general everything went smoothly. In a few places there were minor tensions which arise out of cultural differences, e.g. attitudes to women'.[96]

---

89   Elliott, 'Special Supplement'.
90   *Final Report of Quilapayun Tour*, Papers of GMM.
91   *Vines (Australian Union of Students) to Robertson (CSCP), 12/12/74*, Papers of GMM; *Robertson (CSCP—Syd) to Valenzuela 13th June, 1975*, Papers of GMM.
92   *Final Report of Quilapayun Tour*, Papers of GMM.
93   Elliott, 'Special Supplement'.
94   Ibid.
95   *Robertson (CSCP—Syd) to Valenzuela 13th June, 1975*, Papers of GMM.
96   *Final Report of Quilapayun Tour*, Papers of GMM.

While Robertson politely reflected that Quilapayun were a 'group of personalities', it is obvious the musicians were very vocal chauvinists. They were often very offensive and progressively more unkind the older the woman. Ironically, it was the presence of a woman, Joan Jara, with the band that made the whole tour a musical and political success rather than just a series of exotic folk concerts. Jara had crisscrossed the countryside fulfilling speaking engagements with workers and feminists, activists and politicians. In order to fit all of her activities in to the 10 days allocated, she must have had little or no time to rest.

For example, an evening was organised by women involved in the peace movement and women's organisations such as the Women's International League for Peace and Freedom, Women's Liberation, the Women's Electoral Lobby and the Communist Women's Collective. The gathering was primarily for women and it was hoped that Joan Jara would show a film. Of course, the members of the band were welcomed also, though apparently declined the invitation.[97]

Jara also travelled to Armidale and attended an International Women's Day lunch in Wollongong along with 50 other women,[98] met with the Port Kembla WWFA branch[99] and was called upon to meet with the NSW Trades and Labour Council. While the council was 'not exactly left', they were nonetheless very important for action in New South Wales.[100] Jara also met the Victorian Trades Hall Council, where the Creative Arts Committee organised a reception with 100 unionists in attendance. A later report noted that 'Joan made an outstanding contribution at the [reception]. She was given a standing ovations (which is unusual) by the 150 delegates except for 5 members, said to be of the Clerks Union, who remained seated.'[101] Jara spoke at several meetings in houses, gatherings in Adelaide and met with representatives of the CPA, SPA and ALP and also with students and the church.[102] Meanwhile, the band hosted two workshops for musicians, with 50 attending in both Melbourne and Sydney.[103]

Jara's personal presence and easy cultural similarity with Australians smoothed other problems and boosted the success of the tour. The one event that defined her life, at least publicly, was the loss of her husband. His martyrdom gave Jara

---

97   Though it is unclear if any men took up this offer. *Robertson (CSCP—Syd) to Valenzuela 13th June, 1975*, Papers of GMM.
98   *Final Report of Quilapayun Tour*, Papers of GMM.
99   *Robertson (CSCP—Syd) to Valenzuela 13th June, 1975*, Papers of GMM.
100 Ibid.
101 *Report on the Tour of Inti Illimani (Melbourne 5.4.77)*, Papers of GMM. The clerks were a noted right-wing union. They had even put forward a proposition to stop the use of political strikes at the 1971 ACTU Congress. Schmutte, 'International Union Activity', 85.
102 Jara also attended the reception that was given to farewell Jeria Bachelet, who was leaving Australia to go to live in Europe. It was a particularly moving meeting, with the two widows in attendance. *Final Report of Quilapayun Tour*, Papers of GMM.
103 Ibid.

an air of incorruptibility and moral authority.[104] Though it seems insensitive to discuss and was by no choice of her own, the manner of the death of her husband furnished Joan Jara with a huge amount of moral capital. This alone, aside from her connections in and out of Chile, obliged and propelled her to *use* this immense legitimacy and strategic ability.

The concerts and meetings represented the biggest gatherings in solidarity with Chile that had occurred up to that point in Australia. Both the Sydney and the Melbourne concerts had audiences of 2000 people.[105] The tour resulted in a burst of support for the campaigns in all the cities visited and the tour report declared it to be an 'enormous success politically and artistically'.[106] It also spurred on the organisers to continue with a musical theme.

The second tour of a high-profile Chilean band was that of Inti Illimani in 1977.[107] 'Inti Illimani' means 'condors of the sun' in Quechua, and all members had been students at the Technical University in Santiago.[108] When the coup occurred, they had been outside Chile on tour and had since been living in Rome. In the four years since the coup, Inti Illimani had toured to Washington, Hanoi, Paris, Moscow, Berlin, London, Rome, Caracas, the Hague, Milan, Lisbon, Venice, Havana and Mexico City.[109] The band earned no money personally from the tour, but all their expenses were paid. Any profit was to go to the 'movement for solidarity with Chile'.[110] The tour of Inti Illimani benefited from the Quilapayun tour before it. Less education of the audience was now needed and many Australians now knew of the new song movement.[111]

The main problem was visas. A change in government since the Quilapayun tour in Australia meant it was difficult to obtain entry without extensive travel documentation.[112] Ever conscious of their support base, the CSCP also sought permission from Actors' Equity to allow the Chilean musicians to perform.[113] Again, Robertson was at the helm of the organisation, but this time she was

---

104 'I fully trusted Joan Jara and anyone who thinks that she is … on a narrow sectarian side, doesn't know her.' Robertson Interview, 2009.
105 8, 10 July 1975. *Quilapayun*, Papers of GMM. The United States had bigger concerts, but did not make as much money for the cause. Robertson Interview, 2005.
106 *Final Report of Quilapayun Tour*, Papers of GMM.
107 Inti Illimani also returned in 1985 and 1987. *The Chilean Community in Canberra presents: Inti Illimani in Concert*, Papers of GMM.
108 *Inti Illimani: Chile's Famous Folk Singers, Australian Concert Tour, March 1977*, AMWSU, E262/137, NBAC: ANU, Canberra.
109 *Chile Democrático*3, Sydney, March 1977.
110 Listed elsewhere as the Movement for Restoration of Human Rights in Chile. *Agreement/Contrato*, Papers of GMM; 'Inti Illimani', *Tribune* [Australia], 23 March 1977. The contract was signed mainly to make sure that 'the movement' avoided excessive taxation. *Robertson (CSCP—Syd) to Rivas, 17th January, 1977*, Papers of GMM.
111 *Robertson (CSCP) to Rivas, 10th December, 1976*, Papers of GMM.
112 *Robertson (CSCP—Syd) to Rivas, 17th January, 1977*, Papers of GMM.
113 *Evatt (AAEAA) to Robertson (CSCP—Syd), 23/12/76*, Papers of GMM; *McGahen (CSCP) to Patten (Department of Immigration and Ethnic Affairs), 28th January, 1977*, Papers of GMM.

assisted by a more efficient national organisation. Brian McGahen (Young Communist Movement and subsequently AMWU Research Officer)[114] helped Robertson organise the Inti Illimani tour, as he was unemployed at the time.[115] Inti Illimani sent extensive requests for sound equipment that exceeded the wattage capacity of most Australian venues, and furthermore, 12 microphones were needed and these details stretched the resources, and no doubt the patience, of the organisers.[116] Five hundred posters, and 700 programs were printed.[117] The Electric Record Company looked after the pressing of an Inti Illimani record. They promoted the $6.95 record extensively in Sydney and Melbourne, but the concerts in other States did not benefit from the company's work.[118]

The CSCP had to outlay approximately $9000, and so asked affiliated and friendly organisations for donations.[119] Again, the political and fiscal generosity of trade unions was imperative to the campaign. The fact is, despite the large outlay and difficult liaison with the musicians and the expatriates the music tours were probably the most solid moments of Australia-wide organisation. Support for the tour was given by the AMWSU (Vic.), BWIU, Chilean UP Committee of Australia, Firemen and Deckhands Union (FDU) (Vic.), WWFA, various student groups, Teachers' Chile Solidarity Group (NSW), Miscellaneous Workers' Union (MWU), Federated Engine Drivers and Firemen's Association of Australia (FEDFA), Clothing and Allied Trade Union and Food Preservers.[120] Clearly, little would have occurred without the unions. Every little bit counted, even the $25 donated by the Printing and Kindred Industries Union NSW branch and the WWFA's $100.[121] Funds were also boosted by student and workers' concerts, as well as collections at the interval of the main performances.[122]

In Melbourne, Philip Herington battled to organise the Victorian leg of the tour among his suite of other political activities and 'pestering' from locally based Chileans; but he succeeded above all expectations when the band visited the West Gate Bridge site to play at a stop-work meeting and the workers struck

---

114   'Chile Popular Unity Adopts New Program', *Tribune* [Australia], 1 October 1975.
115   Much of the incoming correspondence to the CSCP Sydney on the topic is addressed to him.
116   *Philip [Herington] (CSCP—Melb) to Brian [McGahen], 25.1.77*, Papers of GMM; *Rod Williams (CSCP—Perth) to Brian*, Papers of GMM.
117   *Philip [Herington] (CSCP—Melb) to Brian [McGahen], 25.1.77*, Papers of GMM.
118   *McGahen (CSCP—Syd) to friends, 23rd February, 1977*, Papers of GMM.
119   *McGahen (CSCP—Syd) to [blank], December 1976*, Papers of GMM.
120   *Report on the Tour of Inti Illimani (Melbourne 5.4.77)*, Papers of GMM.
121   *Kelly (PKIU) to CSCP, 21st March, 1977*, Papers of GMM; *Fitzgibbon (WWFA) to McGahen (CSCP), March 21, 1977*, Papers of GMM.
122   It was made clear that only CSCP material was allowed to be distributed and sold at the concerts: *McGahen (CSCP—Syd) to [all States], Jan 23 [1977?]*, Papers of GMM.

for half an hour to extend the concert. They then passed an excellent resolution and promised to work towards action for Chile in the future.[123] This was the highlight of the trip for the members of the band.

Meanwhile in Perth, the solidarity committee did its best to find a venue for a concert that met the Chilean's requirements, and to be fair, they struggled even to find a typewriter to write their letters on.[124]

Inti Illimani was made to work hard from their arrival in Sydney from Japan on 24 March 1977.[125] They were kept constantly on the move, with press engagements, small performances and large concerts as well as solidarity meetings with Chileans and trade unionists.[126] The tour organised would take in Wollongong (Warrawong Hall, 25 March 1977), Sydney (Town Hall, 26 March), Brisbane (Teachers' Union Hall, 27 March), Melbourne (Dallas Brooks Theatre, 29 March), Adelaide (Norwood Town Hall, 30 March) and Perth (Octagon Theatre, 31 March).[127]

At the Sydney concert, the two most important organisers, Mavis Robertson and Philip Herington, attended, having been saved good seats so they could at last, and at least, enjoy the concert.[128] Tas Bull, the prominent unionist, had been coopted as a compere and did a 'splendid' job under the difficult circumstances.[129]

It was reported in the *Tribune* that almost 10 000 people attended the concert tour.[130] Sykes described in the *Sydney Morning Herald* 'whether you were stirred by their appeal for the return of socialism to Chile, you could not help but be moved by the beauty and power of their material, and the quality and strength of their performance'.[131]

In a letter to the organisers all around Australia after the tour, Mavis Robertson wrote that there was 'no doubt that the tour has been a success both financially

---

123 *Final Report of Quilapayun Tour*, Papers of GMM; *Philip [Herington] (CSCP—Melb) to Brian [McGahen], 25.1.77*, Papers of GMM; *Report on the Tour of Inti Illimani (Melbourne 5.4.77)*, Papers of GMM; *From Philip Herington*, Papers of GMM.
124 Rod Williams did his best to organise the concert there. *Rod Williams (CSCP—Perth) to Brian*, Papers of GMM; *Williams (CSCP—Perth) to Brian, 11-2-77*, Papers of GMM; *Robertson (CSCP—Syd) to Friends, 13th December 1976*, Papers of GMM.
125 *McGahen (CSCP—Syd) to [blank], December 1976*, Papers of GMM.
126 *Inti Illimani Itinerary*, Papers of GMM.
127 'Inti Illimani: Chile's Famous Folk Singers, Australian Concert Tour, March 1977'; 'Inti Illimani', *Socialist*, 2 March 1977, 4; 'Inti Illimani', *Tribune* [Australia]. The group did not travel to Tasmania due to travel costs, although the Tasmanian State Council of the AMWSU did donate $50 and offer to assist in organising the event if it was to go ahead. *Ridley (AMWU Tas State Council) to McGahen (CSCP), 4th April 1977*, Papers of GMM.
128 He was in Sydney for the SPA anti-war conference in that week. *Philip [Herington] (CSCP—Melb) to Brian [McGahen], 25.1.77*, Papers of GMM.
129 *Robertson (CSCP) to Bull (WWFA), 22nd April, 1977*, Papers of GMM.
130 'El pueblo unido jamas sera vencido', *Tribune* [Australia], 20 April 1977.
131 Sykes, 'Inti Illimani's Poetic Message'. Similarly in the report in the *Tribune*, it was written that 'Inti Illimani's powerful combination of music and politics inspired audiences wherever they played, bringing the strength and spirit of the Chilean resistance alive'. 'El pueblo unido jamas sera vencido'.

and politically'.[132] Philip Herington, however, noted in his report that ticket sales in Melbourne were slower than for the Quilapayun tour two years earlier because the passing of time had taken 'the edge off the enthusiasm about Chile', as well as organisational issues and overlapping events (such as the uranium moratoriums).[133] Despite this, the tour was hailed a success, so much so that Chilean music events in the future promised music 'in the style of Inti Illimani'.[134]

Trade unions in Australia were opportunistic just as those in Britain were and just as they were around the world. Though Australia's Chile movement lacked the coherence of that in Britain, trade unions were provided with ample opportunities to use the movement to express their internationalism at little organisational cost. The indirect actions described in this chapter illustrate the symbiotic relationship between radical unions and the Chile committee. Each was being used by the other.

But actions that were light on the use of resources could be undertaken by almost anyone. Did Australian unions have the commitment to put their backs into it and really push in the name of internationalist ideology? And was there anything that the solidarity movement could do to encourage independent union action?

Those within the movement were certainly aware of the challenge. After the tour of Inti Illimani, Philip Herington wrote:

> Our task now is to develop in the coming period a political program of solidarity work which can consolidate the impact that the Inti had and to translate it into [concrete] actions that Australians can do. This demands careful work to spread our message among trade unions, the ALP, Church groups etc.[135]

The following chapters will assess the campaign's success in their work of encouraging trade unions to take action independently.

---

132 *Robertson to 'friends' re: Inti illimani*, Papers of Barry Carr.
133 *Report on the Tour of Inti Illimani (Melbourne 5.4.77)*, Papers of GMM.
134 'Concert for Chile', *Tribune* [Australia], 30 November 1977.
135 *Report on the Tour of Inti Illimani (Melbourne 5.4.77)*, Papers of GMM.

7. 'Twelve Days in Chile', 1974

Steve Cooper sat at a table looking across at a group of Chilean men. They were in a factory called Madeco, a metalworking establishment that Cooper had first visited a year before. The difference was that now Chile, and its workers, had been under military rule for six months. He observed the men closely, and noted that there were several newly appointed 'union representatives', and only one of the old committee.

Cooper asked only one question: 'When you have an industrial disagreement with the boss and you get no satisfaction after exhausting negotiation—what practical action can you take?'

It was a loaded question.

From the tense silence that followed, Cooper surmised:

1. that the position here was the same as they had already been told elsewhere: 'a strike would be suicide'
2. that there was an informer present.

To ease the tension and reduce the potential danger to the workers, they cut the conversation short, and toured the factory: 'On leaving the plant, we took some photos. I conveyed to them that we were aware of the true situation and they seemed rather pleased, but relieved, when I left.'[1]

Cooper had returned to Chile as part of a joint trade union delegation. This chapter describes the lead-up to the delegation, including the factional jockeying between unions and how one resource-rich organisation could exert its political will. It describes the activities of the delegates while travelling in Chile, and the information they discovered. Delegations such as these fulfilled a unique part of the repertoire of action of trade unions in the Chile movement. They were created *by* unionists *for* unionists. Significantly, of all solidarity activities, delegations were the least opportunistic and involved the most organisation and commitment. Interestingly, what the delegates did and found in Chile are not the most important aspects. It was what they could do previous to and post visit that made the delegation significant to the solidarity movement.

This chapter reveals that the size of the union was imperative to its adoption of external political issues: a threshold must be passed for the resources to be available for such an undertaking. The organisation of the delegation further

---

1 *The AMWU Commonwealth Council: Re: Chile Fact-Finding Mission, 7 June 1974*, Plumbers and Gasfitters Employees Union of Australia [hereinafter PGEUA]: Federal Office, N133/203, NBAC: ANU, Canberra.

underlines the importance of strategic individuals in developing external political action within labour unions. It provides several more examples of such individuals at work, including Henry McCarthy and James Baird. Finally, this chapter elucidates the politics of delegate selection and indicates that the use of international social movement delegations as a weapon in local factional disputes was a dangerous strategy.

The arrangement of the delegation was prompted by a throwaway remark during a visit to Australia by the president of the Chilean national airline, Lan Chile. In November 1973, General Germán Stuardos, newly appointed president of Lan Chile, became the first Chilean Government official to enter Australia after the coup. Stuardos was a 'debonair' man, who 'muster[ed] all what urbanity he could to defend the regime and its odious doings, already well known'.[2] According to Derry Hogue in *The Australian*, Stuardos had been a general in the Chilean Air Force during Allende's Government, but had resigned shortly before the coup as a protest against Allende's policies.[3] G. A. Grimshaw, NSW Branch Secretary of the Transport Workers Union of Australia, was more straightforward. He said Stuardos was 'a big shot in the Chilean Government'.[4] Stuardos was visiting Australia acting in the interest of the military junta: petitioning for Lan Chile landing rights and justifying the Chilean military's actions because of the so-called extreme policies that Allende's Government had pursued.

Still, as John Kane has noted in his book *Moral Capital*: 'any attempted legitimation is always potentially vulnerable to someone else's delegitimation.'[5] The junta's efforts to legitimise their rule in the eyes of the world could be undermined by the moral capital of a few if those few were suitably armed. What sort of arms would you need to dent the shiny exterior of a new military government?

In 1973 Lan Chile still flew commercially only to Tahiti, forcing passengers to connect with other airlines in order to travel on to Australia. They were keen to alter this situation.[6] A press conference was to be held for Stuardos and it would inevitably expose him to questioning about what was occurring in Chile. In the days previous to it, AMWU publicity officer Henry McCarthy and Steve Cooper had agreed that journalists should be encouraged to question Stuardos about the abuse of trade union rights. Stuardos's offhand response to one such question produced the opportunity. He said 'we will be lucky if union officials from your country come to Chile and see what has happened and how much happier the

---

2   Derry Hogue, 'Lan Chile Query', email to author, 7 March 2005, copies in possession of author.
3   Derry Hogue, 'Chile Air Line Wants to Land Here', *The Australian*, 22 November 1973.
4   'Unions Free Plane after Chilean Note', *The Australian*, 11 February 1974.
5   Kane, The Politics of *Moral Capital*, 32.
6   *Report re Chile 'Fact-Finding Mission', February 1974*, WWFA: Federal Office, N114/932, NBAC: ANU, Canberra.

people are now'.⁷ Cooper and McCarthy discussed the possibility of a delegation and decided it was a viable option.⁸ McCarthy then drew the attention of his union colleague Jim Baird to the opportunity.⁹

Seizing the opportunity, Steve Cooper, who was working at the Miscellaneous Workers' Union (MWU), McCarthy and Baird, national organiser of the AMWU, banded together to become the Committee on the Delegation to Chile.¹⁰ McCarthy rang the regional manager of Lan Chile in Australia. He demanded that a delegation of unionists be able to see fellow unionists and jails in Chile in order to assess the 'happiness' of the Chilean people as stipulated in Stuardos's invitation. The invitation was formally extended to the AMWU and five other unions as selected by the Australian Council of Trade Unions (ACTU). It was reported in the *Herald* that the unionists would be able to 'go anywhere' and 'see anyone' while in Chile.¹¹ Lan Chile agreed to pay for return flights from Tahiti to Chile for the unionists and 17 January 1974 was set for their departure.¹² Who were these men who swiftly forced the hand of the airline and what was their union like?

The AMWU consisted of 167 445 members in 1971. It was known as a progressive union and was affiliated to the ACTU, State trades councils and to the ALP in every State.¹³ New South Wales had 36 per cent of members.¹⁴ Politically, nine national-level and 30 NSW State-level full-time officials were ALP left or CPA, but there was also an organised opposition within union ranks.¹⁵

The AMWU was the union in which the Sydney Committee of Solidarity with the Chilean People was most firmly embedded, even in those first months. The involvement did not stem directly from the encouragement or efforts of the CSCP, but from a combination of reforms and amalgamations with a mix of new ideology. The AMWU had high membership growth in the very early 1970s, emerging in 1972 as an even larger organisation due to amalgamations.¹⁶ As with other unions in Australia, the AMWU benefited from the ACTU Congress's decision to set union fees at 1 per cent of weekly earnings, which meant a

---

7 Hogue, 'Chile Air Line Wants to Land Here'.
8 Cooper et al. Conversation, 2007.
9 *The AMWU Commonwealth Council, Re: Lan Chile Airlines, 10 December 1973*, PGEUA: Federal Office, N133/203, NBAC: ANU, Canberra.
10 Montenegro, 'La Campaña de Solidaridad con Chile en Australia 1973–1990'.
11 *Herald, 29 November, 1973 in AMWU Commonwealth Council, Re: Lan Chile Airlines*, PGEUA: Federal Office, NBAC: ANU, Canberra.
12 Ibid.
13 Rawson, *A Handbook of Australian Trade Unions and Employees' Associations*, 29.
14 Stephen Frenkel and Alice Coolican, 'Union Organisation and Decision Making', in *Australian Unions: An Industrial Relations Perspective*, eds Bill Ford and David Plowman (South Melbourne: Macmillan, 1983), 146.
15 Ibid., 146–7.
16 Ibid., 51; Bramble, *Trade Unionism in Australia*, 68.

substantial windfall for unions with the large wage rises of 1973–74.[17] The AMWU had only recently shed its ties to the Amalgamated Engineers Union in the United Kingdom, and then it amalgamated with the Ship Wrights and Ship Constructors Union in 1976 to become the Amalgamated Metalworkers and Shipwrights Union (AMWSU).[18] This resulted in its status as Australia's largest union in 1978. The union was consequently still in metamorphosis in 1973–74 at the time of the Chile delegation.

Jim Baird had cut his teeth in the more militant Menzies years. 'In the old days', he recalled in the 1970s, a shop steward 'was often successful by the loudness of his voice and the size of his fist. But that's changed. Now the membership want logical arguments.'[19] The union and its members may have been becoming more sophisticated and the union was definitely becoming more complex. The growing awareness of members described by Baird had caused the union to become progressively more organised. It emerged from its amalgamation with a bulky and rather complicated structure. Its policymaking body was a biannual conference, the participants of which were elected by the rank and file. Sitting below the policy body was a national committee which was made up of 22 members and which met three times a year. Underneath that was the nine-man executive, which dealt with the day-to-day running of the union. As noted, it was dominated by men who were CPA and ALP members, though all CPA members on the executive strenuously denied any interference by the party in union affairs.[20] The AMWU assistant national secretary, Laurie Carmichael was the president of the CPA and secretary, John Halfpenny, was also a member. The union was affiliated to the ALP in every State, but for the CSCP it was perhaps the CPA links that were more operative. The connection and sympathy of the AMWU leadership for the CPA created a reservoir of resources and goodwill for the Chile campaign.

The large AMWU membership provided a generous budget, which allowed for a broad array of committees. These were divided into two types: industrial committees (17) and subcommittees (12). One of the latter was an international committee convened by a national officer. In the early 1970s George Aitkins held this position.[21] There was also an established research office at the union, which had a coordinator and four full-time research officers.[22] It has been noted that a union's research and education capabilities directly affect the type of activism the union undertakes. Given that unions at this time in Australia were

---

17 Hagan, 'The Australian Trade Union Movement', 51.
18 Bray, 'Democracy from the Inside', 85.
19 Pat Huntley, *Inside Australia's Largest Union* (Northbridge, NSW: Ian Huntley, 1978), 69.
20 Ibid.
21 Aitkins was also a WFTU representative. Roe, 'Notes for Speech'.
22 Huntley, *Inside Australia's Largest Union*, v–viii. Cooper would later take up a paid research position at the AMWU (after the delegation returned).

extending their staff capability it is reasonable to hypothesise that the type, scope or method of activism was changing too.[23] In 1973 the AMWU was entering a period of relative prosperity, with a new building being constructed in Sydney and the creation of various new professional administrative positions. These positions provided more man-hours for the union, which not only allowed for adequate attention to the industrial issues but also an overflow of advocacy into social justice issues, such as the Chile movement.

The multiplication of members, officials, employees and funds for the AMWU in the 1970s meant that the representatives of the union attended many more international conferences.[24] Without the membership growth's subsequent multiplication of structure, time, organising and research hours, the delegation would never have gone ahead. The AMWU's action was, in this case, directly related to its size.

If prosperity provided the means, it was the impact of the ideas of the new left that encouraged unions such as the AMWU to take on new causes—some of them social, others international. The extension of union activity into social activism was also driven by key individuals. The AMWU's involvement in the Chile issue, in particular, reflected the influence of several fundamental people in the union—notably, James Baird and Henry McCarthy.

Baird was a boilermaker by trade, whose apprenticeship at Morts Docks in Balmain in Sydney exposed him to an education by the radical left. It was the international nature of the work at Morts Docks and the high concentration of workers with radical left politics that pushed Baird towards the trade union movement.[25] By the 1970s Baird was immensely respected and later in his career became a commissioner of the Australian Conciliation and Arbitration Commission.[26] In the 1970s, he was also convenor of the AMWU publications committee, and before being elected to the national organiser position in 1973 he had been head of the research centre for nine years.[27] Along with Baird's long-term membership of the CPA, this meant he was well aware of the Chilean situation before the coup.[28] He was present at the first meetings of the CSCP

---

23 Deery, 'Union Aims and Methods', 77; Hagan, 'The Australian Trade Union Movement', 51.
24 Commonwealth secretary J. D. Garland said this came down to the far-sighted policies the union undertook in the 1940s and 1950s. Pat Huntley and Ian Huntley, *Inside Australia's Top 100 Trade Unions—Are they Wrecking Australia?* (Northbridge, NSW: Ian Huntley, 1976), 326.
25 Huntley, *Inside Australia's Largest Union*, 65.
26 Rhiannon Lee, 'Death of the Honourable Roy Frederick Turner, AM, A Former Member of the Legislative Council', in *NSW Parliament Legislative Council* (29 June 2004), 10438.
27 Huntley, *Inside Australia's Largest Union*, vii.
28 *Minutes of Meeting of National Council held Professional Musicians Club, Sydney, Wednesday 16 Jan 1974*, AMWU: South Australian State Council, N131/98 Commonwealth Council Minutes AMWSU and AMWU 1973–1977, NBAC: ANU, Canberra. Huntley, *Inside Australia's Largest Union*, 65.

and was a member of its executive and steering committees.²⁹ His prominent position in the AMWU ensured that Chile received constant coverage in the AMWU publications.

In this he had an ally in Henry McCarthy, the national publicity officer of the AMWU in the early 1970s, who was a strategic actor of high importance in the early years of the Chile movement. For example, he endorsed the production of 15 000 leaflets for the demonstration on the first anniversary of the coup.³⁰ In 1973 Baird gained strategic importance after his election (a promotion) to national organiser, but he lost the ability to dedicate time and make on-the-run decisions due to the increase in his union responsibilities. McCarthy could be a little more flexible in his role and the position of head of publishing was by nature influential.

The committee organising the delegation to Chile (McCarthy and Baird, together with Steve Cooper, who was starting to take on a substantial amount of work at the CSCP in Sydney) sought guarantees from the Chilean Government for the safety not only of the delegation's members but also of the Chileans with whom they hoped to meet. The official press statement from the AMWU outlined the guarantees sought, including access to prison areas and freedom to interview people without surveillance from authorities.³¹ The Miners Federation also expressed interest, and ABC Television's *4 Corners* program was to send a crew; however, it all soon ground to a halt.

Although the Chilean Government was willing to give all manner of assurances verbally, the Australian office of Lan Chile received a cable from the Chilean Government stating that it 'did not consider it appropriate to give written confirmation of the guarantee[s]'.³² It was little wonder. The letter sent seeking the assurances had rather cheekily noted that there was a substantial level of resentment of the 'current undemocratic military government in Chile' among trade unions in Australia.³³ A lack of written assurance for this group of unionists implied that the danger to others was very real indeed. The Australians refused to move without the papers and Lan Chile and the Chilean authorities refused to accede to the demands.

As January 1974 came and went, McCarthy, Baird and Cooper began to mobilise the support of trade unionists and the wider community. The AMWU distributed a press statement (thanks to McCarthy's strategic role as publicity officer) titled

---

29   NSW Committee for Solidarity with the Chilean People.
30   The demonstration was to be organised by the CSCP. *Circular. AMWU Commonwealth Council, august 16 1974*, PGEUA: Federal Office, N133/158, NBAC: ANU, Canberra.
31   *Press Statement of the AMWU—7/2/74: What is the Chilean Junta Up To?*
32   *Press Statement by Federal Council Waterside Workers' Fed. of Aust. Re: Chile, Sept 13 1973*, WWFA: Federal Office, N114/932, NBAC: ANU, Canberra.
33   *Press Statement of the AMWU—7/2/74: What is the Chilean Junta Up To?*

'What is the Chilean Junta up to?'. It outlined the fight to get to Chile, and some of the occurrences within Chile that the delegation proposed to investigate.[34] While it may have been Baird and McCarthy pushing AMWU action on Chile, the official AMWU face of international issues was George Aitkins (as head of the International Subcommittee).[35] Aitkins was not a lightweight in the union; he was a WFTU representative and a national organiser with extensive negotiating experience.[36] His position and knowledge would come into play for the Chile cause sooner than anyone expected.

The Chilean Government officially deferred the delegation on 6 February; the AMWU press statement explaining the situation was released on 7 February. The final sentences of the document called for support of the WFTU solidarity with Chile Day on 12 February, and urged the Australian Government to refuse Lan Chile's landing rights. As it turned out, Australian action pre-empted the international boycott plans, but despite their efforts until that point, the metal workers were not the ones who struck the first blow.

At 6 am on Saturday, 9 February 1974, a Lan Chile flight was black banned at Kingsford Smith Airport in Sydney. 'When the plane landed in Sydney on Saturday morning', said Grimshaw, secretary of the NSW branch of the Transport Workers' Union of Australia, 'we decided to take industrial action to show them we were fair dinkum'.[37] The Transport Workers' Union, with support from the AMWU, WWFA, SUA and other unions, refused to touch the plane. It remained unfuelled and unloaded and was parked off to the side of the airport, in an area under air force control.[38] The passengers, and their families waiting in the terminal, resented the union action. George Aitkins noted the irony:

> The 138 passengers refused to leave the aircraft for 3 $^{1/2}$ hours unless their baggage was unloaded. Some 300 relatives and friends demonstrated outside the Custom Hall by slow clapping and chanting 'chasalga' ('let them free') referring of course to the passengers but ironically the protest of the transport workers was to get the Junta to 'let the Chilean trade union and political prisoners free.'[39]

The black ban was hailed as 'possibly the first direct action taken in defence of Chileans by workers in another country'.[40] Australian workers had sensed an

---

34 Ibid.
35 Ibid.
36 Cooper et al. Conversation, 2007.
37 Ibid. Grimshaw was later listed as a member of the delegation; however, he did not travel. *AMWU Commonwealth Council re: Chile Fact Finding Mission, February 22 1974*, WWFA: Federal Office, N114/932, NBAC: ANU, Canberra.
38 Roe, 'Notes for Speech'.
39 *AMWU Commonwealth Council re: Chile Fact Finding Mission*.
40 *Chilean Junta Airliner Grounded, 1974*, AMWSU, E262/137, NBAC: ANU, Canberra.

opportunity and moved rapidly and conclusively. While the plane lay idle on the tarmac, Lan Chile and AMWU representatives Henry McCarthy and George Aitkins met to negotiate its servicing. They used the black ban to highlight their opposition to the military government of Chile, and also as leverage to get the Chilean Government to grant their demands for the delegation. The thickly moustached Aitkins was quite deaf and, so the story goes, he just turned off his hearing aid so he could not hear what the Lan Chile representatives were saying, let alone grant any concessions.[41] The unionist's negotiating experience won out, and the two AMWU organisers were successful: the Chileans were forced to accede to the demands of the trade union delegation. After a delay of 22 hours, the aircraft left Sydney on 10 February 1974.[42]

The Transport Workers' Union action was pivotal in this story. Without it, the delegation may never have travelled. Luis Figueroa and Luis Meneses, Chilean trade unionists who later visited Australia, phrased it explicitly in a special message for the Transport Workers' members of Mascott Airport: 'without your action which banned the Lan Chile Aircraft in 1974, it is possible that we may not be alive.'[43] On an earlier occasion, Figueroa had said 'when that plane was grounded in Sydney the news swept through Chile and from that moment, lives began to be saved in Chile'.[44]

What was essentially an opportunistic, symbolic and short-term action had deep consequences.

Following the blacking of the plane, flushed with success, 13 unions presented a united front against the military junta of Chile. They endorsed a pamphlet that focused on the black ban of the aircraft and the abuse of workers' rights in Chile. The flyer's title was an open declaration of solidarity with 'oppressed people', but the text was focused on trade union rights. This was a textbook case of the manifestation of the socialist ideal of a worldwide working class: 'Oppressed people across the world with a yearning for freedom will take courage from the stand of the airport workers.'[45] The delegation was hardly mentioned, as it was

---

41 I have not been able to find why AMWU went in to negotiate instead of TWU organisers. Cooper et al. Conversation, 2007.
42 *Chilean Junta Airliner Grounded, 1974*. James Baird claimed the plane was boycotted for a month. Baird, 'After the Coup', 7. This copy was given to the author by Steve Cooper, who believes it was written as part of Baird's memoirs before his death. Steve Cooper remembers the boycott as lasting about a week. Cooper Interview, 2005. *The Australian* reported that Australian and Chilean journalists were aboard when it left, and if they were, they were not linked to the delegation as implied in the article. 'Unions Free Plane after Chilean Note'.
43 J. Baird to G. Grimshaw, October 1 1975 and attached letter for Transport Workers' Union Strikers from CUT, September 19 1975, AMWSU, E262/137, NBAC: ANU, Canberra.
44 *Maritime Worker*, 14 May 1977, 7.
45 *Chilean Junta Airliner Grounded, 1974*.

too controversial for all unions to agree. The exclusion of the delegation from the pamphlet was a concession to the SUA, WWFA and AFULE, who all opposed the trip, but supported the boycott of the plane.

Despite the veneer of unified purpose and ideology, soon the cracks were showing in the fragile unity of the plane blacking.[46] Those who objected generally did so on the grounds that taking up the invitation of the military junta implied complicity with fascism, imperialism and capitalism. The AFULE, who had sent a delegate to the Chilean multinational conference before the coup, was firmly against sending a delegation of unionists as guests of the military junta.[47] The Building Workers' Industrial Union (BWIU) also felt that the acceptance of the invitation might lend respectability to the junta.[48] The maritime unions' opposition was based on their belief that the delegation would necessarily have to work *with* the Chilean military in order to express solidarity. They held the view that working within the framework set by the capitalist world only added to its legitimacy. In the words of CSCP activist Mavis Robertson, members of the SPA believed that the delegates would be suborned by the military rulers of Chile, or as Cooper phrased it, 'duchessed'.[49] The SPA affiliates also believed that the military regime would take the delegation 'around like circus ponies', showing them only the places where everything was unaffected by the coup.[50] Their objection was not due purely to their doubts about the usefulness of the delegation, but also to a nuanced ideological difference. Individuals in opposition to the delegation were generally anti-revisionist, pro-Soviet and in the SPA, or unions in which this view predominated.[51]

The SUA's opposition to the delegation was particularly vehement. The Federal Office of the SUA sent a letter to the AMWU stating that 'any acceptance by Australian workers' representatives of the hospitality of the fascist military Junta in Chile is an indictment of our class consciousness'.[52] The SUA sent representatives to every meeting discussing the delegation, and consistently raised their opposition to it. Some members of the AMWU National Council also opposed the delegation at first; however, it was agreed that if the international labour movement organisations supported it, a consensus for support would be reached. According to Baird, 'Henry McCarthy … got to work and through his international contacts was able to secure the support of the' ICFTU, WFTU and the Catholic International of Trade Unions (CITU).[53] The international

---

46 'Seamen Reject Invitation for Fascist Chile General', *Seamen's Journal* 29 (March 1974), 64–5.
47 Ibid.; *Australian Federated Union of Locomotive Enginemen letter to J Baird, March 18 1974*, AMWSU, E262/137, NBAC: ANU, Canberra.
48 *AMWU Commonwealth Council re: Chile Fact Finding Mission*.
49 Robertson Interview, 2009; Cooper et al. Conversation, 2007.
50 Cooper Interview, 2005.
51 Robertson Interview, 2009.
52 'Seamen Reject Invitation for Fascist Chile General'.
53 Baird, 'After the Coup'.

organisations telexed their support within an hour of the requests.[54] The WFTU reportedly said that the delegation would 'greatly help the international solidarity campaign'.[55]

WFTU approval was not long lasting.[56] Believing them to be misled, the SUA sent information concerning the organisation and conditions of the delegation to the WFTU on 15 February.[57] In response, the WFTU did not withdraw support from the delegation, but strongly questioned if the delegation would be allowed to make independent inquiries when in Chile. Yet, in the same letter to the AMWU, they also gave further information on the current union situation in Chile.[58] As both the SUA and the AMWU were affiliates, it appears the WFTU was unwilling to take sides. The opposition to the delegation was a manifestation of local political divisions and probably not important enough for the WFTU to bother with. 'Chile' was being used as a tool for political point scoring and assertion of identity. Mavis Robertson reflected on this, saying, 'well, there is no doubt in my mind that the split in the [CPA] was being played out in international things'.[59] But going out against the delegation was a dangerous stance. If the delegation succeeded they would return heroic. Furthermore, not all the unionists, branches or unions played into the factional disputes.

Despite the federal officers (Elliot, Geraghty, Nolan, Webster and Brennan) all unanimously voting against the delegation, the structure of the SUA allowed branches to have their say, and it was not as simple as branches following national office orders. At a stop-work meeting on 25 February 1974, the Victorian Branch of the SUA discussed the proposal. Members were confused. Comrade Wilson questioned why the SUA national office at first asked for motions in support of the delegation, then in opposition to it. He said: 'Earlier, quite properly, the Federal Office suggests stop work meetings carry resolutions calling for a fact finding commission, comprising members of Parliament and Trade union representatives. To present this as fundamentally different from a fact finding Trade Union group is nonsense.'[60] Whatever the status of those who travelled to Chile, they would need visas, he argued, and thus would have to make contact with the ruling junta. At the Queensland branch stop-work meeting, the motion was put to the assembled unionists. There was a speaker against the motion (that is, for the delegation), and only five ended up voting to endorse the federal

---

54 Ibid.
55 'Australian Mission may Visit Chile', *SPA*, March 1974.
56 'Seamen Reject Invitation for Fascist Chile General'.
57 Ibid.
58 Ibid.; International Committee AMWU, 'Commonwealth Conference—May/June, 1974', in photocopies attached to Roe, 'Notes for Speech'.
59 Robertson Interview, 2009.
60 *SUA (Victorian Branch) Minutes of Stop Work Meeting held Unity Hall Tuesday, 25th February, 1974*, 5, Seamen's Union of Australia [hereinafter SUA]: Federal Office, N38/639, NBAC: ANU, Canberra.

office's stance.⁶¹ The Fremantle branch, however, unanimously carried their resolution endorsing the federal office's position. The West Australian, Port Kembla, Sydney, Newcastle and South Australian branches all carried to support the national office,⁶² but internal SUA dissent and even unified opposition to the action would be little more than a scratch on the history of the delegation.

Leaving behind the disagreement between the unions and the machinations of political factions, the delegation set off for Chile via Tahiti on 23 March 1974. They were almost the only passengers aboard.⁶³ The delegates were Jim Baird (the official AMWU representative), Steve Cooper (endorsed by the MWA), Ron Masterson (Plumbers and Gasfitters Union, Newcastle Branch), Brian McMahon (Transport Workers' Union, Victorian organiser),⁶⁴ Henry McCarthy (travelling as a journalist) and Carmen Bull (translator and Argentinean-born wife of prominent CPA member and WWFA organiser Tas Bull).⁶⁵ Not surprisingly, not one delegate was a member of the SPA.⁶⁶ Many of the delegates were not paid their union wages for the period they were away, but the unions invested funds in the trip and expected results.⁶⁷ Their activities in Chile were to include a meeting with the Minister for the Interior, a visit to a detention centre and multiple factories, and meetings with the ex-minister of labour as well as underground and stranded trade unionists.⁶⁸

Steve Cooper described their arrival in Chile in his notes:

> Night. Santiago patterned with lights as we land, full of forebodings.
>
> The rest of the passengers leave. The plane is well out in the airport. We descend the stairs and cluster at the bottom. It is very dark with a thin, swirling mist.

He continued:

---

61   'Seamen Reject Invitation for Fascist Chile General'.
62   *SUA (WA Branch) minutes of stop work meeting held in Waterside Workers' Federation Hall—Fremantle—Tuesday, 26th, February, 1974*, SUA: Federal Office, N38/639, NBAC: ANU, Canberra; 'Seamen Reject Invitation for Fascist Chile General'.
63   Roe, 'Notes for Speech'.
64   McMahon was a lawyer. *The Commission of Enquiry, 1974*.
65   *The AMWU Commonwealth Council: Re: Chile Fact-Finding Mission*.
66   *Against political exclusionism: For a United Front Against the Repression in Chile—Spartacist League*.
67   Henry McCarthy received 10 days' leave without pay to travel on this delegation. Several unions contributed to his airfare. *Mission to Chile (minutes of CAC Meeting, 18-2-74)*, Papers of GMM; *AMWU Commonwealth Council re: Chile Fact Finding Mission*.
68   The delegation also saw General Schneider's daughters, a bishop who was key to getting interviews with workers and students and so on, interviewed between 30 and 40 people, and took a pocket camera to try to catch images without being noticed by the military. They possibly visited a women's prison, found that soldiers from the south had been sent to the north and vice versa in order to make soldiers more likely to follow orders and Carmen went out after the curfew in attempts to make contacts. They visited the towns of Valparaiso, Santiago, Antofagasta, Tocopilla, Maria-Elena and Chuquicamata. They met with representatives of the CUT, Metal Workers, Textile workers, CEPCH, Railway workers, Sugar Workers, Dockers, Copper Workers, Hospital Employees and Lan Chile's Union. Roe, 'Notes for Speech'; *The Commission of Enquiry, 1974*.

> Out of the mist some soldiers emerge, walking towards us. One is dapper with a moustache. Major Figueroa. But he smiles and politely asks about our trip, and we can relax. We sense he is 'O.K.' given that the city is otherwise crawling with psychotic killers in uniform.
>
> So far, so good.[69]

Relying on gut instinct was a must, as the delegate's grasp of Spanish was, in general, rudimentary.

The highest-profile meeting with the junta was with Oscar Bonilla Bradanovic, an army general and co-conspirator with Pinochet, who later met his death in a suspicious helicopter accident in 1975.[70] He was minister of the interior and he met the Australian unionists dressed in perfect, crisp military uniform. He greeted the Australian unionists by saying, 'you have come from a paradise, and I have just left hell'.[71] Bonilla's idea of hell was the three years of government under Allende, which had represented such hope for the Australian unionists. This poorly disguised, combative mockery must have heightened the tension in the room, a hypothesis that was supported by the language of the report written by David McIntyre, a South American affairs expert from the Australian Embassy in Argentina.[72] Led by James Baird, the Australians tried their best to extract information about the 'hell' they had come to investigate.[73]

The general followed his confrontational opening with a claim that there was 80 per cent popular support for the military government. He then made remarks emphasising the freedom of Australians to form their own opinion on what was happening in Chile. The interview was opened to questions and the Australians began to probe intensely. They sought answers regarding the detention of unionists, the conditions at the Dawson Island prison camp in Tierra del Fuego and confirmation that torture had taken place.[74] At this time Bonilla was still supporting the general facade of the military government: that it was a

---

69 Major Figueroa was not related to the labour leader also named Figueroa. Cooper, 'Journey to Chile. 1974', notes transcribed to one copy on return to Australia, copy in possession of author.

70 Largely believed to be the victim of political cleansing that Pinochet undertook to solidify his own position. Arturo Alejandro Munoz, 'Gral. Bonilla, accidente demasiado sospechoso', accessed 17 April 2007, <http://www.granvalparaiso.cl/columnistas/munoz/bonilla.htm>; *Central Unica de Trabajadores de Chile, Comite Exterior Paris: Un Fraude Escandoloso, September 19, 1980*, Australian Teachers' Federation, Z219 Box 83, NBAC: ANU, Canberra; Burbach, *The Pinochet Affair*, 53.

71 *Conversation with General Oscar Bonilla (Minister of the Interior) and Trade Union Delegation, 25 March 1974*, AMWSU, E262/137, NBAC: ANU, Canberra.

72 *The Commission of Enquiry, 1974.*

73 Baird acted as the main negotiator with Bonilla. He was chosen possibly because he was the only delegate with a national organiser position, and was thus the highest in rank. Baird's aim was getting people back to Australia. Gustavo Martin Montenegro's family came to Australia because of Baird's work. Judy Lyons, 'Chilean Refugee "Tortured, Threatened with Death"', *AMWU Monthly Journal* (1974); Cooper et al. Conversation, 2007.

74 *Press Statement of the AMWU—7/2/74: What is the Chilean Junta Up To?*

benevolent dictatorship forced to act because of the serious Marxist threat to the people of Chile and the world. Bonilla insisted that 'the objectives of the government [were] to reinstate democracy and normalcy'.[75]

Figure 7.1 Australian trade unionists speak with General Oscar Bonilla.

Source: From left: Jim Baird [unconfirmed], Steve Cooper, unknown member of the Australian diplomatic core [possibly Jim Lindsay or David Macintyre], General Bonilla. 'La Patria', Martes 26 de Marzo de 1974, AMWU: National Office, Z112 box 7, NBAC: ANU, Canberra.

A photograph of some of the delegation in the interview with General Bonilla appeared on the front page of *La Patria*, a Chilean newspaper in print at the time. It was part of the strategy of the military government to appear open and transparent to foreign visitors. The caption below the photograph tells the

---

75 *Conversation with General Oscar Bonilla (Minister of the Interior) and Trade Union Delegation, 25 March 1974*, 3.

reader that the visit of the Australian trade unionists was not of a 'political character' and that they did not want to visit Dawson Island Detention Centre. In the extensive files of the AMWU, a cut-out of the article appears. It is circled various times in ink, with the following words scribbled by an unknown hand: 'this is a complete lie. Thats what we *went* for.'[76]

Although the delegates did not visit Dawson Island as they had hoped, they did win a small victory when they were granted permission to enter the Chacabuco Detention Centre.[77] The visit was perhaps the most important aspect of the delegation to Chile, however confused the Australians were about the spelling of its name. Writing Spanish words and names down as they sounded resulted in distinctively Australianised versions of words being used throughout the whole Chile solidarity movement. In this case, the Chacabuco centre was 'Chakabooka', 'Chacabouka' in a report and 'Chacavuco' in a union newspaper, resulting from the Chilean accent, which often leads to confusion of the sounds of 'b' and 'v'.[78]

Despite some uncertainty over the most basic information, the intense feeling of solidarity and the determination of delegates Jim Baird, Carmen Bull and Ron Masterson were obvious as they travelled deep into the Atacama Desert to the detention centre.[79] Chacabuco was a nitrate-mining ghost town, deserted in the 1930s. In 1974 it was surrounded by layers of fencing with wooden guard towers. The buildings were very old and dusty, but rust and decay-free as a result of the dry climate in which they were situated. The freshly painted signs on the outside of the area indicated '*Minas*': mines.

The delegation members procured a taxi to travel the 260 km from Tocopilla in the north of Chile. The detention centre guards carried machine guns and peered cautiously into the vehicle that had appeared out of the desert. They forced the Australians to hand over their passports and then the letter from Minister Bonilla, which 'caused a small stir'.[80] A guard, still carrying his gun, squashed into the car with the delegates as they drove into the camp. Since their arrival in Chile, the list of detained men the delegates hoped to speak to had grown to include academics, metal workers and a number of other unionists and non-unionists; however, only 20 inmates were led out into an enclosed garden area where some small plants struggled against the elements. They sat in a rotunda.

---

76   *Sindicalistas Australianos, 1974*, AMWSU, E262/137, NBAC: ANU, Canberra. Baird later spoke to an aide of the Minister for the Interior, who told him the minister was 'furious that the delegation was doing what it wanted'. Roe, 'Notes for Speech'.
77   Chacabuco was one of the places pointed out by the WFTU as a potential place to visit. *Press Statement of the AMWU—7/2/74: What is the Chilean Junta Up To?*
78   *12 Days in Chile, 1974*, AMWSU, E262/137 'Chile 1974–1977', NBAC: ANU, Canberra; *Chacabooka, 1974*, AMWU: National Office, Z112 Box 7, NBAC: ANU, Canberra.
79   *Chacabooka, 1974*; *The AMWU Commonwealth Council: Re: Chile Fact-Finding Mission*.
80   Baird, 'After the Coup'.

The inmates looked worn out, but clean. They stated that they had received relatively good treatment at Chacabuco, where they were allowed to receive censored letters and visitors too if they had the means to travel all the way into the desert. Although they were all held without charges, the men were relatively happy to be at that particular centre. They thought it was the best camp, used by the junta purposely to mislead foreigners investigating human rights abuses. Jim Baird wrote in a report: 'It was a moving situation at the end, as we decided after 1½ hours to leave. They embraced us and gave us an emotional farewell.'

The Australians walked with the men towards their barracks behind a fence. Furtively, a metalworker pressed a piece of paper into the hand of a delegation member.

> They then halted, all trying to talk to Carmen [the only delegate present with fluent Spanish]. I think to try and convey some last minute thoughts. We bid them farewell and stood and waved as they walked back towards the wire enclosure accompanied by the group of armed guards who shepherded them through a wire gate about 12 ft. wide and 8 ft. high. They stood and continued to wave until at last they were moved towards the huts which were in rows behind the wire.[81]

Later, when the Australian read the note, it said 'we expect a lot of you comrade. We look to you to tell the Australian workers of what has happened.'[82] The delegates were anxious to leave the oppressive and intense environment, and refused the commanding officers' invitation to dine.[83] They drove back into the desert, heading towards the sea and away from 'what can only be described, with all its emotive force, as a concentration camp'.[84]

To make the most of their time in Chile, the Australians had split into smaller groups. Despite this, the chaperones succeeded in taking up chunks of time by insisting on sightseeing and picnics. Still, the delegates succeeded in visiting Luis Figueroa, who was under the protection an embassy in Santiago.[85] Figueroa had been Allende's minister for labour and the president of the CUT, the peak union body in Chile. He spoke at length to the Australian unionists about the crimes of the junta and the present trade union conditions in Chile, reporting that the CUT had been dissolved and its assets confiscated. Trade unionists who remained in office, said Figueroa, were Christian democrats or members of the

---

81   *Chacabooka*.
82   *Discussion with Metal Workers and Building Industry Leaders. Tuesday, 2nd April, 1974*, PGEUA: Federal Office, N133/203, NBAC, ANU, Canberra, 1974, 7.
83   He was an air force officer, trained in the United States. He was eager for company, as he disliked the prison and the desert. Roe, 'Notes for Speech'.
84   *12 Days in Chile, 1974*.
85   The delegates made their way there accompanied by Australian Embassy officials (possibly including Jim Lindsay). Cooper et al. Conversation, 2007; *Minutes of CAC meeting, 27-5-74*, Papers of GMM.

right. Despite what was happening in Chile, it was the failure of workers of the world to develop international action against multinationals that primarily concerned Figueroa. Steve Cooper, hearing this after attending the conference on multinationals the year before in Chile, must have been filled with dismay. Still, Figueroa said 'the fact that this Delegation can talk to the unions and to the people in gaols has created a great lift in morale among the Chilean trade unionist[s]'. He also proposed 'a toast to the delegation and to international trade union unity'.[86]

Delegates met two members of the Confederación de Empleados Particulares de Chile (CEPCH: the Chilean Employees' Confederation) with the aid of the Australian Embassy. Both were Christian democrats and they described the dire situation of workers in Chile, including the blacklisting of UP supporters by employers. Now the mere accusation of political activity could lead to instant dismissal.[87] The report of the conversation described the emerging economic conditions of the workers and the speculation over numbers of dead and missing. It continued: 'Now, to deal with the main problem. Most of the union officials are dead, gaoled or have lost their jobs, therefore cannot be organised.'[88]

The military government had no respect for the organised labour movement, and the military chiefs in each town were given almost unlimited power.[89] For unionists in Chile, the report related that 'the objectives to-day are to survive, to defend our friends, and to achieve freedom for the unions and end the state of war'.[90]

As well as the Madeco factory visit detailed at the beginning of this chapter, Steve Cooper also visited Indumet, a 'small but modern' sawmill equipment manufacturer in the suburb of San Miguel, only 6 km from the centre of Santiago.[91] The factory had been under workers' control until the day of the coup. On that day, a tank and soldiers had broken into the factory and at least 14 workers had been killed. Another version of the story was that *carabineros* attacked the factory and, following CUT orders, the workers offered armed resistance. Three of the policemen died and later the army retaliated. Sixteen workers were disappeared.[92]

---

86 *The AMWU Commonwealth Council: Re: Chile Fact-Finding Mission.*
87 Ibid.
88 *Interview with a Member of CEPCH.*
89 Ibid.
90 Ibid.
91 Ibid.
92 Ibid.; *Maritime Worker*, 18 June 1974, 7.

Cooper remembered the workers he had met a year earlier had all 'seemed to me cordial, intelligent and conscientious ordinary trade unionists doing their best to implement industrial democracy'.[93] Not one of them was left working at the factory when Cooper returned in 1974.

Cooper also met with some surviving members of the Textile Workers' Union of Chile. That union's membership had been predominantly socialist and communist and consequently had suffered heavy losses in the initial repression of the regime. The men sitting across from Cooper shared some of the shocking and painful stories of the terror of life under the dictatorship. Workers had been executed in their workplaces and military personnel killed families and burnt houses if their search for arms was resisted. The men said 'there was a lot of torture. At the national stadium some … were shot. They pulled out fingernails. They castrated men. They violated and raped women and pushed pisco bottles into their vaginas.'[94]

The confronting stories together with the constant tension of being under armed guard must have put immense strain on the delegates.[95] But it also drew them together. 'Saturday night. Shared a room with Ron Masterson', wrote Cooper in his notes. They 'chatted away until shut up by rifle fire nearby. (Silly Ron tries to stick his head out to see what's going on). If the place was bugged, they got our life stories.'[96]

The room may or may not have been bugged, but there were definitely guards. Jim Baird found this out when a cleaner took him aside and gestured towards another room. In it were armed guards.[97] Baird also recalled that on the way to a mine visit, they stopped to admire the scenery and as a result arrived 20 minutes late. The *carabinero* at the gate proceeded to beat the driver for this transgression. The 'interpreter' swiftly pulled out his identification card, and the policeman stopped beating the man, and saluted.[98] People were not who they seemed and not everyone could be trusted. The interpreter was clearly more than a clerk.

In their report in the CPA organ *Tribune*, Baird, McCarthy and Bull wrote that 'the delegation worked tirelessly and with an average of four hours sleep a night to see as much as possible of life in Chile'.[99] They visited the shantytown El Carmen, and Cooper articulated the experience of returning to where he had

---

93 *The AMWU Commonwealth Council: Re: Chile Fact-Finding Mission.*
94 *2.4.74—Textile workers Union of Chile interview, April 2 1974*, AMWU: National Office, z122 Box 7, NBAC: ANU, Canberra.
95 Baird, 'After the Coup'.
96 Cooper, 'Journey to Chile. 1974'.
97 Roe, 'Notes for Speech'.
98 Ibid.
99 Carmen Bull, Jim Baird and Henry McCarthy, 'Chilean Resistance', *Tribune* [Australia], 16–22 April 1974.

been welcomed a year earlier: 'I walked on into the settlement and *asked a worker* about Sergio, Vincente and the twelve others I knew, and he told me they had all been shot. It just felt like the end of everything.'[100]

The delegates were taken to the river where the bodies had been dumped.[101]

Almost 10 days in Chile had passed before the delegation was contacted by any of the banned, underground unions. On 2 April 1974, a secret meeting was set up with representatives of the Chilean underground resistance to the dictatorship. A trusted interpreter accompanied Masterson, Cooper and Baird. One of these men wrote:

> After passing through a number of back streets in Santiago, we came to an old two-storey building, part of a row of buildings, we were ushered into the front room through a hallway to meet two Chileans in their 30s or 40s. A careful exchange of information followed as to our connections and they volunteered that they were among the remaining free leaders who had been the national leadership of the metal workers.[102]

The Australians learned that many unionists had been detained and murdered. The unionists could still use the building, because the Metal Workers' Union had given it to the Archbishop of Santiago, thus preventing the military from confiscating it as they had done with other unions' property. The men had not been home since the coup of 11 September 1973 and were in danger of being detained. They believed that if they returned home, they would not only be captured, but also their families would be persecuted. The unnamed, nervous men proceeded to outline the limited nature of organised opposition to the junta; but after some minutes, they were interrupted: 'we were joined by a very impressive man in his 40s who was introduced to us as a leader of the Building Trades Workers. From the onset, he commanded the discussion with the delegation.'[103]

The building worker was heavily involved in the resistance to the military government. He accused the Chileans who had already left the country of 'running away' and was strongly focused on unifying the forces of the political left and the general populace to fight the military government. The Australian unionists expressed their desire to help the resistance in Chile, but the charismatic man replied that he was looking to political parties for support, not

---

100   Cooper, 'Journey to Chile. 1974'.
101   Roe, 'Notes for Speech'.
102   *Discussion with Metal Workers and Building Industry Leaders. Tuesday, 2nd April, 1974.*
103   Ibid.

trade unionists. The Australians replied: organised resistance could come 'from the militant trade unionists in Australia, who would be able to look for political support from the working class parties'.[104]

The statement seemed to win the trust of the Chilean men. The interpreter present said that the conversation he heard was 'the most open and frank' discussion since the unions had been forced underground months earlier. The Australians wanted to offer the men some form of immediate assistance, so rifled in their pockets to produce all the cash they had to give to the underground unionists. It totalled $100. The Chileans reciprocated by presenting the Australians with three albums of Victor Jara's recordings as the meeting ended emotionally.

The final paragraph of the report places the meeting in an international context and underlines the responsibility that the Australians felt for the Chilean workers and their situation. 'This meeting, taking place as it did in the back streets of Santiago in the bare surroundings of an empty house, for me, was a most moving experience', recalled a delegation member:

> It leaves one with a deep appreciation of the dedication and sacrifices made by these workers in the struggle against the Chilean fascists and the need of those who are free to help them in their life and death struggle, cannot be over emphasised as a part of the world movement for Freedom and Democracy.[105]

The Australians felt their efforts had not been wasted as the underground unionists

> expressed their very deep appreciation of the delegation's visit. They felt that as a result, many trade unionists were alive or free because of the fear by the Junta of adverse international publicity about their anti union actions. They said that in the few weeks prior to us arriving, there had been considerable publicity in the press and progressives everywhere were hoping that we would go back and tell the story of what was happening in Chile.[106]

The story was told.

The delegation returned home from Chile on 4 April 1974 and shortly after produced a four-page broadsheet newspaper entitled *12 Days in Chile*, which was published in seven languages around the world. The paper outlined the activities, findings and successes of the Australian trade union representatives, as well as relaying the message from Chilean trade unionists to take action

---

104   Ibid.
105   Ibid.
106   Ibid.

against the military junta.[107] The paper showed some photos of the delegation in Chile, Chilean children and acts of repression such as book burning. The articles described to the reader the tyranny of the military government, giving accounts of talks with Luis Figueroa and the underground members and visits to shantytowns and factories. They also published a letter to Bob Hawke (at the time the president of the ACTU) from Figueroa and called for more protests by Australian unions. In a brief description of the delegation's achievements, they included the petitioning for the release of political prisoners Olivares and Enriquez (which occurred in the weeks after the return of the delegations). They also listed the retrieval of information and discussions with everyday Chileans as 'solid achievements, going beyond what was possible for representatives of previous delegations'.[108]

They also produced a report that went out to WFTU-aligned unions, even those which opposed the delegation. In it, the delegates reported the broad range of opinions they had encountered, such as one Chilean saying that 'Chileans who have left Chile should not lose touch with those who remain',[109] and another who said that Chileans in exile had 'run away' and were not of any help.[110] Despite this openness, Robertson recalls:

> [W]hen they came back, and the people from the Seamen's union in particular attacked them ... [the AMWU] were the biggest union in the country at the time and ... I think their attitude was to say that 'I don't think we're going to have people telling us that we've done the wrong thing and we didn't achieve anything, when we have!'[111]

Luis Figueroa, ex-minister in Allende's Government, said of the delegation's visit: 'because it reached the Chilean people, [the delegation] is of great international importance and gives great support to the Chileans fighting against oppression, we recognise that their concern is an expression of international solidarity.'[112]

Words such as these must have been tough to swallow by those who had vehemently opposed the delegation. The action was a significant marker in the history of Australian trade union internationalism. It was a product of the size of the AMWU and strategic individuals within it. Without the resources inherent in the membership boom or the individuals connected through politics and common internationalist sentiment, the delegation would not have happened.

---

107 Baird, 'After the Coup'.
108 12 Days in Chile.
109 *Press Statement of the AMWU—7/2/74: What is the Chilean Junta Up To?*
110 Ibid.
111 Robertson Interview, 2009.
112 *12 Days in Chile.*

But it wasn't without social movement links: Steve Cooper, an example of a modern-day faddist, was involved in the union *and* deep within the CSCP. It made him a unique and driven participant in the delegation and the activities that followed. His involvement also exposes a slight flaw in this otherwise seamless classification of the delegation as solidarity *by* unionists *for* unionists. He was clearly linked to the solidarity committee in more than just name. Consequently, the rigidness of the theoretical classification is put to the test when trying to file the delegation as an action of social movement or industrial national unionism. It is true the delegation remained relatively clear of the social movement, but its contribution was relied upon in more than one way by trade unions *and* the movement.

It is hard to determine the exact depth of reaction or influence of the delegation as it formed part of a broad web of solidarity actions that took place across the world. It is certain that the authority, rhetoric and symbolism of such an indirect action was enhanced by the fact that this delegation was one of the only types of action that was *created by* the trade unions, rather than being an opportunistic expression of internationalism.

Mavis Robertson recalled that the delegation 'got fantastic results, I mean, they got unbelievable results when you think about it'.[113] They acted on the ideal of an international working class that was drawn from their own political ideals. The efforts of these men 'resulted in a world-wide exposure of the suppression and victimisation of the labour movement'.[114] Locally, they were able to use their experiences in Chile to raise awareness and accumulate support for the initial wave of the Chile movement.[115]

---

113 Robertson Interview, 2009.
114 *Statement by L. Figueroa and L. Meneses to the Delegates of the ACTU Congress, September 17 1975.*
115 Baird, 'After the Coup'; 12 Days in Chile.

8. 'Not one pound of wheat will go': Words and actions

The *Holstein Express* was crewed by Indonesian seamen, but it sailed under a Liberian flag.¹ Its Australian agents, Dalgety and Patricks, had been charged with the shipment of 600 dairy cows to Chile. In the week of 4 December 1978, the ship attempted to dock in Newcastle to load but was black banned by Australian workers. Union members would not assist with loading the cargoes. They simply refused. After discussion between the workers' representatives and the agents, it was agreed that the ship could anchor outside the harbour in Stockton Bight and receive water and stores.² It remained off Newcastle for two weeks.³

In stop-work meetings on 19 December 1978, the Sydney, Port Kembla, Port Adelaide and Victorian branches of the SUA all passed motions of support for the actions of their Newcastle branch.⁴ And shortly thereafter a white flag was raised by the owners in the form of a communiqué shown to the maritime unions that the ship would depart for New Zealand without cattle if it was able to refuel. The maritime unions allowed the ship to dock and refuel and it set off on 22 December 1978, apparently without cows and apparently for New Zealand. The company was in the middle of a goosestep that spanned the State.

The next day, Don Henderson, secretary of the Firemen and Deckhands' Union, was urgently advised that the ship was in fact at the southern NSW town of Eden loading hay and cattle.⁵ The union delegate at Eden was contacted and subsequently the local fishermen who had been hired to load the cattle stopped work.⁶ The ship's crew and the vendors were forced to load the cattle themselves and the vessel departed for New Zealand on Sunday, 24 December 1978. Don Henderson immediately sent a telegram to the Morgan Lighthouse in New Zealand to ensure that the unions there would boycott the vessel.⁷ In response to the agent's deceptive attempt to circumvent the black bans, the maritime unions of New South Wales placed a blanket ban on all Dalgety and Patricks'

---

1 Extract SWM—Held Tuesday 19th December, 1978—Sydney Branch, SUA: Federal Office, N38/299, NBAC: ANU, Canberra.
2 Federal Office Report No 16/1978, Period ending December 13, 1978, SUA: Federal Office, N38/299, NBAC: ANU, Canberra.
3 'Blow for Solidarity', *Seamen's Journal* 34, no. 1 (January 1979), 2.
4 Extract SWM—Held 19th Dec 1978—Port Kembla Branch, SUA: Federal Office, N38/299, NBAC: ANU, Canberra; Extract SWM—Held Tuesday 19th December, 1978—Sydney Branch; Extract SWM—Held Tuesday, Dec 19, 1978, Port Adelaide, SUA: Federal Office, N38/299, NBAC: ANU, Canberra; Extract SWM—Held Tuesday, Dec 19, 1978, Victorian Branch, SUA: Federal Office, N38/299, NBAC: ANU, Canberra.
5 Montenegro, 'La Campaña de Solidaridad con Chile en Australia 1973–1990', 202.
6 Geraghty, 'Barometer', *Seamen's Journal* (January 1979).
7 Overseas Telegram to Morgan Lighthouse, Wellington, New Zealand from Henderson Firemen & Deckhands 27-12-78, SUA: Federal Office, N38/299, NBAC: ANU, Canberra.

ships. This remained until 4 January 1979 when the agents produced written confirmation that they would not act for any ships trading with Chile.[8] The WWFA chose to believe them.

That year, three classes of livestock worth $570 000 made it to Chile, including 1348 bovine animals and one horse. As this represents many more animals than was reported in the *Seamen's Journal* (only 600), it is possible there was another ship during that year, the *Journal* was misinformed or the *Journal* deliberately played down the size of the shipment.[9] Regardless, the total live animal export to Chile constituted less than 10 per cent of the total $7.6 million exports that made it to Chile in that financial year. So why was this short, ultimately unsuccessful boycott hailed as 'Unions' Chile Solidarity Victory'?[10]

This chapter reconstructs and explains the intricacies of a trade boycott used for political purposes. It delves further into union size, tactical positioning of union labour, strategic individuals and internationalist rhetoric. It explains the influence of these factors on industrial action for external political purposes. While declarations of black ban and boycott action were imperative to some unions' internationalist identity, ultimately jobs were more important than any distant political gain. Consequently, the size of the shipment to be boycotted played a role in the decision-making of a union, where ultimately industrial protection was paramount. Like the engineers in East Kilbride and shipbuilders on the Clyde from past chapters, the key issue in the final instance was jobs—jobs the unions were constituted to protect.

Australian workers in the SUA and WWFA were employed in internationalist professions.[11] The products they dealt with were transnational, and the conditions on the job exposed workers to people of many cultures. Furthermore, in the case of seamen, the cramped conditions on board obliged them to be tolerant. On the ship there was the opportunity to read and on land previous generations of radicals gave new lads their political education.[12] Wharves and ships were radical spaces in the 1970s, but more than that, seamen and wharfies conceived of themselves as radicals. Seamen Paddy Crumlin said of his union: 'The industrial work was complemented by the political work, our identity was with social issues.' [13] The boycott of the Chilean regime was not only a political statement, but also an assertion of identity, and for that reason it was consistently represented as 'successful' by the left press and trade unionists both at the time and subsequently.

---

8   'Unions' Chile Solidarity Victory', *Socialist*, 17 January 1979.
9   'Blow for Solidarity'.
10 Ibid.
11 Diane Kirkby, *Voices from the Ships: Australia's Seafarers and their Union* (Sydney: UNSW Press, 2009), 14.
12 Ibid., 181.
13 Ibid., 413.

Boycotting, for both the Seamen's Union and the Waterside Workers' in Australia, embodied their internationalism: it was a representation of their socialist and humanitarian identities. As John Healy (WWFA) said, 'the fight of the Chilean people cannot be viewed as their fight alone'.[14] The same rhetoric in support of boycotting was also repeated by Chileans in exile who consistently called for the action against the junta by trade unions.[15] For example, visiting the UP in exile, representative Hugo Miranda said, 'I must say that we think the most important way to fight against the military Junta is the way that you have elected; that is to say, the trade union bans, the boycott'.[16]

The seamen and the waterside workers had used boycott action as a political statement before. As recently as December 1972 the Sydney Waterside Workers had banned US shipping in protest against the bombing of North Vietnam. In the same year, the SUA had boycotted the Spanish ship *Pedro de Alvarado* in protest against the antidemocratic policies of the Franco Government.[17] Stretching back into the 1930s, the waterside workers had black banned shipping for a number of causes including anti-Japanese imperialism, anti-Dutch imperialism and anti-apartheid.[18] The anti-Japan actions protested the invasion of China and were known as the Pig Iron Bans, after the main export boycotted. The Pig Iron Bans led to large-scale layoffs in Port Kembla.[19] The name 'the Black Armada' refers to the actions, including boycotts and mutinies, that maritime workers took in the 1940s to support Indonesia's independence from the Netherlands.[20] During the 1960s and early 1970s, there was no shortage of international issues to act upon including the Greek military junta, apartheid in South Africa and of course the Vietnam War. Historian Rupert Lockwood wrote in 1975 that his colleagues of the future would find that during this period, 'the conscience of the Australian people found expression more often on the waterfront than in the nation's legislatures'.[21] Nevertheless, much of the wharfies' internationalism in the 1970s was around 'bread and butter' issues, especially after they joined the International Transport Workers' Federation (ITF) in 1971. The organisers spent a great deal of their time sorting out pay disputes and safety issues for foreign seamen.[22]

---

14 Healy, 'Chile: No Trade with Junta'.
15 For example, see: 'Aid to Chile Struggle', 7. The same rhetoric was used by the ILO: 'ILO Call to Fight Chile Torturers', *Maritime Worker*, 2 September 1975, 7.
16 'Chile: No Trade with Junta'.
17 'Maritime Action on Franco Ship', *SPA*, September 1972. This is not mentioned in the *Sweeney Report*, which cites a WWFA pay dispute due to arsenic spills on this ship. This could have been a later voyage. This possibly indicates that the ban was a one-off. John Bernard Sweeney, *Royal Commission into Alleged Payments to Maritime Unions* (Canberra: Australian Government Publishing Service, 1976), 134.
18 'Apartheid Protest', *Socialist*, 23 November 1977; Sydney Branch Waterside Workers' Federation, *Branch News*, 12 January 1973; Kirkby, *Voices from the Ships*, 37.
19 'Pig-Iron Ban—2500 Employes [sic] May Lose Jobs', *The Age*, 19 December 1938, 19; 'Dismissed', *The Age*, 21 December 1938, 8.
20 Lockwood, *Black Armada*.
21 Ibid., 253.
22 Les Symes, 'Bread-and-Butter Internationalism', *Maritime Worker*, 5 October 1976, 14.

For Chile, however, the WWFA policy was internationalism pure and simple: 'that no Chilean ships and no cargoes to or from Chile will be handled on the Australian waterfront.'[23]

Using the boycott as a political tactic against the Chilean dictatorship had the potential to be effective in various ways. First, there was economic loss as a motivator for change in the junta.[24] Second, the boycott could serve to lift the morale of leftist forces in Chile or at the very least, individuals imprisoned there as well as Chileans in exile.[25] Enacting a boycott was a concrete gesture of worldwide working-class solidarity. Anner notes that left-wing unions are more likely to pursue an internationalist agenda, especially internationalism in its more confrontational forms.[26] This tendency must have been further exacerbated by the fact that the impact of the coup in Chile was first felt in the left and therefore was a 'socialist' issue. No-one was surprised that the SUA and WWFA took action, as they had the reputation of being among the most radical unions in Australia. In fact, Stephen Deery wrote in 1983 that political stoppages in Australia are very few, and mostly from stevedoring, maritime, building and metal industries.[27]

In more than one sense, Australian maritime unionists held a 'unique position in the workforce'.[28] Not only was their identity internationalist but also their physical location was strategic, with a high percentage of primary products and manufactured goods passing through their jurisdiction. This was intensified by Australia's geographic isolation and the topographical distance between cities, which necessitated reliance on sea transport. The maritime unions expressed solidarity through telegrams and letters, as was normal for progressive unions, but the difference between them and other unions was that almost all of their work was a potential direct action on an international issue.

Historian Diane Kirkby has proposed that the internationalism of the SUA was an identification with other individuals: a person-to-person commitment that overcame the difficulties of action.[29] Activist Mavis Robertson remembered:

> There is a cultural history in Australia, perhaps because it is a continent that ... is bound by sea ... that those kind of bans have been more

---

23 'Firmer Chile Junta Bans', *Maritime Worker*, 9 March 1976, 12.
24 'Chile: No Trade with Junta'.
25 Ibid.
26 Mark Anner, 'Industrial Structure, the State, and Ideology: Shaping Labor Transnationalism in the Brazilian Auto Industry', *Social Science History* 27, no. 4 (2003), 627.
27 Deery, 'Union Aims and Methods', 75.
28 Don Henderson, 'The military coup in Chile in September 1973 had little effect on the thinking...' *1993*, Papers of GMM.
29 Kirkby, *Voices from the Ships*, 106.

prevalent in Australia than in some other countries. It doesn't mean that we are more solidarity conscious, it means … that it is a cultural right thing to do.[30]

Both of these conclusions are true in part, but, in the case of the Chile campaign, internationalism was also an assertion of political identity. SUA member John King said, 'because that's what we are, we endeavour to help the underdog'.[31]

The SUA, as outlined above, has a proud history of international action. In fact, their pride was the cause of an exceptionalist attitude within the union. The union's record of international actions was mentioned almost every time their representatives spoke at a function as if they were bastions of true internationalist action. That projection of identity was a simplification of the SUA's actions within the broader union movement. For example, members had declined the invitation to crew the *Boonaroo*, which was shipping supplies and troops to Vietnam for the war.[32] After threats of disciplinary action from the ACTU and a compulsory conference at the Arbitration Court, the SUA allowed members to crew the ship.[33] The choice to lift a ban on the *Boonaroo* showed that however hard-line their leaders were, the SUA was not impervious to pressure from the rest of the labour movement.[34]

In her history of the SUA, Diane Kirkby notes that the seamen had a reputation for being a communist-led union. While many members were politically aware and active, very few were actually card carriers of the CPA or SPA.[35] Leaders, Kirkby asserts, were not elected because of their political affiliation, but because they were good unionists. The SUA was a democratic and collectivist union: democracy was built into the union's procedures and organisation.[36] It was not unusual to have resolutions and letters forwarded from ships, as the SUA was an organisation on the move, literally, and no-one was to be left out.

In 1971 the SUA had approximately 4500 members, though given the mobile nature of their working life, it was impossible to gather every member into a single meeting. The union was affiliated to the ACTU, and State labour councils and to the ALP in all States except the Northern Territory and Tasmania.[37] But the SUA was known to be more radical than those affiliations suggest. The reputation was due in part to its secretary, Eliot V. Elliott, who, as Don

---

30 Robertson Interview, 2009.
31 Kirkby, *Voices from the Ships*, 86.
32 Schmutte, 'International Union Activity', 85.
33 Ibid.
34 Kirkby, *Voices from the Ships*, 51, 52.
35 Ibid., 26.
36 Officials were elected by ballot; port representatives and seamen were elected at stop-work meetings. Ibid., 141.
37 Rawson, A Handbook of Australian Trade Unions and Employees' Associations, 84.

Henderson quipped in 1972, had been in the SUA for 'more years than I even want to think about'.[38] Elliott had been a founding member of the SPA, and before that, a Communist Party member since 1941. He was a Leninist and a supporter of socialist countries until his death in 1984.[39] Elliott was still a trim and fit man in the 1970s, with a carefully tended moustache.[40] Elliott was known to be a straight talker, straight up and down and sometimes humourless, and Don Henderson told Kirkby he was a 'very dogged fighter for human rights, the rights of people everywhere'.[41] He was persuasive and intimidating, and believed SUA members had the opportunity to spread internationalist ideology around the world. Of Chile, Elliott wrote: 'The struggle of the Chilean people is, in our opinion, the struggle of the Australian people, for the struggle of the people everywhere in the world under bourgeois democracy is a common struggle.'[42]

Elliott took a personal interest in the maintenance of the Chile boycott—for example, attending the Sydney branch stop-work meeting to explain the *Holstein Express* dispute.[43]

Stop-work meetings were in fact essential to the functioning of the SUA and to their expression of Chile solidarity. Federal office reports were distributed to branches and then discussed at the monthly meetings, resulting in branches that were very well informed of official union business at the national level.[44] Mick Carr, SUA member, said 'all good trade unionists went to the stop work meetings'.[45] Stop-work meetings were effectively paid for by shipowners, as everyone in port at that time received half a day's paid leave.[46] In these circumstances it was easy to be good. In theory, a deck boy could propose a motion at a meeting that could flow back into union policy, although it was not that often that the rank and file went against the union leadership's recommendations.[47] Similarly at elections, officials were almost always retained. Even so, the discussion at meetings demonstrated consistent strength in anti-Chile dictatorship feeling. By comparison, British seamen were also generally compliant with their

---

38   'Chile: No Trade with Junta'.
39   Rowan Cahill, *Sea Change: An Essay in Maritime Labour History* (Bowral, NSW: Rowan Cahill, 1998).
40   Kirkby, Voices from the Ships, 17.
41   Ibid., 19, 20.
42   Elliott, 'Chile: No Trade with Junta'.
43   *Extract SWM—Held Tuesday 19th December, 1978—Sydney Branch*, SUA: Federal Office, N38/299, NBAC: ANU, Canberra.
44   For example, the SUA Queensland branch called for the national office to continue discussions with the ACTU on the Chile issue so that the ACTU support of the boycott would be reimposed. Extract SWM minutes held Queensland Branch Tuesday May 2nd 1978 ref. 1422, SUA: Federal Office, N38/299, NBAC: ANU, Canberra.
45   Kirkby, *Voices from the Ships*, 145.
46   Ibid.
47   Ibid., 147–8.

leadership's orders; however, they were exposed to much more Chilean trade and consequently the prospective loss of more jobs, which influenced decision-making on the ground.

Members of the SUA were kept informed through the *Seamen's Journal*, which often reported on Chile. Elliott's wife, Kondelia, was in charge of the federal office and the *Seamen's Journal*. Given the control of the administrative hub of the union, the true democratic practice in the union was possibly less robust than has been previously put forward.[48] It was the sort of democracy that Lenin, and Elliott, favoured: democratic centralism. One thing is certain, however, the *Journal* and the stop-work meetings were the main expressions of Chile solidarity within the SUA. Almeyda, executive secretary of the UP in exile, sent a long letter to the SUA that was republished and it served to motivate sailors. He wrote that the solidarity of the SUA saved lives and freed people from concentration camps. Almeyda put it simply: 'the boycott holds back Pinochet's plans to arrest the trade union leaders and make them disappear.'[49]

When the Chilean musical group Inti Illimani attended the Melbourne branch's monthly meeting in April 1977, they spoke about the boycott of wheat and sang two songs. In response, the SUA branch produced and passed a strong resolution;[50] however, the band did not perform for the WWFA Melbourne branch, even though it represented a greater number of unionists with perhaps more strategic power. That branch was dominated by Maoists at the time, who did not like the sound of the Marxist–Leninist singers.[51]

Of the two main unions which enacted the boycott on Chilean goods, the WWFA was far greater in size, industrial power and perhaps also in political influence. The WWFA held the most privileged position from which to implement a boycott action. Not only was stevedoring an unavoidable part in the trade between Australia and Chile, but there was also a law that stated that no member of a foreign crew may be engaged in the stevedoring of a ship.[52] In addition, their membership was larger and more spread out over the continent. For these reasons they had more opportunities to put their boycott into action than the SUA: where Australian-crewed ships were only a small percentage of all that sailed, almost every ship that came into Australia would be touched in some way by WWFA members. In contrast with the SUA, the organisation did not widely publicise its threatened Chile action in its journal despite, or perhaps because of, its actions' potential greater efficacy.

---

48 Kirkby, *Voices from the Ships*, 149, 154.
49 'Trade Boycott—Unidad Popular Chile's Warm Gratitude for S.U.A. Solidarity', *Seamen's Journal* 33, no. 4 (April 1978), 94.
50 Report on the Tour of Inti Illimani (Melbourne 5.4.77), Papers of GMM.
51 Hewett Interview, 2005.
52 *The Navigation Act*, s. 45(1), as quoted in Sweeney, *Royal Commission into Alleged Payments to Maritime Unions*, 132.

In 1976, the WWFA had members in every Australian port working in stevedoring.[53] The union was affiliated to the ACTU (at State and national levels) and the ALP in all States. Between 1965 and 1975, the WWFA membership had fallen from 23 000 to just more than 13 000 due to new technologies on the wharf.[54] Ironically, considering the dramatic loss of members, the 1973 elections started a period of organisational stability for the national WWFA. At the next four elections, Leo Lenane, Tas Bull, Charlie Fitzgibbon and Neil Docker were all re-elected at the national level.[55]

Though the WWFA was often presented as the epitome of the 'communist menace' union, this was not necessarily the case.[56] Card-carrying communists were in fact a minority throughout the WWFA. Margo Beasley noted in her history of the union that although the fact that 'there was a strong ideological base to the WWF's industrial strategy is unquestionably true ... it was much broader than purely communist in inspiration'.[57] Traditional militancy came out of bad working conditions rather than any advanced class consciousness. In fact, the union was a politically diverse organisation. Mavis Robertson remembered that the WWFA at the national level 'was a mixed group of people, and as long as Tas [Bull] was there ... you had a rational kind of leadership, not an irrational one. (They weren't vying for positions to go to Moscow, the last thing they would want to do probably).'[58]

There was also diversity at the lower levels. The Port Melbourne branch was dominated by Maoists and five of its members travelled on a 1975 delegation to China.[59] By contrast, the Sydney branch in particular was not completely dominated by any one party, though there were many CPA and SPA-influenced members. Among the most vocal were probably those affiliated to the SPA.

Stephen Deery commented that of all Australian unions, the WWFA 'has perhaps shown the most persistent level of industrial activity in socio-political issues',[60] and this fact drew criticism from within the union movement. The wharfies were seen as possibly challenging the constitutional government by using industrial tactics to try to influence parliamentary proceedings or foreign policy.[61] In actuality, despite the perception of consistent militant political

---

53 Ibid.
54 Bull, *Tas Bull, An Autobiography*, 141. In 1971, the WWFA had 16 113 members spread over every State of Australia. Rawson, *A Handbook of Australian Trade Unions and Employees' Associations*, 94; Beasley, *Wharfies*, 228.
55 Three-year terms. Bull, *Tas Bull, An Autobiography*, 144.
56 Beasley, *Wharfies*, 140.
57 Ibid., 142.
58 Robertson Interview, 2009.
59 WWFA Melbourne Branch, *Official Branch News*, 28 July 1975.
60 Deery, 'Union Aims and Methods', 75.
61 Ibid., 76.

action by the WWFA, most of the disputes the union was involved in were industrial in nature (for example, for safety or wet weather gear) and the union did not always take up the call to boycott.⁶²

Even with its strong tradition of internationalist sentiment, the WWFA joined the ITF only in 1971. When they did so, Charlie Fitzgibbon, general secretary, was immediately appointed to its executive council.⁶³ It was through the ITF that the WWFA took up a highly publicised flags-of-convenience shipping campaign, which was an economic, industrial and human rights issue. The international movement seemed to benefit from Australia's involvement in general, as Australians (especially in the maritime unions) were willing to act. Australia's geographic position also gave credence to the claim of worldwide support.

About the same time as the union joined the ITF, Tas Bull became federal organiser of the WWFA.⁶⁴ Bull had a strong international bent. You could say that internationalism was one of his passions—which was apt considering his first name (Tasnor) was a conglomerate of Tasmania and Norway, the birthplaces of his parents.⁶⁵ He was a long-term maritime worker and he spent some of his youth abroad as a seaman. Bull had been a member of the CPA until 1956 and joined the ALP in 1974.⁶⁶ He was, at one stage, chair of the Hunters Hill ALP.⁶⁷ Bull was a well-known trade union figure in the 1970s and 1980s, and also worked himself into prominence in the ACTU. His complex web of political connections, strong commitment to internationalism of all types and personal affinity with Latin America made him prominent and useful in the Chile solidarity movement in Australia.⁶⁸ The affinity was due, at least in part, to his wife, Carmen, who was Argentinean.

Tas Bull and his wife travelled to Chile in 1971 for the first anniversary of the election of Allende. They celebrated alongside Chileans in the National Stadium, which later became a concentration camp in the first days of the military regime.⁶⁹ At meetings in Sydney in September 1973, Bull drew on those brief experiences. Yet despite his personal feelings, he remained aloof from the organisational side of the movement. He was not a member of the CSCP and he did not attend

---

62 Tom Bramble has noted the conservative industrial practice of some CPA union leaders and furthermore lists examples of the WWFA's non-support of other strikes such as by the Mt Isa Copper Miners in 1964. Bramble, *Trade Unionism in Australia*, 21, 34.
63 Bull, *Tas Bull, An Autobiography*, 131; *Fitzgibbon (WWFA) to McGahen (CSCP), March 21, 1977*, Papers of GMM.
64 Bull was federal organiser of the WWFA from 1971 to 1983. Rowan Cahill, 'Obituary: Tas Bull (31.01.1932–29.05.2003)', *Labour History*, no. 85 (2003).
65 Ibid.
66 Bull, *Tas Bull, An Autobiography*, 148.
67 Shane Bentley, 'Tribute to Labor Leader Tas Bull', *Maritime Workers Journal*, July 2003.
68 Bull was director of the Cuban Children's Fund until his death, and spent his seventieth birthday in that country. Bull, *Tas Bull, An Autobiography*.
69 Montenegro, 'La Campaña de Solidaridad con Chile en Australia 1973–1990', 226.

committee meetings regularly, if at all. Mavis Robertson remembered that he 'felt things with his heart' about Latin America, but the Chile issue 'was not the centre of his life'.[70] He was sensible in terms of deploying his own, and his union's, resources.

In more than one sense, maritime unions cooperated amongst themselves and took initiative in expressing Chile solidarity. They shared some of the public relations burden of the boycott. Sometimes, they acted under a unified banner called the Water Transport Group of Unions, which also included the Firemen and Deckhands Union of New South Wales (FDU).[71] For example, the group held a buffet lunch in honour of the visit of Chilean Hugo Miranda in July 1977. Miranda had been a senator for eight years and a member of the UP Government. He survived two years as a political prisoner in Dawson Island and after his release resided as an exile in Mexico.[72] As a guest of the CSCP Sydney, Miranda was treated to lunch and spoke to the group along with Benson (SUA Sydney), Elliott, John Healy[73] and Henderson.

Don Henderson verbosely welcomed Miranda:

> Comrade Hugo Miranda is here to acquaint us, if we need to be acquainted, with the problems that are today confronting the progressive forces of Chile and have confronted those people since September 11, 1973.
>
> I remember that day for two reasons: because of the destruction of democracy in that country and the brutal murder of Allende and some of the other people; and because it happens to be my birthday.[74]

Henderson was the secretary of the FDU, a small NSW-based union, whose 670 members (in 1971) mainly worked on the Sydney ferries. While it was affiliated to the NSW Labour Council, the union was not an affiliate of the NSW ALP.[75] Henderson did not attend all meetings of the CSCP, but went to many. He was most active, it seemed, in the *international*-level solidarity scene, as described in Chapter Six. He was often sent to represent the maritime unions at international conferences, and the influence he had within the WWFA and SUA was due to his network of SPA contacts.

---

70 Robertson Interview, 2009.
71 The FDU was described as a 'kindred union' of the WWFA Sydney branch. Waterside Workers' Federation, *Branch News*, 23 February 1973.
72 'Chile: No Trade with Junta'.
73 John Healy, son of Jim Healy, legendary waterside leader and CPA member. 'Jim Healy's Cargo Hook', *Maritime Worker*, 4 November 1975, 5; Bramble, *Trade Unionism in Australia*, 21.
74 'Chile: No Trade with Junta'.
75 Rawson, *A Handbook of Australian Trade Unions and Employees' Associations*, 55.

Henderson had joined the SUA as a deck boy in 1940, and prominent SPA member Eliot Elliott acted as his political mentor.[76] His experiences as a deck boy on a hospital ship during World War II influenced his anti-war stance.[77] By 1947, with the birth of his first child, he had started work on tugs and moved over to the FDU. Henderson joined his local ALP branch at one stage, trying to infiltrate them and spread SPA sympathy, but when the plot was discovered, he was expelled along with 16 other branch members.[78]

Henderson's commitment to Chile and his SPA membership made him an important figure in the first years of the campaign in Sydney. The combination of his political affiliation and the relatively small size of his union allowed him the time and gave him the drive to devote himself to the Chile cause. Henderson occasionally spoke for a more substantial amount of workers and the Australian solidarity movement than his union position actually warranted. To those involved in the SPA faction of the Australian left, Henderson 'was a very important player' in Chile solidarity.[79] To those in the CPA stream, he 'strutted around' on the world stage due to the maritime union and SPA support. His union position was not as fixed or as broadly representative as, for example, Jim Baird of the AMWU, yet he keenly participated in the kind of 'prolier than thou' attitude described by Burgmann.[80] In reality, however, it was the small size of his union that was key in the high level of his involvement: he had time on his hands.

Though his political affiliation meant he probably helped more resident Chilean Communist Party members than people from other groups, activists reminisced that he did try to bridge both the political gap and the gap between union and CSCP.[81] He was 'a nice man', recalled Mavis Robertson, and Ferguson remembered his dedication to the cause.[82]

Well before the Chilean coup, in August 1972, the Waterside Workers' Federation of Australia sent a letter to Salvador Allende. They expressed their admiration for the UP and the Chilean people and their attempts to implement a progressive socialist program. They wrote: 'We are conscious that there are many powerful forces throughout the world and particularly in the North American continent who will do everything within their power to frustrate your efforts to build a new people's democratic society in Chile.'

More than just anti-imperialist sentiment, the Waterside Workers expressed particular sympathy with Chile. The letter continued: 'Our interest is

---

76   Kirkby, *Voices from the Ships*, 19.
77   Ibid., 40.
78   Ibid., 30.
79   Ferguson Interview, 2009.
80   Burgmann and Burgmann, *Green Bans, Red Union*, 54.
81   Robertson Interview, 2009.
82   Ibid.; Ferguson Interview, 2009.

particularly related to the fact that this is the first such effort to build a new society in the Southern Hemisphere and in particular in our own region—the South Pacific area.'[83]

With this support of the UP Government and the general hypersensitivity of the Australian left to capitalist imperialism, it was no surprise that immediately after the coup the WWFA Federal Council released a press statement stating its abhorrence to the happenings in Chile.

But it did not call for a boycott.[84]

At the All Ports Conference on 19 September 1973, the motion was carried with an addendum initiated by the Sydney WWFA branch: that all branches take industrial action against the military government in Chile.[85] This bears close similarity to the manner in which the rank and file from Rolls Royce East Kilbride forced a revision of the original executive's Chile decision in Britain as described in Chapter Four. The WWFA All Ports Conference also declared that the coup proved there had been CIA interference in Chile, and called upon the Australian Government to raise the matter at the United Nations.

Similarly, the National Secretariat of the SUA immediately condemned the coup publicly by publishing a denunciation in the *Seamen's Journal* in September 1973.[86] In the first stop-work meeting after the coup, Sydney seamen urged the federal office to place a boycott on Chilean trade and soon the boycott was official SUA policy.[87] The Committee of Management decision did not directly call for a boycott, but for members to participate in mobilisation against the Chilean Government.[88]

It would be months before any industrial action was taken on ships trading with Chile and the main export affected would be wheat.

---

83 *Letter to President Salvador Allende from WWF of Australia, 4 August 1972.*
84 *Press Statement by Federal Council Waterside Workers' Fed. of Aust. Re: Chile, Sept 13 1973.*
85 Interestingly, the Federal Council passed a resolution that did not call for industrial action, or the mention of it was not published in the Sydney Branch Waterside Workers' Federation *Branch News*. The All Ports Conference is the first official mention of industrial action. *All Ports Conference—extract 26, September 19 1973*, WWFA: Federal Office, N114/932, NBAC: ANU, Canberra; *Maritime Worker*, 23 October 1973, 4; 'Chile: No Trade with Junta'.
86 Montenegro, 'La Campaña de Solidaridad con Chile en Australia 1973–1990', 224.
87 This call for boycott was repeated in the *Tribune*: 'Australian union should also urgently consider a boycott of all Chilean goods imported into Australia and the cutting of communications and other links, with thousands of Chilean workers dead, being tortured and bombed in the factories run previously under workers' control and which they are now so heroically defending, the duty of unions here is clear. Words of solidarity are valuable, but become somewhat hollow if not backed with deeds.' 'Chile Cargo Ban', *Tribune* [Australia], 2–8 October 1973.
88 *1973, National C.O.M Meeting (SUA)*, Papers of GMM. In fact, the first published SUA call for the direct boycott of Chilean trade was after Don Henderson attended the Mexico City International Commission of Enquiry into the Crimes of the Military Junta in Chile. T. A Curphey, 'Need Stressed for More Union Action against Chile Junta', *Seamen's Journal* (May 1975).

The first substantial sale of wheat to Chile in many years occurred in 1966 and remained relatively steady until a significant increase in the early 1970s.[89] This was in part due to an amplification of the area sown to wheat and in the yield per acre, which placed pressure on the Australian Wheat Board (AWB) to find extra markets for the bumper crops. Transport strikes in Chile had caused many local crops to be spoiled and made Chile an ideal customer for Australian wheat.[90]

In 1972 Dr Pedro Bosch, representing the Chilean grain-buying authority Empresa de Comercio Agrícola, visited Australia and negotiated the third sale of wheat to Chile for the 1972 season. He was undoubtedly shown a very good time while he was here, as all business the Australian Wheat Board (AWB) undertook was 'highly personalised'.[91] A total of 600 000 t of wheat was sold to Chile in that year. The contracts secured Chile 7 per cent of the total Australian wheat exports and earned it the ranking of Australia's fourth-largest wheat customer for 1972.[92] In July 1973 Dr Bosch and the AWB negotiated large sales to Chile while the Allende Government was still in power. The wheat was to be shipped early in 1974 but the coup occurred before this could take place.

Wheat was by far the biggest commodity exported to Chile prior to the coup; but even with the large wheat contracts, Chile never reached 0.01 (one hundredth of 1 per cent) of total Australian exports.[93] Other items that consistently exited Australia labelled for Chile included grass seeds of various types, agricultural products such as canned fruits, machinery parts and safety equipment. There were also miscellaneous items such as four breeding sheep in the 1968–69 financial year and artificial limbs in the 1969–70 financial year. The major imports from Chile were marine products both for human consumption (hake fillets) and in the form of meal to be fed to animals or used as fertilisers.[94]

Wheat is an important product to Australia and Australians, not only because of its monetary value, but also because it is an integral part of Australia's psyche. The golden wheatfields, 'boundless plains' and 'nature's gifts', as well as the salt-of-the-earth farmers who 'toil with hearts and hands' were integral to Australia's identity and history (as demonstrated in the national anthem). The first wheat in Australia was sown by convicts on the government farm where the

---

89   The 1966 season is not included on the graph because the amount is only included in bushels (not tonnes). Australian Wheat Board [hereinafter AWB], *Wheat Australia Annual Report* (Melbourne: AWB, various years).
90   Seasons are measured from 1 December of the previous year to 30 November of the year listed. The area sown to wheat was up by 21 per cent in 1974. AWB, *Wheat Australia Annual Report* (1974).
91   Greg Whitwell, Diane Sydenham and AWB, *A Shared Harvest: The Australian Wheat Industry, 1939–1989* (Melbourne: Macmillan, 1991), 237.
92   'Chile Buys Again', *Wheat Australia* 5, no. 4 (1972).
93   The highest percentage was 0.006790475 per cent in 1972–73: Australian Bureau of Statistics [hereinafter ABS], *Australian Exports, Country by Commodity*, ABS 5414.0 (Canberra: ABS, 1973–74).
94   Import statistics and descriptions compiled from ABS, *Australian Imports, Country by Commodity*, ABS 5414.0 (Canberra: ABS, 1965–84).

Sydney botanic gardens are now located.[95] The iconic image of the great Aussie battler was played on by the AWB in its self-congratulatory 1967 publication when it said that the wheat industry started from a 'humble beginning' and from that 'a great primary industry has developed'.[96] In the 1960s wheat made up as much as 15 per cent of the total national income from exports and it continued to be a vital part of the Australian economy.[97]

By the 1970s, Australia was the third-largest wheat exporter in the world. Economic historian Greg Whitwell characterised the period 1974–89 as 'the drive for greater efficiency' in the wheat industry in Australia.[98] In 1978, 70 per cent of all wheat grown in Australia was sold for export, explaining the preoccupation of the AWB with external markets.[99] Chile, especially after the contracts of the Allende years, had become an important wheat customer.[100]

The AWB was a government-controlled authority that had a monopoly on the acquisition and sale of wheat in domestic and international markets.[101] The main objective of the AWB was to raise and stabilise the incomes of Australian wheat growers. While a single desk, State-run enterprise might not maximise profits per se, it does aim to make money secure and regular for its suppliers.[102]

The Wheat Board's composition was shaped by the domestic politics of the era.[103] Four of the board members were selected by the Minister for Primary Industry and the federal acts provided that the minister could 'direct' the board.[104] This rarely happened, and it was more often that Canberra reacted to the AWB's decisions rather than ordering a course of action. There were two published interventions, one in 1967 and one in the early 1970s. Neither had anything to do with Chile.[105] Given the Whitlam Government's insistence that credit be offered to Egypt in the 1970s, and the previous use of the AWB in 1967 as a

---

95   AWB, *Wheat Growing: A Great Australian Primary Industry* (Melbourne: AWB, c. 1967).
96   Ibid., 4.
97   E. J. Donath, 'The Australian Wheat Industry in the 1970s', *Australian Outlook* 23, no. 3 (1969), 296.
98   Whitwell, Sydenham and AWB, *A Shared Harvest*, 191.
99   AWB, *Wheat Australia Annual Report* (1978), 3.
100   I contacted the AWB various times to ask for information or interviews about the boycotts. The AWB did not reply.
101   AWB, *Corporate History*, accessed 30 April 2009, <http://www.awb.com.au/aboutawb/corporate/history/>; Steve McCorriston and Donald MacLaren, 'Single-Desk State Trading Exporters', *European Journal of Political Economy* 21 (2005), 505; Steve McCorriston and Donald MacLaren, 'Deregulation as (Welfare Reducing) Trade Reform: The Case of the Australian Wheat Board', *American Agricultural Economics Association* 89, no. 3 (2007), 638.
102   McCorriston and MacLaren, 'Deregulation as (Welfare Reducing) Trade Reform'.
103   Ibid., 235.
104   Ibid., 236.
105   Ibid.

'tool of foreign policy', it is not a stretch of the imagination to envisage that the contracts entered into with the Allende Government may have had some political element.[106] But it was not necessarily so.

Rather than the elected and selected board members, it was actually the management of the AWB that ran the everyday negotiations of the organisation. They applied their substantial weight to decisions within the organisation. The general manager until 1977 was L. H. Dorman, who had previous experience in international grain companies and had worked at the AWB since 1939, seeing the board through many political decisions. He would turn up at an ACTU meeting in the near future.[107]

The board's attitude to the maritime bans on Chile was that they were 'pointless (as well as being costly and inconvenient)'.[108] If there was a hole in the market, they argued, someone else would simply fill it. Caroline Overington, writing about the AWB scandal in Iraq in 2007, wrote that AWB executives 'were not callous, but, in the course of doing business abroad, Australian executives are routinely forced to deal with all manner of dictators, thugs and murderers … AWB's only interest was trade—specifically, trade that would benefit Australia's … wheat farmers'.[109]

Though written more than 30 years after the wheat trade with Chile's dictatorship started, the words still ring true.

The first direct action taken to enforce the trade union boycott was in May 1974 on two vessels owned by Indomar Limited (Bahamas): *Jag Shanti* and *Star Lily*. This was almost certainly not the first Chilean trade to enter or exit Australia since the coup, but perhaps it was the first time when the balance between ideology, economics and opportunity was perfect. The ships were contracted to load wheat for Chile but were boycotted by the maritime unions in Fremantle.[110] At first the SUA refused to tug the vessels ashore. After prompting by the ACTU, the vessels were tugged, but not loaded.

The Wheat Board organised a meeting with the ACTU, who were significantly less politically radical than the maritime unions. The AWB hoped that this would make them more receptive to capitalist reasoning and that maritime unions would in turn be receptive to the authority of the ACTU. The AWB argued that the wheat to be loaded was covered by the previous contracts signed with

---
106 Ibid., 235.
107 Ibid., 237.
108 Ibid., 236.
109 Caroline Overington, *Kickback: Inside the Australian Wheat Board Scandal* (Sydney: Allen & Unwin, 2007), 5.
110 *Hetherington Kingsbury Pty. Ltd to T. Bull (WWFA) re: Proposed Ban Chilean Cargoes, May 20 1974*, WWFA: Federal Office, N114/932, NBAC: ANU, Canberra.

the Allende Government. They informed the ACTU that the vessels were under the charter of the AWB, and consequently any delay to them was costing the Australian Government. The AWB also argued that Chile could easily acquire wheat from the United States at a cheaper price, reducing the effect of any boycott as a method of punishing the military government.[111] A very similar argument was put to the WWFA in the 1960s when the AWB feared the loss of the East Indies market due to the action the wharfies were taking to aid Indonesian independence.[112]

Hetherington Kingsbury, agents for Maritime Chartering Services Incorporated of Connecticut, who were, in turn, agents for Indomar Limited, pressured the WWFA directly to lift the boycott. The agents said that while they were mindful of the union's aims in holding a boycott, Indomar had 'no involvement in any ideological/political conflict'.[113] Though the WWFA was responsible for the greater part of the wheat boycott, wheat for Chile only made it into the pages of the *Maritime Worker* once.[114] This fits with the general reporting pattern of political action against Chile by the WWFA: very minimal.

The WWFA contacted the Wheat Board because they were concerned about the contractual obligations the board had with the previous Government of Chile. The AWB had, in fact, just signed a new contract with the representative of the new military regime in February 1974 and four more shipments of wheat were set to sail in June of that year. Two vessels had been chartered for this purpose. The WWFA, considerate of the Wheat Board's contractual obligations and the financial consequences that breaking them would have on the Australian Government, offered to load the remaining vessels on the condition that no further contracts were entered into with the dictatorship. The AWB reluctantly agreed to these terms, happy to meet their current contractual obligations, but wounded at the loss of their recently engaged fourth-largest customer.

The maritime boycott was not restricted to ships loading wheat. When the *Esmeralda*, a Chilean naval sailing ship used in the first days of the coup as a torture centre, attempted to visit Sydney in 1974 she was blocked by the WWFA.[115] A year later, in September 1975, Melbourne rank-and-file tug men

---

111 *Memo re: Shipping—Wheat Shipments to Chile, June 3 1974*, WWFA: Federal Office, N144/932, NBAC: ANU, Canberra.
112 Lockwood, *Black Armada*, 228.
113 *Hetherington Kingsbury Pty. Ltd to T. Bull (WWFA) re: Proposed Ban Chilean Cargoes*. Minter, Simpson and Co (Solicitors and Notaries), later contacted the WWFA for information on the boycott of 23–29 May 1974. Indomar tried to sue the AWB for losses. *Minter, Simpson and Co to Fitzgibbon (WWFA), November 11 1974*, WWFA: Federal Office, N114/932, NBAC: ANU, Canberra. Baird recalled that 'Chilean leaders said that the Junta was very anxious to placate Australia, because it desperately needed our wheat'. Baird, 'Chilean Junta on Trial before I.L.O.'.
114 *Maritime Worker*, 4 March 1975, 2.
115 'Block the Esmeralda!', *Tribune* [Australia], 4–10 June 1974, 12; *Maritime Worker*, 10 September 1974, 6. For information on the *Esmeralda*, see: Amnesty International, *Chile: Torture and the Naval Training Ship the 'Esmeralda'*, AMR 22/006/2003 (London: Amnesty International, International Secretariat, 2003).

(SUA) refused to tug another ship, *Austral Entente* (USA), in protest of the United States' involvement in the coup in Chile.[116] This was an entirely opportunistic action on the anniversary of the coup. The Chilean registered *Viña del Mar* was boycotted in Dampier, Western Australia, by the SUA at the end of the 1980s. It was attempting to load 100 000 t of iron ore for Western Europe. It sailed with no cargo nine days after arriving.[117] Conversely, all through the early 1980s shipments of rutile (TiO_2—found mainly in the Murray Basin of Victoria and New South Wales) were successfully sent to Chile. Australia holds 44 per cent of the world's known rutile deposits and thus a substantial portion of the world's market, but this was not a target of union harassment. Boycotting trade with Chile was not without risks for the workers. Section 30K of the *Commonwealth Crimes Act* (1914) outlawed interference with overseas or interstate trade, and the workers doing so could be arrested and potentially jailed. In 1978, the SUA and individuals within the union were summonsed in Western Australia over their bans on Indonesian-flagged ships. The person who initiated action under the *Crimes Act* was a representative of West Farmers.[118]

Section 45D of the *Trades Practices Act 1974* also prohibited secondary boycott, ban or strike action that occurred within Australian workplaces.[119] The individual, the union representative and the union could all be held responsible if this did occur. Interestingly, Section 45DD allowed for boycotts with the purpose of environmental protection, and Section 88(7) stated that the Australian Competition and Consumer Commission (ACCC) could grant permission for a secondary boycott—that is, an industrial action with a non-industrial objective. Without that permission, however, the boycott against Chile was illegal. John Garrett of the SUA recalled the danger of refusing to tug Chilean ships: the *NSW Crimes Act* was still in force and the NSW Liberal Government (1965–75) was active in oppressing any political activity that was not in the national interest.[120] Margo Beasley noted that in the 1950s when Jim Healy of the WWFA was arrested due to political actions on the wharves, it was only due to the fact that those campaigns were 'major and effective interventions

---

116 'Chile Venceremos', *Tribune* [Australia], 16 September 1975; *Carr (Co-Convenor, Australian CSCP) to the President (Continuing Liaison Council World Congress of Peace Forces) 27.10.75*, Papers of Barry Carr.
117 Montenegro, 'La Campaña de Solidaridad con Chile en Australia 1973–1990', 204; 'Chilean Registered Vina del Mar', *Seamen's Journal* 35, no. 3 (April 1980), 55. The agents for the *Vina del Mar* asked the SUA if they would be able to load again in 1981. The SUA refused. 'Chile Alert', *Seamen's Journal* 36, no. 2 (February 1981), 43.
118 *Extract SWM Minutes Victorian Branch 31/1/78. ref. 628, 31 January 1978*, SUA: Federal Office, N38/299, NBAC: ANU, Canberra; *Extract SWM Minutes W.A. Branch 31/1/78 Ref. 676, 31 January 1978*, SUA: Federal Office, N38/299, NBAC: ANU, Canberra.
119 Primary boycotts are actions taken with the purpose of protesting industrial concerns in that place of work. Secondary boycotts are with aims that do not fall into that category. Bramble, *Trade Unionism in Australia*, 104.
120 Kirkby, *Voices from the Ships*, 105.

in international affairs'.[121] She was referring to the Dutch shipping ban, which also put substantial pressure on the AWB. If this is true, perhaps the relatively small amount of trade with Chile protected the workers to some extent.

The law was not the only negative pressure on maritime unions. There was considerable insistence that they drop their black ban on trade with Chile in a number of forums, not just with the Wheat Board and shipping agents. Don Henderson reported that there were 'verbal conflicts with farmers' organisations, reactionary politicians and their supporters' on various occasions.[122] Resistance to the boycott came with two main arguments: concern about the boycott's humanitarian impact and anxiety about its effect on Australian business. It soon became clear that support for the boycott of Chilean trade was not a given even among unionists.

In the first instance, the ACTU's attitude had been to support the boycott; but by 22 January 1975, representatives of the Storemen and Packers, Marine Stewards, Federated Shipwrights, the WWFA and the SUA, plus Bob Hawke and Harold Souter of the ACTU, met with three representatives of the AWB.[123] Hawke had called the meeting immediately upon receipt of a letter from the then chairman of the AWB, Jack Cass, requesting it.[124] The ACTU representatives, in a slightly ambiguous position, tried to mediate between the unionists and the Wheat Board representatives. The AWB maintained that wheat was the only product that was exported to Chile in any substantial amount (see Figure 8.1). AWB general manager Dorman argued that cutting off the supply of wheat because of the boycotts could harm the long-term export market for Australian wheat. Wilson of the SUA, Tas Bull of the WWFA and Campbell of the Federated Shipwrights (soon to amalgamate with the AMWU) stood firm. There would be no wheat shipments to Chile, despite the supposed humanitarian and business concerns.[125]

The shipments already negotiated were sent, and no wheat was thereafter contracted to Chile, as demonstrated in Figure 8.1. With the exclusion of wheat from the export list, the total value of exports to Chile dropped to an all time low

---

121 Beasley, *Wharfies*, 152.
122 'Wider Union Bans on Chile Junta', *Modern Unionist* 3, no. 1 (1975).
123 The AWB representatives were chairman, J. Cass OBE; general manager, L. Dorman OBE; and South Australian grower representative, T. M. Saint. *Australian Council of Trade Unions RE: Exports of Wheat to Chile, Jan 20 1975*, WWFA: Federal Office, N114/932, NBAC: ANU, Canberra; *Australian Wheat Board to Hawke RE: Chile, January 20 1975*, WWFA: Federal Office, N114/932, NBAC: ANU, Canberra.
124 Sir John Cass, NSW wheat grower, was selected as chairman by outgoing Minister for Primary Industry and Country Party leader, Ian Sinclair, against the previous chairman's wishes. Cass was the first chairman who took an active interest in the day-to-day running of the AWB. Whitwell, Sydenham and AWB, *A Shared Harvest*, 239.
125 *Minutes of Meeting of Unions with Representatives of the AWB to Chile held in the ACTU Board Room on Wednesday. 22nd January, 1975, commencing at 2.15pm*, WWFA: Federal Office, N114/932, NBAC: ANU, Canberra; *'General Secretary', February 7 1975*, WWFA: Federal Office, N114/932, NBAC: ANU, Canberra.

of only $157 000 in 1976.[126] The reduction was dramatic, but the WWFA was aware that a small amount of trade was slipping through, and in the *Maritime Worker* asked all branches to redouble their efforts.[127]

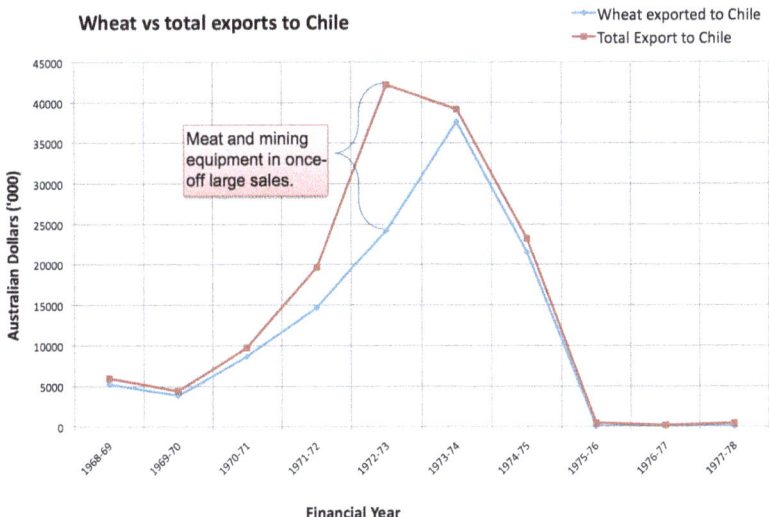

Figure 8.1 Wheat Percentage of Total Exports to Chile, 1968–69 to 1977–78.

Source: ABS, *Australian Exports, Country by Commodity*.

Some of the goods may have been exported by being transhipped—that is, labelled for another place before being sent to Chile.[128] In 1977 John Healy reminded the maritime workers to be on the lookout: 'At a couple of terminals they tried to sneak containers that had been shipped via Europe. Some of our boys have been very alert and they noticed Chilean copper and we said, "that goes back on the ship and goes back where it came from".'[129]

Despite transhipping, the efficiency of the maritime unions' stranglehold on trade led to the intensification of pressure aimed at them. Stewart A. Anderson, president of the Bendigo Trades Hall Council, a trade unionist and the ALP candidate for Bendigo in the heart of Victoria's golden triangle, sent a concerned letter to the AMWU detailing his apprehension about the moral and political

---

126   ABS, *Australian Exports, Country by Commodity* (1975–76, 1976–77, 1977–78).
127   'Firmer Chile Junta Bans'.
128   Henderson, *'The military coup in Chile in September 1973 had little effect on the thinking…'*, 1993.
129   Healy, 'Chile: No Trade with Junta'.

implications of a ban on wheat shipments to Chile. Acknowledging that a guarantee could not be given that the wheat would reach the needy, he still wondered: how could the democratic situation in Chile improve with no bread?[130]

The accusation that denying wheat to Chile was in fact starving the Chilean people was rebutted by the AMWSU Commonwealth Council in a standard letter. In it the union argued that the ILO and the UP in exile had requested boycotts on basic materials to Chile, and that the military government had not restored subsidies for low-income earners to purchase grain, therefore little would get through to the workers.[131] In information circulated in 1977 by the CSCP, it was noted that the wheat sold to Chile was used for fodder. That is, it would be eaten by animals, not humans, and 'it will fatten up meat for the tables of the wealthy'.[132] The AMWSU, WWFA and SUA stood by the assertion that bans on trade to Chile were a valid method of putting pressure on the military government and the humanitarian repercussions of the boycotts were non-existent.

A similar response was given to the Continental Overseas Corporation (USA) on 28 October 1974. Buyers in Chile had approached the company to import Australian meat. The 1972–73 financial year had seen a substantial amount of meat ($5.1 million) exported to Chile.[133] Australian exporters therefore backed the 1974 proposal of approximately 1000 tonnes of frozen meat (approximately one-fifth of the 1972–73 meat export to Chile), and the Australasian Meat Industry Employees Union supported the sale, but the WWFA was defiant.[134] The Continental Overseas Corporation telexed the Department of Agriculture seeking advice, which wrote to the Department of Labour and Immigration, which in turn wrote to the WWFA.[135] The Continental Overseas Corporation had expressed common concerns over the boycotts: that it was damaging their business, Australia's reputation and her long-term export prospects.

Putting forward a similar argument in a separate union and business alliance, a representative of the Federated Cold Storage and Meat Preserving Employees Union of Australia wrote to the ACTU enclosing a letter from the general

---

130 *Stewart Anderson to Fitzgibbon (WWFA), January 20 1975*, WWFA: Federal Office, N114/932, NBAC: ANU, Canberra.
131 *AMWU Commonwealth Council to S. Anderson, Branch Secretary, Bendigo RE: Chilean Grain Boycott, February 6 1975*, WWFA: Federal Office, N113/932, NBAC: ANU, Canberra.
132 *The trade Boycott of Wheat Sales to Chile, March 1977*, Papers of GMM. This fact is backed up by the statistics that note that only unmilled wheat went to Chile. This is considered unfit for human consumption. ABS, *Australian Exports, Country by Commodity* (1974–75 – 1988–89).
133 ABS, *Australian Exports, Country by Commodity* (1972–73).
134 This is even though their representatives had signed petitions for the release of political prisoners in Chile: Clodimoro Almeida, Anselmo Sule, Pedro Felipe Ramirez and Luis Corvalan. Sule later visited the WWFA offices in Sydney. *Letter to Cardinal Monsignor Silva Henriquez, May 15 1974*, WWFA: Federal Office, N113/932, NBAC: ANU, Canberra; 'Chilean Terror', *Maritime Worker*, 27 May 1975, 6.
135 *From Department of Agriculture, Canberra. to M. Ryan, Department of Labour and Immigration, Melbourne, RE: Meat to Chile, October 28 1974*, WWFA: Federal Office, N114/932, NBAC: ANU, Canberra.

manager of Murray Goulburn Cooperative Company, about exports to Chile. The general manager recalled that before the dictatorship, Australia had been exporting dairy products to Chile, and this had all but come to a stop due to the WWFA ban (which he specifically mentioned rather than 'maritime', unwittingly leaving a tantalising hint as to the effective player in this action).[136] This trade had topped $605 805 in 1972–73 from a low of $3000 in 1968–69.[137] In 1980, Chile would import 21 000 tonnes of dairy product from the European Economic Community. It was argued that up to 40 per cent of that could be replaced with Australian product owing to the decreased transport costs across the southern hemisphere. The Cold Storage and Meat Preservers did not see a point in denying Chileans' food or Australian workers' opportunities.[138] It was a familiar refrain: external political gain outweighed concerns for employment.

ACTU president, Bob Hawke, told the SUA in 1979 that trade was being diverted around the boycott to other countries to our detriment.[139] He tried to assure the SUA that the international labour movement would act eventually against the Pinochet regime.[140] He argued that continued pressure from the SUA would reduce the influence of the forthcoming two-day international boycott to be organised by the International Confederation of Free Trade Unions (ICFTU). Elliott, however, was already on the record as saying that 'the Chile wheat ban is a matter of principle before earning'.[141] Similarly, Henderson of the Firemen and Deckhands believed government and business put profit before people, and 'it is one thing to pay lip service to freedom and democracy, it is another thing if you are talking through your pocket'.[142] The AMWU published a pamphlet that declared: 'nothing exported to Chile is for [the workers], it is for the elite minority who live in luxury while millions are persecuted and starved.'[143]

Peter Nolan, secretary of the ACTU, was explicit in a circular to the 15 unions involved in sea transport in 1978. Not only was the boycott detrimental to workers in Australia, but also there had been a threat of legal action from farmers' associations. He questioned why boycotts had not been placed on other regimes and attempted to weaken the moral position of the maritime unions. For example, why was there a blanket ban on Chile and only a partial ban on Indonesia? The final point Nolan made was that although international

---

136   *Gallagher (Secretary Federated Cold Storage and Meat Preserving Employees Union of Australia Vic/Tas Branch) to Nolan (Secretary ACTU), 19 August 1980*, ACTU, N147/285 'Bans on Chile, 1978–1979', NBAC: ANU, Canberra.
137   ABS, *Australian Exports, Country by Commodity* (1968–69, 1972–73).
138   *Gallagher (Secretary Federated Cold Storage and Meat Preserving Employees Union of Australia Vic/Tas Branch) to Nolan (Secretary ACTU), 19 August 1980*.
139   Hawke had also had some sort of confrontation with Henderson in early 1978 over the Chile boycott issue. *Extract SWM Minutes Victorian Branch 31.1.78 Ref. 628, 31 January 1978.*
140   'Hawke Opens Conference', *Seamen's Journal* 34, no. 3 (March–April 1979), 54.
141   Montenegro, 'La Campaña de Solidaridad con Chile en Australia 1973–1990', 206.
142   Henderson, *'The military coup in Chile in September 1973 had little effect on the thinking...', 1993.*
143   Amalgamated Metalworkers and Shipwrights Union (Australia), *Chile!*.

organisations condemned the regime, why were Australia and New Zealand the only ones holding a boycott? Even Eastern-bloc countries had continued to trade with Chile.[144] Despite the increased pressure, the maritime unions refused to lift their blanket boycott on trade with Chile and this stance had grassroots support within the unions.[145]

Defiance in the face of the ACTU, which had gained huge membership in this period due to the incorporation of white-collar unions, was not unusual. Despite a union membership rate sitting at 58 per cent of Australian workers in 1975, the ACTU was 'a federation without the institutional capacity to direct and coordinate a structurally decentralised union movement'.[146] For example, in 1966 the SUA had ignored the ACTU ruling that there was to be no union interference with ships carrying goods to Vietnam.[147] It was a case of history repeating itself as after a brief period of encouragement, the ACTU released a statement that it supported 'the aims and not the methods' of the boycott.[148] The ACTU was pressured by its own more right-wing affiliates, as well as business and political interests.[149] Furthermore, the ACTU was, in general, not willing to go against the Government, because losing a Labor government was believed to be detrimental to all Australian workers.[150] In 1975 the congress heard Chilean trade unionists Luis Figueroa and Luis Meneses speak, but it had little effect: it seems the confederation stayed neutral from late 1975 to early 1977.[151] Soon, however, the ACTU's attitude changed and it began to try to have the boycott lifted.

By the ACTU Executive Meeting of February 1977, the consistent pressure finally provoked a debate.[152] The delegates from the AMWSU and BWIU voted against the lifting of the boycott; importantly, Charlie Fitzgibbon (WWFA) was not present at the meeting. Fitzgibbon was the unionist who originally proposed the motion to support the boycott in 1973–74. In his absence, the

---

144 'Ban on Indonesian and Chilean Trade', *Seamen's Journal* 33, no. 1 (January 1978), 14.
145 'Committee No. IV', *Seamen's Journal* 34, no. 3 (March–April 1979), 75.
146 Hagan, 'The Australian Trade Union Movement', 51; Chris Briggs, 'The End of a Cycle? The Australian Council of Trade Unions in Historical Perspective', in *Peak Unions in Australia: Origins, Purpose, Power, Agency*, eds Bradon Ellem, Raymond Markey and John Chields (Sydney: The Federation Press, 2004), 242.
147 Beasley, *Wharfies*, 218.
148 Kirkby, *Voices from the Ships*, 53.
149 The ACTU was capable of providing leadership on some political issues, such as the uranium debates of the 1970s. See, for example, the WWFA's decision to ship uranium: 'Unions' Policy', *Maritime Worker*, 29 March 1977, 9; Hagan, 'The Australian Trade Union Movement', 52–3.
150 It was 'too big a price to pay'. Hagan, 'The Australian Trade Union Movement', 52.
151 *Agenda Paper, Australian Congress of Trade Unions, 15 Sept – 19 Sept, 1975*, ACTU, S784/2/21, NBAC: ANU, Canberra; 'First Aid to Chile', *Maritime Worker*, 4 January 1975, 12.
152 *The trade Boycott of Wheat Sales to Chile, March 1977*. An example of a letter pressuring the ACTU to drop the boycott can be found at: *D. Eather (Vice President, Queensland Graingrowers Association) to Hawke (ACTU), 29 July 1977*, National Farmers Federation: Australian Primary Producers Union, N18/779, NBAC: ANU, Canberra; *AWB to Hawke RE: Chile, January 20 1975*, WWFA: Federal Office, N114/932, NBAC: ANU, Canberra; *AMWU Commonwealth Council re: Chile, January 22 1975*, AMWSU, E262/137, NBAC: ANU, Canberra; *Australian Metal Workers' Union Commonwealth Council, RE: Chile, January 28 1975*, WWFA: Federal Office, N114/932, NBAC: ANU, Canberra.

majority supported lifting the ban, adding that the decision would not be put to the congress. With that, the boycott was no longer sanctioned by the ACTU. The ACTU had decided that the only people who were being harmed by the boycott were Australian workers, and the ban was ineffectual because it was being carried out only by Australia and New Zealand.[153]

The council's about-face caused waves of defiance throughout the SUA, the BWIU and the AMWSU.[154] John Healy responded bitterly, arguing that the ACTU had tried to 'smash the ban, to lift the ban, to allow trade with Chile' even though international protests against the Pinochet regime and industrial action around the world were on the increase, including those by the ICFTU with which the ACTU was affiliated.[155] Between February and the next meeting of the ACTU in December, the CSCP lobbied trade unionists with detailed arguments about why the boycott should remain. Steve Cooper wrote that the boycott was supported by the CUT, WFTU, ICFTU, World Confederation of Labour (WCL), ITF and the ILO. Further, Bob Hawke, president of the ACTU, was also the federal president of the ALP, whose conference *supported* the ban on trade.

At stop-work meetings members of the SUA made statements demonstrating the high level of idealism and ideology among its members. The Sydney branch, for example, said: 'Australia's trade with Chile never was important or vital to any section of our people, and our continued boycott will enhance the overseas and national democratic principles of the Australian people.'[156]

For some SUA members international brotherhood took a higher priority than the tension between Australian unions, which was exacerbated by their boycott. At an SUA Sydney branch stop-work meeting, Pat Sweetensen (SPA) admitted that the seamen did not want to be isolated from the Australian trade union movement, but 'we also have international responsibilities to our suppressed comrades'.[157] The SUA reserved the right to continue it because the repression continued in Chile.[158]

John Healy, leader of the WWFA Sydney branch, echoed SUA sentiments. He said, 'as far as the W.W.F. is concerned, [wheat] will never be handled until

---

153 *Minutes of the ACTU executive meeting held in the ACTU boardroom, Melbourne, from Monday. 12th December, 1977 to Friday, 16th December, 1977 commencing at 2.15pm: Second Session, Fourth Session and Resolutions*, ACTU, N147/622, NBAC: ANU, Canberra.

154 Henry McCarthy returned from Algiers with support messages for the boycott. Henry McCarthy, 'Boycott the Junta', *Tribune* [Australia], 22 February 1978.

155 Healy, 'Chile: No Trade with Junta'.

156 *Extract SWM Minutes Sydney Branch 31/1/78*, SUA: Federal Office, N38/299, NBAC: ANU, Canberra.

157 *Extract SWM Minutes held Sydney Branch 2nd May 1978*, ref. no. 1493, SUA: Federal Office, N38/299, NBAC: ANU, Canberra. See also *Extract SWM Minutes held Port Kembla 2nd May 1978*, SUA: Federal Office, N38/299, NBAC: ANU, Canberra.

158 *Federal Office report No 8/1978 Mey* [sic] *26, 1978*, SUA: Federal Office, N38/299, NBAC: ANU, Canberra.

democracy is restored in Chile'.[159] Leo Lenane, federal organiser, repeated that attitude in July 1977: 'the way to remove the trade bans in Chile is through restoration of democracy in that country.'[160] In the *Maritime Worker* of 27 September 1977 and the *Seamen's Journal* of February 1978, it was reiterated that the ban was still in place.[161]

What seems like a cut-and-dried story is, however, much more complicated: inconsistencies exist in this narrative that only appear with very close examination of all sources. First, the ACTU Executive Meeting minutes of 20 March 1978 note that Fitzgibbon of the WWFA voted along with the other members to *lift* the ban.[162] Second, late in 1978 the ACTU received notice from shipping agents of barley being shipped to Chile.[163] The content of the letter suggests previous communication. Letters started to flow, seeking confirmation of the WWFA's position.[164] Further, Gethin, of the Farmers' Union of Western Australia, wrote to the ACTU stating that his members were worried about the WWFA *reinstating* the ban on Chile.[165] The last mention in the *Maritime Worker* of the ban being policy was in mid October 1977, but the mention was one sentence only, and relegated to the corner of a page.[166]

So, was the boycott still in place?

The WWFA was going through a general weakening in the 1970s. The organisers had other things on their minds such as containerisation, job layoffs, contracts, amalgamations and the stagflation of 1974–75, which led to increased employer pressure in all industries.[167] Margo Beasley wrote:

> The Australian waterfront was widely regarded as a shambles by 1976. The cost of surplus labour had reached record levels and no matter how

---

159   Healy, 'Chile: No Trade with Junta'.
160   *Lenane (WWFA) to CSCP, 7th July, 1977*, Papers of GMM.
161   'International Aid', *Maritime Worker*, 27 September 1977, 3; 'Indonesia, Chile Bans', *Maritime Worker*, 18 October 1977, 4; 'Seamen Continue Boycott on Trade with Chile', *Seamen's Journal* 33, no. 2 (February 1978), 35.
162   *Minutes of the ACTU Executive meeting held in ACTU board room, Melbourne from Monday, 20th March, 1978 to Wednesday 22nd March 1978, commencing at 9.30am*, ACTU, N147/623, NBAC: ANU, Canberra; *Nolan (ACTU) to ACTU Officers and Secretaries of all Affiliated Unions, April 18 1978*, SUA: Federal Office, N38/299, NBAC: ANU, Canberra.
163   *Erhard Schwazrock, Coarse Grains Manager, Continental Overseas Corporation to Nolan ACTU, 6 December 1978*, ACTU, N147/285, NBAC: ANU, Canberra.
164   For example: *Gallagher (Secretary Federated Cold Storage and Meat Preserving Employees Union of Australia Vic/Tas Branch) to Nolan (Secretary ACTU), 19 August 1980*. CONAUST wrote to the SUA noting the WWFA's lifting of the boycott, and seeking the SUA policy: *CONAUST to Federal Secretary SUA, Re: Chilean Flag Vessels, May 12 1978*, SUA: Federal Office, N38/299, NBAC: ANU, Canberra.
165   *P. J. Gethin, Director of Industrial Relations (The Farmers' Union of WA Inc) to Nolan (ACTU), 197(9)*, ACTU, N147/285, NBAC: ANU, Canberra.
166   'Indonesia, Chile Bans'.
167   Bramble, *Trade Unionism in Australia*, 75.

quickly the stevedoring industry shed employees, there were always either too many left for the work available, or those that were left were inefficiently used because of the way the industry was structured.[168]

The *Seamen's Journal* does not mention the WWFA lifting the boycott. Neither does it mention it holding the boycott in place. The mentions of waterside boycott after the wheat incidents are left to non-specific sweeping statements except for the case of the *Holstein Express*. For example, the Sydney Waterside Workers reinforced the rhetoric of the ban after Humberto Elgueta spoke to their meeting on 10 October 1979, but the promotion of the WWFA boycott faded.[169] According to trade statistics, so did the WWFA's stranglehold on trade to and from Chile.

There was a lull in both import and export activity with Chile from the 1975–76 to the 1977–78 financial years caused by the WWFA boycott, and the ACTU's support of it. These three years, after the existing wheat contracts were filled by the AWB, were when the WWFA and ACTU advertised their Chile boycott. Interestingly, the small amount of trade that did get through was primarily scientific and allied health machinery. These were shipped in relatively equal amounts before, during and after the WWFA boycott. The SUA may have stopped at least one shipment of iron ore in 1980, but shipments of grass seed made it through the ports every year of the dictatorship (except one). Trade with Chile never ceased, despite the best efforts of radicals. The total exports to Chile dropped from a high of $42 million in 1972–73 to a low of $157 000 in 1976–77. This reduced the rate of trade to pre-Allende levels.[170] Imports also hit a low in 1976–77, but the variation in those figures was not as marked (see Figure 8.2).

With the change in stance of the ACTU and the weakening of the WWFA's boycott in practice in 1977 and 1978, exports rose sharply. Major exports to Chile now included coking coal, malting barley and, in 1982–83, wheat. In addition, imports rose, with the highest being in the 1980–81 financial year, with $6.5 million worth of goods arriving in Australia.[171] The traditional imports of fish, fertilisers and fishmeal were entering and also on one occasion parts for arms in 1976–77. Despite this, trade with Pinochet's Chile never again reached the zenith of the early 1970s, though it did experience a spike due to a particularly good malting barley shipment year in 1979–80.

---

168 Beasley, *Wharfies*, 237.
169 It is unlikely, however, any substantial amount of Chile–Australia trade travelled through Sydney. 'Chile Bans Stay', *Tribune* [Australia], 10 October 1979.
170 In 1963–64 it was $142 000.
171 Import statistics and descriptions compiled from ABS, *Australian Imports, Country by Commodity* (1965–84).

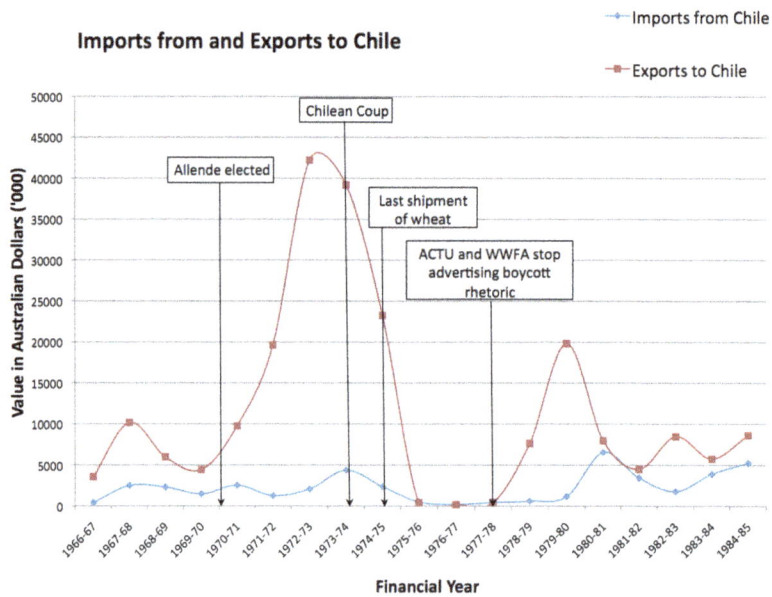

Figure 8.2 Comparison of Imports from and Exports to Chile, 1966–85.

Source: ABS, *Australian Exports, Country by Commodity*.

While the Wheat Board agreed not to ship wheat, the Australian Barley Board (ABB) had made no such commitment. The ABB was a government statutory authority that had been established under the *National Security Act* of 1939. Similar to the Wheat Board, it was a legislative requirement that all growers sell their barley to the ABB.[172] Barley had been grown in Australia since the first European settlement. In the 1960s, bulk handling had become the norm for Australian wheat and barley and had contributed to the loss of jobs on the waterfront.

In January 1973 Britain entered the European Common Market and this created a problem for the ABB, as it no longer enjoyed the benefits of trading with Britain without import taxes.[173] This was also coupled with an increase in barley production and a bumper crop in the USSR in 1976–77.[174] As a result, the Barley Board was searching for new markets. The 1978–79 season was a

---

172 The first chairman, Herbert Tomlinson, had a long career, working previously with Dalgety & Company, the same company which would test the maritime boycott in 1978 attempting to export cattle. Pauline Payne and Peter Donovan, *The Australian Barley Board: Making the Right Moves, 1939–1999* (Adelaide: Australian Barley Board, 1999), 97; also 17.
173 Ibid., 79.
174 Ibid., 94.

bumper crop in Australia and this was reflected in the largest shipment of barley to Chile, in the 1979–80 financial year.[175] Due to the bumper season, the ABB sold 136 505 t to South American countries, and the export records say that in the 1979–80 financial year all of it went to Chile.[176] In 1978, barley had the highest international selling price of all coarse grains.[177] Most of Australia's barley crop was grown in South Australia and Victoria. As the major brewers of Melbourne bought most of the barley from their own State, it was likely the barley shipments to Chile were exiting via one of the South Australian ports where the ABB had facilities.[178]

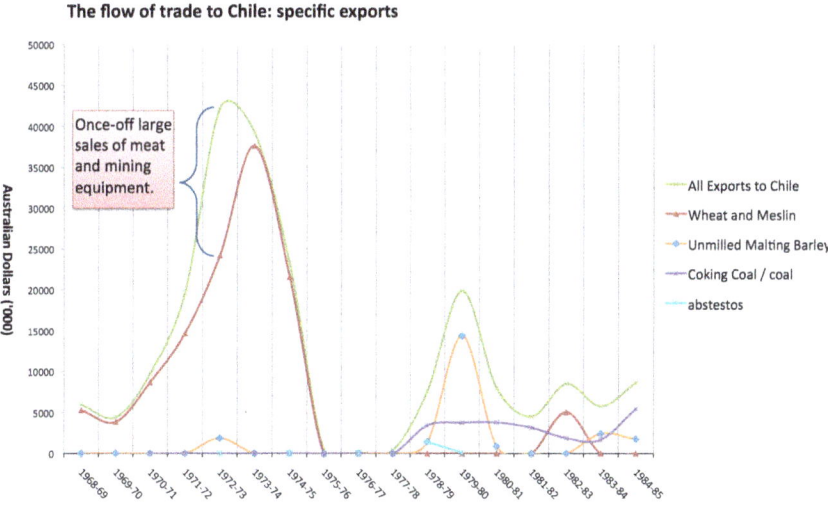

Figure 8.3 Specific Exports to Chile, 1968–85.

Source: ABS, *Australian Exports, Country by Commodity*.

From Figures 8.2 and 8.3 (assembled from trade information collected by the Australian Bureau of Statistics), it is obvious that the WWFA, not the SUA, had real power when it came to boycotts. The rhetoric of internationalism may have been stronger, or at least more vocal, in the SUA, but the strategic position of the WWFA allowed it to be much more effective. Its larger membership had

---

175   ABS, *Australian Exports, Country by Commodity* (1979–80).
176   Some 142 574 t of barley went to Chile. Payne and Donovan, *The Australian Barley Board*, 94; ABS, *Australian Exports, Country by Commodity*.
177   Australian Bureau of Agricultural Economics, *Coarse Grains Situation and Outlook* (Canberra: AGPS, 1978).
178   Port Lincoln, Wallaroo, Port Giles, Port Adelaide or Ardrossan.

more contact with Chilean trade than Australian-crewed ships ever could. But this strategic position also exposed the WWFA to more pressure than the SUA experienced.

Other than the odd burst of rhetoric, such as from the Sydney branch president, John Healy—'[t]here will not be one pound of wheat go, there will not be one point of cargo come in'[179]—the WWFA did not publicise their Chile commitment.[180] They kept their members informed of events in Chile and petitions via the *Maritime Worker* and circulars, but there was no dramatic call to arms as in the Seamen's Union.

The WWFA was carrying many campaigns at the time, including anti-apartheid and contra the Greek junta. The WWFA was also under constant pressure to take up campaigns due to their efficiency in boycotting. Mavis Robertson recalled one occasion when Tas Bull said to her: 'Listen Mavis, if someone else comes through this door and asks me to put a ban on something else, whether it's this or that … none of my members will ever get a day's work, and sometimes we just have to do things symbolically.'[181]

This was a significant admission. The wheat boycott was the main action, allowing the WWFA to claim the moral high ground. It was a powerful symbolic action. After that, jobs came first.

Despite its limitations, the boycott was, many times over, heralded as the cause for freedom of Chilean political prisoners. It was appreciated by many throughout the world such as the CUT in exile, which sent thankful telegrams.[182] Luis Corvalan, on his release from Dawson Island, said the maritime workers' boycott was 'an inspiration to the people of Chile'.[183] A world away from Chile, in Wollongong, Doreen Borrow of the local Chile Solidarity Committee wrote: 'We live with the certainty that the Chilean People will one day live in dignity and with full human rights. That day *will* come because of the united actions of the working class throughout the world. Included among these are our honoured comrades in the S.U.A.'[184]

Kirkby called it 'shared humanity', and this sentiment is an echo of E. V. Elliott's insistence that the Chilean and Australian workers were 'brothers in struggle'.[185]

---

179 Published in an SUA publication.
180 Healy, 'Chile: No Trade with Junta'.
181 Robertson Interview, 2009.
182 Original text reads: '*agradecemos y felicitamos por beoycot contrat el transitoria debe condisionarse a liberación de los prisionros politicos y sindicales* [sic].' Telegram from CUT to WWFA, January 1975, WWFA: Federal Office, N114/932, NBAC: ANU, Canberra.
183 Relayed via Frida Brown, an SPA member who was in Moscow. 'Luis Corvalan Thanks SUA for Solidarity with Chile Workers', *Seamen's Journal* 32, no. 2 (February 1977).
184 'Restore Democracy in Chile', *Seamen's Journal* 38, no. 8 (September 1983), 233.
185 Kirkby, *Voices from the Ships*, 16; Elliott, 'Chile: No Trade with Junta'.

But it was easy for Elliott to say 'solidarity has no national or geographical boundaries',[186] or for Henderson to state that 'we believe by isolating the Junta we will help the people of Chile to restore the democratic freedoms that Comrade Allende and many thousands of his countrymen have given their lives for'.[187]

The FDU and the SUA's real influence on trade with Chile was negligible, and thus their members' exposure to criticism or potential jail was also far less. The SUA could enjoy using Chile as a 'feather in their internationalist cap' from the relative safety of their position, when it was unlikely that Australian-crewed ships would sail to Chile. The most contact they were likely to have was through tugboats.[188] When trade did pass through, perhaps tug men turned a blind eye, just as many other unionists in Australia must have.

For example, wheat was transported by truck to regional silos. As soon as it arrived at the silo the wheat was the property of the AWB. From those regional silos it was transported in stages by train to ports. There were 17 wheat export ports in Australia.[189] Given that hides, coal, meat, wool, dairy products, clothing, manufactured goods, minerals, canned foodstuffs and cars were sent to Chile, the TWU,[190] AFULE,[191] ARU,[192] AMWSU, Amalgamated Engineering Union, Miners Federation, Australasian Coal and Shale Employees Federation, Food Preservers' Union of Australia, Wool Brokers' Staffs Association, Australasian Meat Industries Employees Union, the Federated Cold Storage and Meat Preserving Employees and Australian Textile Workers Union, to list just a few, all may have had workers who mined, moved or manufactured goods bound for Chile.

In other words, the majority of Australian workers did not take a stand.

Given this inconsistency between rhetoric and reality in the activities of the Australian labour movement, and the fractured nature of the branch structure of the WWFA, the fact that the 'ban stayed on so long, was a miracle', to use

---

186 E. V. Elliot, 'On Course!', *Seamen's Journal* (May 1974).
187 'Wider Union Bans on Chile Junta'.
188 Tug 'seamen' were congratulated as members of the SUA, but were actually in the main members of the FDU. For example, John Garrett, who incidentally was also the official SPA representative to the CSC. Kirkby, *Voices from the Ships*, 105.
189 AWB, *Wheat Growing*, 11, 12, 14.
190 The TWU did boycott at Mascott Airport as described in Chapter Seven. *J. Baird to G. Grimshaw, October 1 1975 and attached letter for Transport Workers' Union Strikers from CUT, September 19 1975.*
191 AFULE expressed their solidarity through getting Chilean enginemen jobs. They also supported Chileans in coming to Australia. *Australian Metal Workers' Union Commonwealth Council, Re: Chile, 30/1/75 and attachments dates 6/1/75 and 3/1/75*, January 30 1975, AMWSU, E262/137, NBAC: ANU, Canberra; *Mr Sergio Marambio—age 32, 1974, Australian Federated Union of Enginemen*, 8/3/38 Box 136, Melbourne University Archives: Australian Federated Union of Locomotive Enginemen Collection, Melbourne; *Memo re: Appeal from ALP for finance to bring ex-Senator Sule to Australia*, April 9 1975, WWFA: Federal Office, N114/932, NBAC: ANU, Canberra.
192 In 1975 the ARU offered 'practical support' to the Chile cause. *Programme Results—Chilean Trade Union Delegation to Australia, 11–20 September 1975*.

the words of Mavis Robertson.[193] It was a ban chiefly in name, but the symbolic nature of the boycott does not imply it was useless. Rhetoric, especially from the WWFA and ACTU, scared shipping companies from attempting to trade Chilean goods.

The so-called miracle continued in 1978, when the live-cattle shipment on the *Holstein Express* was boycotted by determined maritime unionists. Was this really a 'union victory', as hailed by the SPA organ?

The 1978–79 financial year was the start of the upward swing of trade with Chile. The SUA's harassment of this one vessel in a wave of trade may seem relatively futile or a gesture and little else. Yet, the *Holstein Express* incident was symbolic of so much more for the SUA: it was support for the Chilean people, but more than anything, it was a self-affirming action by the seamen whose identity rested on their radical internationalist ideology. Henderson argued, speaking of the SUA: 'In fact, we see ourselves—quite rightly, I believe—as among the most progressive sections of the trade union movement of this country. We also see ourselves as internationalists and we involve ourselves in all issues of economic and industrial matters.'[194]

For the waterside workers, it was slightly different: 1978 had been a hard year. The negotiations for the contract of 1978–80 had stalled. In April of that year there had been a nationwide stoppage on the waterfront over the use of non-union labour to load ships.[195] 'Scabs' had crossed a picket line set up by the Australasian Meat Industry Employees Union (AMIEU), who had supported the sale of frozen meat to Chile in 1974. They were protesting live export of animals from Australia, as it resulted in the loss of their members' jobs. The WWFA respected their picket lines, even though the AMIEU had questioned the Chile ban in 1974, even supposing it meant less work.

Tensions were high in the WWFA, and anti-solidarity scabs were on the top of the blacklist. The WWFA official organ framed the *Holstein Express* incident as typifying the deception of the companies and the non-union labour involved. The article noted that $1000 in compensation had been received by the watersiders of Port Kembla for the work to load the cattle that should have been undertaken by union labour.[196] Should the workers have accepted the money in light of their boycott on Chile? For the WWFA, it wasn't about Chile anymore.

The WWFA Sydney branch saw the *Holstein Express* episode in terms of anti-scabbing and national-unity rhetoric rather than one centred on Chile solidarity

---

193 Robertson Interview, 2009.
194 'Chile: No Trade with Junta'.
195 'No Non-Union Wharf Labour!', *Maritime Worker*, 18 April 1978, 1.
196 'Eden Compensation', *Maritime Worker*, 13 February 1979, 5.

or an internationalist identity.[197] This was a clear case of a union using the Chile issue as a tool for their own more pressing political and industrial objectives. The relaxation of the overall ban pointed to a resource rationalisation by the union. The boycotts became a risk inordinately larger than the benefit of maintaining the blacking activities.

The SUA, on the other hand, whose communist identity and rhetoric were consistently advocated in relation to the Chile boycott, had no trouble maintaining their stance. In fact, they used the boycott to express their exceptionalist political identity: 'principle before earning', Elliott had said. Because of a small membership, however, and those members' lack of contact with Chilean trade, the Seamen's boycott, for all its political zeal, was anticlimactic.

The WWFA was in the right industrial position and had the right leadership to give a base to the boycott; however, over time, the international socialist rhetoric that had formed the base of the black ban faded and industrial conditions required more imperative, strategic and political attention. As the boycott took a low and sinking profile in the union and the ACTU, so the grip on trade to Chile loosened. When Hugo Miranda noted 'Australian watersiders prefer action',[198] he did not know how true those words were: they undeniably preferred their jobs.

---

197 Waterside Workers' Federation, *Branch News*, 2 January 1979.
198 'Chile Junta Victim Thanks Watersiders', *Maritime Worker*, 26 July 1977, 11.

Conclusion

> I am thinking of Diane, of Angie, Mike, Jerry, Bill, Adrian, Jeannie, Mavis, Peggy … People that you surely do not know. I think that we have never adequately thanked them.[1]

On 3 June 2009, at the Moneda Palace in Santiago, Joan Jara rose to give a speech of thanks. She looked at Michelle Bachelet, the then President of the Republic of Chile. They had both been victims of the military dictatorship. The president had just signed the papers that would grant Jara Chilean citizenship. Jara finally—officially—joined a people she had talked about as her own for almost her entire adult life.

Jara told of the responsibility she felt when she left Chile after the coup and the death of her husband: solidarity work had given her something to live for. She spoke of the tours she made with Inti Illimani and Quilapayun. She said a generation of students heard of the coup in Chile and it 'changed their vision of the world, and also changed the rhythm of their lives'. She spoke of the friends she made in exile, of many of them who gave years of their lives in support of the fight for Chilean democracy.

Among that list appeared two of the most prominent members of the solidarity movements in Britain and Australia: Mike Gatehouse and Mavis Robertson. Both have featured extensively in this book. These two activists, among many others, gave time, gave up income and also devoted ideological and emotional support to the Chile cause.

While I have argued that union action for Chile was constrained by the availability of resources, opportunities and primary union aims, these individuals acted very distinctly. They participated in the movement far beyond the time it was personally, politically, economically and emotionally useful for them to do so. They were motivated by ideology and/or a deep unrest over the abuses of the Pinochet regime (though the order of those reasons varied). The Chile campaigns in both Australia and Britain owed their success in part to these sorts

---

1 'Pienso ahora en todas aquellos amigos del exilio. Muchos de ellos dieron años de sus vidas en apoyo a la larga lucha por la restauración de la democracia en Chile. Para una generación de jóvenes universitarios en muchos países el golpe militar en Chile cambió su visión del mundo, cambió también el rumbo de sus vidas. Pienso en Diane, en Angie, Mike, Jerry, Bill, Adrian, Jeannie, Mavis, Peggy … y tantos, tantos otros de diferentes culturas, idiomas. Personas que seguramente Uds. no conocen. Pienso que nunca les hemos agradecido adecuadamente.' Joan Jara, 'Joan Jara recibe nacionalidad chilena por gracia en Palacio de la Moneda, jueves, 04 de junio de 2009', *Fundación Víctor Jara*, accessed 19 August 2009, <http://www.fundacionvictorjara.cl/nacionalidad.html>.

of organisers, including Mavis Robertson, Steve Cooper and Mike Gatehouse, who 'attached an exalted significance' to their cause.[2] I used Hamer's term 'faddists' to describe them in this book, but not in any pejorative sense: their importance to the movement was crucial. It was their *duty* to work for Chile and it was the right thing to do. Parkin has suggested that a 'status inconsistency' (the gap between skill level and actual income that is filled with a sense of duty or honour) was in fact a motivator for radical activists, and the cases contained within these pages would support that notion.[3] The great positive force and energy that the hyper-committed 'communicators', as Waterman would call them, brought to their chosen cause gave the impetus needed to organise and ultimately harness the power of the labour movement.[4]

While many comparisons draw conclusions on a theoretical level, which I shall do too, the parallel study of these two campaigns also elucidated some much more personal similarities. In fact, there were uncanny similarities within the personnel of the Chile movements in Australia and Britain through all the levels of organisation. Mike Gatehouse and Steve Cooper were both quiet, highly educated and hardworking. They were not necessarily very well connected themselves, but had the ear of people who were. They came to the campaigns after spending time in Chile during the Allende administration. Steve Hart and Andrew Ferguson were both passionately involved in politics. They were both from leading labour families with relatives in representative positions in government. Mavis Robertson and Alex Kitson were both strategically connected to the upper hierarchy of the labour movement, although Kitson's connections were more institutionalised than Robertson's. Furthermore, Robertson used her network for Chile on a much more regular, albeit less formal, basis. Judith Hart MP and Senator Anthony Mulvihill were used in both countries to furnish the campaigns with legitimacy in the public eye. Allan Angel was similar to Barry Carr: they were scholars of Latin America in universities with similar politics. Both spoke Spanish and acted as key communicators between sections of the Chilean exile community and their host countries. George Anthony and Brian Nicholson in Britain and Henry McCarthy and James Baird (and to a lesser extent, Tas Bull) in Australia played comparable roles: their politics and career courses were very different, but they were used to give the campaigns the seal of rank-and-file trade union approval. There is really only one who has no exact counterpart in the movements. It was the moral authority of Jack Jones

---

2 Also mentioned were Diane Dixon and Angela Thew, both of whom were interviewed for this thesis. Hamer, *The Politics of Electoral Pressure*, 1.
3 Parkin, *Middle Class Radicalism*, 53, 184, 189.
4 Waterman, *Globalization, Social Movements and the New Internationalisms*, 247.

that placed him in an important position in the hierarchies of the movement. If Bob Hawke had showed interest in the Chilean situation, he may have held a similarly privileged position.[5]

Their ideology differed, sometimes significantly, but they all shared a sense of moral purpose: a common belief in the justice of actions against the regime in Chile. They were also bound by the momentum of the cycles of protest established during the early 1970s. This primarily followed an annual calendar with a focus around key labour movement and historical Chilean dates. As is ascertained in Chapters Two and Six, the 11 September demonstrations were the main point around which activities clustered each year. Years of higher than normal activity appeared on significant anniversaries or around events such as the Chilean plebiscite of 1980. The campaigns' focus and rhythm were also shaped by a long cycle of activist succession. There were few, if any, activists who remained imbedded in the social movement's structure for the duration of the dictatorship, and very interestingly, the first major change of personnel occurred at roughly the same time in Australia and Britain at the end of the 1970s.

The cycles were comparable and the roles fulfilled strikingly similar, but one of the most obvious differences between the two campaigns was the integration of exiles into the committees. In both cases, the integration of migrants into the structure of the campaign was problematic, but the CSC in Britain was more successful in sustaining its broad front. This was achieved by effectively denying voting rights to exiles. Mike Gatehouse remembered:

> The Chilean People were in Chile, they were not here. The Chilean political parties were in Chile, they have external representation. But, if you involve them, then it ceases to be a solidarity campaign and becomes an exile movement. And we were absolutely clear that that would be wrong.[6]

He went on to say that those campaigns that integrated Chileans floundered very quickly, and his observations are supported by the Australian example. In Australia, the attempted broad front collapsed under the disparate pressures of the two sets of political factions; however, to place the blame for this completely at the feet of the exiles would be hasty and incorrect, as politics on local, State, national and global levels also impacted on the Australian Chile campaign. Furthermore, due to the size of the population, there was more pressure to integrate Chileans in Australia, if only to have more hands on deck to help with organising.

---

5   Bramble, *Trade Unionism in Australia*, 82.
6   Gatehouse Interview, 2007.

The size of the movement also influenced the depth of bureaucratic structure. In Australia, where the left was much smaller and split among distant cities, a national organisational framework was attempted but never achieved. Instead, the Australian campaign relied more heavily on the networking abilities of individuals. While the need for a formal structure for the campaign was less necessary in Australia, it did expose the movement to the dangers of instability and potential collapse if a strategic individual ceased participation. The British Chile Solidarity Campaign created a more complex organisational framework, at both local and national levels, and was much more stable because of it. By creating a self-perpetuating network of affiliates, the British campaign successfully exploited the bureaucratic and organisational (industrial national) based nature of the trade unions and enabled the systematic capture of a critical mass of supporters.

Thus the main difference in trade union involvement in Chile solidarity campaigns between Britain and Australia was the more ad-hoc nature of Australian unions' and unionists' involvement, compared with the more structured and hierarchical nature of the British trade union integration. Despite the British campaign's ability to capture more mass support, the individuals with strategic knowledge of, and connections with, the labour movement were the most important acquisitions of the campaigns in both countries.

This book has provided a road map through the concurrent complex structures of the labour movement in Britain and Australia tracking the idiosyncratic paths between them taken by privileged actors—privileged, that is, by their knowledge of the organisational topography of the labour movement. These strategic individuals could bridge labour movement hierarchies and carry the Chile cause further than it otherwise might have achieved. The campaigns used these individuals to boost their positions within the hierarchy of aims of the labour movement. Inversely, some individuals used the movement to promote themselves. In Britain, George Anthony is a case in point: he reached an organising position above his usual level within the labour movement hierarchy, and also extended his own network and influence.

The exchange between individuals and the campaigns did not end there. Moral capital—that incalculable yet imperative resource as defined by Kane—was reciprocally granted between the campaigns and participants. While the moral capital of one person, such as Jack Jones, could be captured and used in order to legitimise the campaign, the reverse was also true. Though, the cause itself did not bestow moral authority on its participants per se, their involvement—that is, their stated aims and fulfilment of those aims—added to that individual's store of moral capital. In the case of many individuals in the campaign, this could then be transferred into other organisations or positions in the future to benefit their careers.

While elucidating similarities between individual trajectories, this comparative study has also established a repertoire of activities on the historical record. This book has moved towards developing a typology of actions used by trade unions for external political causes in the 1970s.[7] The majority of actions within that repertoire were indirect, and the majority of indirect actions were organised outside trade unions by either local or international solidarity organisations. These actions, described in Chapters Two and Six, included demonstrations, local and international conferences, cultural activities, tours and donations. The two movements' repertoires were strikingly similar, though not identical, and often where they did differ it was due to scale.

Externally organised indirect actions took advantage of the opportunistic nature of union internationalism. Essentially, when a progressive union was petitioned for aid in the form of conference attendance, or support for a demonstration, they had no trouble fulfilling that request. These types of indirect actions against Chile, along with letter writing, telegram sending and resolution passing, represented the majority of solidarity actions in both Britain and Australia and most importantly had a minor impact on union resources. Indirect actions like this allowed unions to express their internationalist ideologies with little organisational expenditure and without risk to their members, and fittingly, the solidarity movement sought to routinise these actions into union business wherever they could.

Other so-called indirect actions attempting to create change in Chile through public pressure included delegations and they were organised from within unions with little interference from social movements. Of all the Chile actions undertaken by unions, these were the least opportunistic because the union had to create their own opportunity to travel. Delegations were a substantial and high-risk undertaking: it could never be known what the outcome would be and there was physical danger to the delegates and the people they met. Delegations such as those sent from Australia in 1974 and by the NUM in 1977 were extremely high-profile forms of solidarity that served the unions, Chileans and the solidarity movement very well, despite the fact they generated factional infighting in the union movement.

There were difficulties of sustaining or even starting a direct action for an external political goal. The only direct industrial protests that took place in solidarity with Chile were boycotts and scattered stop-work meetings, as described in Chapters Four and Eight. Essentially, the availability of union resources and the degree of threat to unions' primary aims had an inverse relationship to the likelihood of action occurring. That is, the more activities were seen to require union resources (in organising time or money) or impinged upon the union's

---

7   Though not in its entirety.

main aims, the less likely it was that unions would take that action.[8] Solidarity with Chile was a just cause, but notwithstanding its role in fulfilling a sense of moral obligation and an ideological imperative to internationalism, it was still remote from the unions' raison d'être.

As such, action for Chile needed almost *no* impediment for it to occur. Unions were risk averse. For this reason, the Chile campaigns in both Britain and Australia comprised mainly routine events. These were endorsable and easily undertaken by the labour movement without draining resources or imperilling jobs, wages or conditions. An exception to this was the grassroots boycott in East Kilbride, which was, significantly, pulled into line by the union hierarchy. Similarly, the unilateral action of the wharfies in Australia soon drew the ire of the peak union organisation. This suggests that with few exceptions, those most keen on preserving union business were to be found in its upper hierarchy.

It can be concluded, after examining the case studies and how they fit into the existing categories of political action, that international activity in unions is contingent on the sum of the incentives, capacities and impediments to the action.[9] The CSC and CSCP were extremely successful mobilisers as they undertook activities that had little or no organisational cost for the unions and thereby made the expression of union internationalism easy. The Burgmanns have noted that militancy thrives in a favourable industrial climate, and the research contained within these pages provides highly detailed case studies that support this view.[10] As long as industrial stability was not threatened, radical unions reacted favourably to the possibility of action for Chile.

It is evident throughout this history that actions undertaken by trade unions in solidarity with Chile were largely opportunistic, whether that opportunity was provided by an external source (such as participating in an organised international conference) or by the union's industrial location (such as the Waterside Workers boycott). But also, below the opportunity, an ideological or moral sense of obligation to the cause was needed. The campaigns worked hard to sustain the sense of obligation and build a pool of goodwill towards the Chile cause. Left-wing unions were more likely to pursue an internationalist agenda and did not see a limit to their legitimate concerns.[11] Their ideological concerns for the worldwide proletariat or socialism, peace or nonviolence predisposed them to actions for Chile.[12]

---

8   Deery, 'Union Aims and Methods', 61. Though it has been noted in other places how hard it is to actually quantify union aims: Peter Gahan, '(What) Do Unions Maximise? Evidence from Survey Data', *Cambridge Political Economy Society* 26 (2002), 279–98.
9   Schmutte, 'International Union Activity', 65.
10 Burgmann and Burgmann, *Green Bans, Red Union*, 14.
11 Anner, 'Industrial Structure, the State, and Ideology', 627.
12 Plowman, 'The Victorian Trades Hall Split', 306.

Ideology, however, also caused the impure motives for some individuals' and organisations' involvement in the movement. 'Chile' was used to gain local political capital or as a weapon for internecine disputes. This was tantamount to a commodification of the Chile issue for political capital. It did not, in general, stop events from occurring or unions from taking internationalist actions but, as we have seen, it sometimes tempered action. It reduced solidarity effectiveness by self-censoring, limiting aims and ultimately resulting in the degradation of the broad front.

It's hard to place rogue behaviour into the theoretical models of trade union action retrospectively applied by social scientists: to them, union actions with internationalist aims manifested as direct or indirect and union or social movement organised actions. The case studies published here demonstrate that industrial national unionism and social movement unionism existed concurrently within organisations. The case studies highlight the inability of static theoretical models to explain actions over time.

The role of pragmatism should not be underestimated, when it comes to union interaction, and more specifically union internationalism. And pragmatism is hard to work into a structural political model.

Unions or unionists who desire to reach a political goal used the methods that were appropriate and available to them, regardless of that method's abstract place in a theoretical model of union organisation. Each union and every union action was idiosyncratic, influenced by a huge range of factors. The forces at work on the decision for international political action or inaction by unions are too complex to be attributed to an 'ideal type' of union decision-making and it should not be assumed that there was a unity of purpose behind them.[13] The union activity that did take place for Chile could not be divided exactly into categories of direct and indirect political activity, social movement and industrial national unionism. The four categories overlapped.

In sum, I have put forward three overarching findings in this history and reiterated them in this conclusion. The first covers the factors that must be present for internationalist action to occur within a union: opportunity, ideology/moral convictions and little or no risk to union core aims and resources. The second finding concerns the manner in which individuals and the campaigns attracted legitimacy and moral capital in a self-perpetuating and mutually beneficial manner. Finally, this work suggests that existing theoretical models of union action require revision in order to be useful in understanding the relationship between solidarity campaigns and trade unions.

---

13 Deery, 'Union Aims and Methods', 60.

But quite aside from the arguments, this book has restored trade union international action to its rightful place in the history of the labour movement. High-profile strategic individuals and committed faddists were a minority in the movement. The majority of those who expressed solidarity were trade unionists.

The fact that they acted *at all* was a condemnation of the junta, and the *very existence* of a social movement denounced the crimes of the junta and increased pressure on the regime. If they did not succeed in restoring democracy, they certainly won a number of small victories, and one of those small victories was to do with trucks.

The slogan 'no truck with the Chilean junta' embodies the importance of unions to the Chile solidarity campaigns. The slogan itself stemmed from the first half of 1977 when rank-and-file Northampton lorry drivers declared they would not touch Chilean goods. On several occasions, they had refused to touch cargo at the Liverpool docks, and soon they produced stickers for their cabs that pronounced: 'NO TRUCK WITH CHILE!'

News of their boycott and slogan spread to London, and the CSC office recognised an opportunity. Stickers were circulated through the campaign's affiliates bearing the slogan (see Figure 1), and as a result, by 1979 the stickers were slapped on cabs and cars all around Britain. The stickers of the Northampton lorry drivers, though humble in conception, had a national and in turn international impact.[14]

Take a sticker, or take any one of the activities for Chile in isolation, and they can seem futile, or simply symbolic. But as Jack Jones said in 1975: 'The routine and often modest activities of the campaign of solidarity with the people of Chile against the Junta when "totalled across the world" have made a very important contribution to easing the repression of the regime.'[15]

The stickers were one small victory of many in the Chile solidarity movement.

---

[14] *CSC Annual report, 1977; Annual General Meeting 1979: Draft Programme of Activities for 1979*, CSC, CSC/1/14, LHASC: Manchester; *Stick by Chile in the Cab, the Highway*, May 1979, CSC, CSC/7/14, LHASC, Manchester.

[15] 'How Solidarity has Helped Chile Fight', *Record* [TGWU], February 1975, 5.

Figure 2 A float hastily constructed for a workers' parade in Glasgow by Chilean refugees.

Source: From the Collection of Manuel Ocampo, Glasgow (Undated).

Appendix

Dramatis personae

Allende, Hortensia	Widow of Salvador Allende
Allende, Salvador	President of Chile, killed on the day of the military takeover
Angell, Alan	Academic, Academics for Chile; Chilean expert
Anthony, George	CSC Joint Chair with Brian Nicholson; CPGB; AUEW
Atkins, George	AMWU organiser
Bachelet, Michelle	A young woman at time of coup, her father was tortured to death. She and her mother fled to Australia. She went on to become President of Chile.
Baird, James (Jim)	AMWU, peace activist, travelled to Chile in 1974; gave evidence to ILO; internationalist
Barbour Might, Dick	Friend of the CSC
Beausire, William	Disappeared dual British–Chilean citizen
Binns, Peter	IS leader
Bolger, Bob	WWFA Sydney Branch
Bower, Celia	Association for British Chilean Friendship
Boyd, John	AUEW
Browne, Anne	CCHR, JWG; accompanied NUM delegation
Bull, Carmen	Tas Bull's widow; Argentinean by birth; used by CSCP for translation
Bull, Tas	WWFA organiser; ALP; long-term social activist
Bunster, Alvaro	Ambassador to Britain during the Allende administration; during the dictatorship was a popular speaker around Britain
Bustos, Manuel	CUT, Textile Workers of Chile; emerged after the coup as a union leader
Carr, Barry	Academic, Latin Americanist; communist sympathies; key individual in Melbourne solidarity movement
Carstairs, Susan	CCHR
Cassidy, Sheila	Detained in Chile; British subject, went on to become symbol of the irrationality of the Chilean regime
Clancy, Pat	BWIU

Collins, Jack	NUM representative to the CSC; CPGB member
Cooper, Steve	Key organiser for the CSCP in the early 1970s; lifelong unionist; AMWU in the 1970s; BLP left
Cornejo, Pedro	CUT representative to Britain; originally adopted by NUPE Hammersmith
Corvalan, Luis	Secretary-General of the Communist Party of Chile; imprisoned after coup
Creighton, Colin	Sociologist; Hull Chile Solidarity
Dixon, Diane	Key activist for Chile in Scotland and England; CPGB
Elgueta, Humberto	CUT leader; teacher
Ferguson, Andrew	ALP; radical left; organiser for the CSCP in the latter half of the dictatorship
Figueroa, Luis	President of CUT
Fitzpatrick, Barry	NATSOPA journalist; involved in the CSC as a union representative over many years; travelled to Chile in the 1980s as part of the Labour Movement Delegation
Garrett, John	SPA member on the CSCP
Gatehouse, Mike	Key organiser for the CSC; CPGB
Georges, George	ALP; sympathetic to Chile cause; leader of demonstrations
Gillies, Dougal	East Kilbride Works Committee member
Gonzalez, Mike	Academic, Glasgow; Latin Americanist
Hargreaves, John	TUC International Department
Hart, Judith	BLP MP; active in Chile and Latin American causes
Hart, Steve	Employed as organiser for Liberation; son of Judith
Hawke, Bob	ACTU and ALP president
Healy, John	WWFA Sydney Branch leader; son of Jim Healy, legendary WWFA leader
Heffer, Eric	BLP MP Liverpool constituency; sympathetic to Chilean cause
Henderson, Don	FDU unionist with deep interest in Chile activities
Henfrey, Colin	CSCP organiser, Liverpool; academic
Hulme, Ken	Trade union organiser for the CSC; activist; CPGB member at time of involvement
Hutchinson, Gordon	Local committees and refugee portfolios within the CSC; JWG
Jagers, Pat	WWFA Sydney Branch, SPA aligned

Jara, Joan (Turner)	Widow of Victor Jara; dancer; activist; owned Chile Records, a company that promoted Chilean new song
Jones, Jack	TGWU; Spanish Civil War
Keenan, John	Shop steward at East Kilbride Rolls Royce factory; BLP; AUEW; STUC
Kitson, Alex	Scottish, executive officer of the TGWU; treasurer, CSC; involved in TUC and BLP
Levy, James	Oxford academic with speciality in Chilean labour; organiser for Academics for Chile
Lewis, Jeannie	Australian folk musician
Little, Jenny	BLP international department
McCarthy, Henry	AMWU and peace activist
McGahey, Mick	Scottish miners' leader
MacIntosh, Duncan	CSC distribution organiser
MacIntyre, Jim	TGWU; STUC
McKay, Jane	Scottish communist leader; imperative to Glasgow Free Chile Committee and STUC
McKay, Ted	NUM delegation member, 1977
McKie, Joe	NUM delegation member, 1977
Martin, Billy	AMWU national organiser; involved with the Chile movement from about 1978 onwards; Martin was given (according to Steve Cooper) a Golden Sombrero by the Latin American Community in Australia for service to the community
Medina, Tony	Chilean refugee to Australia; a key communicator
Mitchell, Adrian	Poet, playwright from Britain; activist in peace and disarmament causes
Moorhead, Glenn	AFULE member, SPA aligned
Mulvihill, Tony	ALP MP, sympathetic to the Chilean cause
Murray, Len	General secretary, TUC
Nicholson, Brian	TGWU member; joint secretary of the CSC; CPGB
Nolan, Jim	STUC
Parry, Steve	National Union of Students UK; CPGB
Plant, Cyril	TUC; ILO
Robertson, Mavis	CSCP organiser; CPA member; long-term peace and women's liberation activist
Sol, Raul	Charismatic Chilean journalist in Britain

Somerville, Bob	Rolls Royce East Kilbride Works Committee
Thew, Angela	Academic, Merseyside Chile Solidarity Committee
Toon, Ken	NUM delegation member, 1977
Tyndale, Wendy	Human rights activist; CCHR employee; afterwards employed by British Christian Aid
Wheelwright, Ted	Professor at University of New South Wales; Latin Americanist; popular for media interviews
Woddis, Jack	CPGB cadre
Young, Amicia	London Trades Council

Bibliography

Manuscripts

Glasgow Caledonian University Archive

'Chile and Scotland: 30 Years On.' Paper presented at the Witness Seminar and Open Forum Series (No. 3). Saltire Centre, Glasgow Caledonian University, Saturday, 29 November 2003.

Sandy Hobbs Papers.

Scottish Communist Party.

Scottish Trades Union Congress.

Scottish Trades Union Review.

476 East Kilbride Trades Council 1978–1982.

Labour History Archives and Study Centre, Manchester

Chile Solidarity Campaign.

Chile Solidarity Campaign. People's History Museum Collections.

Labour Party—Eric Heffer Papers.

Labour Party—Judith Hart Papers.

Marx Memorial Library, London

Morning Star Photo Collection.

Melbourne University Archives

Australian Federated Union of Enginemen.

Australian Federated Union of Locomotive Enginemen Collection.

Victorian Trades Hall Council.

Modern Records Centre, Warwick University

Amalgamated Engineering Union.

Amalgamated Union of Engineering Workers.

British Leyland Trade Union Committee.

Chile Committee for Human Rights.

Confederation of Shipbuilding and Engineering Unions.

Coventry Trade Union Council.

Etheridge Papers: Communist Party.

Etheridge Papers: Longbridge Shop Stewards.

Iron and Steel Trades Confederation.

National Union of Seamen.

Oxford Chile Joint Committee.

Trades Union Congress.

Trades Union Congress (BLP International Department).

Transport and General Workers.

National Museum of Australia, Canberra

Elsie Gare Collection No. 1.

Noel Butlin Archive Centre, Canberra

Australian Council of Trade Unions.

Amalgamated Metal Workers Union.

Amalgamated Metal Workers and Shipwrights' Union.

Australian Teachers Federation.

National Farmers' Federation: Australian Primary Producers Union.

Plumbers and Gasfitters Employees Union of Australia.

Seamen's Union of Australia.

Trades and Labour Council of the Australian Capital Territory.

Waterside Workers' Federation of Australia.

Rolls Royce East Kilbride, Scotland

Rolls Royce East Kilbride Shop Stewards Papers, held in the Shop Stewards' Office at Rolls Royce, East Kilbride.

Whitlam Institute, University of Western Sydney

Prime Ministerial Collection.

Personal Collections

Papers of Barry Carr, Melbourne.

Papers of Colin Creighton, Hull.

Papers of Mike Gonzalez, Glasgow.

Papers of Gustavo Martin Montenegro, Canberra.

Papers of Manuel Ocampo, Coventry.

Papers of Mick Wilkinson, Hull.

Oral History Interviews and Personal Communications

Copies of all interviews and personal communications in possession of author.

Angell, Alan. Interview by Ann Jones. 30 August 2007.

Anthony, George. Interview by Ann Jones. 22 August 2007.

Carr, Barry. Interview by Ann Jones. 5 March 2009.

Cooper, Steve. Notes from a conversation with Ann Jones, Billy Martin (AMWU organiser, Chile activist, 1980s) and Pat Johnson (AMWU organiser of the present day). 21 May 2007.

Cooper, Steve. Phone interview by Ann Jones. 12 October 2005.

Dixon, Diane. Interview by Ann Jones. 4 September 2007.

Ferguson, Andrew. Phone interview by Ann Jones. 27 February 2009.

Fitzpatrick, Barry. Interview by Ann Jones. 28 August 2007.

Gatehouse, Mike. Interview by Ann Jones. 3 August 2007.

Gatehouse, Mike. Interview by Ann Jones. 13 August 2008.

Gatehouse, Mike. Email to Ann Jones. 26 July 2009.

Hewett, Andrew. Phone interview by Ann Jones. 23 September 2005.

Hogue, Derry. 'Lan Chile Query'. Email to Ann Jones. 7 March 2005.

Hulme, Ken. Interview by Ann Jones. 1 September 2007.

Keenan, John. Interview by Ann Jones. 8 September 2008.

Levy, James. Interview by Ann Jones. 12 March 2009.

McKay, Ted. Letter to Ann Jones. 1 November 2007.

McKay, Ted. Letter to Ann Jones. c. 21 July 2008.

Nolan, Jimmy, Antony Burke, Hugo Santillar, Angela Thew and Anthony Santamera. Discussion with Ann Jones. 9 August 2008.

Robertson, Mavis. Interview by Ann Jones. 31 January 2005.

Robertson, Mavis. Interview by Ann Jones. 6 February 2009.

Somerville, Bob MBE. Interview by Ann Jones. 27 July 2007.

Newspapers, Union Journals, Magazines

Amalgamated Metal Workers' Union Monthly Journal (Australia). 1973–75.

BBC News Online (UK). 23 October 1998.

Branch News (WWFA, Sydney Branch). 1973–80 (incomplete).

Building Worker (Australia). 1973–75.

Chile Fights (UK). 1973–89.

Daily Post (UK). 1998.

Direct Action (Socialist Youth Alliance, NSW). 1973–80.

El Mercurio (Chile). 2003.

Glasgow Herald. 1974, 1976.

Guardian (Manchester). 1973–80.

Harbour News (Firemen and Deckhands' Union, NSW, Australia). 1973–76.

Honi Soit (Australia). 1975.

Labour Weekly (UK). 1973–80.

Maritime Worker (WWFA, Australia). 1973–80 (incomplete).

Maritime Workers Journal (MUA, Australia). 2003.

Morning Star (London). 1973–80.

Official Branch News (WWFA, Melbourne Branch). 1973–80 (incomplete).

Seamen's Journal (SUA, Australia). 1973–83.

Socialist Worker Online (Australia). 2004.

SPA (Australia). 1972–74.

Spectator (UK). 1975–76.

Sydney Morning Herald. 1975, 1977.

Tharunka (Australia). 1975.

The Age (Melbourne, Australia). 1938.

The Australian. 1973, 1974.

The Independent (UK). 2004.

The Mail (UK). 21 December 2006.

The Modern Unionist (Australia). 1975.

The Socialist (Australia). 1973–79.

The Times (London). 1973–90.

Tribune (Australia). 1973–79.

Tribune (UK). 1973–79.

Wharfie (Brisbane). 1973, 1974.

Wharfie (Melbourne). 1973.

Workers News (Australia). 1974, 1975.

World Trade Union Movement (review of the WFTU). 1973–76.

Posters and Campaign Printed Material

Chile Solidarity Campaign (UK). *El Arte para el Pueblo*. London: Chile Solidarity Campaign, 1974.

Chile Solidarity Campaign (UK). *Inti Illimani, John Williams in Concert for Chile*. Poster. Manchester: Chile Solidarity Campaign.

Chile Solidarity Campaign (UK). *No Arms Sales to Chile*. Poster. Manchester: Chile Solidarity Campaign.

Chile Solidarity Campaign (UK). *Pete Seeger and Quilapayun: In Concert for Chile*. London: London Caledonian Press, 1978.

Thew, Angela, Joan Jara, Bob Braddock, Diane Dixon and Joyce Horman. *Commemorative Programme for the Premiere Screening of Cruel Separation*. Liverpool: Merseyside Chile Solidarity Committee, 2008.

Theses

Montenegro, Gustavo Martin. 'La Campaña de Solidaridad con Chile en Australia 1973–1990: Un estudio histórico sobre el movimiento de solidaridad australiano durante la dictadura militar en Chile.' Masters diss., University of New South Wales, 1994.

Schmutte, Ian. 'International Union Activity: Politics of Scale in the Australian Labour Movement.' Masters diss., University of Sydney, 2004.

Scott, Andrew. 'Modernising Labour: A Study of the ALP with Comparative Reference to the British Labour Party.' PhD diss., Monash University, 1999.

Wilkinson, Michael. 'The Influence of the Solidarity Lobby on British Government Policy towards Latin America: 1973–1990.' Masters diss., University of Hull, 1990.

Unpublished

Baird, Jim. 'After the Coup: The Trade Union Delegation to Chile.' 2004.

Cooper, Steve. 'Journey to Chile. 1974.' 1974.

Roe, Julius. 'Notes for Speech: 30th Anniversary.' 2003.

Published Reports

Amalgamated Metalworkers and Shipwrights Union (Australia). *Chile! A Report from the International Commission into the Crimes of the Military Junta in Chile, held in Algiers in January, 1978*. Sydney: The Harbour Press, 1978.

Americas Watch Committee. *The Vicaría de la Solidaridad in Chile: An Americas Watch Report*. New York: Americas Watch Committee, 1987.

Amnesty International. *Violence, Torture and Detention in Chile*. London: Amnesty International, International Secretariat, 1973.

Amnesty International. *Chile: Torture and the Naval Training Ship the 'Esmeralda'*, AMR 22/006/2003. London: Amnesty International, International Secretariat, 2003.

Arbitrary Arrests and Detentions in Chile: 4th Session of the International Commission of Enquiry into the Crimes of the Military Junta in Chile, Helsinki, 28–29 March 1976. Helsinki: Finlandia House, 1976.

Australian Bureau of Agricultural Economics. *Coarse Grains: Situation and Outlook*. Canberra: AGPS, 1978.

Australian Bureau of Statistics. *Australian Exports, Country by Commodity*, 5411.0. Canberra: Australian Bureau of Statistics, 1968–69 – 1979–80.

Australian Bureau of Statistics. *Australian Imports, Country by Commodity*, 5414.0. Canberra: Australian Bureau of Statistics, 1965–84.

Australian Wheat Board. *Australian Wheat Board: Annual Report*. Melbourne: Australian Wheat Board, 1966–89.

Australian Wheat Board. *Wheat Australia Annual Report*. Melbourne: Australian Wheat Board, 1974–80.

Campero, Guillermo. *Trade Union Responses to Globalization: Chile*. Report for Labour and Society Programme. Geneva: International Labour Organisation, 2001.

Chile Defence Committee. *Glasgow Chile Bulletin Number One*. Glasgow: Chile Defence Committee, 1974.

Chile Defence Committee. *Resolution to Glasgow Chile Defence Committee A.G.M.* Glasgow: Chile Defence Committee, 1974.

Chile Solidarity Campaign. *Chile: Trade Unions and the Coup*. Edited by Chile Lucha. London: Chile Solidarity Campaign/Chile Lucha, 1973.

Chile Solidarity Campaign. *Chile Fights 8*. London: Chile Solidarity Campaign [Chile Lucha], 1974.

Chile Solidarity Campaign. *Chile Fights 9*. London: Chile Solidarity Campaign [Chile Lucha], 1974.

Chile Solidarity Campaign. *Chile Solidarity Campaign: Annual Report*. London: Chile Solidarity Campaign, 1974–80.

Chile Solidarity Campaign. *Chile and the British Labour Movement: Trade Union Conference Report*. London: London Caledonian Press, 1975.

Chile Solidarity Campaign. *Chile Fights: Chile—Trade Unions and the Resistance 11*. London: Chile Solidarity Campaign [Chile Lucha], 1975.

Chile Solidarity Campaign. *Chile Fights* 29. London: Chile Solidarity Campaign [Chile Lucha], 1978.

Chile Solidarity Committee. *Chile Now: Initial Report of the Labour Movement Delegation*. London: Chile Solidarity Committee, 1984.

Cofre, Hernan. *NUM Annual Conference, 1978*. Torquay: National Union of Mineworkers, 1978).

National Union of Mineworkers. *Annual Report and Proceedings for the Year 1973*. England: National Union of Mineworkers, 1973.

National Union of Mineworkers. *NUM Annual Conference, 1974*. Llandudno: National Union of Mineworkers, 1974.

National Union of Mineworkers. *Annual Report and Proceedings for the Year 1977*. England: National Union of Mineworkers, 1977.

National Union of Mineworkers. *NUM Annual Conference, 1977*. Tynemouth: National Union of Mineworkers, 1977.

National Union of Mineworkers. *NUM Annual Conference, 1978*. Torquay: National Union of Mineworkers, 1978.

National Union of Mineworkers (UK). *Report of the National Union of Mineworkers Delegation*. England: NUM, 1978.

National Union of Mineworkers. 'Trade Union and Human Rights in Chile & Bolivia.' In *Report of the National Union of Mineworkers Delegation*. England: National Union of Mineworkers, 1978.

Report of the Annual Trades Union Congress (UK). Enfield: Trades Union Congress, 1973–89.

Scottish Trades Union Congress (STUC). *STUC Trades Union Congress Annual Report*. Glasgow: STUC, 1973–89.

Sweeney, John Bernard. *Royal Commission into Alleged Payments to Maritime Unions*. Canberra: Australian Government Publishing Service, 1976.

Trades Union Congress (TUC). *Notes of Proceedings at a Conference on Chile held at Congress House, Great Russell Street London, on Thursday, 24th April, 1975*. England: TUC, 1975.

World University Service (WUS). *WUS Annual Report*. London: WUS, 1972, 1975, 1980.

12 Days in Chile. Sydney: Amalgamated Metal Workers' Union, 1974.

Books

Angell, Alan. *Politics and the Labour Movement in Chile*. London: Oxford University Press, 1972.

Association for International Co-operation and Disarmament (Sydney). *The Asian Revolution and Australia*. Sydney: Times Press, 1969.

Australian Wheat Board. *Wheat Growing: A Great Australian Primary Industry*. Melbourne: Australian Wheat Board, c. 1967.

Barnes, Denis, and Eileen Reid. *Governments and Trade Unions: The British Experience, 1964–79*. London: Heinemann Educational Books, 1980.

Beasley, Margo. *Wharfies: A History of the Waterside Workers' Federation of Australia*. Sydney: Hallstead Press, 1996.

Beckett, Andy. *Pinochet in Piccadilly: Britain and Chile's Hidden History*. London: Faber & Faber, 2002.

Benn, Tony. *Tony Benn: Against the Tide*. London: Arrow Books, 1989.

Bramble, Tom. *Trade Unionism in Australia: A History from Flood to Ebb Tide.* Melbourne: Cambridge University Press, 2008.

Bull, Tas. *Tas Bull, An Autobiography: Life on the Waterfront.* Sydney: Harper Collins, 1998.

Burbach, Roger. *The Pinochet Affair: State Terrorism and Global Justice.* London: Zed Books, 2003.

Burgmann, Meredith, and Verity Burgmann. *Green Bans, Red Union: Environmental Activism and the New South Wales Builders Labourers' Federation.* Sydney: UNSW Press, 1994.

Burgmann, Verity. *Power and Protest: Movement for Change in Australian Society.* St Leonards, NSW: Allen & Unwin, 1993.

Burgmann, Verity. *Power, Profit and Protest: Australian Social Movements and Globalisation.* Crows Nest, NSW: Allen & Unwin, 2003.

Byrne, Paul. *Social Movements in Britain.* London: Routledge, 1997.

Cahill, Rowan. *Sea Change: An Essay in Maritime Labour History.* Bowral, NSW: Rowan Cahill, 1998.

Carr, Barry. *Labor Internationalism in the Era of NAFTA*: Past and Present. Miami: Latin American Labor Studies Publications, 1995.

Cassidy, Sheila. *Sheila Cassidy: Audacity to Believe.* London: Collins, 1977.

Castle, Barbara. *The Castle Diaries: 1974–1976.* London: Weidenfeld & Nicolson, 1980.

Chavkin, Samuel. *Storm Over Chile: The Junta Under Siege.* Westport, Conn.: Lawrence Hill & Company, 1985.

Chun, Lin. *The British New Left.* Edinburgh: Edinburgh University Press, 1998.

Coates, David, Gordon Johnston and Ray Bush, eds. *A Socialist Anatomy of Britain.* Cambridge: Polity Press, 1985.

Coates, Ken, and Tony Topham. *Trade Unions in Britain.* London: Fontana Press, 1988.

Cockcroft, James D., ed. *Salvador Allende Reader: Chile's Voice of Democracy.* Melbourne: Ocean Press, 2000.

Cohen, Robin, and Shirin Rai, eds. *Global Social Movements.* London: The Athlone Press, 2000.

Collier, Simon, and William F. Sater. *A History of Chile: 1808–1994*. Cambridge: Cambridge University Press, 1996.

Crick, Michael. *Scargill and the Miners*. Middlesex: Penguin Books, 1985.

Edelstein, David, and Malcolm Warner. *Comparative Union Democracy: Organisation and Opposition in British and American Unions*. Westmead, UK: Gower, 1975.

Ensalaco, Mark. *Chile Under Pinochet: Recovering the Truth*. Philadelphia: University of Pennsylvania Press, 2000.

Fitzpatrick, Brian, and Rowan Cahill. *The Seamen's Union of Australia, 1872–1972: A History*. Sydney: Seamen's Union of Australia, 1981.

Ford, Bill, and David Plowman, eds. *Australian Unions: An Industrial Relations Perspective*. South Melbourne: Macmillan, 1983.

Gilbert, Tony. *Only One Died*. London: Kay Beauchamp, 1974.

Gorman, John. *Banner Bright: An Illustrated History of the Banners of the British Trade Union Movement*. London: Allen Lane, 1973.

Gormley, Joe. *Battered Cherub*. London: Hamish Hamilton, 1982.

Greenland, Tony, ed. *The Campaign Guide 1977*. Westminster: Conservative and Unionist Central Office, 1977.

Hamer, David. *The Politics of Electoral Pressure: A Study in the History of Victorian Reform Agitations*. Sussex: Harvester Press, 1977.

Howell, David. *The Politics of the NUM: A Lancashire View*. Manchester: Manchester University Press, 1989.

Huntley, Pat. *Inside Australia's Largest Union*. Northbridge, NSW: Ian Huntley, 1978.

Huntley, Pat, and Ian Huntley. *Inside Australia's Top 100 Trade Unions—Are they Wrecking Australia?* Northbridge, NSW: Ian Huntley, 1976.

Jensen, Paul. *The Garotte: The United States and Chile, 1970–1973*. Aarhus: Aarhus University Press, 1988.

Jones, Jack. *Jack Jones: Union Man. An Autobiography*. London: William Collins & Sons, 1986.

Kane, John. *The Politics of Moral Capital*. Cambridge: Cambridge University Press, 2001.

Kay, Diana. *Chileans in Exile*. Wolfeboro, NH: Longwood Academic, 1987.

Keane, John. *Global Civil Society?* Cambridge: Cambridge University Press, 2003.

Kirk, Neville. *Comrades and Cousins: Globalization, Workers and Labour Movements in Britain, the USA and Australia from the 1880s to 1914*. London: Merlin Press, 2003.

Kirk, Neville. *Labour and the Politics of Empire: Britain and Australia 1900 to the Present*. Manchester: Manchester University Press, 2011.

Kirkby, Diane. *Voices from the Ships: Australia's Seafarers and their Union*. Sydney: UNSW Press, 2009.

Laybourn, Keith. *A History of Trade Unionism c. 1770–1990*. Phoenix Mill, UK: Alan Sutton, 1992.

Leslie Brown, Christopher. Moral *Capital: Foundations of British Abolitionism*. Oakland, NC: University of North Carolina Press, 2006.

Lockwood, Rupert. *Black Armada*. Sydney: Australasian Book Society, 1975.

Logue, John. *Toward a Theory of Trade Union Internationalism*. Kent: Kent Popular Press, 1980.

Loveman, Brian. *Chile: The Legacy of Hispanic Capitalism*. New York: Oxford University Press, 2001.

Maloof, Judy. *Voices of Resistance: Testimonies of Cuban and Chilean Women*. Kentucky: University Press of Kentucky, 1999.

Marsh, Arthur. *Trade Union Handbook: A Guide and Directory to the Structure, Membership, Policy and Personnel of the British Trade Unions*. Westmead, UK: Gower, 1980.

May, Timothy. *Trade Unions and Pressure Group Politics*. Westmead, UK: Saxon House, 1975.

Miller, Rory. *Britain and Latin America in the Nineteenth and Twentieth Centuries, Studies in Modern History*. London: Longman, 1993.

Milligan, Stephen. *The New Barons: Union Power in the 1970s*. London: Temple Smith, 1976.

Moody, Kim. *Workers in a Lean World: Unions in the International Economy*. London: Verso Press, 1997.

Munck, Ronaldo. *The New International Labour Studies: An Introduction*. London: Zed Books, 1988.

Munck, Ronaldo, and Peter Waterman, eds. *Labour Worldwide in the Era of Globalization: Alternative Union Models in the New World Order*. Basingstoke, UK: Macmillan, 1999.

O'Lincoln, Tom. *Into the Mainstream: The Decline of Australian Communism*. Sydney: Stained Wattle Press, 1985.

Overington, Caroline. *Kickback: Inside the Australian Wheat Board Scandal*. Sydney: Allen & Unwin, 2007.

Pakulski, Jan. Social Movements: *The Politics of Moral Protest*. Melbourne: Longman Cheshire, 1991.

Parkin, Frank. *Middle Class Radicalism: The Social Bases of the British Campaign for Nuclear Disarmament*. Manchester: University of Manchester Press, 1968.

Payne, Pauline, and Peter Donovan. *The Australian Barley Board: Making the Right Moves, 1939–1999*. Adelaide: Australian Barley Board, 1999.

Power, Jonathon. *Amnesty International: The Human Rights Story*. Oxford: Pergamon Press, 2001.

Press, Mike, and Don Thompson, eds. *Solidarity for Survival: The Don Thompson Reader on Trade Union Internationalism*. Nottingham: Spokesman, 1989.

Rawson, D. W. *Unions and Unionists in Australia*. Hornsby, NSW: George Allen & Unwin, 1978.

Rawson, Donald William. *A Handbook of Australian Trade Unions and Employees' Associations*. Canberra: Research School of Social Sciences, The Australian National University, 1973.

Shipley, Peter. *Revolutionaries in Modern Britain*. London: Bodley Hear, 1976.

Sigmund, Paul E. *The United States and Democracy in Chile*. Baltimore: The Johns Hopkins University Press, 1993.

Solidarity Committee of the German Democratic Republic. *Chile at Heart: International Solidarity Reflected in Posters*. Berlin: Solidarity Committee of the German Democratic Republic, 1980.

Souter, Gavin. *A Peculiar People: William Lane's Australian Utopians in Paraguay*. St Lucia, Qld: University of Queensland Press, 1991.

Tarrow, Sidney. *Power in Movement: Social Movements, Collective Action and Politics*. Cambridge: Cambridge University Press, 1994.

Tarrow, Sidney. *Power in Movement: Social Movements and Contentious Politics*. Cambridge: Cambridge University Press, 1998.

The GDR's Fervent Solidarity with the Courageous Chilean People. Berlin: Panorama DDR, c. 1973.

Thompson, Willie. *The Left in History: Revolution and Reform in Twentieth-Century Politics*. London: Pluto Press, 1997.

Transport and General Workers Union National Executive Council. *The Story of the T.G.W.U.* London: Transport and General Workers Union, 1977.

Uren, Tom. *Straight Left*. Milsons Point, NSW: Random House Australia, 1994.

Walker, John. *Left Shift: Radical Art in 1970s Britain*. London: I. B. Tauris, 2002.

Waterman, Peter. *Globalization, Social Movements and the New Internationalisms, Employment and Work Relations in Context*. London: Continuum, 2001.

Whitwell, Greg, Diane Sydenham and Australian Wheat Board. *A Shared Harvest: The Australian Wheat Industry, 1939–1989*. Melbourne: Macmillan, 1991.

Willets, Peter, ed. Pressure Groups in the Global System: *The Transnational Relations of Issue-Orientated Non-Governmental Organizations*. London: Frances Pinter, 1982.

Wilson, John. *Introduction to Social Movements*. New York: Basic Books, 1973.

Wrigley, Chris. *British Trade Unions Since 1933*. Cambridge: Cambridge University Press, 2002.

Book Chapters

Adams, Carol J. 'Woman-Battering and Harm to Animals.' In *Animals and Women: Feminist Theoretical Explorations*, edited by Carol Adams and Josephine Donovan. Durham, NC: Duke University Press, 1999.

Allende, Salvador. 'The Role of the Armed Forces.' In *Salvador Allende Reader: Chile's Voice of Democracy*, edited by James Cockcroft, 86–8. Melbourne: Ocean Press, 2000.

Anner, Mark. 'Local and Transnational Campaigns to End Sweatshop Practices.' In *Transnational Cooperation Among Labor Unions*, edited by Michael E. Gordon and Lowell Turner, 238–55. Ithaca, NY: ILR Press, 2000.

Ashwin, Sarah. 'International Labour Solidarity after the Cold War.' In *Global Social Movements*, edited by Robin Cohen and Shirin Rai, 101–16. London: The Athlone Press, 2000.

Baxter, John L. 'Early Chartism and Labour Class Struggle: South Yorkshire 1837–1840.' In *Essays in the Economic and Social History of South Yorkshire*, edited by Sidney Pollard and Colin Holmes. Barnsley: South Yorkshire County Council, Recreation Culture and Health Department, 1976.

Berger, Herbert. 'The Austro–Chilean Solidarity Front, 1973–1990.' In *Transatlantic Relations: Austria and Latin America in the 19th and 20th Centuries*, edited by Gunter Bischof and Klaus Eisterer, 225–38. Innsbruck: Studienverlag, 2006.

Briggs, Chris. 'The End of a Cycle? The Australian Council of Trade Unions in Historical Perspective.' In *Peak Unions in Australia: Origins, Purpose, Power, Agency*, edited by Bradon Ellem, Raymond Markey and John Chields, 236–60. Sydney: The Federation Press, 2004.

Cohen, Robin, and Shirin Rai. 'Global Social Movements: Towards a Cosmopolitan Politics.' In *Global Social Movements*, edited by Robin Cohen and Shirin Rai, 1–17. London: The Athlone Press, 2000.

Deery, Stephen. 'Union Aims and Methods.' In *Australian Unions: An Industrial Relations Perspective*, edited by Bill Ford and David Plowman, 60–92. South Melbourne: Macmillan, 1983.

de Martino, George. 'The Future of the US Labour Movement in an Era of Global Economic Integration.' In *Labour Worldwide in the Era of Globalization: Alternative Union Models in the New World Order*, edited by Ronaldo Munck and Peter Waterman, 83–96. Basingstoke, UK: Macmillan, 1999.

Foster, Kevin. 'Small Earthquakes and Major Eruptions: Anglo–Chilean Cultural Relations in the Nineteenth and Twentieth Centuries.' In *Democracy in Chile: The Legacy of September 11, 1973*, edited by Sylvia Nagy-Zekmi and Fernando Leiva, 41–51. Brighton: Sussex Academic Press, 2005.

Frenkel, Stephen, and Alice Coolican. 'Union Organisation and Decision Making.' In *Australian Unions: An Industrial Relations Perspective*, edited by Bill Ford and David Plowman, 145–77. South Melbourne: Macmillan, 1983.

Gordon, Richard and Warren Osmond. 'An Overview of the Australian New Left.' In *The Australian New Left: Critical Essays and Strategy*, edited by Richard Gordon, 3–40. Melbourne: Heinemann, 1970.

Hagan, Jim. 'The Australian Trade Union Movement: Context and Perspective, 1850–1980.' In *Australian Unions: An Industrial Relations Perspective*, edited by Bill Ford and David Plowman, 30–59. Melbourne: Macmillan, 1983.

Harrod, Jeffry, and Robert O'Brien. 'Organized Labour and the Global Political Economy.' In *Global Unions? Theory and Strategies of Organized Labour in the Global Political Economy*, edited by Jeffry Harrod and Robert O'Brien, 3–28. London: Routledge, 2002.

Hyman, Richard. 'Class Struggle and the Trade Union Movement.' In *A Socialist Anatomy of Britain*, edited by David Coates, Gordon Johnston and Ray Bush, 99–123. Cambridge: Polity Press, 1985.

Kushner, T., and K. Knox. 'Refugees from Chile: A Gesture of International Solidarity.' In *Refugees in an Age of Genocide: Global, National and Local Perspectives during the Twentieth Century*, edited by K. Knox and T. Kushner, 289–305. London: Frank Cass, 1999.

McAdam, Doug, John D. McCarthy and Mayer N. Zald. 'Introduction: Opportunities, Mobilizing Structures, and Framing Processes—Toward a Synthetic, Comparative Perspective on Social Movements.' In *Comparative Perspectives on Social Movements: Political Opportunities, Mobilizing Structures, and Cultural Framings*, edited by Doug McAdam, John D. McCarthy and Mayer N. Zald, 1–22. Cambridge: Cambridge University Press, 1996.

McCarthy, John D., and Mayer N. Zald. 'Resource Mobilization Theory.' In *Social Movements in an Organizational Society*, edited by Doug McAdam, John D. McCarthy and Mayer N. Zald, 15–48. New Brunswick: Transaction, 1987.

Mansfield, Nicholas. 'Radical Banners as Sites of Memory: The National Banner Survey.' In *Contested Sites: Commemoration, Memorial and Popular Politics in Nineteenth-Century Britain*, edited by Paul Pickering and Alex Tyrell, 81–99. Aldershot, UK: Ashgate, 2004.

Martin, Gerald. 'Britain's Cultural Relations with Latin America.' In *Britain and Latin America: A Changing Relationship*, edited by Victor Bulmer-Thomas, 27–51. Cambridge: Cambridge University Press, 1989.

Miliband, Ralph. 'The Coup in Chile.' In *The Socialist Register 1973*, 451–74. London: Merlin Press, 1974.

Munck, Ronaldo. 'Labour in the Global.' In *Global Social Movements*, edited by Robin Cohen and Shirin Rai, 83–100. London: The Athlone Press, 2000.

Plowman, David. 'The Victorian Trades Hall Split.' In *Australian Unions: An Industrial Relations Perspective*, edited by Bill Ford and David Plowman, 303–43. South Melbourne: Macmillan, 1983.

Press, Mike. 'International Trade Unionism.' In *Solidarity for Survival: The Don Thompson Reader on Trade Union Internationalism*, edited by Mike Press and Don Thompson, 17–25. Nottingham: Spokesman, 1989.

Press, Mike. 'The People's Movement.' In *Solidarity for Survival: The Don Thompson Reader on Trade Union Internationalism*, edited by Mike Press and Don Thompson, 26–47. Nottingham: Spokesman, 1989.

Rustin, Michael. 'The New Left as a Social Movement.' In *Out of Apathy: Voices of the New Left Thirty Years On*, edited by Robin Archer, Diemut Bubeck et al., 117–28. London: Verso, 1989.

Taylor, Richard. 'Green Politics and the Peace Movement.' In *A Socialist Anatomy of Britain*, edited by David Coates, Gordon Johnston and Ray Bush, 160–70. Cambridge: Polity Press, 1985.

Thompson, Don. 'Solidarity for Survival.' In *Solidarity for Survival: The Don Thompson Reader on Trade Union Internationalism*, edited by Mike Press and Don Thompson, 107–11. Nottingham: Spokesman, 1989.

van der Linden, Marcel. 'Proletarian Internationalism: A Long View and Some Speculations.' In *The Modern World-System in the Longue Duree*, edited by Marcel van der Linden, 107–31. Boulder, Colo.: Paradigm, 2005.

Velazquez, Patria-Roman. 'Latin Americans in London and the Dynamics of Diasporic Identities.' In *Comparing Postcolonial Diasporas*, edited by Michelle Keown, David Murphy and James Procter, 104–24. London: Palgrave Macmillan, 2009.

Walker, Kenneth. 'Australia.' In *Comparative Labor Movements*, edited by Walter Galenson, 173–242. New York: Prentice-Hall, 1952.

Waterman, Peter. 'The New Social Unionism: A New Union Model for a New World Order.' In *Labour Worldwide in the Era of Globalization: Alternative Union Models in the New World Order*, edited by Ronaldo Munck and Peter Waterman, 247–64. Basingstoke, UK: Macmillan, 1999.

Waterman, Peter. 'Trade Union Internationalism in the Age of Seattle.' In *Place, Space and the New Labour Internationalisms*, edited by Peter Waterman and Jane Wills, 8–32. Oxford: Blackwell, 2001.

Waterman, Peter, and Jill Timms. 'Trade Union Internationalism and a Global Civil Society in the Making.' In *Global Civil Society 2004–5*, edited by Helmut Anheier, Marlies Glasius and Marty Kaldor, 178–202. London: Sage, 2005.

Willets, Peter. 'Pressure Groups as Transnational Actors.' In *Pressure Groups in the Global System: The Transnational Relations of Issue-Orientated Non-Governmental Organizations*, edited by Peter Willets, 1–27. London: Frances Pinter, 1982.

Willets, Peter. 'Introduction.' In *Pressure Groups in the Global System: The transnational Relations of Issue-Orientated Non-Governmental Organisations*, edited by Peter Willets, xii–xv. London: Frances Pinter, 1982.

Journal Articles

'Actions Protest Repression in Chile.' *Direct Action: A Socialist Fortnightly*, no. 70 (20 September 1974): 6.

Adams, Patrick. 'Deadly Politics: Salvaging Memories in Santiago.' *Duke Magazine* (September–October 2005).

Anderson, Perry. 'Internationalism: A Breviary.' *New Left Review* 14 (March–April 2002): 1–12.

Angell, Alan. 'International Support for the Chilean Opposition 1973–1989: Political Parties and the Role of Exiles.' *The International Dimensions of Democratization* (2001): 175–201.

Angell, Alan, and Susan Carstairs. 'The Exile Question in Chilean Politics.' *Third World Quarterly* 9, no. 1 (1987): 148–67.

Anner, Mark. 'Industrial Structure, the State, and Ideology: Shaping Labor Transnationalism in the Brazilian Auto Industry.' *Social Science History* 27, no. 4 (2003): 603–34.

'Ban on Indonesian and Chilean Trade.' *Seamen's Journal* 33, no. 1 (January 1978): 14.

Bentley, Shane. 'Tribute to Labor Leader Tas Bull.' *Maritime Workers Journal*, July 2003.

Berger, Stefan, and Greg Patmore. 'Comparative Labour History in Britain and Australia.' *Labour History*, no. 88 (2005): 9–24.

'Blow for Solidarity.' *Seamen's Journal* 34, no. 1 (January 1979): 2.

Bray, Mark. 'Democracy from the Inside: The British AUEW(ES) and the Australian AMWSU.' *Industrial Relations Journal* 13, no. 4 (2007): 84–93.

Cahill, Rowan. 'Obituary: Tas Bull (31.01.1932 – 29.05.2003).' *Labour History*, no. 85 (2003): 250–2.

'Call for World Trade Union Action against Chile Junta.' *Seamen's Journal* 30, no. 3 (March 1975).

Callaghan, John. 'Industrial Militancy, 1945–1979: The Failure of the British Road to Socialism?' *Twentieth Century British History* 15, no. 4 (2004): 388–409.

'Chile Alert.' *Seamen's Journal* 36, no. 2 (February 1981): 43.

'Chile Buys Again.' *Wheat Australia* 5, no. 4 (1972): 1.

'Chilean Registered Vina del Mar.' *Seamen's Journal* 35, no. 3 (April 1980): 55.

'Committee No. IV.' *Seamen's Journal* 34, no. 3 (March–April 1979): 75.

Curphey, T. A. 'Need Stressed for More Union Action against Chile Junta.' *Seamen's Journal*, May 1975.

Deery, Phillip, and Neil Redfern. 'No Lasting Peace? Labor, Communism and the Cominform: Australia and Great Britain, 1945–50.' *Labour History* 88 (2005).

Donath, E. J. 'The Australian Wheat Industry in the 1970s.' *Australian Outlook* 23, no. 3 (1969): 294–7.

Elliott, Della. 'Special Supplement: Quilapayun Singers in Australia—The True Voice of Chile.' *Seamen's Journal* 30, no. 7 (July 1975): 165–8.

Elliot, E. V. 'On Course!' *Seamen's Journal* (May 1974).

Elliott, E. V. 'Chile: No Trade with Junta: Support the Resistance.' *Seamen's Journal*, July–August 1977.

Forman, Ross G. 'When Britons Brave Brazil: British Imperialism and the Adventure Tale in Latin America, 1850–1918.' *Victorian Studies* 42, no. 3 (1999–2000): 455–87.

Gahan, Peter. '(What) Do Unions Maximise? Evidence from Survey Data.' *Cambridge Political Economy Society* 26 (2002): 279–98.

Geraghty, Pat. 'Barometer.' *Seamen's Journal*, January 1979.

Hanagan, Michael. 'An Agenda for Transnational Labour History.' *International Review of Social History* 49 (2004): 455–74.

'Hawke Opens Conference.' *Seamen's Journal* 34, no. 3 (March–April 1979): 54.

James, Leighton, and Raymond Markey. 'Class and Labour: The British Labour Party and the Australian Labor Party Compared.' *Labour History*, no. 90 (2006): 23–41.

Jones, Ann. '"Sindicalistas Australianos": A Case Study of International Trade Unionism.' *Labour History* 93 (November 2007): 197–212.

Kirk, Neville. 'Why Compare Labour in Australia and Britain?' *Labour History* 88 (2005): 1–7.

'Luis Corvalan Thanks SUA for Solidarity with Chile Workers.' *Seamen's Journal* 32, no. 2 (February 1977).

Lyons, Judy. 'Chilean Refugee "Tortured, Threatened with Death".' *AMWU Monthly Journal*, 1974.

McCorriston, Steve, and Donald MacLaren. 'Single-Desk State Trading Exporters.' *European Journal of Political Economy* 21 (2005): 503–24.

McCorriston, Steve, and Donald MacLaren. 'Deregulation as (Welfare Reducing) Trade Reform: The Case of the Australian Wheat Board.' *American Agricultural Economics Association* 89, no. 3 (2007): 637–50.

Moody, Kim. 'Towards an International Social-Movement Unionism.' *New Left Review* i, no. 225 (1997): 52–72.

Patmore, Greg, and David Coates. 'Labour Parties and State in Australia and the UK.' *Labour History* 88 (May 2005): 121–40.

Peetz, David, and Barbara Pocock. 'An Analysis of Workplace Representatives, Union Power and Democracy in Australia.' *British Journal of Industrial Relations* 47 (2009).

'Restore Democracy in Chile.' *Seamen's Journal* 38, no. 8 (September 1983): 233.

Robertson, Alec. 'A Communist's New Guinea. "Essentially the Same … as Vietnam".' *New Guinea and Australia, The Pacific and South-East Asia* 6, no. 2 (1971): 6–16.

'Sad Untimely Loss—Death of Luis Figueroa Reminder Chile Struggle Still to be Won.' *Seamen's Journal* 31, no. 11 (November 1976).

Saunders, Robert. 'Chartism from Above: British Elites and the Interpretation of Chartism.' *Historical Research* 81, no. 213 (2008): 467.

'Seamen Continue Boycott on Trade with Chile.' *Seamen's Journal* 33, no. 2 (February 1978): 35.

'Seamen Reject Invitation for Fascist Chile General.' *Seamen's Journal* 29 (March 1974): 64–5.

Steele, J. 'Big Success of Brisbane May Day Commemoration.' *Seamen's Journal*, May 1974.

'Stop Repression in Chile—Sept 11.' *Tharkuna* 21, no. 21 (1975).

'The ACTU Stands for United Action.' *World Trade Union Movement (Review of the WFTU)*, no. 1 (January 1976).

'Trade Boycott—Unidad Popular Chile's Warm Gratitude for S.U.A. Solidarity.' *Seamen's Journal* 33, no. 4 (April 1978): 94.

Waterman, Peter. 'Adventures of Emancipatory Labour Strategy as the New Global Movement Challenges International Unionism.' *Journal of World-Systems Research* x, no. 1 (2004): 216–53.

'Wider Union Bans on Chile Junta.' *Modern Unionist* 3, no. 1 (1975).

Wilkinson, Michael. 'The Chile Solidarity Campaign and British Government Policy towards Chile, 1973–1990.' *European Review of Latin American and Caribbean Studies* 52 (June 1992): 57–74.

Newspaper Articles

Aarons, Eric. 'Chile Resistance Fighters' Visit.' *Tribune* [Australia], 7–13 May 1974.

'Action against Chile is Urged.' *The Australian*, 11 October 1973: 10.

'Action against U.S. over Chile.' *Tribune* [Australia], 18–24 September 1973: 3.

'Aid to Chile Struggle.' *Maritime Worker*, 14 May 1974.

'Apartheid Protest.' *Socialist*, 23 November 1977.

'Australian Communists Look at Chile Events.' *Tribune* [Australia], 6–12 November 1973.

'Australian Mission May Visit Chile.' *SPA*, March 1974.

'Australian Speaks at Santiago.' *SPA*, June 1973.

Baird, Jim. 'Chilean Junta on Trial before I.L.O.' *Tribune* [Australia], 12 November 1974.

Bentley, Shane. 'Tas Bull (1932–2003).' *Green Left*, 18 June 2003.

Birnberg, Benedict. 'Government Accused of International Banditry.' *The Times*, 14 June 1978: 14.

'Block the Esmeralda!' *Tribune* [Australia], 4–10 June 1974: 12.

'Blocking of Arms for Chile Beset by Legal Difficulties.' *The Times*, 17 May 1974.

Bull, Carmen, Jim Baird and Henry McCarthy. 'Chilean Resistance.' *Tribune* [Australia], 16–22 April 1974.

'Chile Analysed.' *Tribune* [Australia], 23–29 October 1973: 10.

'Chile Bans Stay.' *Tribune* [Australia], 10 October 1979.

'Chile Bars Jack Jones.' *Observer*, 1 December 1975.

'Chile Cargo Ban.' *Tribune* [Australia], 2–8 October 1973.

'Chile Engine Crates Found.' *Morning Star*, 16 August 1974.

'Chile Export Ban Stays.' *Socialist*, 4 June 1975.

'Chile Inflation and Repression Hit all Sectors.' *Tribune* [Australia], 3 September 1974.

'Chile Junta Victim Thanks Watersiders.' *Maritime Worker*, 26 July 1977: 11.

'Chile One Year After.' *Workers News*, 19 September 1974: 2.

'Chile Popular Unity Adopts New Program.' *Tribune* [Australia], 1 October 1975.

'Chile Recognised but not Approved.' *The Australian*, 12 October 1973: 10.

'Chile Venceremos.' *Tribune* [Australia], 16 September 1975.

'Chile Waves.' *Guardian* [Manchester], 4 October 1973.

'Chile will get Warships.' *The Times*, 9 April 1974.

'Chile Winds.' *Guardian* [Manchester], 15 November 1973.

'Chile, Bolivia: "Their problems should be our problems ... their achievements will be our achievements".' *Miner*, June–July 1977.

'Chile: Scanlon Acts.' *Tribune* [UK], 10 May 1974.

'Chile: Solidarity Expressed in Aust. Meetings.' *Tribune* [Australia], 30 July 1974.

'CHILE: World Campaign of Solidarity Launched.' *Tribune* [Australia], 9–15 October 1973.

'Chilean Folk Artists to Visit.' *Socialist*, 18 February 1977.

'Chilean Guests' Appeal! "Keep up the Fight, Venceremos!"' *SPA*, June 1974.

'Chilean MP Tells of Torture after Allende Overthrow.' *The Times*, 3 September 1975.

'Chilean Terror.' *Maritime Worker*, 27 May 1975: 6.

'Chilean Thanks for Australian Help.' *Maritime Worker*, September 1975.

'Chilean Workers' Leader Dies in Sweden.' *Tribune* [Australia], 15 September 1976.

'Chileans Reclaim "Blacked" Rolls-Royce Engines.' *The Times*, 28 August 1978: 2.

'Commission Calls on Chile to Halt Political Reprisals.' *The Times*, 29 June 1974.

'Communist Party of Australia. Fighting Multinationals.' *Tribune* [Australia], 4–10 September 1973.

'Concert for Chile.' *Tribune* [Australia], 30 November 1977.

'Conference Decisions: Chile.' *Tribune* [UK], 12 October 1973.

Cooper, Steve. 'Fighting the Transnational Companies.' *Tribune* [Australia], 24-30 July 1973.

Cooper, Steve, and Henry McCarthy. 'Chile—Internal Strife—Solidarity.' *Tribune* [Australia], 16 July 1974.

'CSC.' *Tribune* [UK], 30 September 1977.

'Dismissed.' *The Age*, 21 December 1938: 8.

'Eden Compensation.' *Maritime Worker*, 13 February 1979: 5.

'Editorial: May Day—Internationalism.' *Socialist*, May 1974: 3.

'El pueblo unido jamas sera vencido.' *Tribune* [Australia], 20 April 1977.

'Engineers Defy Call to Stop Work on Chile Warships.' *The Times*, 16 May 1974.

'Engineers Stop Work on Frigate for Chile.' *The Times*, 14 May 1974: 1.

Faux, Ronald. 'Docks Watch by Workers for Chilean Engines.' *The Times*, 29 August 1978: 2.

'Figueroa Speaks.' *Socialist*, 24 September 1975.

'Firmer Chile Junta Bans.' *Maritime Worker*, 9 March 1976: 12.

'First Aid to Chile.' *Maritime Worker*, 4 January 1975: 12.

'Former Miner Tells of Pinochet Horror.' *Mail*, 21 December 2006.

'Frigates for Chilean Junta: Why the Government Must Think Again.' *Tribune* [UK], 19 April 1974.

Garland, Nicholas. *Daily Telegraph*, 17 May 1974, © Telegraph Media Group Limited 1974, The British Cartoon Archive, University of Kent, <www.cartoons.ac.uk>.

'Govt. Told: "Don't Recognise Chile".' *Tribune* [Australia], 9–15 October 1973.

Groser, John. 'Mr Heffer to Face Wilson Rebuke over Chile.' *The Times*, 15 April 1974.

Hamilton, Alan. 'Mr Hayward Rebukes Cabinet on Chile Ships.' *The Times*, 19 April 1974.

Hatfield, Michael. 'No Policy Reversal on Ships for Chile.' *The Times*, 25 April 1974.

Hatfield, Michael. 'Callaghan Rebuke over Warships.' *The Times*, 2 May 1974.

Hennessy, Peter. 'Government will Issue Export Licences for "Blacked" Engines Soon.' *The Times*, 19 July 1978: 4.

Higgins, Jim. 'AUEW Election.' *Spectator*, 1975.

Higgins, Jim. 'AUEW: Decline of a Union.' *Spectator*, 1975.

Higgins, Jim. 'Trade Unions: Democracy at the Top.' *Spectator*, 1975.

Higgins, Jim. 'Amalgamating the Engineers.' *Spectator*, 1976.

Hogue, Derry. 'Chile Air Line Wants to Land Here.' *The Australian*, 22 November 1973.

Homes, David. 'CPA, SPA Sectarianism in Chile Defence.' *Direct Action*, 2 September 1974.

'How Solidarity has Helped Chile Fight.' *Record* [TGWU], February 1975: 5.

'ILO Call to Fight Chile Torturers.' *Maritime Worker*, 2 September 1975: 7.

'Indonesia, Chile Bans.' *Maritime Worker*, 18 October 1977: 4.

'International Aid.' *Maritime Worker*, 27 September 1977: 3.

'Inti Illimani.' *Socialist*, 2 March 1977: 4.

'Inti Illimani.' *Tribune* [Australia], 23 March 1977.

'Jim Healy's Cargo Hook.' *Maritime Worker*, 4 November 1975: 5.

Jones, David. 'When You Look into the Eyes of a Mother Who has Lost a Son, You Can Tell Who is Telling the Truth and Who is Not.' *Daily Post*, 12 November 1998: 18.

Keatley, Patrick. 'Stronger Line on Chile Demanded.' *Guardian* [Manchester], 6 January 1976.

Kelly, Stephen. 'Chile: NUM Sees Repression and Union Solidarity at First Hand.' *Tribune* [UK], 13 May 1977: 16.

'Libs Look to Junta: The Chilean Connection.' *Tribune* [Australia], 3 December 1975.

McCarthy, Henry. 'Boycott the Junta.' *Tribune* [Australia], 22 February 1978.

MacKay, Neil. 'The Scot Who Humbled Pinochet Tells His Story.' *Sunday Herald*, 2002.

McKinlay, John. 'Chile Pays Debts to Get Clyde Sub.' *Glasgow Herald*, 27 August 1976.

McKinlay, John. 'Chile Wants More Ships from Britain.' *Glasgow Herald*, 28 August 1976.

'Maritime Action on Franco Ship.' *SPA*, September 1972.

Maritime Worker, 23 October 1973: 4.

'Miners on the March.' *Miner*, July–August, 1978: 11.

'Ministers Accused of Retreat on Chile.' *The Times*, 23 May 1974.

'No Non-Union Wharf Labour!' *Maritime Worker*, 18 April 1978: 1.

'Open File.' *Guardian* [Manchester], 3 October 1973.

Our Political Staff. 'Mr Benn Joins Attack on Sale of Warships.' *The Times*, 9 May 1974.

Pattinson, Terry. 'Lord Scanlon: Charismatic Trade-Union Leader.' *Independent*, 28 January 2004.

Perman, Raymond. 'Ban on Work for Chile May Be Widened.' *The Times*, 15 May 1974.

'Pig-Iron Ban—2500 Employes [sic] May Lose Jobs.' *The Age*, 19 December 1938: 19.

'R-R Engines Can Go to Chile.' *The Times*, 21 July 1978: 2.

'Remembering Chile's Brave Fight.' *Morning Star*, 11 September 1978: 3.

'Removal of Aero Engines a Commercial Matter.' *The Times*, 28 July 1978: 4.

'Report from Chile.' *Tribune* [UK], 17 June 1977: 11.

Reuters. '50 Nations in Movement to Oust Chile Junta.' *The Times*, 1 October 1973.

Robertson, Mavis. 'Moscow World Peace Congress.' *Tribune* [Australia], 13–19 November 1973.

Robertson, Mavis. 'Protest on Chile Claim.' *Tribune* [Australia], 27 November – 3 December 1973: 10.

Robertson, Mavis. 'Expressing Thanks.' *Tribune* [Australia], 16–22 April 1974.

'Rolls-Royce Nears Deal on "Blacked" Chile Jets.' *Telegraph*, 1 September 1974.

'Rolls-Royce Workers Free Aero-Engines Overhauled for Chile.' *The Times*, 19 August 1978: 3.

'Saved Chileans to be Allowed Here: Success for Mrs Hart.' *Morning Star*, 16 September 1975: 5.

Singer, Angela. 'Mystery Clouds Movement of Chile Engines.' *Guardian* [Manchester], 28 August 1978: 2.

Singer, Angela. 'RAF Denies Any Involvement in Removal of Chile Aero-Engines.' *Guardian* [Manchester], 29 August 1978: 24.

'Solidarity Call to World Trade Union Movement.' *Socialist*, April 1975: 3.

'Solidarity Meetings with Chilean Workers.' *Tribune* [Australia], 2–8 October 1973.

'Solidarity with Chile.' *Tribune* [Australia], 4–10 September 1973.

'Solidarity with Chile on September 11.' *Socialist*, September 1974: 1.

'Solidarity with the Chilean People.' *Tribune* [Australia], 18–24 September 1973: 12.

Spiers, Bill. 'Frigates Deal a "Betrayal" of Chilean People.' *Tribune* [UK], 19 April 1974.

Staff Reporter. 'Marchers Protest over Arms Sale to Chile.' *The Times*, 6 May 1974.

'Stepping Up Chile Solidarity.' *Socialist*, 20 July 1977.

'"Stop Aid" Demand as NUM Men Visit Bolivia and Chile.' *Miner*, May–June 1977: 1.

'Strengthen Solidarity.' *Socialist*, 8 October 1975.

Styron, Rose. 'Chile: The Spain of Our Generation.' *Honi Soit*, 1975: 12.

'Support Chilean Workers in their Struggle to Free their Country from Fascism.' *Tribune* [Australia], 16 September 1975.

'Sydney Committee for Chile.' *Tribune* [Australia], 23–29 October 1973: 2.

'Sydney: Slogans in English and Spanish …' *Tribune* [Australia], 18–24 December 1973: 3.

Sykes, Jill. 'Inti Illimani's Poetic Message.' *Sydney Morning Herald*, 26 February 1977.

Symes, Les. 'Bread-and-Butter Internationalism.' *Maritime Worker*, 5 October 1976: 14.

Taft, Bernie. 'Chile and Mass Consciousness.' *Tribune* [Australia], 16–22 October 1973: 8.

'Toon to Testify on Chile to UN Group.' *Miner*, July–August 1977: 1.

'Trade Union Stops Return of Jet Engines to Chile.' *The Times*, 10 June 1978: 2.

'Trotskyists Profit from Munoz Campaign.' *Socialist*, 15 September 1976.

'Unions' Chile Solidarity Victory.' *Socialist*, 17 January 1979.

'Unions Free Plane after Chilean Note.' *The Australian*, 11 February 1974.

'Unions' Policy.' *Maritime Worker*, 29 March 1977: 9.

Varas, Florencia. 'Chile Threat to Stop Copper Sales to Britain.' *The Times*, 30 March 1974.

'Wanted: A Million Pencils for Cuba.' *Tribune* [Australia], 12 July 1961.

'Welcome to Sergio Insunza!' *Socialist*, May 1974: 1.

'Wider Bans on Chile Junta.' *Modern Unionist* [Australia], 1975.

'World Conference on Chilean Fascism: Call to Isolate the Military Junta.' *Building Worker*, October 1973.

Online

Australian Government. 'Australia's National Anthem.' <http://www.itsanhonour.gov.au/symbols/anthem.cfm>.

Australian Wheat Board. 'Corporate History.' Accessed 30 April 2009. <http://www.awb.com.au/aboutawb/corporate/history/>.

Gatehouse, Mike. 'Testimony: Detainee Remembers Chile 1973.' *BBC News Online*, 23 October 1998. Accessed 28 July 2009, <http://news.bbc.co.uk/2/hi/special_report/1998/10/98/the_pinochet_file/198743.stm>.

International Federation of Chemical, Energy, Mine and General Workers' Unions (ICEM). 2000. 'Ann Browne: A Tribute.' In ICEM News Release No. 8/2000,ICEM. Accessed 22 August 2008. <http://www.icem.org/en/5-Mining-DGOJP/437-Ann-Browne:-A-Tribute>.

Jara, Joan. 'Joan Jara recibe nacionalidad chilena por gracia en Palacio de la Moneda, jueves, 04 de junio de 2009.' *Fundación Víctor Jara*. Accessed 19 August 2009. <http://www.fundacionvictorjara.cl/nacionalidad.html>.

'John Dugger Born 1948.' *Tate Collection*. <http://www.tate.org.uk/servlet/ViewWork?cgroupid=999999961&workid=4042&searchid=13877&tabview=text>.

Lippard, Lucy. 'Spinning the Common Thread.' A World of Poetry—Anthology Preview. <http://www.worldofpoetry.org/cv_t2.htm>.

Mark, Imogen. 'Ann Browne.' *Guardian News and Media Limited*. Accessed 9 January 2009. <http://www.guardian.co.uk/news/2000/feb/15/guardianobituaries2>.

Munoz, Arturo Alejandro. 'Gral. Bonilla, accidente demasiado sospechoso.' Accessed 17 April 2007. <http://www.granvalparaiso.cl/columnistas/munoz/bonilla.htm>.

'"The Walrus", Hugh Scanlon: From Awkward to Ermine.' *Socialist Worker Online*. Accessed 7 February 2004. <http://www.socialistworker.co.uk/art.php?id=622>.

Government Documents

Dyer, Ron. 'Death of Former Senator James Anthony Mulvihill.' In *NSW Parliament Legislative Council* (8 March 2001): 12449.

Report of the Chilean National Commission on Truth and Reconciliation, vol. I/II. Notre Dame, Ind.: University of Notre Dame Press, 1993.

Rhiannon, Lee. 'Death of the Honourable Roy Frederick Turner, AM, a Former Member of the Legislative Council.' In *NSW Parliament Legislative Council* (29 June 2004): 10438.

Snedden, Billy. 'Whitlam Government: Want of Confidence Motion: 23 October 1973.' In *Hansard Parliamentary Debates (House of Representatives)* 86 (1973): 2482–8.

Wentworth, Hon. William Charles et al. 'Adjournment: National Anthem—Health Insurance Scheme—Decentralisation—Land Transactions—Political Parties, 25 October 1973.' In *Hansard Parliamentary Debates (House of Representatives)* 86 (1973): 2767.

Music

Bragg, Billy. 'Days Like These.' *The Peel Sessions Album*. UK: Strange Fruit, 1991.

Index

Aarons, Eric 181
Aarons, Laurie 163, 168, 184
Adelaide 191, 193, 195, 198, 223, 249
Adopt a Prisoner 63, 72, 76, 77-82, 84, 85, 89, 95, 266
Adopt a Town 66
Allende, Hortensia 54, 55, 56, 58, 60, 61, 68, 69, 71, 75, 129, 133, 138, 181, 265
Allende, President Salvador 1-3, 5, 6, 43, 72, 118, 234, 251, 265
  perceptions of 2, 6, 29, 72, 155, 157, 159, 163, 164, 165, 166, 182, 183, 184, 202, 212, 251
Allende, Isabel 185
Amalgamated Metal Workers' and Shipwrights Union 187, 197, 198, 204, 242, 244, 245, 251
Amalgamated Metal Workers' Union 9, 155, 158, 162, 163, 164, 165, 183, 185, 188, 190, 191, 194, 197, 220, 233, 241, 243
  delegation organisation 202-211
  formation of/structure 203-205, 220, 240
Amalgamated Union of Engineering Workers 34, 45-46, 53, 55, 56, 57, 58, 59, 64, 65, 71, 72, 74, 75, 85, 90, 94, 119, 120, 122, 128, 131-137, 146, 148, 149, 150
  formation of/structure 124-127
Amnesty International 27, 31, 77
Angell, Alan 43
anniversary *see* demonstrations
Anthony, George 41, 45-48, 75, 256, 258
Arms Industry
  Australia, 247
  UK 117, 119, 127-131, 140, 146, 191
Art *see* banners, music, mural
Association for British Chilean Friendship 29, 30, 74, 85
Association for International Cooperation and Disarmament (Sydney) 163-164, 165, 193
Association of Cinematograph, Television and Allied Technicians 30, 34, 85
Association of Scientific Technical and Managerial Staffs 46, 54, 85, 90
Association of Teachers in Technical Institutes 85
Australian Federated Union of Locomotive Enginemen 156, 188, 209, 351
Australian Labor Party 156, 157, 158, 169, 172, 174, 177, 184, 187, 191, 193, 195, 199, 203, 204, 227, 230, 231, 232, 233, 241, 245

Bachelet, Michelle 255
Baird, James (Jim) 165, 181, 183, 185, 186, 202, 203, 204-206, 207, 209
  in Chile 211-221
Baker, Jack 165
banners 40, 57-58, 63, 64, 65, 72, 76, 88, 130
  strip banner 69-71, 75
Barbour Might, Dick 26, 29, 95
barley 346-349
Beausire, William 79, 80
Benn, Anthony (Tony) 122, 130, 131, 133
Binns, Peter 38
black ban 36, 38, 45, 48, 84, 93, 94, 114, 122, 127, 128, 133, 134, 140, 141, 144, 146, 148, 149, 150, 161, 190, 216, 223, 224, 225, 240, 252, 253, 259, 260, 262
  jets, Scotland 117-151
  Lan Chile, Sydney 207-209
  lorry drivers, UK 1, 262
  shipbuilders, Scotland 146-150
Bolger, Bob 183
Bonilla, General Oscar 212-214
Bower, Celia 29, 37
boycott *see* black ban
Boyd, John 72, 73, 125, 132-4, 150
Brisbane 181, 193, 198
British Labour Party 30, 31, 33, 34, 39, 42, 44, 45, 50, 53, 54, 56, 57, 58, 64, 66, 68, 80, 93, 94, 105, 121
  conference 107, 112
  International Department 43, 52, 55
  parliamentary 31, 105, 119, 128, 130,

135, 144
  policy on arms for Chile 128-131, 135, 137
Brown, Bill 163
Browne, Anne 97-105
Builders Labourers' Federation 162, 163, 166, 183
Building Workers' Industrial Union 163, 166, 178, 188, 191, 197, 209, 244, 245
Bull, Carmen 189, 211, 214, 217
Bull, Tas 163, 164, 166, 189, 198, 211, 230, 231, 240, 250, 256
Bunster, Alvaro 30, 70, 72, 73, 148

Callaghan, Jim 84, 86, 129, 130, 131, 140
Carmichael, Laurie 163, 204
Carr, Barry 161, 170, 172, 256
Carstairs, Susan 37, 79
Cassidy, Sheila 31, 79, 140
Catholic International of Trade Unions 209
Central Unica de Trabajadores (Trades Union Congress of Chile) 28, 43, 51, 72, 73, 85, 88, 95, 144, 177, 181, 186, 190, 211, 215, 216, 245, 250
Chile Action Committee (Sydney, AUS) 182-184
Chile Committee for Human Rights (UK) 28, 31, 75-79, 81
  see also adopt a prisoner
Chile Solidarity Campaign (UK) 1, 16, 28, 63-64, 69, 71, 258
  formation of/structure 28, 74, 30-49, 76-77
  relationship with trade unions 30-59, 63-64, 73, 82-87, 89, 90, 93, 94-95, 97, 104, 105, 115-116, 123, 126, 135, 138, 169, 260
Chile Solidarity Campaign Commission (UK) 36
Chile Solidarity Campaign Executive Committee (UK) 33, 34, 56, 97
Civil and Public Services Association 34, 75, 79, 81, 85
Clancy, Pat 191
Collins, Jack 90, 97, 104, 114
Commission of Enquiry into the Crimes of the Military Junta 106, 186, 189, 234
Committee for Solidarity with the Chilean People (AUS) 162, 209, 260
  formation of/structure 164-184
  relationship to trade unions 164-184, 190, 197, 203-205, 221, 231, 233, 245
Communist Party of Australia 6, 156-160, 163-168, 170, 171, 172, 176, 183, 184, 195, 203, 204, 205, 210, 211, 217, 227, 228, 230, 231, 232, 233
Communist Party, Chile
  in Australia 166, 172, 173, 175, 176, 178, 194, 233
  in the UK 25, 75
Communist Party of Great Britain 5, 31, 32, 34, 37, 38, 39, 45, 46, 56, 57, 58, 64, 65, 74, 76, 80, 90, 92, 97, 118, 141, 118, 109, 118, 120, 121, 122, 127, 135
Conferences on the Chile issue
  Australia 168
  International 108, 155, 184-189
  UK 33, 44, 45, 50, 82-87, 90, 95, 112-113, 123, 136
Cooper, Steve 155-156, 157, 159, 163, 164, 168, 169, 173, 190, 245, 256
  delegation to Chile 201-221
  leaves CSCP 175-177
Cornejo, Pedro 71, 72, 85, 95, 109, 144
Corvalan, Luis 109, 189, 191, 242, 250
Coup d'etat 1-7, 25-27, 43, 118, 157-159, 255

dairy (Australian export) 223, 243, 251
delegation to Chile
  from Australia 201-222
  from the UK 89-116
demonstration 33, 38, 68, 81, 161, 182, 257, 259
  Australia, September 1973 163-165
  Australia, September 1974 182-184, 206
  UK, 11 September 1974 49, 54-59, 64-66, 70-71, 75, 134
  UK, 1 May 1974 63
  UK, September 1976 66-67
  UK, September 1983 66

UK, July 1978 139
UK, September 1979 145
Dugger, John 69-71, 75
Dixon, Diane 76, 150, 256

East Kilbride 68, 116, 117-151, 224, 234, 260
Electrical, Electronic, Telecommunications and Plumbing Union 65
Elgueta, Humberto 133, 247
Eurocommunism 158, 164, 178
　see also New Left
ex-patriots, Chilean
　Australia 7, 10, 170-179, 181, 197
　UK 32, 39, 65, 74-76, 78-82, 88, 108-109, 116, 133
Faddist 27, 28, 37, 58, 156, 221, 256, 262
Federated Engine Drivers and Firemen's Association of Australia 176, 197
Ferguson, Andrew 159, 172, 174, 176, 177-178, 233, 256
Figueroa, Luis 8, 50, 85, 88, 133, 185, 189, 190, 208, 215, 216, 220, 244
Firemen and Deckhands Union 181, 188, 197, 232, 233, 251
Foot, Michael 131
Foreign and Commonwealth Office (UK) 51, 53
Furniture, Timber and Allied Trades 34

Garrett, John 239, 251
Gatehouse, Mike
　Chile 25-29
　UK 29, 31, 32, 37, 38-40, 45, 49, 54, 55, 80, 109, 110, 255, 256, 257
General and Municipal Workers Union 91
Georges, George 184, 185, 187
Gill, Ken 56, 58, 68, 126
Gillies, Dougal 133, 134, 142, 144
Glasgow 57, 64, 78, 116, 122, 128, 134, 136, 141, 144, 263

Hargreaves, John 52-54
Harrison, Greg 165
Hart, Judith 30, 31, 34, 44, 57, 58, 61, 65, 70, 75, 128, 130, 256
Hart, Steve 30, 31, 37, 75, 56
Hawke, Bob 11, 12, 174, 191, 220, 240, 243, 245, 257
Hawker Hunter, see jet engines
Healy, John 225, 232, 239, 241, 245, 250
Heath, Edward 130
Heffer, Eric 64, 129
Henderson, Don 166, 185, 187, 189, 191, 194, 223, 232, 233, 240, 243, 251, 251
Henfrey, Colin 37, 38
Hogue, Derry 202
Hulme, Ken 37, 38-40, 43, 52, 72, 73, 84, 106
Hutchinson, Gordon 39, 65

immigrants see ex-patriots
industrial national unionism 15, 16, 18, 20, 21, 87, 115, 221, 261
International Confederation of Free Trade Unions 4, 13, 50-51, 89, 107, 113, 115, 156, 185, 186, 188, 209, 243, 245
International Conference of Solidarity with Chile 84
International Federation of Miners 98, 104
International Labour Office 51, 107, 111, 112, 185, 186, 191, 242, 245
International Marxist Group (UK) 32, 34, 56-58, 133
International Socialists (UK) 38, 39, 56, 57, 65, 82
International Telephone and Telegraph Company 29
International Transport Workers' Federation 53, 111, 225
internationalism 8-21, 35, 54, 74, 86, 89, 95, 1-5, 110, 123, 157, 178, 199, 220, 221, 226, 227, 231, 249, 259, 260, 261
Inti Illimani 68, 70, 71, 75, 196, 197-199, 229, 255
Iron and Steel Trades Confederation 75, 270

Jara, Joan (Turner) 8, 31, 74, 75, 192-196, 255
Jara, Victor 25, 70, 74, 192, 194, 219
jet engines, boycott of 117-151, 224, 234, 260
Joint Working Group (UK) 28, 98
Jones, Graham 38, 39

Jones, Jack 30, 42, 45, 50, 51, 53-57, 88, 89, 111-116, 126, 136, 137, 256, 258, 262
Jones, Mike 163

Keenan, John 120, 121, 123
Kitson, Alex 33, 41-45, 48, 57, 58, 75, 84, 85, 86, 135, 141, 169, 256

Labour Party Young Socialists (UK) 34, 65
Lan Chile 183, 184, 202, 203, 206-208
Lenane, Leo 163, 230, 246
Levy, James 165, 176
Lewis, Jeannie 193, 255
Little, Jenny 42, 55, 56
Liverpool 30, 37, 43, 54, 64, 68, 85, 149, 262
London Co-operative Society 31, 32, 34, 58, 61

MacIntosh, Duncan 37
Madrid 107, 108, 185, 186
march *see* demonstration
maritime boycott 161, 223-254
Martin Montenegro, Gustavo 7, 170, 212
May Day 63, 71, 89, 90, 100, 101, 181
McCarthy, Henry 187-190, 202-211, 217, 245, 256
McCarthy, Rory 149
McGahen, Brian 163, 190, 197
McGahey, Mick 93, 109, 110
McKay, Jane 37
McKay, Ted 96, 97-111
McKie, Joe 99, 105
McLeod, Ken 165, 168
Melbourne 170, 181, 182, 184, 191, 192, 193, 191-199, 229, 230, 238
migrants *see* ex-patriots
Miscellaneous Workers' Union 197, 203
Mitchell, Adrian 75
Moorhead, Glenn 156
Movimiento de Izquierda Revolucionaria – Movement of the Revolutionary Left 74, 172, 173
Mulvihill, Tony 157, 169, 170
mural 70-73
Murray, Lionel (Len) 52, 105

music 63, 70, 74, 75, 85, 165, 192-199, 229

National Association of Local Government Officers 34, 80, 85
National Association of Teachers in Further and Higher Education 34, 75, 78, 80
National Graphical Association 34, 59, 75, 90
National Organisation of Labour Students 34
National Society of Operative Printers and Assistants 30, 34, 68, 80, 85, 90
National Union of Dyers, Bleachers and Textile Workers 75
National Union of Gold, Silver and Allied Trades 34, 85
National Union of Mineworkers 57-58, 63, 64, 65, 78, 85, 96, 98, 141, 169, 259
  delegation to Chile 89-116
  relationship with CSC 90
  structure 90-94
National Union of Public Employees 30, 34, 50, 72, 75, 85
National Union of Railwaymen 34, 85
National Union of Seamen 34, 68, 85, 119, 270
  direct action 148, 149
National Union of Sheet Metal Workers 30, 34
National Union of Tailors and Garment Workers 34
Navy Day 64
New Left 4-6, 16, 19, 20-21, 32, 36, 63, 159, 160, 172, 183, 205
New Song 192-196
  see also music
Newens, Stan 34, 130
Nicholson, Brian 33, 38, 41, 44, 45-49, 69, 85, 150, 256
Nolan, Jim 43, 54
NSW Builders' Labourers Federation 162, 163, 183

O'Sullivan, Frank 163
Owens, Joe 163
Oxford 35, 43, 64, 143

Pacific Steam Navigation Company 149
Peace Movement (Australia) 168, 176, 185, 195

Perth (Australia) 198
Pinochet, Augusto 135
    coup d'etat 1-7, 25-27, 43, 118, 157-159, 255
    image of 26, 72, 117, 151
Plant, Cyril 1, 3, 123
Post Office Engineers Union 85
Presidential Palace, Chile 1, 3, 118, 123, 255
Price, Malcolm 163
prime ministers (Australia) 157, 158, 174, 236
prime ministers (UK) 53, 84, 86, 128, 129, 130, 131, 133, 140, 151
protest *see* demonstrations

Quilapayun 75-76, 192-196, 199, 255

refugees *see* ex-patriots
resolutions 12, 29, 44, 51, 55, 79, 91, 92, 94, 105, 122, 129, 131, 138, 141, 146, 161, 163, 210, 227
Robertson, Mavis 157, 169, 255-256
    biography of 166-168
    communism 210, 166
    on Chileans in Australia 171-178
    on trade unions 166, 226, 230, 233, 250, 252
    peace movement 184-185
    tours of musicians 192-199
Rolls Royce (company) 119-121, 122, 127, 128, 132, 133, 138-139
Rolls Royce East Kilbride Shop Stewards 65, 117-151, 224, 234, 260

Scotland 30, 35, 91, 117-151
Scott's Shipbuilders (Scott Lithgow) 129, 148
Scottish Trades Union Congress 72, 127, 129, 131, 146, 148, 149, 150, 129, 149
Seamen's Union of Australia 160, 162, 165, 166, 181, 187, 188, 194, 207, 209, 210, 211, 223-253, 243, 246, 251
    identity and structure 224-229
shipbuilding (UK) 119, 146-149
social movement 16-18, 63, 64, 68, 71, 86, 87, 89, 90, 108, 110, 116, 181, 191, 202, 221, 257, 261, 262
social movement unionism 18-20, 59, 63, 68, 71, 86, 87, 89, 90, 108, 110, 116, 181, 191, 202, 221, 257, 261, 262
Socialist Party of Australia 5, 156, 158, 159, 160, 163, 163, 165, 166, 172, 175, 178, 181, 182, 183, 187, 188, 191, 195, 198, 209, 211, 227, 228, 230, 232, 233, 245, 250, 251, 252
Socialist Workers' League (Aus) 182, 184
Socialist Workers' Party (UK) 32, 34
Society of Graphical and Allied Trades 34, 75, 85, 90
Sol, Raul 32, 65
Somerville, Bob 118-124, 134
Spartacists League 182, 183, 184
Steen, Laurie 165
Stockholm 191
strike
    in Australia 190, 239
    in Chile 17, 201, 235
    see also black ban
submarines 127, 129, 131, 133, 146-150

Thatcher, Margaret 151
Thew, Angela 37, 43, 256
Toon, Ken 97, 99, 100, 106-107, 109
    delegation to Chile 89-116
Trades Union Congress (UK) 41, 42, 28, 50-58, 84, 89, 94, 95, 104, 105, 107, 112, 114, 115, 126, 136, 140, 146, 156
transnationalism 14-15
Transport and General Workers' Union 10, 31, 34, 38, 42, 43-46, 50, 53, 54, 55, 57-59, 64-65, 75-76, 78, 85, 88, 90, 105, 111, 112
    boycott/black ban 114, 119, 120, 126, 130, 132, 135, 136, 137, 138, 141, 149
Transport Workers' Union (Aus) 29
trips to Chile *see* delegations
Trotskyites 32, 38, 56, 184

Unidad Popular – the Popular Unity Government
    Australia 157, 158, 163-164, 170, 171-172, 173, 181, 183, 197, 225, 229, 232, 233, 234
    Chile 1-3, 26, 157
    international 185, 242 (UK) 29, 32, 51

Union of Construction, Allied Trades and Technicians 30
Union of Shop, Distributive and Allied Workers 30, 34, 75
University of London students 34

Waterside Workers' Federation of Australia 158, 162, 163-164, 165, 166, 183, 188, 191, 194, 195, 197, 206, 207, 209, 211, 223-253, 260
wheat 223-253
Wheelwright, Ted 164
Whitlam, Gough 157, 158, 174, 236
Woddis, Jack 32
World Federation of Trade Unions 4, 13, 155, 156, 185, 186, 188, 204, 207, 209, 210, 220, 245
World University Service (UK) 28, 43

Yarrow's Shipbuilders 129, 148, 149
Yorkshire 58, 64
Young, Amicia 46
Youth Communist League (UK) 34, 40

www.ingramcontent.com/pod-product-compliance
Lightning Source LLC
Chambersburg PA
CBHW040934240426
43670CB00033B/2978